To Rachel,
Here's to late ~~night~~ guitar
jams & hangin out.
Hope you like my ~~book~~!

—

THE WILD BLACK YONDER

The Inside Story of the Secret Trip to the Edge of Space
for the Highest Balloon Flight and Skydive of All Time

JARED LEIDICH

Edited by Andy Wolaver, Nancy Casey
Illustrated by Jenna Westbrook

FIRST EDITION

Book ISBN: 978-0-9976919-0-0

Library of Congress Control Number: 2016913636

DEDICATION

...

This book is lovingly dedicated my incredible parents,
Mike and Cheryl Leidich.

Boundless exploration of our planet through a
childhood of adventurous travel gave me the desire
to send people to even deeper exploration. Tinkering,
building, and fixing countless machines with you, Dad,
and observing your passion for humanity, Mom, gave me
the first tools I needed to do it.

TABLE OF CONTENTS
...

PROLOGUE

...

By Alan Eustace

I had just arrived at 135,890 feet after a very relaxing and unbelievably beautiful two-hour and seven-minute ride to altitude. I was enjoying the view when I heard the voice of my flight director, Sebastian Padilla, say, "I will need positive acknowledgement from the pilot to begin the countdown sequence."

Before then, almost all of my communication had been done by bending my left leg, which could be seen at mission control by a downward-facing low-resolution camera. Now Sebastian was asking me to actually speak. I went through the complicated machinations to activate the push-to-talk switch. It's not easy in a bulky spacesuit. First I tucked in my right elbow, then rotated it up in a swimming motion to turn the shoulder bearing into the right position. Then I pushed the elbow out and up and extended the forearm, until my hand could finally reach over the top of the environmental unit and my fingers gently squeezed the toggle switch. I pushed it forward into transmit mode. The radio beeped. From hard experience, I knew this meant that there was a conflict in the channel and I wouldn't be able to transmit. I waited a second and tried again. Another beep. I had never had two beeps in a row, and this one was happening at the worst possible time. I tried again. A third beep. Finally, on the fourth try, I hit the push-to-talk toggle switch, and there was no beep. As calmly as I could, I spoke into the microphone: "Pilot ready for release." I was slightly tired from the effort, but Sebastian gave me no time to recover—"5 . . . 4 . . . 3 . . . 2 . . . 1," and away I went, falling silently, accelerating rapidly.

It was almost four years before this moment that I first had the idea of a completely self-contained system for freefalling from the stratosphere—and surviving. I was visiting Skydive Perris in southern California in an effort to update my long-dormant skydiving skills. Although I had over 500 jumps, the last one was in 1984, over 30 years ago. I was at Perris Valley to get requalified, in hopes that I'd get the chance to be one of the first people to jump out of a Gulfstream 550. My skydiving instructor was Luigi

Cani, one of the most experienced skydivers on the planet. We hit it off immediately. The training went really well. Skydiving really is like riding a bicycle: it's not easy to forget how to do something that terrified and thrilled you at the same time. More importantly, skydiving was just as much fun as I remembered, even at the age of 55!

When I got back to Palo Alto, Luigi called me with a personal request. He had a potential sponsor for an attempt to break Joe Kittinger's record for the world's highest freefall, 102,800 feet, set on August 16, 1960. It was a record that had not been broken for 50 years, easily the most coveted and difficult record in skydiving history. Everyone knew that Red Bull was mounting an attempt. Because I'm an engineer, pilot, and skydiver, Luigi asked me to join him and Dick Rutan at Mojave airport to check out a capsule that was left over from Dick's attempt to fly a giant helium balloon nonstop around the world. The capsule was massive: almost 14 feet high and 12 feet wide. It could only be entered through a tiny porthole on the top. It wasn't even close to finished, and it was very expensive.

Luigi asked what I thought. I told him that if it was me, I'd scrap the entire capsule idea and replace it with something more akin to scuba diving. Why deal with the complexity and weight of the capsule when the suit of the person inside has to work independently anyway? I had read about the history of high-altitude skydiving, and capsules had been the weak link in many of the previous attempts. In 1962 the Russian military test pilot Pyotr Dolgov was killed when he broke his facemask exiting his capsule. Kittinger had trouble getting out of his seat on his first high-altitude attempt in 1959, which caused a premature release of the drogue parachute. The drogue wrapped around his neck, causing a spin that rendered him unconscious. He only regained consciousness under canopy. Just three years after Dolgov's death, Nick Piantanida couldn't release himself from the capsule oxygen system and had to ride down with the capsule from 120,000 feet, hanging on tightly, since he had already released his seatbelt and couldn't reattach it. The canopy had huge oscillations, but he managed to hold on, only to die on his next attempt.

Luigi's funding fell through, but I couldn't let go of the idea of eliminating the capsule and attaching a scuba-diving-like system directly to the balloon. It seemed so simple, so elegant, so beautiful, and much safer than any of the previous attempts. It could also be done at a fraction of the cost. With Luigi's permission and encouragement, I started researching the concept on my own. After a year and thousands of Google searches, I had convinced myself that it was possible. A smarter man would have declared success and moved on, but I wanted to build it—and more importantly, I wanted to fly it.

Anxious to find out if my analysis was fatally flawed, I asked my friend Peter Diamandis, CEO of the X Prize Foundation, if he knew of anyone who had the space and environmental system expertise to evaluate my calculations. He gave me an introduction to the man who would change my life: Taber MacCallum. I didn't know it at the time, but Taber and his wife, Jane Poynter, were two of eight people in Biosphere 2, an experiment to see if a completely isolated and self-sufficient human community could live for two years without any interaction with the outside world. In Taber, I found a lifelong adventurer and a kindred soul. When we talked on the phone, not only did he not shoot holes in my idea, he was so excited that he invited me down to visit his company, Paragon Space Development Corporation, to consult with his best engineers. I learned that Paragon made exposure suits for toxic environments and environmental systems for spacecraft: the perfect combination for this crazy idea.

With Paragon signed up, we worked to fill out the team. I recruited Julian Nott to consult on the balloon, United Parachute Technology to advise on the parachute, and Don Day Jr. to confer with on the meteorology. Taber recruited ILC Dover for the spacesuit and Jon Clark to head our new aeromedical team. The core team was formed—and the rest is history.

Fast-forward four years to December 2015

We completed the world record jump over a year earlier, and Jared Leidich and I are having breakfast at the San Carlos Airport Cafe, having just flown around San Francisco in my Aircam, a two-person, amphibious, home-built, open-cockpit airplane. Although Jared had never flown a plane, he was a natural, and did almost all of the flying.

Jared built the environmental system for my project. He's one of the most talented engineers I've ever known, and was one of my closest friends on the project. He's young, but man, is he smart. After breakfast, he casually reaches into his backpack and produces a packet, surprising me with the news that he had been writing notes throughout the project and this is the first draft of a book. I'm the first person he's told, and he anxiously waits for my reaction.

I break into a huge grin and give him a huge hug! I'm thrilled beyond words. Our jump involved so much history that I feared was going to be lost forever.

I excitedly took the book home and immediately started reading. It was way better than even my highest expectations. It offered me the rare chance to see the project from a completely different perspective. The failed tests that they never told me about came to life, and I relived the many successes. This is the story of the engineers behind the scenes; I couldn't put it down.

I came away with an even greater appreciation for what this amazing team accomplished. It made me so proud, and so grateful, to have shared those three intense years with this group of individuals. I'll never forget their incredible intellect, experience, creativity, and resilience. We started as strangers, and parted as family. I love these men and women for sharing my dream and making it come to life. They never forgot that I was a man in his fifties with a wife and two young kids. They agonized over every detail so that I could be safe. How do you repay that?

When Jared asked me to write the prologue to this book, I couldn't say no, although I'm way more afraid of writing than I am of jumping from 135,890 feet. I hope you enjoy the book as much as I did. I hope it inspires the next generation of engineers, scientists, and explorers to push the boundaries the way the Apollo project inspired my generation.

I'm reminded of the slightly modified Alan Kay quote: "It's easier to invent the future than it is to predict it." Enjoy!

CHAPTER 1

...

The Very Beginnings

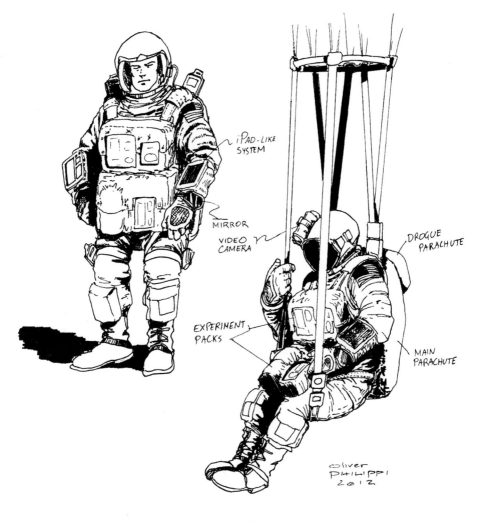

iPAD-LIKE
SYSTEM

MIRROR

VIDEO
CAMERA

DROGUE
PARACHUTE

EXPERIMENT
PACKS

MAIN
PARACHUTE

oliver
PHILIPPI
2012

A second space age is beginning. The first took humans to the moon, and it started with aeronauts skydiving from the edge of space out of giant plastic balloons. This space age aspires to take us to Mars, and it, like the first, is being kicked off with journeys to the boundary that divides the atmosphere from space, followed by a descent in eye-widening freefall across dozens of miles back to Earth. In life they say, "The sky's the limit." That's true unless you're a stratospheric skydiver. In that case, space is the limit, and then the ground. In that order.

October 2011: First Contact

It was a normal day in the cubicle-filled, basketball court–sized Paragon Space Development Corporation office in Tucson, Arizona, when our CEO, Taber MacCallum, told us that he had been contacted by a vice president of Google regarding the design of a spacesuit life-support system. The executive, Alan Eustace, wanted to ride up into the stratosphere tethered to a balloon and skydive home. Taber gave us the news at our weekly engineering meeting surrounded by the 35-person engineering team. He was clearly excited about the idea.

A shelf along one wall of Taber's office boasted motorcycle racing trophies. He often sported a gold hoop earring, and when he came to the office on weekends he wore rock and techno T-shirts. His engineering education did not include four years at a traditional university. It began aboard a research vessel where he roamed the Earth's oceans working in a floating laboratory. During this time, he connected with a group of people building a self-contained glass enclosure in the desert that they would call Biosphere 2. When the massive structure was eventually built, it was occupied for two years and 20 minutes by Taber and seven other people. Since then Taber's entire career has focused on ways to support human life in environments other than Earth's standard atmosphere. He is a fountain of ideas for inventions and contraptions that allow frail, weak humans to live outside the warm bath of air we need to stay alive. He never quits. He pushes hard and with direction. That direction is humans toward space. He wants to go to Mars—and I believe he will. His relentless positivity and refusal to acknowledge any difficulty in any problem inspires and drives me. He and Alan hit it off instantly, of course. They were both crazy.

Most small to medium-size aerospace contractors get a loony phone call every now and again from someone wanting to do something ridiculous in space. Those calls typically don't get past the assistants, who know that funding trumps imagination in such discussions. When Taber's assistant heard that the wild idea was coming from a short-list Google exec with piles of money, she put him through to Taber. The two of them had an instant nerd fest, rattling through the ins and outs of spacesuit life support, becoming ever more giddy with anticipation. Taber made it fully clear that building a suit to do what Alan wanted would be difficult and expensive. But this was Taber's area of expertise, and he was able to tell Alan in that one phone call that the thing he wanted to do was entirely possible.

Even so, when I heard the announcement, I dismissed it as a neat encounter but a long shot. Ideas are everywhere in the space business yet realities are next to nonexistent. Few projects get close to completion, even fewer finish, and none get done at the cost or schedule originally envisioned. The following week, I was surprised to hear that the business development team was going to write a proposal to build a suit that the Google exec would wear on a voyage up to the top half of the stratosphere, where he would float, then cut loose for a skydive through some 20 miles of atmosphere. When he reached normal air, a skydiving parachute would open and set him gently down on the ground. The suit Alan envisioned was unique. He wanted it to be totally self-supporting—no capsule around him, no gondola holding extra equipment, just a suit and a tether. Everything he needed to stay alive would be attached directly to his body.

In space-nerd terms, Alan wanted a multi-pressure, long-duration spacesuit capable of a stratospheric exploration mission without an umbilical. The long-duration exposure to changing pressures and temperatures which this mission called for would make it unlike any others. Such a project would be a noble addition to space technologies, skydiving, and aviation. It was after a year of paper studies, that Alan had approached Taber for advice.

January 2012, Tucson, Arizona: The Proposal

Alan stayed in touch. After some sweet-talking from Taber, whom he had originally contacted only for advice about life support, Alan asked for a feasibility study and a proposal for building him his suit, tasks he had originally intended to oversee himself.

The business development team wrote a proposal to address the biggest challenges of what Alan wanted to do. The first major problem was the extreme cold of the middle part of the trip, which would require a liquid-heating system built from scratch and a whole lot of batteries to power it. In addition to the cold, the lack of air in the upper stratosphere would give rise to potential problems with overheating during the second half of the mission. The next problem was oxygen. Because one goal of the mission was not to leave anything behind, Alan couldn't jettison his oxygen tanks; he would have to skydive with the tanks strapped to him. Thus conserving oxygen would be of the highest importance so that those tanks could be as small as possible.

The proposal team solicited Taber and an analyst to take a first stab at feasibility. If those studies suggested it could be done, they would write a paper describing how our company could build the life-support pack for the suit. When the project analyst finished crunching the numbers to approximate the overall mass of the oxygen needed and the total power required to keep the pilot warm, he would send these two values to the person on the business development team moving into the lead role of the effort: Gary Lantz.

Gary is the person I picture when I think of new age entrepreneurs. He was a bright-eyed lover of new engineering with glasses and long brown hair which he wiped back regularly. He liked to talk, and did so with a leaning relentlessness that was both gripping and rather terrifying if you weren't ready for it. His big ideas blossomed in front of your eyes as he spoke. He had a long history in aeronautics and aerospace, starting out in airplanes, and mid-career moved into the space and space life-support field. His cool-guy vibe provided a contrast to the mechanical-pencil-wielding nerds that filled the rooms he worked in. His disposition would upturn many a mood; the days we rode under his banner were never boring. Like Taber, he was an idea man, but he didn't think as big. Because they had a similar drive, and both considered the project their baby, he and Taber seemed to be perpetually slightly annoyed with each other.

I got my first detailed introduction to the fundamentals of our mission over some beers with Taber. I was surprised to learn that unlike all other spacesuits, this one would require a heating system but no cooling system. Spacesuits used in low Earth orbit (where the space station is) need cooling systems. When a person works, the metabolic processes that convert food to power create heat. On Earth this heat is pulled away from our bodies by the atmosphere. Because space is a vacuum, it has very little ability to absorb heat. Therefore, even though space is technically very cold, a body in space has no way to get rid of the heat of work, or heat absorbed from the sun. Spacesuit-cooling systems use a liquid-cooling garment, which is like long underwear with little tubes in it that circulate cold fluid next to a person's skin. That fluid is cooled in the suit life-support pack using a sublimator, a sort of swamp cooler for space. When the water in the sublimator vaporizes, energy leaves the system, cooling the person down.

Why, then, were we proposing a spacesuit architecture with a heating system—a first in the spacesuit world? The middle of the atmosphere is extremely cold and, unlike space, it is not a vacuum. In the middle part of Alan's journey, the air would be thick enough to absorb more heat than is produced by the pilot's body, making him get too cold.

Unlike suits used on the space station, this suit would not need a cooling system. Our target altitude appeared to coincide with a region in the atmosphere which I will call "THEA," an acronym for Thermal Human Equilibrium Altitude. THEA is the band where the human metabolic heat load roughly matches the cold atmosphere's ability to remove heat from a system occupied by a person. Functionally, that means that below this region, a suit spending long durations in the atmosphere would need a heating system, and above it a cooling system would be necessary. Per our calculations, we estimated that this band is right around 130,000 feet.

Because this was so close to our target altitude, the system would be idle at that height and the pilot would be at a comfortable temperature without active thermal control. Not only did this equilibrium make our suit system feasible, the concept itself is elegant. This band is the one place other than the ground where our atmosphere is not thermally hostile; it's not too cold and not too hot. With enough oxygen, a pilot could remain at this height for a long time in relative thermal comfort. The thermal control center could be pretty simple. We would take a liquid thermal garment normally used to cool astronauts in spacewalks and integrate that with a heater on a controller.

The next major challenge was sizing the oxygen system. The oxygen system would be unique to the suit regardless of the style because the mission would be carried out in a way none before had. The team considered what it would take to use current spacesuit technology to supply a suit with oxygen for about four hours, the amount of time we were assuming the mission would take. Ordinarily a stratospheric skydiver would breathe from giant tanks in their gondola or capsule until they switched to tiny bail-out bottles they would use for the few minutes it took to get down. The team made an assumption that, as in a typical suit, oxygen would flow continuously into the helmet through an umbilical or hose providing vital gases and liquids to a pilot from a mother ship, or in this case, from a life-support pack. Under this assumption, the suit would use a high volume of oxygen. This would be doable, assuming liquid oxygen was used, so this was the idea that was proposed.

The last problem that would have to be addressed seemed the easiest to solve: how to manage lots of extra weight under our parachute canopy. The system would weigh about 450 pounds, while normal sport skydiving parachutes are made for weights topping out at about 250 pounds. To solve this problem, the team proposed a parachute system like that made for tandem skydiving, since those parachutes are designed to hold the weight of two people. Such parachutes can handle the speeds and loads being considered and would solve the problem of mounting the life-support pack. If we used a tandem system, the life-support pack could hook to the tandem mounting straps as if it were a person. Using a tandem-style rig in this way was not uncommon for what are called "gear jumps" (jumps using tandem rigs with heavy gear instead of a second person).

With those three big questions out of the way, the proposal was written. Graphs plotted atmospheric temperature against suit interior temperature to describe visually how the temperature would remain comfortable and warm in the suit while the outside temperature plummeted to negative 70 degrees Fahrenheit. Graphics also showed how the liquid oxygen system would flow for a full four hours, and how the off-the-shelf parachute system would softly return the pilot to the ground. Sketches showed a pilot wearing a soft chestpack and hanging from a custom sitting harness connected to a standard tandem skydiving system all suspended, exposed, from a giant balloon. The system would remain in that state until it got to an altitude where it would float steady for a couple hours and then release the pilot to fall with all his gear back to Earth. Finally, the pilot would swing under his parachute to settle to the ground at the end of the flight, presumably sliding in on his butt.

Despite the fancy graphics, the 30-page proposal was very dry. The business development team read Alan correctly: as a calculating person inspired more by truth than sparkle. His background upheld that assessment. He earned a PhD in computer sciences from the University of Central Florida—not an Ivy League school. Yet he had become a short-lister at Google. Despite an obvious daring side that seemed to conflict with this calculating personality, the team assumed he would be wowed by accurate, unshakeable numbers, not dazzled by glamour.

Alan and Taber continued to hit it off. Stepping out of standard CEO protocol, Taber had taken a special interest in this project and had become immersed in the technical details and relationships at the gritty level. The bulk of the proposal was composed by just two people. They made the pitch. The team proposed a one-year project to lift Alan Eustace in a budget spacesuit with accompanying life support to the top of the stratosphere and then drop him back to Earth.

February 2012: Assembling the Team

On a Tuesday morning in early February Taber told me that the insane proposal to drop a Google executive from the edge of space had been accepted. He asked me to join the four-person team that would make the stratospheric spacesuit. I immediately agreed. Although we all knew that this team would quickly grow, at its inception it felt elite; it was an exhilarating feeling.

Gary Lantz, who had been a major part of the proposal effort, would be the program manager. He dove in on day one with pages of requirements and direction to start the design. Gary spearheaded the overall endeavor and Christie Iacomini led the effort to create the detailed design of the suit system for most of the architectural development process

Christie was an intimidatingly motivated person. She had worked at NASA for the better part of a decade before moving to Arizona to finish a PhD, and then came to work at Paragon Space Development Corporation to run programs designing the life-support systems for next-generation spacecraft. A 70-hour week doing battle with aerospace type A astronaut program washouts was her day-to-day. Her technical grounding was unshakeable—no questions unanswered, no stone left unturned. She stayed ahead of us, clearing obstacles that would interfere with our work and defining the requirements that would splay first into diagrams, then computer models, then paper drawings, then finally into the components of metal and space-age plastic that made up the life-keeping elements of our spacesuit to be. Christie's role was unique in that she was both a member of team StratEx and a high-level manager of the company as a whole. She never joined the team as full-on as the others.

Another designer, Zane Maccagnano, joined the team shortly after work began. He worked in concert with Christie through the creation of the schematic describing what we intended to design and build. Zane wore the same leather coat through most the program. His high-energy persona and confident, confrontational, matter-of-fact style of conversation found either conflict or compliment (but not much in between) on most occasions. With his near-compulsive obsession with the intricacies of what he designed, he was a born aerospace designer. He interpreted everything literally, combing the seas of information and possibility for the tiniest glitch that could bring down our suit. Zane and I did most of the detailed physical design of the life-support pack and life-support systems.

That left me. I was young and relatively new. I had worked at Paragon since leaving college two and a half years earlier. I was 26 years old. I had worked in human spaceflight since 2003, when I won a high school internship at Lockheed Martin working on NASA's Orbital Space Plane. During that project I wore my first spacesuit. I stayed in the industry all through college, working on satellites and life-support systems. I rode on NASA's zero gravity airplane twice. Through my collaboration with the NASA scientist who mentored me in our zero gravity experiments, and the NASA water labs, I landed a job at Paragon Space Development Corporation, a company specializing in space life-support systems. When this project started I was selected as one of the designers. It seemed Gary liked me. I like to think I was a skilled engineering designer, but I was no doubt fresh, learning as much as doing.

That was the crew: two managers, two designers, and Taber. We operated from the very beginning in a fairly unusual way. There was a core team whose members spent most their time together. That core team would very quickly grow to include contractors from other companies who worked with us full-time. Company boundaries didn't matter. We got huge amounts of support from surrounding people in the office at Paragon, but as the project progressed the dividing line between being on the project and not would grow bolder. The first design task was to define the architecture of the suit we were to build.

March 2012: Defining an Architecture

As Alan breathed and sweated in the suit, he would produce toxins that would poison him if allowed to build up. The basic structure of a spacesuit made to provide air and manage toxins in a vacuum has three potential architectures. The first is called a "flow-through" system where air is constantly pushed through the suit and then driven away, either out to space or back into a mother ship. The second, a "demand-regulated" system, works like a scuba-diving system: on an inhale it gives the wearer some air, and on the exhale it dumps that air overboard. The third type of system is called "recirculating." A recirculating system cleans the exhaled air and returns it to the person wearing the suit. The relative complexity and the quantity of breathing gas needed are inversely proportional: the more complex the system, the less gas is needed.

Gas Consumption Vs. Complexity

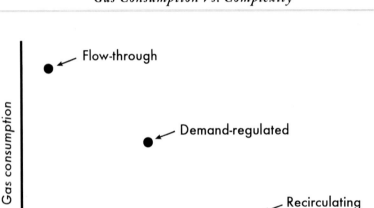

Architecture Types

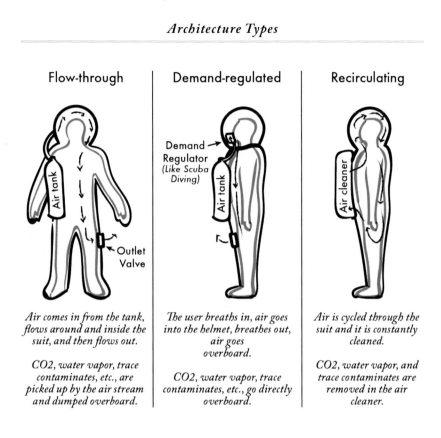

Flow-through	Demand-regulated	Recirculating
Air comes in from the tank, flows around and inside the suit, and then flows out.	*The user breaths in, air goes into the helmet, breathes out, air goes overboard.*	*Air is cycled through the suit and it is constantly cleaned.*
CO_2, water vapor, trace contaminates, etc., are picked up by the air stream and dumped overboard.	*CO_2, water vapor, trace contaminates, etc., go directly overboard.*	*CO_2, water vapor, and trace contaminates are removed in the air cleaner.*

The architecture in the original proposal was a "flow-through system." Toxins built up from breathing and sweating were to be swept away by a constant stream of air flowing from a tank, swirling around Alan's body, and then flowing out of the suit. The gas stream washing away the toxins would also contain the oxygen he would breathe. An outlet valve would regulate both the pressure inside the suit and the flow rate of air moving through the suit. Although enormous quantities of stored gas would be necessary to maintain the constant airflow for carrying toxins away to space, this architecture was the one preferred by most spacesuit designers. It was simple. It didn't have many life-critical components, and in the event of an abort it would leave the pilot with a suit full of fresh air to last the trip down. Several suits using that type of architecture existed. It worked.

As we crept up on the start of sizing and defining components for the build, we had to pause. We had proposed a flow-through architecture because it was simple and cheap, but without knowing for certain it would work. Although we knew that a flow-through system would consume more oxygen than the others, just how much more hadn't been clear. It wasn't looking good. The thought of reconsidering other architectures was aggravating. It would overturn weeks of work and possibly aggravate Alan as well. At this point he could have pulled the plug pretty painlessly. We feared he might view us as amateurish if we changed our minds just a few weeks in. But the flow-through architecture proved to have a fatal flaw.

Because flow-through systems use so much air, the proposal had relied on the use of liquid oxygen, which takes up some 800 times less volume than the gas form. The difficult reality, however, was that liquid-oxygen systems only work in one orientation: you can't turn them upside down, or even sideways. Skydivers do turn upside down and sideways sometimes. We had no choice but to take a step back and conduct a study comparing the three architectures to determine which system would truly work for our suit. This was a task which we had told Alan was already done.

Tensions quickly began to rise as opinions hardened around each of the three architectures. The company happened to be in a bit of a lull at the time, which allowed more people to participate in this particular debate than was probably healthy. In very few programs, even building suits in other contexts, is the use of a device to support a human in an otherwise deadly environment so personal. This suit would be used by someone we knew, and we were building it completely from scratch without guidelines set by actual experience. Accusations were flung. Choosing the wrong architecture would kill Alan. Changing the architecture would invalidate the proposed cost of the program.

I was the one given the task of doing the actual mathematical study of how much oxygen would be consumed throughout the mission for each of the three system types. People wanted the study to give the answers they wanted to see. I just did the math. As a young, relatively inexperienced engineer, I think I was viewed—rightly—as a workhorse carrying out the will of others.

The night before the meeting intended to put the issue to bed was a long one. I refined the code used to derive the numbers approximating mixing gas streams flowing into a constantly changing volume at variable sinusoidal rates. By the start of the new day, I was in the office, Taber checking my work as we produced what would become our guiding analysis for the arduous design process ahead. We added graphs and conclusions to a report describing my methods and recommendations for going forward.

We presented a proposal to use a demand-regulated system. The meeting was tense, a showdown orchestrated by the advocates of the chosen system. This was probably inevitable, since the team as a whole was headed nowhere toward a solution. The numbers in the analysis favored a demand-regulated system over the flow-through architecture of the original proposal.

The design team scurried into action, and within a few days of the meeting enough work had been done that it would be hard to go back. We were rocketing off toward a demand-regulated spacesuit design. The program was overhauled and re-costed in the months following the architecture change. Already, this system looked almost nothing like what was first proposed.

As expected, the cost of the revamped system was considerably more than estimates for the first one. In addition, during this process we had a rude awakening, appreciating more fully the cost of quality control than we had at the time of proposing the project. Someone had to inform Alan of these cost increases. It became clear that Gary, who was originally opposed to the change in architecture, would have to force a smile and explain that the program had gotten more expensive almost as soon as the work began. For Gary that was the beginning of the end. I know very little about the discussions that took place, so the actual events of the final unfolding remain a mystery to me.

What I do know is that at our next major program meeting a couple months later, a fellow design and thermal engineer, Sebastian Padilla, a steady problem-solver with a decade of history at the company and a reputation for having incredible emotional stamina, would sit in and start to learn the ropes. Gary, who was largely responsible for the very existence of the program, had resigned.

The early team and advisors gathering for a weather balloon launch at one of our first meetings as a full team. (Photo by Volker Kern.)

The original project manager, Gary Lantz, taking a break from one of the program's notoriously long early meetings. (Photo by Volker Kern.)

Alan trying on a spacesuit for the first time in the ILC Dover Suit Labs in Houston.

CHAPTER 2

...

Building a Knowledge Base

A t the time we started this endeavor, four people had ascended to the stratosphere with the intention of freefalling down. Two of them died. Of the two jumpers who survived, one narrowly escaped death. Little was published about the experience of the other surviving jumper. We know he exited a gondola in the stratosphere over Russia and lived, but not much else.

The atmosphere can be considered in layers delineated by temperature inversions, as shown in the following figure. The troposphere is the atmospheric layer where all humans live and where the activities of all living things—except astronauts and aeronauts—occur, including the vast majority of aviation. Starting from the ground, as the altitude increases, the temperature decreases until the tropopause is reached. The tropopause marks the end of the troposphere and the beginning of the stratosphere.

In the stratosphere, as altitude increases, the temperature rises. At increasing altitude, as the temperature goes up and the air pressure drops, the environment becomes more thermally accommodating to people because the air is less cold and there is less of it to absorb heat from the body. The stratosphere ends at the stratopause. Above that point the layer named the mesosphere begins. Here, as altitude increases, temperatures decrease. Without an engineered cooling system, a person cannot survive outside of a spacecraft in the mesosphere; despite the lowering temperatures, they would overheat. The air is too thin to remove heat from a person's body at the rate it is produced. Partway through the mesosphere, at 100 kilometers, is the Karmen line, where the atmosphere is too thin for aerodynamic flight. This is sometimes considered the start of "space."

Above the mesosphere is the thermosphere where, like the stratosphere, temperature increases as altitude increases. At this point, however, temperature starts to become a rather abstract concept because there is virtually no air to make ambient temperature relevant. Above the thermosphere is the exosphere. In the exosphere, where there is no air, traditional methods of measuring temperature no longer work. Engineers measure temperature changes above the mesosphere by considering "radiative sink temperature," or the temperature that something will reach from radiating alone. By that measure, in the exosphere, temperature decreases infinitely into the depths of deep space, approaching absolute zero, the coldest a thing can get.

Circa 1960: The History

Prior to the space race that brought Americans to the moon, there was a race to explore the stratosphere. Before people left the surface of the planet strapped into rockets, they did so strapped into balloons. Both the US and Russia sent people to the stratosphere in the 1960s, but the United States went first, and went higher.

Layers of the Atmosphere and Historical Jumps as of 2011

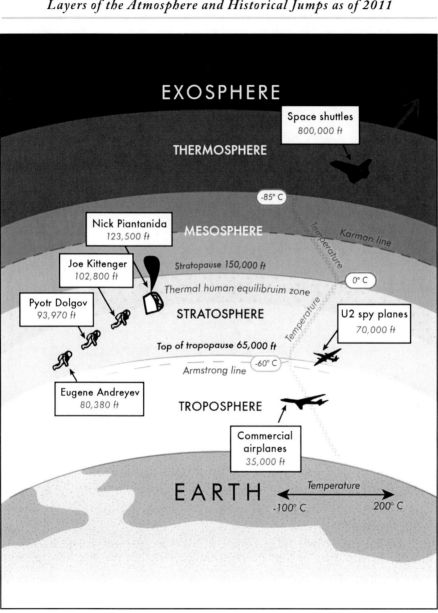

The first drops from the stratosphere were performed by Colonel Joseph "Joe" Kittinger as part of a project called Excelsior, which means "ever higher." The project was spearheaded by John Paul Stapp, who was particularly interested in space bailouts as an alternative way for astronauts to return to Earth if they found themselves in a dysfunctional spacecraft too far from home.

When a person is subjected to low air pressures, their insides push out harder than the outside air pushes in, creating numerous dangerous physical effects. Joe wore a partial-pressure suit, an architecture that has since been abandoned, to manage this pressure difference. There is no fundamental reason that the pressure that is normally exerted on a person's body by compressed air can't be exerted by something physical like tight fabric, which is exactly what partial-pressure suits used. The gloves and helmet of the suit were pressurized with air, and the rest of the pressure was created by tubular bladders under painstakingly laced fabric pressing on an aeronaut's skin, ideally at 14 pounds every square inch, mimicking the pressure created by air at sea level.

Joe launched from Roswell, New Mexico, and ascended in an open metal structure, or gondola, carrying oxygen and equipment in November 1959. He ascended to over 76,000 feet above the desert under a zero-pressure polyethylene balloon. He then performed some closeout tasks before stepping off the edge of the gondola for the jump. Most notably, he had to disconnect from the big oxygen tanks and switch to his smaller onboard bottles. Upon exiting the gondola, he became the first person to freefall from the stratosphere.

When a person exits a gondola in the stratosphere, they will encounter a period of relative weightlessness. The aeronaut will float for a while because there is no air to oppose their motion. They are falling, but without any air it looks and feels forceless, much like an astronaut floating outside a spaceship.

This period will present a serious entanglement hazard for a parachute, so Joe's system included a timer that would let him fall for a while before a small stabilizing parachute called a drogue came out. After Joe stepped off the edge of the gondola, the system would wait 12 seconds, then spit out the drogue parachute. By then he would be in thick, moving air.

While disconnecting his oxygen tanks, Joe accidentally pulled the lanyard that initiates the timer on his drogue parachute. He stepped into the black sky with the timer partially run out, and the drogue came out before he was moving fast enough for the air to inflate the mini-parachute and pull it away from him. He floated in space.

While he was floating, the drogue parachute bridle wrapped around his neck. The spacesuit prevented the fabric from choking him, but without a functioning stabilizer, and wearing a restrictive partial-pressure suit that forced him into a sitting position, he entered a violent spin. The stabilizing parachute was an extraction chute intended to pull out the main parachute. It was now tied to his neck. The main parachute had no mechanism to open. Joe blacked out and woke up under his reserve parachute, which had opened automatically near the ground. Joe nearly died.

Joe returned to the stratosphere in December 1959, ascending to over 74,000 feet. This time he successfully returned without using his reserve parachute.

Half a year later, Joe ascended for the third and final time. Soon after launch, his glove failed but he opted not to tell the ground crews. His hand swelled to twice its normal size but his skin never ruptured. He was able to disconnect himself from the capsule and execute his jump from 102,800 feet. It was August 16, 1960, and when Joe successfully landed on the desert floor, he set the record for the highest skydive of all time. His record would stand for over 50 years.

Two years after Joe's final drop, on November 1, 1962, two men from the Russian military, Pyotr Dolgov and Eugene Andreyev, boarded a Volga balloon gondola in Volsk, Russia, with the intention of ascending into the stratosphere and freefalling back. The balloon ascended successfully and crossed into the black of the stratosphere. Eugene jumped first, from 80,390 feet, and successfully completed his flight. Pyotr let the balloon ascend higher before exiting the gondola at 93,970 feet. He was found dead on the ground in the desolate flatlands of southeast Russia with a broken facemask in a depressurized suit, killed by exposure to vacuum. Pyotr was testing an experimental pressure suit and that pressure suit's facemask had apparently collided with the gondola and failed. Even if Pyotr had lived, however, he would not have broken Joe's record.

The only other stratospheric skydiving attempt before the current era was mounted by an unlikely truck driver and exotic animal dealer named Nick Piantanida. Nick was a recreational skydiver who set out to break Joe Kittinger's record for the highest balloon flight and skydive of all time. Nick raised money and built legitimacy piecewise. He had a gondola built. It was roughly the size of a phone booth and housed oxygen and other support equipment not needed in freefall. He convinced the military to loan him a high-altitude pressure suit that was normally used in U2 spy planes. Like Joe, Nick would make three attempts at the stratosphere.

On his first attempt, in 1965, Nick's balloon successfully launched but did not survive the ascent. The balloon encountered a wind shear that reportedly tore open the thin plastic and was damaged such that the mission could not continue. Nick separated from the ruptured balloon at under 20,000 feet (still in the troposphere) in his gondola under a large parachute and then exited the capsule to ride his personal parachute to a safe landing in the city dump.

Nick's second flight attempt, in 1966, resulted in a successful launch and ascent to 123,500 feet. At the time this was the highest balloon flight ever performed. At altitude as Nick prepared to jump, he was stopped by a stuck oxygen quick-disconnect valve. The jammed valve connected him to a large oxygen tank and thus functionally locked him to the gondola. Nick was forced to remain in the gondola for a trip down from the stratosphere under the gondola parachute. Unfortunately, Nick had already removed his seatbelt and could not refasten it in the pressurized suit. He was forced to cling to the capsule as it descended 23 miles, surging and bucking, threatening to toss Nick out to flail from the end of his oxygen hose. He survived the trip and became the unofficial highest balloonist of all time, but he did not break any freefall records. He wasn't even officially awarded any ballooning records because he had landed with his gondola parachute, not the balloon, a condition of the record-keeping organization for balloon flight.

In that same year Nick attempted the feat one more time. His third and final flight ended when ground personnel heard a loud rush of air across the voice microphone and remotely cut him down by activating a radio-controlled release mechanism just above 57,000 feet. Nick may have been suffering from a severe case of decompression sickness, the same ailment that can happen in scuba diving when divers go from a high pressure to a low pressure. Nitrogen dissolved in the blood bubbles out. This can result in potentially severe confusion as the bubbles block blood to the brain. Nick was either very confused or very poorly trained; it was speculated he had opened his helmet in the stratosphere. He reached the ground in a coma from which he would never wake.

Fast-forward to 2011. It is 45 years since Nick's death, and he remained the highest-flying balloonist in history, while Colonel Joseph Kittenger still held the record of highest skydiver. Alan Eustace was beginning to gather information on ways to ascend and freefall from the stratosphere. At the same time, the Red Bull Stratos program was also hard at work on a new method to accomplish the same thing.

In all the previous drops, Alan saw the supporting vehicle as the weak point. Joe's gondola had pulled his timing cord early, nearly killing him. Nick's vehicle tethered him to his oxygen tank and prevented his record jump. Pyotr's capsule had likely bashed a hole in his facemask. Getting rid of the vehicle was Alan's biggest innovation. Without it, the system was lighter and the balloon far smaller. A smaller balloon might not have sheared in Nick's first mission. Smaller balloons mean safer launches.

The designers of the Red Bull Stratos program did not have this revelation. They were working in a nearly opposite direction. They were the first team to produce a fully pressurized capsule, whereby a person could survive without a suit as long as the door was not open. They would need one of the biggest balloons available to lift the heavy system, which included both the large pressure vessel and a functional spacesuit for the descent.

Alan took notes on the failures of the past and incorporated modern learning from what could be seen of the Stratos program and its team's difficulties in producing the complex capsule system. The statistics were daunting. Half of the men who went to the stratosphere to freefall back died in the attempt. Nobody who considered this a coin toss with death was going to try this again.

Despite space diving's morbid history, suit technology, space medicine, and the art of operations had all seen major advances since those early jumps. These advances, along with the game-changing idea to skip the vehicle, were enough for a team to convince themselves that the historical odds weren't relevant.

Suits don't have helmets that can be opened in a vacuum anymore, so a modern suit would not have allowed Nick's demise. Modern helmets are made of incredibly durable polyethylene instead of acrylic or glass, which can shatter or crack when impacted, eliminating the deficiency that led to Pyotr's death. The parachute problem that nearly killed Joe would still need to be solved, but such a problem wouldn't have arisen if Joe had not been in a gondola. Both Nick's and Pyotr's deaths are suspected to have been linked with decompression sickness that prevented them from thinking clearly at the time they made their mistakes. Modern space medicine experts understand that condition much better now and can take precautions to prevent it. Operationally, teams are more rigorous than in the past. Nick was said to have been smoking a cigarette in his spacesuit prior to his final flight—at the moment when his procedures said he should have been pre-breathing. A proper pre-breathe would have helped prevent the decompression sickness which may have contributed to the confusion that led him to open his helmet in a vacuum.

Alan knew the history and would not repeat the mistakes of earlier teams. He would be smarter. Failures in the eerie past of stratospheric skydiving would give birth to the idea of taking on the stratosphere outside of a vehicle.

April 2012, Denver, Colorado: Wind Tunnel Testing

Word reached us that the aspiring world record holder for the Red Bull Stratos project, Felix Baumgartner, was complaining to the engineers working on his suit about the tiny chestpack that was being added to the spacesuit he planned to wear in his jump. That pack was a few inches tall and wrapped around the center part of his chest, protruding a few inches outward. Our suit needed a chestpack also, but because Alan would fly totally exposed for the whole mission, our chestpack had to do a whole lot more than Felix's and therefore would have to be much bigger and heavier.

The question was straightforward: if one of the world's most well-known skydivers was having so much trouble staying stable with a tiny little chest bump, how on earth would our much less experienced (and older) skydiver manage the highly dynamic plunge through the sound barrier attached to a 150-pound personal life-support system?

This question was impossible to ignore in our meetings about stability and what the skydive would be like inside a pressurized spacesuit with a voluminous, massive chestpack. We decided to test the thing in a vertical wind tunnel.

The Red Bull Stratos team didn't exactly know who we were. We knew of them because they were intentionally generating a media hurricane, building energy for the big jumps that were planned to happen the same year as these wind tunnel tests. The Stratos program had been plagued by some fairly well-known political and technical issues that were constantly threatening to shut them down. We knew this because it was in the news. We had no idea if their schedule would hold. It didn't really matter to us either way.

Taber first brought up the idea of doing a wind tunnel test in a meeting where I wasn't present. To call this man an optimist would be an understatement. He is known for building elaborate, inspiring pictures of how easy every step will be. In his eyes, we're always on the verge of incredible success. What is so invigorating in the meeting room can be a disaster for the people on the ground who have to build whatever thing he dreams up. His mentality plays a huge role in his company's success; that type of attitude fosters self-fulfilling prophecies. I was the engineer often charged to actually do the extremely difficult thing that was proposed as easy. Sometimes, while agonizing over the design and construction of an "easy to make" machine, I'd find myself reciting pep talks through gritted teeth: "He is truly a brilliant engineer and leader. I aspire to be like him someday." I never truly doubted him.

Taber's disposition was in full force when he haphazardly, and without really consulting the program manager, proposed to add an early-stage vertical wind tunnel test to the project. For that test we would build a ground life-support pack roughly representing our anticipated flight pack and fly it in a wind tunnel, piloted by Alan.

I had encountered Alan in a few prior meetings, but these tests would be my real opportunity to get to know the driven, science-fueled aviator behind all of this. Given his accomplishments, his means, and what he was about to attempt to do, Alan came off as remarkably down to earth. He was of average height, fit, and simmered with a constant excitement about the next idea that was about to surface. He was like Taber in his ambition and in his ability to confidently minimalize outlandish problems. Alan was the son of an engineer who grew up in Florida, surrounded by the space program. He could see the launches of the space shuttle from his house if he couldn't make it to Cape Canaveral. Throughout his time at major computer companies and eventually at Google, he remained inspired by the space program of his childhood. He became an aviator, working up to the flying of his own Cessna Citation business jet and various other experimental aircraft. He was an avid skydiver at a time when skydiving was much scarier than it is today. Alan is a passionate man, and I found him exciting to be around once I got over the awe of his reputation and general presence.

In Taber's mind this wind tunnel test was already straightforward and painless. We would throw a scuba-diving tank onto a spacesuit and outfit it with a scuba-diving-style demand regulator for breathing air. We'd strap some weights to the suit, attach a shell to cover the whole thing up, then toss it into a wind tunnel, sit back, and see how the pilot managed.

At this point my title was the "Design, Integration, and Testing Lead" for the growing team, and so I was tasked to design the system. I would work with the engineer Ryan Lee, who led the suit team. Ryan was a full-time employee of ILC Dover but, like many of the contractors, would come to spend virtually all his time with us on Project StratEx.

He and his close cohorts probably made up the most qualified spacesuit team alive. ILC Dover designed the white extra vehicular activity (EVA) suits used by NASA astronauts outside the International Space Station. Before that, they had designed the well-known Apollo suits that danced on the moon. At NASA, Ryan supervised astronauts on EVA from mission control. He was deeply drawn to space exploration and had followed his inclination with action, becoming a major player in the world's modern space-exploration efforts. He smiled often from behind his brown goatee and had the ability to keep someone calm and level while enduring the intense claustrophobia of entering a spacesuit. I was lucky to become friends with him and to work with this savant of spacesuit design.

A vertical wind tunnel is essentially a big tube, about the size of the fuselage of a passenger airplane, standing on end with big fans pushing air through it. We chose a wind tunnel outside Denver, Colorado. That particular wind tunnel was "recirculating," meaning that the air traveled in a big loop, pulled upwards through the usable portion of the tunnel by a bank of fans that then pushed it through massive air ducts, recirculating it through two U-turns before pulling it through the tunnel again. The advantage of this recirculating style (as opposed to one where the air is sucked in by fans, then blasted up and out into the open) is that the air can be climate controlled, giving the operators more control of air density to better report things like relative air speed, an important value we were trying to find. Minute for minute, a wind tunnel is a cheaper way to get airborne at 120 miles per hour than jumping out of an airplane, and you don't need a special license or lots of training to use it.

Elite skydivers train in wind tunnels like this. First-time fliers such as thrill-seeking teens and even children fly in them as well. Within this controlled environment, ordinary people can experience floating for the first time, or skydivers can attempt new maneuvers or special body positions. It was a big change of pace for us NASA contractors to leave our protocol-driven cleanroom testing facilities and head to the wind tunnel to be jostled by elementary school kids all jacked up on Mountain Dew at their wind tunnel eighth birthday party. We used the "party room" to prep our million-dollar spacesuit for the tunnel tests. The experience was a fun and enlightening introduction to what is called "commercial space."

About four weeks before the tests, I got my briefing on the product I would have to design and build to take into the tunnel. The suit crew had offered up a spare ILC Dover launch, entry, and abort (LEAI) suit for the tests. My design team, along with the suit group, would have to design a ground life-support system to be used in the tunnel. It had to represent the size and mass of the actual system and also be capable of pressurizing the suit while keeping the pilot in a cool bath of fresh oxygen. To do this, we had to come up with a reasonable size and mass for the system. After that, we needed to figure out how we were going to pressurize, cool, and get new air to the suit. We had to fit that in a space that represented the correct size and shape of the anticipated flight system.

The plan was to begin talking to the suit team about how the suit was normally operated, and then work backwards to determine which of its components the temporary life-support pack would need. Once those components were identified, we had to figure out how to structure them. After that, we could add the extra weight to make our pseudo-pack feel like the actual pack. Then all we had to do was fly it. Simple.

The LEAI suits normally run off an umbilical, a tube that carries vital fluid between a mother ship and the suit. We planned to connect our life-support pack to the suit using the port where the umbilical leading to the mother ship normally hooked. This was a latch with two hoses for water and two for air, which we would use to flow air into the suit at a known rate and provide a loop of cooling water. Air would enter the suit through one air port and exit the suit through the second. We could control the pressure inside the suit by installing a pressure gauge and a valve on the air exit port. The two water lines were to be connected to an ice-pack system that was originally designed for cooling bomb suits. The ice-pack system would cool and circulate water through Alan's special long underwear.

Wind Tunnel Rig

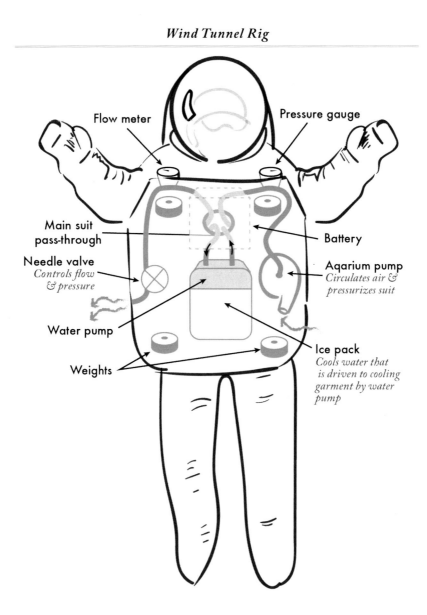

Flow meter

Pressure gauge

Main suit
pass-through

Battery

Needle valve
*Controls flow
& pressure*

Aqarium pump
*Circulates air &
pressurizes suit*

Water pump

Ice pack
*Cools water that
is driven to cooling
garment by water
pump*

Weights

As we determined the details of the wind tunnel suit, an engineer named Jacob Dang and I were also designing both the metal frame that would hold everything and the attachment system to secure this frame to the suit. The frame was a metal rack which had two hooks intended to secure it to the rings on the front of the parachute pack. Making the rigid frame mate to the soft parachute pack proved difficult. Ultimately, we were able to make a rigid frame that flexed on hinges to provide enough movement to attach the hooks. The rigid rungs of the pack between the hinges was where the life-support components connected, along with a few steel disks to make up for the weight of the oxygen tanks. This pack would work in a wind tunnel but not in space because the air it was providing to the pilot was being pulled in from the room at the pump inlet in the pack. It appeared to work just fine on the ground, though.

Jacob was a designer and draftsman who took the steadfast approach to problem-solving: he sat in his cubicle and worked until the job got done. He was the man who made the blueprints. In his quiet, head-down way, he influenced every aspect of the design process.

From the outset, the plan was to use the straps on a tandem skydiving parachute rig but instead of attaching a skydiver, attach all of our life-support equipment. To implement this, we would need to bring in the newest core member of the team, a parachute expert.

As we wandered the parachute factories of the American South, we found that most of the designers we encountered had a common distinguishing feature: they were from South Africa. South Africa is one of the few countries in the world outside the US with a vibrant parachute industry, and some of their engineers had emigrated here. I also suspect that South African culture lends itself to parachute engineering because there are presumably fewer rules to impede the design process and fewer liability problems with parachute users. The South Africans we met were just the right flavor of crazy to build and test new parachute systems. They had moved to America over the last decade and were building parachute systems at the most distinguished parachute-manufacturing facilities in the world. Since we would use a fairly standard tandem skydiving parachute for our first versions of the system, we contacted the makers of the world's most popular tandem skydiving setup, United Parachute Technologies. That's how Daniel "Blikkies" Blignaut joined the team.

Blikkies had spent his life skydiving and building parachute systems. He had jumped from an airplane over 8,000 times, during many of those jumps wearing brand-new gear he had personally designed and built. He was a bold South African with the mouth of a sailor and the brain of a flung-hair laboratory scientist. His countless parachute system innovations had unquestionably saved lives. Though he was wildly animated among friends, he avoided the spotlight and made no splash in the parachute world. Yet most of the glam-faced parachutists blowing up YouTube wear gear he has built.

Blikkies was part of the engineering team at United Parachute Technologies that was normally in charge of special projects like this. He would remain a full-time employee of United Parachute Technologies, but as the program grew, and especially at its end, the vast majority of his time would be spent on Project StratEx.

The skydiving rig we used for our wind tunnel tests had "DO NOT JUMP" embroidered on the back. I am sure that was for good reason, but it was adequate for our test. We adapted this tandem rig so as to hook the equipment where the second person would normally go.

Blikkies added the final touch to the chestpack: a cover that kept everything tidy and provided space to mount four feet onto the back of the frame. The feet created a solid surface at the front of the pack so that while the suit bounced around and collided with the wire mesh floor of the tunnel, it didn't crush the life-support equipment.

Once the pack was built, we spent two days walking through the schematics of the system and reviewing the fundamentals of the design, preparing for our first big meeting of all the advisors. At the meeting we demonstrated the ability of the new life-support pack in the center of a crowded room. The brand-new red suit with the wind tunnel chestpack hung from an aluminum pull-up bar that was being used as a makeshift gantry so the person in the suit wouldn't have to hold up the heavy equipment. I was that person. I felt the onset of claustrophobia as I pushed through the rubbery inside of the suit and considered calling the whole thing off right before they latched the helmet down. After the helmet was locked, air flowing on my face made me feel better. Blikkies took measurements while other team members poked, prodded, and asked me to perform various movements.

After my suit session, Alan took a turn. Moving his arms around, he accidentally knocked the chestpack's main power switch to the off position. Inside the pressurized shell I'm sure things fell quickly, eerily silent as the suit powered down. The suit was filled with plenty of breathable air, so Alan was not in any immediate danger, but it was necessary to get the helmet off quickly before carbon dioxide started to build up. Under Ryan's signature calming instruction, Alan had to wait while the power status was verified and then the suit depressurized through the outflow valve so that the helmet could be removed. Ryan didn't have time to explain all the details to Alan. The helmet came off into Ryan's hands, revealing Alan's calm but frightened face—at the time he had little idea what was going on. It was a look I would come to understand firsthand myself.

We saw Alan flinch in that demonstration. As Ryan calmly started giving instructions to get the suit buttoned back up and resealed to continue work, Alan kindly let him know that we were done for the day. We had what we needed, so nobody pushed back. The parachute team had their measurements to finish the mock rig. We would meet next in Colorado to test the system in the blasting winds.

We moved all the equipment out in two days. Multiple crates the size of golf carts were shipped across the country with "critical space equipment" stamped on the side. Parts came from Houston Texas, and from Tucson, Arizona, where our early build and test processes took place. We had a gantry, the suit, a big scale for weighing the equipment, a communication system, cooling packs, coolers, tools, straps, and two pickup truck loads of spare parts and buckets of things we might need if something went wrong. I drove from Tucson to Denver with the huge batteries that would power our pump. While we unloaded, kids were laughing and enjoying their first wind tunnel visit. Our test would take place at night.

The engineering team shuffled across the street to a hotel to begin preflight tests on the suit. I'm fairly certain we are the first team ever to unpack a NASA-certified LEAI suit in a hotel room, another hallmark of the uniqueness of our program. It was thrilling to work through the preflight checks in such an incongruous place.

We inflated the suit both to integrate the final hooks and to do a "structural," making sure nothing was wrong with the suit fabric or bladder envelope. Then, with the suit inflated and half the team preparing boxes to move down to the wind tunnel, everything went dark: a power outage. Once again I got the feeling that what was happening to us had never happened to anyone before. We put on headlamps, monitored the final steps of the suit test, and started ferrying boxes down pitch-black stairwells to running cars on the ground level. The slightly panicked safety officer (who was actually the temporarily reassigned project engineer Norman Hahn) watched and waved us past while we carried load after load of heavy equipment through the dark, silent hallways.

Norman was just coming into the project. The project engineer was charged with overseeing everything: he approved all documents and attended all meetings. Norm worked in a big automotive company before coming to Paragon, where he worked out of Colorado like me. Norm was likely chosen as the project engineer because he was somewhere between a bureaucrat and a scrappy creative engineering type. He was a good choice for a makeshift safety officer. He would play that role regularly.

Lights flickered back on as we were pulling up to the wind tunnel. Just in time. The staff had cleaned up and prepared for us so we could move equipment straight upstairs. The building had large bay windows so we had to place things awkwardly in a back corner to avoid generating attention should passersby see a spacesuit hanging in a window.

We started things off by firing up the tunnel and letting the skydivers take a couple sessions in the wind. This was a veiled way for us to do a pre-evaluation of Alan's freefall skills. We hadn't quite gauged his personality yet and weren't sure how he would respond to any skepticism about his ability to fly in a tunnel. He easily saw through our scheme and put us at ease: "I know you're worried; I'm worried too!" He suited up and went for a fly.

This was one of the world's most advanced vertical wind tunnels. The lead instructor, Derek Vanschboeten, was not only the head coach in the tunnel but an accomplished freefly skydiver. He was one of the main reasons we had picked this particular wind tunnel. On top of his impressive skydiving history, he had also worked as a support SCUBA diver at NASA's Neutral Buoyancy Lab, a giant swimming pool used to train astronauts by suspending them in water as if they were weightless. Thus he had direct experience working with spacesuits and understood the rigors of that process. The level of detail associated with maintenance, cleanliness, and general handling of a spacesuit can be very frustrating for people without that experience.

Upon arriving, we realized that Derek happened to be nearly the exact same size as Alan and me, five foot, 10 inches and 170 lbs. This meant that Derek could also wear the suit. So we deliberated with him and decided that he should fly the suit for its first test. He was undoubtedly the first person ever to don an LEAI space suit and fly in a vertical wind tunnel with just two hours' notice.

We started through the preflight checklists and got Derek suited up outside the tunnel. We moved the big life-support pack inside where we would hook it up as he lay down over it, suspended on some gymnastics mats. After he was in the suit and hooked up, we would turn on his cooling, turn on the air system, close up the helmet, pull the mats, and exit the tunnel.

In the first round, everything went as planned in the suit-up. We got Derek in the suit with relative ease and were able to connect the life-support tubing without a problem. The hooks gave us trouble, as they had every time, but we wrestled them on. We hit the big red switch on the side of the suit and Derek's hair flipped up over his forehead as the air began to flow out. After a very nervous thumbs-up, we pushed the helmet bubble closed and locked it down. The suit techs and I scrambled to get the sneaker-marked mats out from underneath and pulled into the anteroom. The colossal fans above the tunnel drowned out all other sound and we stared with nervous apprehension through the observation window while the scene livened in the wind.

When a wind tunnel starts, the straps begin to whip. Any tail of webbing or loose fabric begins to flap, and then to slap. The roar increases and combines with screeches of wind catching on corners. The wind-speed dial passes 60, then 70 miles per hour. Soon it's windier in that tunnel than in hurricanes or tornadoes as the speed exceeds 110 miles per hour. The suit and pilot visually appear to lighten, rocking and slightly bouncing, while the wire mesh holding everything offloads and returns to flat. Finally, at around 130 miles per hour, the suit begins to lift up off the mesh. When that moment came, everyone couldn't help but smile as the monster suit and pack hovered gently a few inches off the pad. We knew the idea would work. This thing could fly.

That was, of course, just the beginning, the first minute of two all-nighters testing every facet of the mock suit in flight. In the first round, as Derek held his hover for the first few seconds, we saw our first flaw. Presumably because of the broad, flat front surface on the suit, we started to see a phenomenon known as vortex shedding, where high-pressure zones build up and then relieve, creating a back-and-forth rocking motion. In our case, that process had an unfortunate resonance. The time it took the high-pressure zone to build and relieve was about the same amount of time it took the pilot to rock back and forth, causing the motion to persist and keeping the pilot in a light continuous wobble in the air.

Our second major problem quickly presented itself. We had attempted to place the oxygen tank simulators on the pilot's back for this test to keep the chestpack lighter. Derek started drifting slowly to the side, and as soon as he started encountering this light turn, we found a scary problem with having big tanks on the backpack. When Derek began to turn, he stuck an arm out in the normal fashion, expecting to counteract the tilt. He kept turning, then spinning. Everyone on the bench stood up. The spin bordered on violent, threatening to slam him into the wall. Another instructor, who was in the sealed anteroom attached to the tunnel, jumped in and threw out a leg, colliding with the suit and arresting the spin. The tunnel was quickly powered down and we freed Derek to digest our first live test. He had made it about five minutes, the time it takes for someone to freefall from the stratosphere.

When Derek came out of the tunnel, we dove into the video and identified what we thought caused his out-of-control spin. When a human body is falling at 120 miles per hour and the person sticks an arm out, they tilt to the side. That tilt puts their bent legs into the wind, causing them to spin like a helicopter blade. Normally a skydiver can rearrange their arms and upper body into a position that will counteract the motion. This type of turn-arresting is a focus of normal skydiver training, and for an instructor it is second nature. A skydiver who sticks their arm out with their palm facing down would expect to turn so that their thumb moves forward. A human body is typically wider (side to side) than it is thick (front to back). But in our suit, the life-support pack, parachute pack, and tanks make the body profile far larger in the "thick" direction, so when an arm is extended the skydiver tilts as expected, but the chest catches more air on the side than the legs. This makes things that normally happen behind a skydiver's center of gravity happen in front of it. The chest helicopters instead of the legs. Everything is reversed. In order to fly this suit, an experienced skydiver must act directly opposite to all of their training and muscle memory when counteracting a tilt.

We ran our second test after making some significant changes to the suit. Blikkies tore apart the tank holders on the parachute pack and we set the tanks aside, replacing their weight with extra metal disks in the front pack.

To address the vortex shedding and wobbling (which we had come to call "potato chipping"), we added little pieces of yarn called telltales all over the front of the chestpack. These would point in the direction of the wind so we could physically see the vortices shedding. The telltales would point back and forth as the high-pressure zones relieved over the edge of the pack.

As the clock ticked toward the following morning, we worked through our suit-up process again. We laid Derek down and hooked him up for the second time, hitting the big red switch and sealing him in. As the pack filled, Derek worked through skydiving motions, feeling around the space he had to work with. During his arm waving, his thumb snagged the power cord and everything unexpectedly powered down. The suit was depressurized, the helmet pulled off, the situation explained, and Derek sealed right back in. We reconnected the suit and the chestpack and were able to continue.

The second flight felt more relaxed. There were two turns that had to be arrested by the other instructors, but this time they were less severe. There was some rocking and the telltales verified what we had suspected: the flat surface was allowing pressure to build up. We made a design note to add a crest to our flight suit so that the compressing air could escape in even rivers running off the two sides of the pack. This time we didn't stop until we planned to. It was time for another debrief, dinner, and preparations for our real pilot, Alan, to ride the red stallion spacesuit into the wind.

Nobody had planned for dinner. It was 1 a.m. and we were all starving. We roamed around town looking for any open restaurant . No luck. At a gas station we managed to procure frozen burritos and Starbucks Frappucinos (Red Bull being strictly off limits). Again, I was aware of the odd clash of environments: a senior vice president of Google, the chief engineer for ILC Dover's spacesuit division, a world-champion freeflyer, and a rough handful of ex-NASA engineers and contractors silently chewed frozen gas station burritos in the party room of Skyventure Colorado, mentally preparing to button up a space shuttle LEAI suit and levitate its pilot in double hurricane-force winds before morning came.

After dinner, Alan went in the tunnel for the first time. After twice watching Derek, a muscular young skydiver, struggle to maintain control in the pressure suit, it was hard to drum up confidence in our 55-year old pilot.

For our first test with Alan, we took all the extra weight off the system and pulled the oxygen tank simulators off the parachute pack so that we were running as light as we could. This would require less wind speed to levitate, put less weight on Alan's arms, and make it easier for the instructors to intervene in the slower air. We took the liquid-cooling garment off the instructor and put it on Alan. We replaced the ice packs in the cooling system, laid the chestpack on the mats in the tunnel, and Alan suited up. He lay on the pack and we hooked up the umbilical ports with his water and air supply, then clipped down the chestpack. We ran our cooling test, but there was no flow—we had a problem.

We pulled Alan off the pack and then proceeded to troubleshoot the cooling system into the morning. Nothing we did seemed to work; there just wasn't any flow through the system. We'd seen repeated issues with the quick disconnects that connect the long underwear to the suit not fully engaging and staying sealed so we worked them over and over, with no success. We pulled the central cooling pack off. We tried jumpering the system, short-circuiting the water loop with an external tube to try to isolate where the problem was. Still no flow. We finally took the whole thing apart on the carpeted floor of the waiting area and worked the problem back to the source at the ice packs. It still refused to move water. We dug deeper, removing the covers, and found that the entire length of tubing running under the insulation was frozen solid. How could the system have gotten so cold? We eventually discovered that a last-minute decision to switch to dry ice in order to keep the ice reliably cool had supercooled the water in our system to well below freezing. When the hoses were hooked up, they froze everything in contact with them. We were lucky we hadn't lost the entire pump assembly.

Finally understanding the problem, we thawed the other packs out until there was liquid water present, ensuring that the remaining ice was near freezing, not below it. We tried the pumps and they ran well. Within an hour, we reassembled the system on the mats at the bottom of the tunnel, being careful not to let any parts roll too far sideways and fall through the mesh and into the giant ducting below.

The final tests showed signs of life in all the systems, so we closed Alan in, adjusted the straps, and stepped back to watch his first-ever flight in a spacesuit. The wind built up while the suit techs and I stayed glued to the scene from the small anteroom. The air groaned as the speeds rolled up over 100 miles per hour and we saw the now-expected offloading of the mesh so that the suit was just barely supported. The suit skimmed in a light circle before the wind-speed indicator slid past 140 miles per hour and Alan lifted into the air.

He flew the suit like he'd done it a hundred times. Rocking lightly, he flew at an angle with his head high above his feet at 30 degrees. Perhaps because the pack was lighter than it had been with the instructor, the suit found equilibrium in a position that didn't shed air with the same type of pulsing. Alan bounced off the mesh and made a couple of laps around the room, each time flying higher, reaching the edge of the observation window. We cleared the bench and hugged the glass as he drifted high into the tunnel. The extremely tense but flawless run finished without a single spin event; the tunnel assistants barely touched Alan once.

When we spoke afterwards, it was clear that Alan had outdone even Derek, the weathered instructor, surprising us all with an incredible run. Perhaps his having less experience and instinctive control than Derek actually worked in his favor. Maybe it was the lessened weight or the chance to observe before he got in. Despite the success, he was clearly exhausted and more beat up by the run than he let on.

Alan was satisfied with his night. We took some pictures of deep indentations on his arms where the suit bearings were digging into the front of his biceps. We took more notes, reviewed videos, tinkered with hardware, tightened straps, loosened straps. Derek took one more run.

We were starting to suspect that some of the spinning issues were a product of the pack shifting from side to side, forcing an asymmetry in the system's windward profile. The pack-shifting issues appeared ultra-sensitive, threatening more potentially severe spins. In the instructor's final run, we also started experimenting with the center of gravity of the pack, shifting it by moving weights up or down in the pack and causing a very visible change in the stable position of the suit while hovering in the air.

Alan left for the night before Derek's final run to sleep and prepare for more time in the tube the next night. Derek was also exhausted at the end of the session. He too had deep indentations on his arms, and his shoulders were near their breaking point; he needed to go home and sleep. It was definitely a successful night, but flying in the suit with the pack had quickly proved to be a brutal process. This was consistent with reports from our astronaut advisors: wearing a spacesuit is really hard.

As the sun rose, Blikkies, Derek, and I made our way to a little café for breakfast. Blikkies had a tradition he'd followed over years of parachute testing: drinking a cold beer in the rising sun after all-night tests. He hadn't doubted the participants would survive this test, Blikkies said, but traditions are traditions. We hadn't walked on water, but we had levitated a 450-pound spacesuit into the dry, thin Colorado air. We toasted an amazing night with one beer and two orange juices.

The next day we all slept like hungover college kids until 4 in the afternoon, then it was back to the lab. We were once again jostled by partying children making their way out the door as the wind tunnel closed down its regular business hours. After the kids were gone, we could move our mobile suit station up to the second floor. Derek had ended up working most of the day in the tunnel, but he was still revved up and ready to go for more flying, an activity he was volunteering to do for free.

Although the plan had been to have Alan fly the suit for the testing, most of the tests (except one each night) ended up being flown by Derek. We were all still gauging Alan's abilities. This testing was the team's first chance to assess whether he had what it would take to do this thing. Currently it was not looking good. Our planning was less than optimal, and it seemed he got to the tunnel totally beat. Of course, he was a VP of a tech firm, not a professional skydiver. And, strangely, he did seem to bow out of the testing each night, which gave us pause. Then he surprised us all, tipping the scales back toward the making of a legend, by having the best run yet in the tunnel.

We hadn't considered using Derek to test the suit until the day we started, and we still didn't know whether Alan would have made it through the tests if Derek hadn't stepped in to do the initial ones. It was literally heavy lifting. Derek was the only one to ride the suit at full weight, and it was quite possibly the heaviest manned system ever flown in a vertical wind tunnel. We were awed by Alan's ability to fly the suit nearly flawlessly, but we were less than inspired by his lack of motivation to get in and fly.

On night two, we had fewer big boxes to check but many more little boxes to mark off. We had answered the question of whether an inflated spacesuit with a giant chestpack could skydive: it could. Now we would use all the remaining time to conduct test after test in order to identify crucial limits for the design team.

We first had to determine how much effort we designers would have to expend to keep the center of gravity near to the natural human center of gravity. To do this we would fly the system, moving the weights to all the extremes to see how this affected flight. We flew once with the suit weighted heavy to one side (left to right), again with the suit weighted high (toward the belly button), and finally with the suit weighted low (toward the groin).

We hit our stride a few tests in. In a growing rhythm we banged out two tests with Derek flying, showing the effects of left/right and high/low center of gravity. Moving the weights all to the right side resulted in a system that was highly difficult to stabilize. In order to fly straight, Derek had to keep one arm stuck straight out all the time to catch more air on the heavy side. Presumably this was the only way to stop the system from leaning toward the heavy side of the pack and turning him into a propeller.

The low center of gravity test, which brought the center of gravity down away from the belly button, was performed by Alan. It was expected to be the easiest of the remaining tests. If that one looked good, we would test high center of gravity flying. If these tests didn't show a significant change to the suit's ability to fly, the design team would have total freedom in where to locate the high/low center of gravity for the system, which would make our lives that much simpler down the road.

After a long debrief with Derek, Alan suited up again. The process of getting into the suit was getting easier each time. We weren't freezing lines or pinching hoses, and we streamlined the strapping process so the pack looked even each time we strapped it on. We hauled the life-support pack into the tunnel and laid it on the mats while Alan once again donned the red suit. This time the suit techs had removed the cover layer from the suit so we could see the bearings and try to better identify which bearing was digging into people's arms. The suit looked more machinelike with the covers off, the visible metal joints and restraint buckles reminding us just how complicated the suit really was.

Alan walked into the tunnel and lay on the pack. We fastened it. Once ready to fly, we gave the signals to the tunnel folks and walked away. I had an independent pitot tube air-speed reader that we would take measurements with to try to gauge how fast Alan would fall in thick air. The two instructors huddled against the edges.

Normally the instructors will ride right in the middle of the tunnel with the students, and because a person laid out like a skydiver catches so much more wind than a vertical person, an instructor can stand up in the tunnel without flying into the air. But because our system was so heavy and required much higher air speeds than a normal skydiving session, the instructors would have to stay near the walls and float in if necessary to intervene while the suit was flying. If they tried to walk on the mesh the air would lift them up. The very edges were the only safe place; the closer they got to the subject, the fiercer the fury. When Alan started to turn, they would pounce in. With arms sucked against their chest—weirdly tight, with their elbows inside the profile of their chest—they could get a knee into the center of the channeling air stream. The spacesuit would bash into that knee and rock back to normalcy. During the collision, the instructors would start to lift into the air and spend a moment standing on nothing but a channeling vortex of 150-mile-per-hour wind while they rode the edge swirl back to the wall. There, the pressures dropped and they would be set back onto the mesh.

The instructors waited along the edges and Alan rode in a more heavily angled but generally stable flight, with only a couple of instructor interventions. The flight was again gentle and benign, and we couldn't dismiss what that meant. Alan could fly that suit. We had reinforced our biggest victory with another stable flight.

We debriefed for over an hour, ate a far more organized 3 a.m. snack of donuts and fruit, and pulled together for the final runs.

Alan again departed early. After his run he was encouraged and excited but battered. Perhaps the biggest takeaway from the testing would be the brutality of the process itself. While Alan had the skills to fly, he did not appear physically ready for the flight—or the training, for that matter.

Next Derek got back in with the weight moved up high on the chestpack. This flattened out the system. With the weight up high, the surface of the pack drew perpendicular to the wind and caused it to potato chip back and forth more, but the effects were manageable. Strangely, Derek encountered another fairly violent spin. These had been subsiding throughout the flights.

When he came out, we discovered he had a growing injury that was affecting him more then he'd let on. The bearing that had been digging into his shoulder previously was causing a lot of pain. He was starting to turn because he was nursing a hurt arm. He was too weak to keep himself stable. We'd reached the end of our testing for that night, but we had accomplished what we wanted. We had our last data point.

We were all careful to be cautious in our excitement. It was enough to know the suit could fly without spiraling out of control. And on this morning we all drank beer.

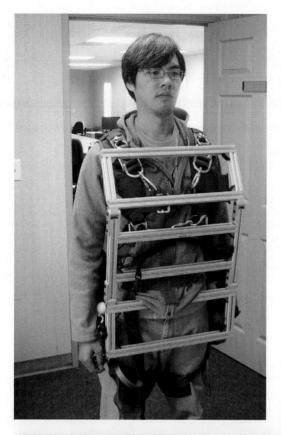

*Engineer Jacob Dang
modeling the first
chestpack frame prototype.
This frame was used
to hold the life-support
components for wind
tunnel testing.*

*Alan Eustace with Ryan
Lee and Dave Graziosi
connecting the wind*

*tunnel life-support pack to
the suit in preparation for
wind tunnel testing.*

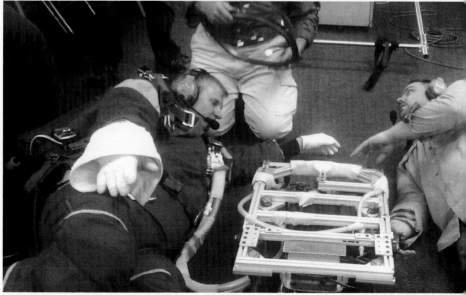

Alan having a 1 a.m. donut in his spacesuit between wind tunnel testing sessions.

Alan Eustace flying a launch, entry, and abort ILC Dover spacesuit in a vertical wind tunnel at Skyventure Colorado in Parker, Colorado.

CHAPTER 3
...
Design and Build

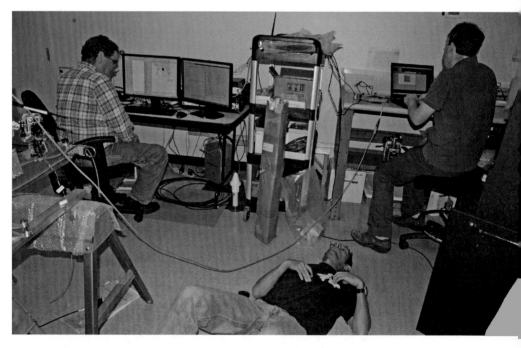

Despite popular conceptions about aerospace technology, the design of this spacesuit was the result of feverish persistence—not genius. Occasional strokes of lucky brilliance are fleeting. Most of the tens of thousands of hours it takes to make something brand new are spent grinding away at a never-ending series of small, time-consuming problems which are taken on in the only way they can be: one at a time. Building a spacesuit is like making gravel in a third world country: you hit a rock with a hammer, and then you hit it again, and then again, and you keep hitting it until the big rock is lots of little rocks. Then you get a different big rock and start again.

Design is meticulous and slow. It is an intentionally dry and sober process of double, triple, and quadruple checking. By the end of the process of designing the suit for this mission, I had shared some 3,000 hours of my life with over 1,000 parts in the chestpack system. Every nut, bolt, washer, dab of glue, and solvent cleaner had been given its due consideration.

May–June 2012: Design

Engineering designers start big and end small, refining an overarching idea into specific requirements. Faced with a requirement for a spacesuit that was fully self-contained and capable of bringing a person to the stratosphere and back, we ask, "How high?" and we ask, "When?" That process continues; we beat at the rock until the questions become smaller, even tiny. "Should we have six suit hinges or seven?" One day we were all discussing block diagrams of spacesuit architectures and then two years later we found ourselves arguing over how to verify the composition of the type of metal in one of our bolts.

As we dug into the project in May 2012, our new leader, Sebastian Padilla, transitioned into his role as the project manager while the old project manager, Gary, phased out. Sebastian, a tall, soft-spoken engineer, was more senior than any person at the company except the founders. Sebastian had a deep understanding of the engineering process and an ability to quickly grasp complex problems. This, coupled with a remarkable philosophical and emotional steadiness, made him the rock at the foundation of the engineering team. Most people never have and probably never will see Sebastian visibly angry or even agitated. In his slow, calculated way, he gave answers straight up, whether they were hard or easy to hear. Sebastian loved the grind and he loved good beer, good food, and good company. He moved easily into his role and stayed tall during a job that included far more stressful moments than glorious ones.

The project was broken into four groups called integrated product teams: the pressure suit team (the actual spacesuit), the equipment module team (the chestpack), the recovery system team (the parachutes), and the flight vehicle team (everything else that flew to space but didn't come down with Alan). There were other focus areas that had their own leads, but their work crossed the boundaries of multiple product teams. This included the avionics group (the flight computer and communication systems) and the environmental control and life-support group, which researched and implemented components inside both the life-support pack and the suit itself. That group had the most critical job of keeping Alan in a safe environment inside the suit.

The pressure suit team was initially led by the analyst who worked on the proposal. In serious efforts to keep the team small, that analyst was crossed over from his day job as a thermal modeling engineer. Ultimately he didn't fit as a team lead, so he was replaced by Christie just a few weeks into the work. She was then in charge of both the spacesuit soft goods and the overall life-support architecture.

The flight vehicle team would be headed up by the lean, always-smiling John Straus, who returned to Arizona from another job to join the project. This team would, understandably, grow to be the biggest team on the project. During the first upsizing of the program, my responsibilities narrowed so that I was in charge just of the life-support chestpack and the parachute system. The parachute system would almost entirely be the job of Blikkies at the parachute company. I would monitor the interfaces and design the attachment rigging between the parachute pack and the flight vehicle John was designing. The design and management of the life-support pack was my major role at the outset.

During the creation of the wind tunnel system, we had to approximate the volumes and masses of all the major system components in order to simulate them in the tunnel. That process had given us a head start on figuring out the basic shape of our pack. This, in combination with the ongoing work by Christie and Zane to identify the life-support system components, left us ready to start the real beef of the design. We had been at the process full-time for about three months at this point. While I was devoting most of my time to getting ready for the wind tunnel, Zane and Christie had been refining the life-support system and had already started contacting vendors about purchasing items with long lead times.

The wind tunnel testing had given us a few fundamental design clues for making a suit system that would fly. Spacesuits are more like machines than a thick pair of coveralls. They are rigid when inflated, move at distinct hinge points, and are heavy. The control options in a spacesuit are extremely limited. This, along with what we were learning in the tests, got us started.

First, we knew that the tanks had to go on the front. With the tanks on the back along with the parachutes, the system profile was too thick. This thickness made the system confusing to control because the pilot had to reverse his instincts. This was potentially destabilizing and put the system at risk of turning sideways in flight or rocking back and forth until it made its pilot nauseous. (Nausea might seem like no big deal for an elite pilot, but vomiting into a facemask is.)

The wind tunnel testing also gave us a key clue regarding suit and pack alignment. The tiniest misalignment between the pack and the suit would cause serious spin potential. To minimize this risk, the pack would need to be rigidly connected to the suit.

On top of those big lessons, we had learned that right-to-left mass symmetry was critical, so we would have to closely control how far the chestpack's center of mass was from the full suit system's center of mass. We learned that the system flew better with mass low in the pack, but that it was not critical. Lastly, we knew our maximum allowable total system mass. We knew that lighter was better, but the instructor was able to fly when the pack weighed a full 180 pounds, making the entire system (including the pilot) weigh 500 pounds. While it was hard on the arms, the system was actually more stable when the pack was heavier. At least we had our mass ceiling.

In addition to designing the chestpack, I became involved in the suit design as we began the task of integrating the two frames. Originally, the suit was to have a hard wedge that would stop the six-pound helmet bubble from resting on the user's head while the suit wasn't inflated. We were able to eliminate that wedge when we decided to integrate the two frames, because the chestpack could hold up the bubble. With this, we stumbled into what turned out to be a very elegant design in which the suit and chestpack shared a structural frame. Later, the frame was further integrated to accept the parachute straps too. We ended up conceiving the system as a single unified person-shaped spacecraft instead of a separate suit, chestpack, and parachute. That integration, along with a painfully thorough stress analysis verifying the frame wouldn't break under the high load of a parachute opening, gave us a buildable spacesuit.

Suit Assembly

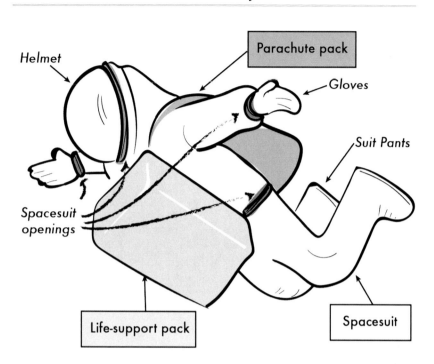

Helmet

Parachute pack

Gloves

Suit Pants

Spacesuit openings

Life-support pack

Spacesuit

The idea is always simple: by using a single frame and leaving the front chest surface with one flat plate on which to mount the life-support equipment, we had a malleable design platform. We could start to build the frame and move forward on the suit without knowing the full details of what was in the life-support pack. This got the big parts into the machine shop quicker. Jacob tackled the final drawings for the central frame, and within weeks of flying our wind tunnel suit, we had hacked its life-support system to scavenge parts for more prototyping and started building the real deal.

June–August 2012, Tucson, Arizona: Building the Suit

The chestpack came together with the suit in one unified model almost immediately. We worked long hours. The metal and plastic took form block by block inside our computers. Hours of staring at the computer model of the chestpack made the suit begin to look like a person with an opened chest, guts spilling out.

We ate, slept, and breathed suit design. Sleepless, Ryan and I exchanged emails about midnight epiphanies and physical illness stemming from our worries over what would and wouldn't work. The teams worked in concert, creating something brand new from conceptual foundations in a very short amount of time. Team boundaries melted as the tubes and wires crossed back and forth between the product teams. We displaced ourselves to each other's cubes, offices, and cities, filling white board after white board with childish spacesuit drawings that curved downwards so as not to spill off the edges of the boards.

The processes of designing and building were always blended. Just days after the wind tunnel testing, the suit team started cutting fabric for what they would call a "pattern verification unit," which is a cheaper, faster prototype used to make sure everything fits. The chestpack team started cutting the frame components a few weeks later, and by that time the chestpack was covered with its bright yellow aeroshell in the computer models. Our first parts were arriving. Soon it would be time to set the main structural frame at the suit facilities.

We chased down components in order: from longest lead time to shortest. We made phone calls. We negotiated deals and glad-handed salesmen in attempts to get parts faster. Parts rated for military use in space got ordered first. We contacted the US Air Force to see if we could swap our place in line for theirs so we wouldn't have to wait so long for things to come in. They said yes. We kept moving.

The computer models morphed day by day from a floating 3D mass of fake cubes holding the place of parts-to-be to complex representations of real-world components. We considered a part "frozen" when it was designed to the extent that we thought it wouldn't change anymore. Next, we would go to review and make sure the other teams agreed the part looked good. Then we would order it. If we discovered that parts on order or a component we were building conflicted with another component or something else on order, we took the hit. We would try to return a part or alter it, but if we couldn't, we moved forward. By not waiting for the design to be fully complete before we started building, we were able to fill the long months it took for the parts to get there with useful progress.

We were a bane to workers on the receiving floor, confronting them with stacks upon stacks of parts that needed inspections. If Alan had been waiting to see if we were really going to follow through, that waiting was over. Within a few weeks of the wind tunnel tests, there was no turning back.

The central frame of the suit would be put together at the ILC Dover suit labs in Houston. We had assembled the first parts of the thick suit skeleton while performing our first set of tests and validating our approach to assembly. We couldn't predict the exact shape of the inflated suit, yet the frame had to have that shape or else the inflation forces of the suit would pre-tension the structure. So we built an adjustable metal frame that was to be installed when the suit was inflated.

The life-support pack was the most complex item in our construction frenzy. It had four major parts: an avionics box, the oxygen tank assemblies, a display panel, and a fluid system hub driving the liquids of the suit. It was all closed in by an aeroshell, a fiber-filled new age plastic, the chestpack skin.

We started the build of the life-support back at our factory in Tucson, Arizona, with the avionics box. Building this box involved weeks of cramming and re-cramming packaging. We were trying to fit a Chevy engine in a Porsche, filling every square centimeter with meticulously placed components. Nothing could be accessed without taking everything apart. The bottom of the box was the communications computer that managed the data signals to and from the ground, turning the data into neat little packages and sending them off in abrupt high-powered bursts. The system on the ground had to be precisely time-synchronized with the system in the air, so that each side of the communication duo knew when to listen and when to shout. A GPS signal would be used for this to take advantage of the extremely precise time stamps GPS needs to operate.

Above the communications computer was a row of densely packaged ultra-high-efficiency primary batteries that would power the whole suit. These batteries could handle temperatures down to negative 70 degrees Fahrenheit and had an unmatched efficiency for both their size and weight. Finally, mounted on the wall of the box was a smart-data-acquisition board that took in all signals from sensors throughout the suit, conditioned and processed them, and passed the data to the communications computer to package up and send back to Earth.

We mounted two big heat exchangers on top of the box to warm the computer when it got too cold and to carry heat away when the batteries got too hot. The heat exchangers also warmed the oxygen going to Alan's helmet. Because the heat exchangers moved oxygen, they were extremely clean. When we assembled the heat exchanger for the first time, we learned the hard way that steel pipe fittings require a tiny bit of grit and natural oil to lubricate the connection. When we tightened the oxygen fittings onto the heat exchangers, they froze together (a phenomenon called galling). We had to smash them apart with wrenches and hammers, destroying the parts and setting us back two weeks while we waited for new ones.

Working in our cubicles and along the walls of the engineering floor of our buildings, we filled notebooks with math and spreadsheets to predict how much heat we would produce and how much heat we would need. We wanted to balance heat production and heat sink to make a toasty little home for all the electronics. Aluminum was cut and re-cut. Vendors were badgered to get us our hardware. In a bright white room in the basement of the Paragon headquarters with a white linoleum table and stacks of parts and toolboxes, we bolted it together. When it didn't fit, we built it again. We would model it, cut it, build it, try it, and repeat until everything fit. Then we'd make sure it worked—and when it didn't, we would start that process all over again.

Meanwhile, a rising-star technician, Esteban Garcia, was working his way onto the scene. Esteban was a charismatic Spanish go-getter who was new to the company but quickly making himself crucial to the build. We got in a strange but fun habit of singing his name opera style whenever he entered a room, grandly and obnoxiously announcing his entrance. He mounted up the aeroshell assemblies for the protective skin on our life-support pack. The base shell was molded from big plastic blocks that were cut with a computerized milling machine to make the flowing, aerodynamic chest plate that covered the guts of the life-support pack. Esteban outfitted the shells with voice radios by mounting modified walkie-talkies to the inside of the shell with rubber and stainless steel straps rated for extreme temperatures. He cut custom holes to hold the mounts that would secure the suit into the cart or "sedan" it would launch from. He installed a single shiny access door for passing life-support tubes and wires into the pack for ground support. At launch, the tubes would be withdrawn. The door had a little steel locking latch to keep it closed through a supersonic flight.

Placing the oxygen tanks in the life-support pack came next. Oxygen equipment is special because it has to be kept incredibly clean. The tank assemblies started with high-pressure tanks used by firefighters. These thin aluminum tanks were then wrapped with carbon fiber strands and coated with a special resin to make them extra light. The assemblies were outfitted with pressure regulators to step down the pressure the first time from the extremely high pressure in the tank to the somewhat lower pressure in the lines that go into the suit. I donned a white bunny suit with booties, hairnet, beard net, and gloves, and working inside a pressurized clean room attached special adaptors between the tank throat and the regulators. Next we added pressure sensors, thermal epoxied tank temperature sensors and finally topped it off with boxy metal covers to protect everything in a rough landing on the desert floor. If the tank stem were to snap off on landing, the tank would become a cold gas thruster launching Alan across the ground.

We added an LED display panel to the top of the chestpack that would show Alan the essential sensor readouts from the suit. Our now very busy avionics expert, Dan McFatter, took the lead on designing the readouts themselves while we designed and built the housings, panel boards, and mounts.

Dan had gained experience in production floor electronics and automation in the US and China before he moved into spacecraft avionics. He was working on the manufacturing floor of Paragon when he was tapped to lead the avionics team. A calm engineer, his nerdy flare was quickly sparked in any conversation featuring ideas about advanced monitoring and control systems or complex spacesuit avionics. Within the first few weeks of becoming involved, he cranked stunted, barely-there-on-paper avionics concepts into a functional flight computer system.

The displays had to be LED instead of the usual liquid crystal because liquid crystal freezes and fails in the extreme cold. We ran experiments with different tinted sheets of Plexiglas and investigated what combination of LED brightness and tinting made a display that was visible in the glaring sun. Another piece of electronics still needed to be tucked away somewhere, a module to control the temperature of the fluid system by flipping a heater on and off. The underside of the display panel made a plate where it could be mounted just below and outside the helmet bubble where the risk of fire was small. Design. Model. Cut metal. Build. That cycle persisted over and over again. As one build got finished, another would begin, and when a new thing screwed up an old thing, we'd redesign both of them.

Building the fluid system was the final challenge. The thermal fluid system would warm Alan in the cold (on his journey) and cool him in the heat (while hooked up to ground control). It was just plumbing: little pipes hooking a pump to tubes, tubes to sensors, sensors to heat exchangers, heat exchangers to ground-connection ports and everything to two fittings on the pressure suit that would attach to the liquid-filled long underwear and carry heat energy to or away from Alan's body. It would also need an overflow accumulator to accommodate the expansion of the fluid volume or a leak. When connected, fluids would move about in a web of tubes, a vascular maze.

The heater assembly was late and nothing fit the first time. We had to drill new holes in the mounting panel because the original design didn't include enough margin for threaded pipe fittings to seat at unknown spacing. The fittings muscled down but the assembly didn't match our paper models. We changed the paper. We changed the metal. Finally it all bolted down, a nest of tubes, sensors, fittings, and accessories. The full design process took about 11 months. Much of what is described in the coming chapters happened alongside this effort.

Neither the build nor the testing truly ended until the program did. Nothing works for sure until everything works for sure. These couple months gave us a beast to tame. We would transform it from ugly and gnarly approximations into a beautiful white working spacesuit. All my life I've wanted to be an inventor. In those months, I became one.

2012: Who's in Charge?

There was no government agency to regulate the build of our system. While the system was actually flying we would be mostly under the supervision of the Federal Aviation Administration (FAA), but they did not oversee our engineering. We ultimately would license our suit and flight system as an "experimental aircraft" that would be investigated by the FAA for flight worthiness. Their responsibility was to ensure public safety, not pilot safety. If we made a system that was going to kill its pilot, no one was going to stop us as long as that system wasn't going to hurt anyone else in the process.

Our project was partially like NASA and partially like the new "commercial space" companies coming into existence, although it was regulated by neither. As a group, we had very tight ties to NASA. Several of our employees came from NASA and most of us had spent some time working there as contractors. Our company's financial health depended on NASA contracts. NASA wrote the specifications for human space travel. However, we were a commercial operation apart from NASA, and this particular project was not under NASA's wing. We had no direct obligations to follow their specs—and to a large extent we didn't. We walked a line between the specifications from the deep bureaucracies at NASA and the new Wild West of space transportation. When walking such a ridge, you fall easily and painfully off the edge, first to one side and then the other.

We had to find our way in a maze of red tape, oversight, and what we learned from experience. As a designer of things made to keep people alive, I was, like many, haunted by the risk of failure and avoidable oversight. Advice, especially in the form of a specification written by a bureaucratic government agency, is a blessing until it overwhelms a situation and the simple act of finding and attempting to follow all the prewritten guidelines buries the project. Yet this is a designer's only verifiable line of defense. We knew, however, that a process in which designers wade through thousands of pages of paperwork searching for their partially applicable guide for making something takes months or years and produces marginal but repeatable results. We also knew that engineers using the creative process of their messy brains and applying fundamentally understood principles to their very specific problems have produced some of the greatest machines made by humans.

The number of human-ferrying crafts NASA has set out to build and never finished is astonishing. In the five-plus years I'd been working around the manned space program, I directly worked on or worked with information from six spacecraft concepts that NASA had started and failed to finish, despite huge investments in each. My life has touched the X-38, a spacecraft intended to carry humans to low Earth orbit, abandoned after substantial work and effort. Next was the orbital space plane, dropped after substantial design and prototyping to be replaced by the crew exploration vehicle as part of George W. Bush's Constellation (the moon, then Mars) ambition, which was itself abandoned when Bush left office in favor of a more modest vehicle named Orion. The Orion program was downgraded to a crew return vehicle for the International Space Station, then upgraded to the multi-purpose crew vehicle, which now ambiguously seems to be referred to again as Orion. The Orion program did manage to get a prototype to space, but it was mostly empty and not all that similar to what the actual vehicle was advertised to be. In 15 to 20 years, none of these vehicles has left the ground with a person inside.

There was a lesson in all this. NASA is a source of inspiration, and their feats guide and inspire true space nerds in a way we don't expect others to understand. That said, today is not NASA's day for manned spacecraft. Something they did wasn't working and we had to figure out what it was and avoid it at all costs.

In our case, avoiding the very strict, multi-billion dollar NASA spaceflight standards allowed us to win the contract in the first place. Alan was not about to pay NASA prices for his suit. Lifting those standards also made the program a hotbed for strong opinions about how the design should be carried out. We constantly walked the line between laborious specification-driven process and freeform engineering. We didn't have much choice.

There was also the element of risk. It couldn't be avoided. NASA had become increasingly more risk averse since its inception and so would never have built our suit. John F. Kennedy let the world know the first missions to another celestial body would be incredibly dangerous, implying that safety was secondary to more pressing and glorious goals. A handful of people worked as astronauts on the Apollo program and some died. Of 135 space shuttle missions, two broke apart, killing everyone inside.

None of the dangers are hidden from the folks who ride rockets, especially today, when most astronauts are engineers or pilots involved in the building of the rockets they ride on. They are consenting, willing participants and should have the right to make their own choices about how much risk they are willing to take in any particular mission. Of course an organization shouldn't hide risks from someone accepting a mission, but beyond that I don't see a moral conflict in dangerous spaceships like the folks running NASA do. The safety standards of government spacecraft have relentlessly crept up over decades to the point that a human-carrying spaceship made to their specifications cannot be made with the money and time they have.

I saw us as explorers going into the unknown, where unknown things may happen. Our acceptance of more risk than NASA was evident in a simple change to the initial requirements for system fault tolerance. Fault tolerance describes the number of things that can fail before something bad happens. NASA generally requires a single-fault tolerance to a loss of mission and a dual-fault tolerance to a loss of life. This means that two things must fail before causing the end of a mission, and three things must fail to result in loss of life. We carried no-fault tolerance to a loss of mission, and a single-fault tolerance to loss of life. Thus a single failure could end the mission and two failures could result in Alan's death.

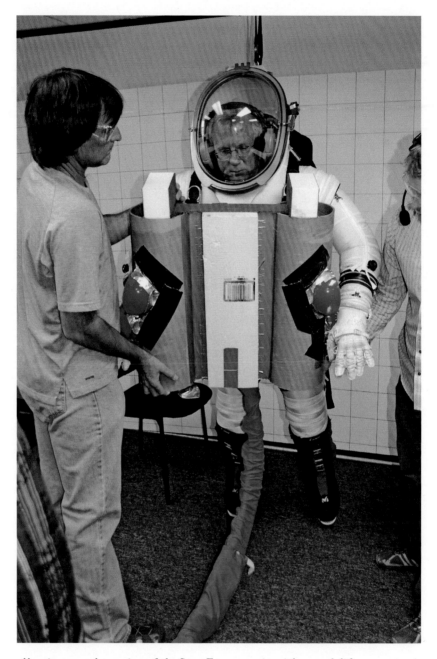

Alan in an early version of the StratEx spacesuit with a mock life-support suit evaluating reach and sizing.

A photo of the dummy assembly used for structural testing of the main suit frame.

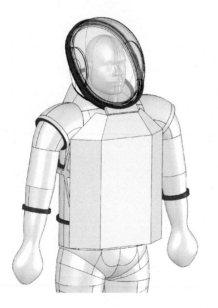

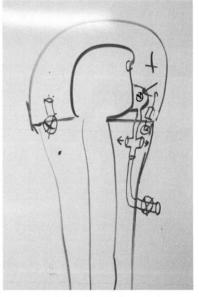

Early shots of the suit design. Computer models were used to create fabric patterns that were then turned into the actual spacesuit.

One of thousands of white board sketches used to communicate the always-changing life-support architecture.

CHAPTER 4

...

Human Testing

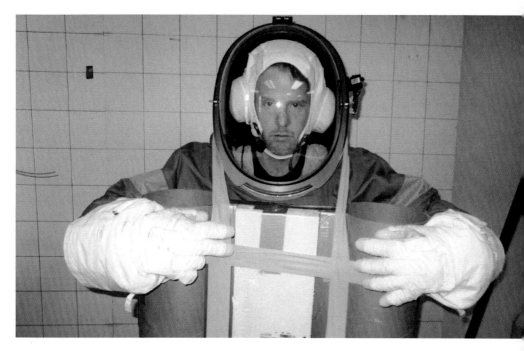

Making machines that strap to flat metal surfaces is difficult enough, but building a machine to closely surround a breathing, talking, sweating, freezing, oil-secreting, particulate-producing, pooping, peeing, vomiting, thinking machine is a challenge of a different nature. Aside from being hard to build, it's also really hard to test. The only option is to use a real live person.

Alan was a busy executive, so a couple of candidates were identified to serve as a pilot analog, and I was one. I was nearly identical in anatomical shape to Alan, and as I was one of the key members of the team, things would be logistically easy if I could stand in for him on some tests. Plus, I had already spent time in the red loaner suit and I didn't freak out. Lastly, because I was already on the life-support design team, I knew the systems well and could hopefully be versed in the possible failure modes so that I could respond appropriately in time to keep myself from getting hurt if something went wrong. I seemed like a good fit. I was extremely excited at the opportunity. I contained myself as best as I could during the selection process. If I was to be a human test subject for the program, I wanted to be selected because I was truly the right choice. The call belonged to Christie and Ryan, the suit and life-support lead from Paragon and the suit lead for ILC Dover.

September 2012: Choosing a Pilot Surrogate

We had decided to make a custom suit, one that would fit Alan alone. A standard spacesuit has adjustable joint locations and extendable sections so it can fit a variety of people, whereas our suit was manufactured without adjustability. Making the suit for one person meant the channels could be slim, and no extra fabric would be bunched up at the end of an adjustable section. During our pattern-verification testing, Alan went to the suit facilities for the first round of sizing. I was sent to be sized up as well, to see if Alan's space suit would fit me.

At the suit lab, the technicians had me change into tight-fitting long underwear. Two lanky guys walked in and introduced themselves. They cracked jokes, which didn't diminish their aura of experience as they fished tools out of a briefcase. You wouldn't find measuring tools like these in a hardware store. They were probably the same ones from the 1970s that measured the spacewalkers who braved the darkness in decades past. They had skull calipers to measure head size, pelvic risers to measure crotch height, and long-stemmed locking indicators to capture a half page of data about my hands—knuckle lengths, finger spans, and palm length. They would take 54 different measurements. This was the only test I've ever taken where my ability to pass was completely beyond my control. I so wanted to wear that suit, but it all depended on the size and shape of my bones, muscle, and fat.

They casually had me move about to accommodate their measuring as they filled a full page of their checklist. I wanted badly to know how it was going and if they saw any issues. Now and again they would point at different measurements and murmur to each other. I was sure they were judging whether I measured up right, saying things like "Look how long that middle finger is compared to that pinky; it will never fit into the normal glove." The process rolled on. They navigated coolly around the pelvic region measurements, asking me kindly at one point to "shift the boys to the other side." I tried to act easy and natural, but I'm fairly certain it was obvious I was just a nervous kid all psyched up about the idea of putting on a spacesuit.

Ryan walked in the suit lab and started to chitchat with the suit technicians as they packed up the instruments. They laid down the piece of paper I had been longing to see since the process began: Alan's measurements. We peered down the checklist, item by item, noting differences. I knew that it would be okay if some of the measurements were off in one direction, but not in the other. For instance, shoulder width could be too narrow but not too broad, crotch height could be too high but not too short, and on and on. We measured up almost identically. Almost. Every measurement was within what Ryan thought would be an acceptable limit except for one: wing span. I learned that day that I have exceptionally long arms for my anatomy. In total, they were four inches longer than Alan's; they would never fit. I would be kept out of that space suit by my stupid baboon arms.

My heart sank as I heard them talk. They chewed over that one measurement. They took the tapes out and measured again to make sure it wasn't a mistake; it wasn't. I remembered back to my fourth grade teacher telling me I should be a boxer because my arms were so long.

It appeared the conversation was over. I tried to mimic their cool demeanor. It just wasn't realistic that I could jam an extra four inches into the suit; the laws of physics apply.

I think Ryan must have called Christie to talk about the sizing and the outcome while we were packing up. I don't know where the suggestion came from, but somewhere in that 20 minutes everything changed.

What had been built so far wasn't the actual suit, it was a pattern-verification unit for understanding the size and shape of a suit built specifically for Alan. The real build was yet to come, which meant that minor changes were still on the table. They mulled it over for a day and then decided to consider adding an adjustable arm section to the suit. Suit techs made adjustable suit components all the time. They would discuss it with Alan, ask him if having an on-site test subject was worth the added cost and complexity of putting a two-inch-long adjustable-length collar into each of the suit arms at the wrist.

It was official. I was available as a human test subject for the program. We had a huge amount of work to do in the field of human factors and system sizing that could now be done with a real human analog. We dove in.

October 2012: Initial Suit Testing

What followed was a series of terrifying and exhilarating pre-delivery acceptance tests using a space shuttle LEAI suit and then various versions of Alan's suit. We wanted to test various suit pressures and establish initial geometries for all the pilot interfaces. This testing was performed at the

ILC Dover suit labs in Houston, Texas. It was mostly Ryan and me with the on-site suit team. Christie and Zane came on occasion. We built a cardboard chestpack that was relentlessly updated and rebuilt as the design progressed. We would update the design, try it in the suit, and see if it worked, change something on the suit, test again—and again and again.

We had multiple design efforts going on at once. In the chestpack that went on the front of the suit, we repeatedly encountered the extreme difficulty of accommodating human interfaces to something as bulky and mechanical as a spacesuit. I would design a display panel thinking it would be perfectly visible from inside the suit and then I would climb in and try it, only to find that almost none of it was in view. I designed two different sets of push-to-talk switches and pilot heater-control switches that the pilot couldn't reach. On the third try, we got them so the pilot could reach them, but they were inconveniently mounted to the oxygen tanks, requiring that they be removed every time we changed the oxygen bottles.

As we battled with these basic problems of three-dimensional geometry, we had an ongoing discussion with the flight doctors about suit pressure. The longest of those suit runs would be a test that assessed mobility in the suit at multiple different pressures. Doctors are usually in favor of high suit pressure because it reduces the chances of decompression sickness. Most doctors suspected that decompression sickness was more common than NASA's or the Air Force's record logs would show because pilots were incentivized not to report it for fear of being marked as more susceptible to the ailment and therefore grounded. Unlike doctors, suit people like low suit pressures because it makes the suit less rigid and offers more freedom of movement. To reconcile the competing interests, we performed a suit test in which I donned an early version of Alan's suit and assessed mobility at three different pressures. We found that higher pressures didn't appear to affect mobility much. We set the pressure controllers to a new pressure of 5.4 pounds per square inch (psi) instead of the old 3.5 psi (5.4 psi is the natural air pressure at an altitude of 25,000 feet). This, coupled with our rigorous pre-breathe protocol, would make decompression sickness next to impossible. Our suit would be the highest-pressure US spacesuit ever used in practice.

Alan came for one early test addressing whether a suit could withstand the ground impact of a parachute landing. NASA labs were designed with suit-suspension systems meant to avoid the potentially catastrophic disaster of a suited astronaut falling down, yet we had to know what would happen when the suit smashed to the ground at the end of a parachute flight. To test this, we suited Alan up and pushed him down. We made him fall backwards onto a mattress over and over again. We found that when Alan landed on his back, he compressed the drink bag inside the pressurized suit envelope, sending a water jet to his uvula that choked him. Thus began an arduous process of deciding if and how the suit would include a drink bag. We never would have learned things like this without these scrappy sessions. Despite the serious concerns we had about suited astronauts falling down, the suit turned out to do a good job protecting its contents.

These testing sessions culminated in a duration test in which we would settle lasting concerns about the overall length of the proposed suit-up and flight-preparation process. Ordinarily a suit wouldn't be pressurized through all the suit-up procedures, but we wanted a rigid, static system where the straps couldn't move, so we pressurized as soon as the parachute pack was put on. Advisors from NASA cautioned that wearing a suit in a full-gravity environment for that long could cause the pilot a damaging loss of blood circulation. We coupled the long-duration tests with an investigation on hang orientation. First I, and then Alan, spent one-hour sessions hanging vertically, then horizontally, and then at 45 degrees between the two. We had heard that Russian cosmonauts preferred 45 degrees and facedown when they did long runs at 1G, and their experience was validated by our tests. At a 45-degree angle it was easy to shift around and relieve pressure points. We did the final long-duration tests in that 45-degree orientation. Alan and I each spent four hours pressurized, hanging from a steel gantry staring at a wall while Ryan sat in a folding chair monitoring the process.

Wearing a spacesuit is much more intense than I could ever have imagined. Feelings of power and protection mingle with a crippling sense of bondage. Inside that alternate pressurized atmosphere you feel invincible. Should the room spontaneously fill with poison gas, or someone burst in with a pressing desire to fight you, you'd be safe. In a quite opposite sense, you are trapped. You cannot move without deliberate mechanical motions and there is no chance of shedding the suit in a hurry. That process takes tens of minutes. The suit techs told us that the first thing most people feel when they enter a spacesuit for the first time is panic from claustrophobia, so much so that some subjects refuse to wear the suit again. That claustrophobia almost derailed Felix Baumgartner's attempt at stratospheric glory.

November 2012: Suit Acceptance Testing

Some of the greatest works of civil engineering are the arches of ancient Roman aqueducts. These feats of hydraulic, structural, and geotechnical engineering weren't understood again until just a few hundred years ago. An aqueduct needs to maintain a certain slope in order to keep water moving at the proper rate. The stone channel can't go up and down as it traverses the countryside or the water would simply spill out. So the Romans had to build bridges over the valleys. In some cases, these rock structures were tens or even hundreds of feet high, composed of a series of stacked arches. The weight on the lowest arches was crushing. Arch construction used what's called a keystone, which allows the rocks' own weight (rather than mortar) to keep the structure from collapsing. Wooden beams held the arch in place during construction. When the artfully shaped keystone was slid into a tight lock at the top, the wood braces could be removed. According to legend, when those braces were pulled off and the creaking rocks shifted into place, the designer of the arch and keystone was ordered to stand beneath it—if the design failed, the engineer would be crushed by his own failure.

This was not unlike stories I heard from one of my early mentors, a veteran of space exploration design, who witnessed the build of the space shuttle and station. In the "olden days" of aviation, he and the handful of engineers responsible for the build of a certain new aircraft ran the checks and flew the maiden voyage themselves. Not only did they understand the system better than anyone on the planet, they considered it part of their job to share the risk of a catastrophic failure.

Everyone on the engineering team in an adventure like ours eventually stands beneath the arch, some of us more literally than others.

We had to test the system that supplied breathable air to our pilot. We had chosen a demand-regulated architecture: when the user breathed in, the pressure in the helmet dropped, causing a valve to open and restore the pressure by supplying some air. This type of system requires a very uncomfortable neck dam, a sort of rubber gasket around the user's neck which seals the helmet area away from the rest of the body.

The neck dam was required by the operating principles of human lungs. Lungs don't pressurize when you inhale; they expand to contain the volume of air taken in. This means that when a person breathes inside a pressurized space suit, the relative volume of the person's body changes to accommodate the moving air, so the pressure inside the suit doesn't change. Without a pressure drop inside the suit, there is no way for a demand-regulated system to tell when the oxygen tanks should add fresh oxygen to the system. The neck dam seals the head into its own separate cavity so that when the lungs expand below the seal, the air in the space above the seal reduces in pressure, causing the valve to open so oxygen flows into the helmet area. The pilot breathes through a facemask that allows fresh air in through a one-way valve; a tube directs the pilot's exhaled air into the musty space below the neck dam where the user's body resides as they breathe out.

If the air supply shuts off inside one of these spacesuits, the user is one breath away from the panic of suffocation. In a fully evacuated head bubble, empty lungs would try to vomit up through the mouth. This risk helped keep the choice of a demand-regulated system furiously debated throughout the program.

In the first architectural study of breathing-gas systems, mass estimates for three different architectures of spacesuit were approximated. The results clearly favored the use of a demand-regulated suit architecture. In the early tests we used flow-through-style suits because this was the type of suit the techs were able to loan us. During some of the tests with the suit that would be used in the program, we pressurized it like a flow-through system by rigging the cooling ports for the water lines as an air inlet and running without cooling. This was a testament to the familiarity and comfort that everyone had with flow-through systems.

Demand-Regulated Architecture

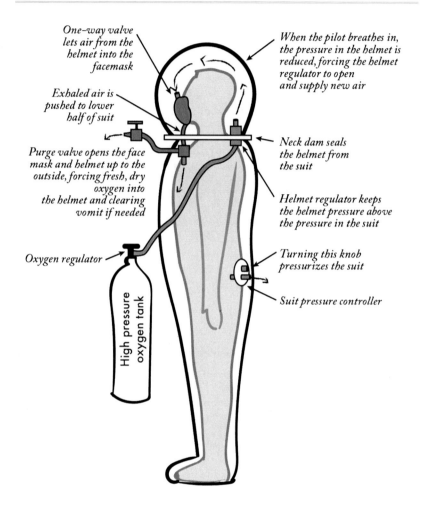

One-way valve lets air from the helmet into the facemask

Exhaled air is pushed to lower half of suit

Purge valve opens the face mask and helmet up to the outside, forcing fresh, dry oxygen into the helmet and clearing vomit if needed

Oxygen regulator

High pressure oxygen tank

When the pilot breathes in, the pressure in the helmet is reduced, forcing the helmet regulator to open and supply new air

Neck dam seals the helmet from the suit

Helmet regulator keeps the helmet pressure above the pressure in the suit

Turning this knob pressurizes the suit

Suit pressure controller

In November 2012 the suit was put into flight configuration as a demand-regulated system. A small team headed to the suit labs for a few technical meetings and a final checkout session before we would take possession of the suit for its life in operational use.

Ryan, Blikkies, and two suit technicians spent the morning laying out the equipment on plastic card tables surrounding a heavy metal gantry and two large air tanks pressurized to over 2,000 psi to supply air to the suit I'd wear for the test. They wandered around the room routing hoses, preparing the parachute systems, and setting valves. This would be the first manned test of the complete system. In a small curtained-off area, I donned the special long underwear threaded with tubes and sensors.

The techs helped me pull the suit pants over the liquid-cooled inner layers. I took a big breath before sliding into the top half of the womb-like suit torso. My head pulled through the soft grip of the rubber neck dam. We closed up, and prepared to lock down the helmet bubble. We were especially nervous about the high-pressure supply lines that go inside the suit to the regulators. If those lines were set up wrong or failed, the resulting pressures could be fatal. We put a pressure gauge on a port connected to the head region of the suit to monitor the pressure in the helmet. After a second walk-through of the details, we prepared to close the helmet. I was about to take the first breath ever from the newly manufactured, newly designed suit.

It took some effort to keep my breathing under control. My breaths already felt stunted with the facemask clamped over my mouth. Ryan pushed the bubble down onto the broad seal and locked it on with its clipping latch. My head was sealed in and I took the first breath from inside the cocoon.

It was weird but okay. When I inhaled, the regulators made a loud flowing sound. It was hard to push air through on the exhale, and the exhaust valve made an annoying vibration. On the second breath, my head came to pressure, the mask bit down a bit, and a wave of nervousness came over me as I thought about those high-pressure tubes. I told the operators that the mask felt pressurized. They reacted quickly by turning off the main air valve, cutting the air supply to the suit and preventing the possibility of an overpressure event.

The moments after the technicians shut off my air remain a blur in my mind. When that air line shut, something went very wrong inside the suit and nobody knew what it was. I felt pressure all over my head, and the mask sucked onto my face unnaturally hard. As the mask sucked down, water started spilling from the small drink tube filling the mask. I swiped my arm in the "end test" signal. The team jumped into emergency egress procedures.

In that moment we all thought that there was an overpressure event in the helmet. We would later learn that what happened was exactly the opposite. When the techs had closed the air line to avoid a high-pressure event, I ended up in an airtight fish bowl with a one-way line for air to leave and no way to get air back in. A vacuum was forming in the helmet.

The increasingly different pressures between the head region and lower body region of the suit had caused the neck dam to flip upside down and squeeze tighter and tighter around my neck while the drink bag port opened to free-flow water into the mask. Most critically, there was no air in the evacuated helmet.

My next attempted breaths were deep and panicked, but they pulled against nothing but a mask half full of water. I opened my mouth wider like a beached fish, gasping ever harder while the operators pulled the latch to unlock the helmet. Nothing happened. The helmet was stuck. With a vacuum in the head of the suit, the atmospheric pressure was now clamping the helmet down. Other operators rushed over to help. Blikkies struggled to hold me up as I stumbled backward. Finally, after about 15 seconds and three sets of hands pulling on it, the helmet banged opened.

Condensation blasted the surface of the helmet bubble as the pressure equalized and I took a glorious breath of thick, wet Houston air, then babbled some nonsense from my oxygen-starved mind. The team flipped the mask away from my face and water spilled down the front of the suit. I was safe but startled. We had experienced firsthand what happens when someone in a demand-regulated suit runs out of air: instant suffocation.

There was a purge valve on the side of the suit that could have been opened to equalize the pressure at the head of the suit, but that valve had been naively blocked off when we added the gauge to monitor pressure in the helmet. We called Zane and Christie to include them in our reconstruction of what had occurred. The incident was truly just a procedural mistake; we shouldn't have turned off the air valve. We decided to go ahead and finish the tests. The suit techs turned the tanks back on and got me ready to go back in. I was scared.

I struggled to keep my breathing under control as I reentered the suit that had just tried to strangle me. Once again Ryan clicked the helmet down onto my head. I reminded myself that this time the air would stay on, and that the purge valve was clear so that if something bad happened it would be opened in an instant. The suit techs had scissors at hand in case we found ourselves in another confusing situation without an easy way out. Plan C was to stab through the suit at the wedge behind my head. That would relieve any pressure differentials—and hopefully they would miss my neck.

The test went without incident. With experience to guide me, I knew that the mask was supposed to suck slightly to my face from the pressure differential between the head region and the body region. Ryan kept his eyes locked with mine. Knowing he would save me if things took another turn for the worse, I found my calm and breathed.

Everything appeared to work. I did basic mobility checks. We exercised the purge valve which hissed air out of a tube on my hip. In a span of tens of minutes, I slowly rolled down from a state of extreme nervousness to one of tranquility. The sound of rushing air and flapping valves became soothing.

It was a day of mixed feelings. We were exhilarated over the successful test; we had used the real oxygen system and it worked. At the same time, we had experienced the ugly beginnings of a suit suffocation. At the time we didn't understand how the technicians were actually able to remove the helmet. The tiniest amount of pressure difference across a helmet that large can create enormous forces. From that point forward in the program, Ryan would say a prayer before every major test.

Watching the video later I felt detached, like the face in the suit wasn't mine. The audio system broadcast one loud gasp, and the bulky gloved hands of the suit began to bat at the helmet in slow mechanistic motions.

Late November 2012: Safety Stand-Down I

A "safety stand-down" is an idea carried over from the military. In a safety stand-down, everyone stops working while an investigation takes place to sort through everything that happened. In team meetings, the leaders repeat dozens of times that the stand-down isn't about assigning blame, it's about avoiding repeat mistakes. We worked within our available emotional capacities to try to uphold that principle.

One thing we learned in those sessions was that nobody really knew who was in charge during tests. During the test in which I had started to suffocate, we had assumed that because we performed the test at the suit facilities, the suit techs were in charge. But that was not clear.

In the days after the event, when the remainder of testing was being completed, it was unclear how the "incident" should be reported. We weren't even sure it actually was an "incident." Alan was told about what had occurred the next day because he was about to go into the suit and needed to know the risks. At the suit headquarters, the Houston crew and I discussed design changes for installing an anti-suffocation valve.

Days passed, but we didn't report the event to management. After the test, I left the suit labs in Houston to work with Blikkies at the parachute factory in Florida. Christie, at the time the integrated product team lead for the suit, was aware of what had occurred. Upon returning to company headquarters in Tucson, I called a meeting to discuss details and next steps, but Christie didn't respond. In hindsight, I understand that the notice was too short to give her a chance to participate.

At this meeting, when I was probably still a bit too revved up about the situation, I spilled the whole "brush with blackout." It was then promptly reported to the safety officer, making for a clumsy and embarrassing reporting of the situation on all of our parts, mostly mine. The safety team felt the incident should have been reported immediately.

This incident cut deep. The debate over suit architecture, which had been heated at the beginning of the program, was revived. Some said the incident proved that a demand-regulated system was itself a flaw. Others argued that the real cause of the incident was the turning off of a valve. I found myself tugged between two camps feuding over what my brush with suffocation really meant, and who was to blame.

Because the program involved a human life, these debates between generally well-tempered engineers became much more animated and personal than usual. It was hard to be detached in discussions that sometimes involved my own safety and well-being. People said things they probably shouldn't have.

When we began the project, chances to participate were coveted. We were the best and brightest, and our job was the most fun. This incident was the start of a change. The import of the dividing line between being part of the team and not being part of it grew as the risks and liabilities associated with this crazy endeavor began to outweigh the potential glory of success.

The event was technically classified as a "near-miss" because it was not clear (even to me) whether I had lost consciousness or not, and because the technicians were able to remove the helmet instead of resorting to more extreme measures like puncturing the suit. It was not elevated to the more serious classification of "incident," which would have triggered even more paperwork and reporting effort.

On the surface it appeared that our system was not fault tolerant. The shutting of one valve resulted in the pilot suffocating. However, it was argued that the suit had two oxygen tanks, so turning off one would not suffocate the pilot, and the purge valve outlet we had blocked with a pressure sensor could have alleviated the issue.

To complicate the matter even further, through the long development process of the suit systems, we had made a series of decisions regarding how the suit integrated to the parachute packs. Those decisions had some cascading effects that impacted the oxygen architecture. To keep the parachute alignment precise, we wanted the suit rigid from the start of every mission, so that the parachute straps would line up accurately. We had learned in the wind tunnel that this was the only way to avoid a misalignment between the suit and pack that could induce a violent spin. This meant we pressurized the suit on the ground using a special valve, rendering the use of a traditional anti-suffocation valve impossible.

Little was resolved after the safety stand-down. Opinions varied. Some regarded the event as a serious incident in the suit; others did not. To some it appeared that we had tried to cover it up. Blame didn't really fall on me, because I wasn't the one in charge of reporting such an incident, and in my clumsy way I had ultimately reported it. Yet I still regret not communicating clearly and quickly with Christie about it. She later told me that she had not grasped the seriousness of the event, and never had any intention of communicating the details to the safety team, though she didn't fault me for doing so—she thought it was the right thing to do. She said she regretted not being present at the test to understand what had actually happened.

Months earlier, Christie had worked on a proposal for another project in which she would be the project manager. The proposal was accepted during the time of this debacle, and she left to assume the other position. She maintains that the suffocation incident had nothing to do with her leaving. She moved on. It was certainly not an easy time.

Preparing for initial oxygen testing.

Three people struggle to remove the helmet from the suit after an operational failure left the suit without oxygen and its occupant suffocating inside.

Testing out suit mobility at one of several different pressures to understand the trade-off between decompression sickness risk and ease of movement.

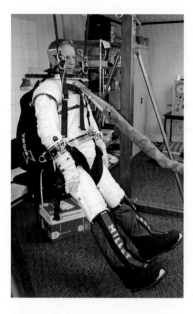

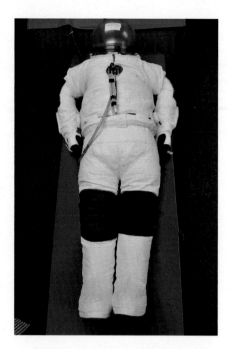

Alan trying on the final patterns for the StratEx pressure suit before the life-support system was added.

One of the first suit-inflation tests. There is no one inside the suit; it is being pressurized using a thermal fluid port.

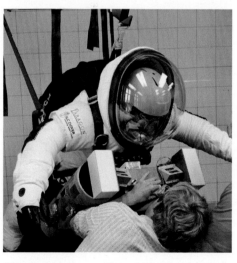

A team of Paragon engineers receiving the pressure suit in Tucson after its initial testing was completed at the Houston suit labs.

Testing out our cardboard life-support pack to establish an appropriate size and position for the pack.

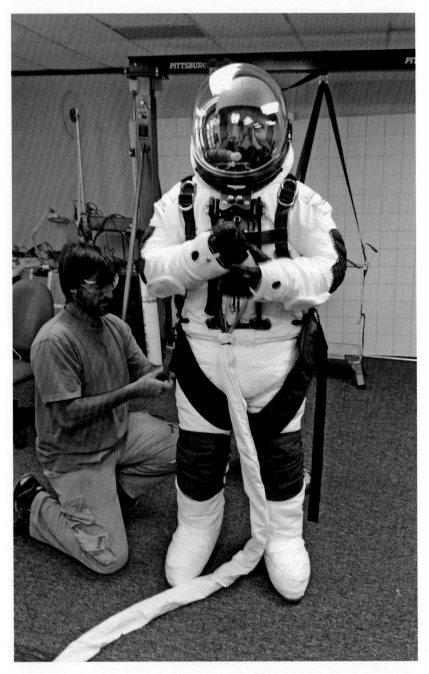

Using the suit for the first time with the final flight cover layers installed.

CHAPTER 5
...
To the Sky

O ne of the biggest problems with dropping someone from the stratosphere lies in finding a parachute system that will carry them safely back to Earth. During the build of this system, I interfaced with one of the largest and most well-known parachute manufacturers on the planet, United Parachute Technologies, which was contracted to develop, test, and integrate the parachute system for the StratEx suit.

We had to work through the dangers inherent in dropping a parachute system through the changing air densities of the atmosphere between

135,000 feet and the ground. I count the solution to this problem among our list of greatest accomplishments.

The atmosphere gets lighter and lighter as it extends from the dense thick air we swim in near the ground to the nearly nonexistent single molecules roaming in a fashion physicists call "free molecular flow" at the edges of the atmosphere on the border of space. That thinning out doesn't happen evenly. The higher you go, the faster the air thins. By the time Alan reached 90,000 feet (two-thirds of the way to the target altitude), more than 99% of the air surrounding the planet would be underneath him. This exponential relationship between altitude and air density causes a unique problem for ultra-high-altitude skydivers.

When an object falls in the presence of a gravitational field, it will accelerate at a uniform rate until it encounters an opposing force. In a parachute drop, that opposing force is drag from the atmosphere. The amount of drag will be proportional to the density of the air the object is falling through. This results in a very problematic phenomenon when falling from the stratosphere. A falling body will experience unopposed acceleration through the very thin air at the beginning of the journey, gaining extreme velocities, and then will slow down rapidly, possibly violently, when it reaches the denser zones of the atmosphere. What this meant specifically for us was that unattended, Alan's body would first find itself gaining outlandish speed in relative zero gravity, followed by a period of fierce deceleration upon reaching the denser air closer to Earth. In all cases for this type of jump, the very large main parachute that the pilot will land under is deployed close to the ground, once the pilot is falling at normal speeds.

This phenomenon can be visualized by examining the terminal velocity for a falling body at any given altitude and the actual predicted velocity of that body, as shown below. Terminal velocity is the speed at which the drag forces an object experiences are equal to the gravitational forces. Within the thick part of the atmosphere, where it is approximately all the same density, a falling object will accelerate until it reaches terminal velocity and then remain at terminal velocity. From the stratosphere, however, a falling body will accelerate toward its terminal velocity and then pass it, spending a period of time going faster than terminal velocity while it decelerates. Terminal velocity is a misnomer when a thing is falling through air with changing densities. In a high school physics class a student may learn that a falling object will never go faster than terminal velocity, but that is not true when something falls from the stratosphere. Because the air in the atmosphere is changing density as the thing falls, the terminal velocity is also changing. When the object is moving slower than terminal velocity, the gravitational forces are higher than drag forces, so the object will speed up; when it's going faster than terminal velocity, the drag forces are higher than the gravitational forces, so the object will slow down.

Velocity of a Human Shape From 135,000 Feet

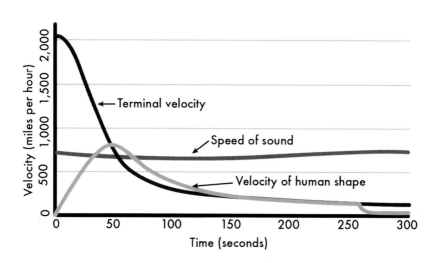

This is how I found myself alongside two charismatic South African parachute engineers breathing pure oxygen in front of the open door of an airplane at 18,000 feet, pushing 10-foot-long concrete missiles out the back of a plane.

Late October 2012: Ballistic Dart Testing

Because spacesuits are so restrictive to basic motion, even an experienced skydiver would lose control when hurtling down from the stratosphere in one. Alan and Derek, the instructor, struggled hard to maintain control in the wind tunnel. Stratospheric skydivers often use a drogue, a stabilization parachute much smaller than the one used to land. It keeps the orientation of a jumper somewhat fixed, typically in a chest-to-Earth orientation, so that they won't lose control. Both our program and the Red Bull Stratos program started with the intention of including this drogue chute in the pack, to be used only if an instability occurred. We considered using the stabilization chute through the whole mission right from the beginning, but after running into some technical problems with that approach, we stuck with the deployable drogue architecture through this testing.

A stratospheric skydiver feels zero gravity upon departing from the balloon, not because they are in orbit around the Earth like a spacecraft, but because they are freefalling in a vacuum; there is no force opposing their motion. Relative zero gravity causes problems because parachutes, especially stabilization parachutes, are prone to getting their lines tangled when they're floating around weightless. Waiting for the low-G portion of flight to end before deploying a drogue is an option, but it causes some other big problems, most notably the extreme speed of the system at the end of the low-gravity float. In addition, purely for enjoyment, Alan hoped to complete the drop without deploying the stabilization chute, a desire which pushed us to delve deep into the mechanics of parachutes and to investigate their opening under some wild conditions.

The velocity and relative acceleration profile of a stratospheric freefall is harder on parachutes than it is on pilots. The acceleration is about two times regular earth gravity, which a pilot can withstand but would cause a typical parachute to fail. We needed a custom parachute that could handle this skydiver version of an atmospheric reentry.

I took on the math of trying to figure out just how much different our deployment would look from a normal one near the ground, while Blikkies dove into the build of an ultra-robust stabilization chute he thought could survive the violent deployments we had in store.

Deriving exact predicted loads for an untested parachute was a murky process. I scraped together declassified papers from the Navy and reports from NASA on ways to predict opening loads and came up with some very crude approximations. We dug through actual high-altitude opening load data from parachute manufacturers and made best-fit curves to help us guess what would occur in an even higher deployment. Ultimately, after coming to terms with the relative complexity and variation in the problem, we decided to test our system by making a test mass heavier than our system mass and getting it moving at three different speeds before deploying a drogue parachute. From those three speeds we would derive what the force across the parachute was in each case, theoretically establishing a maximum allowable load for the drogue parachute. From the maximum allowable load, we could calculate our anticipated load during a worst-case deployment and determine whether or not the parachute Blikkies built was strong enough to save our pilot at the peak of his deceleration. In the unfortunate event our testing showed the parachute would not suffice, we would at least have a limit to apply to our operational constraints. We would know the range of altitudes at which our pilot would need to refrain from activating his stabilization parachute for fear it (and he) would not survive the opening.

Blikkies built his three parachutes from bright orange cloth with different levels of structural support. They were all the same geometry, inflating to make an upside-down teardrop shape. The strongest of the three was built with radial and longitudinal tear-arrestors, giving it the look of an elongated globe. The parachute company tested them on tandem jumps at their local drop zone. The jumps went smoothly.

After the low-altitude testing, we performed the final test with "darts," heavy cylinders with fins, a nose cone, and a parachute in the back that we pushed out of an airplane. At a certain altitude a computer in the dart deploys a parachute which brings it to the ground. We used a two-stage parachute. The first of the two parachutes was the test article, the drogue, and the second was a larger, cruciform-style parachute whose sole purpose was to avoid a heavy impact that would destroy the flight data.

Our analyst generated numbers for our dart speeds at different sizes and masses, and we decided on 10-foot-long cylinders, weighing about 600 pounds, dropped from altitudes ranging from 12,000 to 18,000 feet above sea level. These would reach speeds ranging from about 350 miles per hour to the mid-500s before the drogue deployed. If a parachute failed, the unit could hit that ground at speeds of over 700 miles per hour.

We planned to build the dart units at our facility near the drop area and then drive them up to the test site. Blikkies loaded up all the parachutes, fins, nose cones, and additional hardware while I collected the giant tubes, rod steel, machined plates, threaded rod, and concrete that we would use. We started building the units only a week before we had the airplane scheduled. It was a tight window.

We packed the cylinders with steel, both for structure and additional mass, and capped them with two-inch-thick steel plates that would ensure that the parachute couldn't rip the end cap off the dart. We worked into the night and right through our "fallback" days on the weekend. On a warm summer Saturday night, with the concrete in place, we bolted the caps, hoisted the darts onto our trailer, and strapped them down in preparation for transport to the test site. In the process I accidentally set off the building alarm. The police officers who arrived to follow up stared long and hard at our heavy cylinders. I don't know if their investigation would have become more complicated if we had already fitted the darts with their fins and nose cones.

Dart Functionality

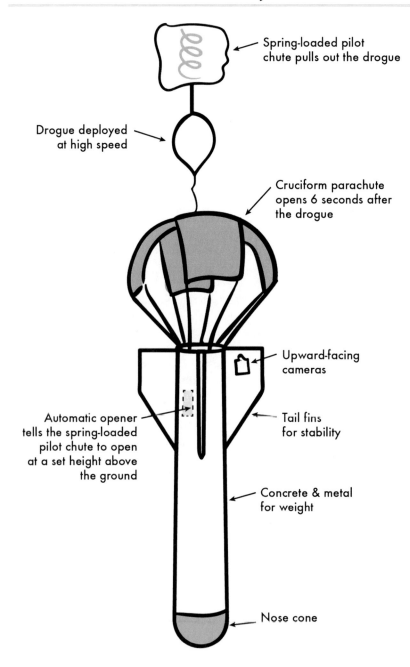

Spring-loaded pilot
chute pulls out the drogue

Drogue deployed
at high speed

Cruciform parachute
opens 6 seconds after
the drogue

Upward-facing
cameras

Automatic opener
tells the spring-loaded
pilot chute to open
at a set height above
the ground

Tail fins
for stability

Concrete & metal
for weight

Nose cone

Blikkies went ahead to prepare our hangar, and a few hours later I transported the 1,800 pounds of dart bodies in a trailer. The training facility that would host our jumps was located on the grounds of a small municipal airport in Coolidge, Arizona, next to a tiny desert town and coincidentally also just a few miles away from one of the largest skydiving facilities in the country. The folks who ran the facility directed me to a massive hangar big enough for C-130 military cargo airplanes. The bay doors towered dozens of feet above the truck as I drove into the immaculately clean space.

Over the next day and a half, we slowly assembled the giant darts and deployment ramp piece by piece. It was a wild departure from office life to be staging these drops in a massive empty hangar at a remote facility. Outside the hangar, two mechanics were testing a new engine on a C-130, blasting out hurricane-force winds. Inside, we worked without talking. We attached the rear clips, programmed the computers, installed the parachutes, set the end caps, and painted half of each body orange so we could determine the rate of spin. The deployment ramp was bolted together with dozens of rollerblade wheels on a wooden frame. As the sun rose on our second day in Coolidge, a beastly, boxy airplane backed into the hangar to start the loading process.

The first day of testing started with a drop from 12,000 feet, with the parachute deploying at about 4,000 feet. At these altitudes, the drogue would deploy at a velocity of around 400 miles per hour in much thicker air than when a drogue would be deploying in stratospheric flight, approximating the forces which would occur at faster speeds in thinner air. The darts were heavier than our flight system. We had projected that success in these circumstances would imply a likelihood of success in the real conditions.

We loaded the deployment ramp into the plane using straps hooked to cleats that mounted to the aircraft floor. We then loaded the dart itself by muscling it onto the ramp with the crew and pilot and strapping it down to the ramp using the cleats. A diver from the jump school briefed us on the drop zone. It was a small pond surrounded by empty flatlands and accessible by backcountry roads. We would aim for the flatlands around the pond. Once we got to altitude, we would unstrap the dart, leaving it floating on the deployment wheels. The diver from the jump school would spot the drop site by hanging his head over the open tailgate of the airplane while we hung onto the dart. At a green light from the pilot, we would push it out, and Blikkies, the other diver from United Parachute Technologies, and the diver from the training facility would all jump out to spot and help with tracking. I wore a parachute so I could walk around freely with the door open, but did not intend to leave the plane. I would land with the aircraft, get the truck, and find the divers and the dart in the desert.

The pilot fired up the engines and bumped along the rough old taxiway to the main runway with the eight-foot-wide tailgate door open. The ground, just a few feet away from us, slid out from under the aircraft to aviation speeds and then fell away. It was amazing to watch.

I clamped onto my seatbelt with a death grip as we climbed through the first 1,000 feet. If I went out before 2,000 feet, I knew a parachute wouldn't save me. The landscape unraveled with the broadest aerial view I had ever been exposed to. At 2,000 feet we unlatched our seatbelts and started walking through a dry run of the whole process, practicing what positions each of us would be in, what order we'd go in, who got what straps, how to signal for the spot, and so on.

Once we reached our target altitude, the pilot turned us on a linear path toward the drop zone, leveled off, and illuminated a yellow light above the door, meaning we could start preparing to release the payload. From this point forward the pilot couldn't let the aircraft pitch lest we lose control of the now unstrapped dart. We held it tight, rocking the deployment ramp back and forth gently to reassure ourselves of the gentle, controllable resistance of the deployment wheels. The divers tightened their helmets, felt for their deployment handles, and psyched up for a high-speed chase with a flying missile. Blikkies gave me a wild-eyed glance and yelled something he would shout multiple times throughout this program: "Stay in the plane!" The dive school instructor then lay on the tailgate hanging his head into the 120-mile-per-hour winds while mentally interpolating horizontal drift so he could signal the drop at the exact right moment.

He pumped his torso up as if he were going to pop to his feet and help us push. We sucked the dart back in preparation for the big push, only for him to lie down again, waiting just a little longer. Finally, he rocked all the way up to his feet and it was time.

"Ready." We pushed the nose forward a foot or so into the open space behind the plane and stopped. "Set." We pulled the dart back on the wheels so the nose drew back inside. "Go!" We pushed full force, and the concrete whale slipped silently into the invisible gushing currents.

The parachute-destroyer fell to its fate. I filmed from the front of the airplane and the others lay on the tailgate to watch it fall. About 20 seconds after pushing the dart off, the three divers popped back up and leapt one after the other out of the plane. Jumping out the back of an airplane causes a diver to pitch forward into the relative wind, so each one got a quick upside-down glance at me before zooming away.

As soon as the last diver was gone, I refastened my seatbelt, shot a glance at the pilot, and fixed a deep stare on the horizon, eager to know the results.

Immediately upon landing, I jumped in the truck and drove on pitted roads for half an hour to the pond, where the divers were waiting with their parachutes. The somber crew was standing over a confusing little hole in the ground. The system had failed.

More accurately, the thick bridle strap connecting the parachute to the dart had failed. The parachute had snapped away from the dart, leaving it to accelerate to the ground: 10 feet of solid concrete, metal, and plastic had burrowed itself into the dirt, leaving a clean hole and a shockingly small debris field. The ground around where the dart had penetrated was hot to the touch. We dug several feet down to find the back end of the dart, and removed our flight computer, fin cameras, and the expensive swivel coupling that connected the parachute to the rear plate. I had a new appreciation for the physics of the whole event, but we had used up one of three test articles and didn't have any numbers.

We spent the rest of the day updating the design for the parachute bridle and reinforcing the lines on the two remaining darts for a test the next day. In order to leave the testing with any data at all, we had to have at least one successful deployment. We added 4,000-pound webbing to both sides of the bridle. We made the attachment rigging strong enough to hold a heavy truck dangling in the air and then some.

The airplane was expensive, so to save money, we decided to drop two darts in one flight that time. We revised our second-day flight plan to another low-altitude flight (12,000 feet). If that was successful, we would skip the intermediate altitude and go straight to 18,000 feet for the last drop. To do that, we had to know if the low-altitude deployment had worked before going forward with the high-altitude one. One of the divers would chase the first dart and signal back to the plane if we were good to go with the high-altitude drop. This would put the first jumper on the ground near the drop site when the second dart came screaming in. He would stand near the pond a safe lateral distance from the linear drop run, hopefully well away from the projected impact site.

I rushed to rework all our calculations incorporating the data from the day's flight into the 18,000-foot drop. With new data available, the analysts honed the drift numbers to increase our chances of hitting the target from three miles off the ground. The new numbers came back as the night closed out. We were ready for the next day's tests.

The two parachute engineers, including Blikkies, carried on their South African traditions with vigor in the US. No circumstance would preclude grilling sausage and drinking beer in this context. This was our last night on site and one of the engineers had procured the necessary South African sausage and a case of beer. Never mind that we were planning to climb into a plane 10 hours later, inhale pure oxygen, and chase missiles through the sky. Now the schedule dictated that we would drink beer and eat sausage outside our casitas near the flight facility.

We were on our feet packing the last bits of gear as soon as the plane pulled in. We strapped it all down, again wasting no time. The plane pulled out under engine power and taxied hard straight into a takeoff. I marveled again at the beauty of the ground dropping away out the gaping door. We were getting to 12,000 feet in around 10 minutes, rising about 1,000 vertical feet per minute, the same rate a balloon rises. This is what Alan would see, but with a wider angle. At 12,000 feet we leveled out and were given our yellow light to ready the payload. The dive school instructor began his silent calculations for dropping the dart into a 500-foot square from an airplane going 120 miles an hour thousands of feet up. The green light flashed and it was time again.

Just like before, it was an elegant, delicate process. The dart laid softly onto the winds running down the belly of the plane, flew straight forward for just a moment, then nosed down for its screaming descent. The three engineers lay on the tailgate staring intently at the shrinking dot. They rose to a crouch for just a second, then Blikkies jumped up and pumped his hand, yelling, "YEAHHHHH, YEAH!" just loud enough for me to hear. I smiled and pumped my fist too. They saw both parachutes deploy from the plane; it was a success.

The first jumper quickly dove out for the chase, and the rest of us sat down for the climb to 18,000 feet. The first diver radioed up to the plane that both parachutes had deployed properly. We had positive results. It was a conservative test (in engineering-speak, "conservative" means built and tested with proper margin), but we had the number we needed to justify a safe drogue deployment region. Now we would go for glory and see if the parachutes would hold together at full speed. This drop was predicted to spit the first parachute out at around 550 miles per hour, and if successful would validate the system's use in the most violent parts of a stratospheric profile.

After the first drop, the three remaining people on the plane would have to pull the dart onto the deployment track and roll it forward. Maneuvering a 600-pound cylinder in a moving airplane with the doors open and an oxygen hose clamped between your teeth isn't impossible, but it is not easy. The dart went out over a bigger skyline. The last two divers went right behind it, and I was again alone in the back of the aircraft. I lay on the tailgate trying to spot the deployment. I lost the mark after about 20 seconds. I chomped back down on my oxygen hose, latched my seatbelt, and shot a thumbs-up to the pilot to go ahead and descend.

Half an hour later, I was in the truck heading to the impact sites. We saw one victory and another failure. The second dart had ripped its parachute hardware to pieces and again plunged deep into hard desert, but the first dart was a beauty: clean drogue deployment, clean second parachute deployment, and all systems intact. We gathered the flight computer, which would tell us the actual velocities and altitudes at deployment, and packed it with the fin cameras into the pickup truck. The trainer from the military school eventually took the cylinder home to use for smoothing his driveway.

The 18,000-foot drop article was buried even further underground than the first. We had to dig six feet to get to the back of the 10-foot-long cylinder. The first diver, who had been on the ground as it came in, reported hearing a loud boom just before he heard the impact. We were excited to think the dart had broken the sound barrier, but it turns out that the boom was likely the big parachute coming out and breaking. The aluminum disk holding the drogue parachute to the back of the dart had sheared in half, immediately releasing the big parachute at full speed, putting a massive load on the system. A set of two heavy nylon straps strong enough to hang four pickup trucks had snapped clean. The dart blasted into the ground and buried the nose 16 feet into the hard-packed desert. As we dug for the tail of the missile, we found chunks of fins in the earth directly behind the tube. It was apparent that during the impact, instead of the fins breaking against the ground and peppering the surrounding landscape with fin bits, they splintered into chunks and got sucked into a dirt vortex formed behind the hard tube as it entered the ground. It swirled the earth behind it like a cannonball being dragged through water.

Covered in dirt, hot, and exhausted, we made our way home. Right before arriving in Tucson, we got a call that Alan was in town and offering to buy everyone dinner. We slapped the dirt off our jeans and walked into a fancy downtown restaurant to tell stories of wild drops and deep penetrations.

Early 2013: First Stratospheric Flights

Some of the first tests performed by the launch team involved using groups of small weather balloons. The team was exploring the idea of carrying Alan to altitude under a long string of multiple rubber balloon clusters instead of one huge plastic balloon. These tests were the first rodeo for a leader in the program, Dr. John Straus, who set up and executed the tests as the head of the flight vehicle Integrated product team.

John was a lanky, sarcastic, soft-spoken jokester who got shit done. He was always too humble. A PhD with a specialty in computational fluid dynamics, John knew nothing about stratospheric balloons the day he took the job. But he nailed it from day one.

We were originally planning to use a zero pressure polyethylene balloon to get to altitude. They are called zero pressure balloons because they never pressurize. Made of an extremely thin polyethylene plastic reminiscent of garbage bags, they are only slightly filled with helium at launch. After launch, the balloon rises into the air, expanding as the surrounding air pressure decreases. Right as the balloon becomes totally full, it starts to pressurize and big vents at its base open. Helium dumps out into space until the balloon doesn't want to rise anymore. Because the balloon will vent until it stops rising, the design of the balloon decides how high it will go, not the amount of helium that is put it in (as long as there is enough helium to make it rise). Weather balloons, on the other hand, are made of a stretchy latex material that expands more as the balloon rises until it gets to altitude and pops, sending a constellation of little chunks of latex trickling down to the Earth.

We had trouble procuring a zero pressure balloon for manned flight. With the Red Bull Stratos project moving forward alongside ours, the issue of whether large balloon companies were willing to make balloons for use in human flight had already made the rounds at all the major outlets. The answer John and the launch crew was getting was, "No, we won't make you a balloon if you're going to put a person under it." Virtually every company that makes large high-altitude balloons was contacted in the process, and they all said no—except one.

The Tata Institute of Fundamental Research in Hyderabad, India, would make us balloons. They had made several in the past for our mentor and balloon advisor Julian Nott, who had been ballooning for several decades and held dozens of ballooning records. The company had an excellent track record. They made good balloons. However, they were not able to meet our wildly aggressive schedule, and waiting was not an attractive option. So the mob of twitchy idea-havers started having ideas.

The first concept for the cluster approach came from an aeronaut, Audouin Dollfus, who ascended to over 40,000 feet in 1945 under a long string of latex balloons. He used a long cable with clusters of three balloons spaced widely enough that when the balloons rose and expanded, the clusters would not squish into each other too tightly. The sets of three balloons would, however, touch each other.

Alan was also inspired and intrigued by a YouTube and TED conference sensation, Jonathan Trappe, who had gone to the sky under giant clusters of colorful helium balloons. Since he hadn't left the breathable atmosphere, he fell short of our target, and he didn't wear a spacesuit, but he did leave the ground by a substantial margin and safely return to it later. He even made is across the English Channel. What he used were essentially latex weather balloons, colored brightly like party balloons. From far away they looked like a group of celebratory gifts that had accidentally hauled someone—a clown, perhaps—into the air. So many childhood dreams of floating away on balloons no doubt attracted attention to the cluster approach.

A team set out to investigate the feasibility of using a cluster or chain of latex weather balloons instead of a zero pressure polyethylene balloon for the mission. These could be bought easily and openly over the Internet, and the companies that sold them didn't ask questions, alleviating the timeline and political issues associated with procuring a zero pressure balloon.

Studies were done and concepts were born. Early in the process, another engineer and I visited our avionics supplier, which also manufactured small weather balloons to carry their avionics packages to altitude. In a meeting that was officially about other business, we floated the idea of using a bunch of these little stretchy balloons instead of one giant balloon to lift something heavy. Their response inspired little confidence: they promised that in the cold of the upper stratosphere the balloons became brittle, and when the balloons touched each other, they would pop from contact. We reported the news; the launch team kept investigating. We were developing what Alan called a "healthy disrespect for the impossible." It was painful and we screwed up all the time, but it was exciting. Alan and Taber took down the walls that bound our problems, and we had a license to experiment and prove other people right or wrong. This time we would prove the experts right. Latex cluster balloons are a bad idea for stratospheric flights.

At the height of this effort, John convened the balloon team in southern Arizona at a little town with a dry lakebed to test some theories. They looked at the general difficulty of filling little balloons, and filling lots of them together.

The possibility of using hydrogen as a lift gas was also investigated on this trip. Hydrogen is a lighter molecule than helium and therefore a more efficient lift gas. Hydrogen is also less expensive than helium and that, coupled with lower balloon volumes, could decrease the overall expense, but there were concerns that when mixed with oxygen it could ignite. The balloon team filled latex balloons with hydrogen and used clumps of matches to try to make the balloons explode. It appears that concerns about hydrogen were overblown. In the first attempt to blow up a balloon, the hydrogen rushing out the hole extinguished the matches. In a later attempt the matches succeeded with an anticlimactic ignition. A film of flame rushed along the boundary of the balloon where the hydrogen met the oxygen— and then went out. The pictures were impressive, but the tests raised no real fear of ignition were we to use a hydrogen-filled balloon.

The team continued with experiments investigating whether a bunch of little hydrogen-filled balloons would work. From a logistical standpoint, filling those balloons could be feasible but hugely difficult. Wild ideas had formed about stringing the balloons out in an elaborate chain between two larger balloons to keep them away from the ground during inflation. Teams on the ground would let out miles of line as the system rose.

The general view of the team, including me, was that this was a dangerous departure from the task at hand, and that going to such altitudes under a cluster of weather balloons would be an incredible effort on its own. There was a legitimate fear that not only would the idea eventually prove a failure, but that the program would not survive that type of tangent. John was at the whim of two pathological optimists (Alan and Taber) who were impossibly blind to the low-level difficulties that plagued the rest of us.

After the attempts to explode hydrogen balloons at the dry lakebed, John put together a set of tests sending single clusters of balloons to the stratosphere to investigate balloon interaction. He used three balloons that suspended a single payload. The tests marked a major milestone: John and his team executed our first stratospheric flights. Cameras flew to the stratosphere with the balloon clusters and took breathtaking pictures of the world from above and also astounding footage of the balloons exploding on contact with each other when they got cold and brittle. These tests were valuable in furthering the team's ability to launch small payloads for development purposes. They succeeded in demonstrating that we could not reliably get far into the stratosphere under a cluster of latex balloons.

After these tests, we were back on our original track. The hair pulling over balloon choice could momentarily end. We would proceed on the assumption that somehow we would procure a massive zero pressure polyethylene balloon. It looked like we would have to settle for the Indian company that had made Julian's balloons years earlier, the one with the show-stopping lead times. But it turned out that the leadership's optimism about cluster balloons was matched only by their optimism about our overall schedule; ultimately we took far longer to develop the system than the balloons took to deliver. The first of the big balloons arrived over a year before we were ready to use any of them.

High-speed ballistic dart being prepared for drogue parachute testing in Coolidge, Arizona.

The landing site for a ballistic dart that worked.

High-speed ballistic dart testing inside the aircraft at 18,000 feet over Coolidge.

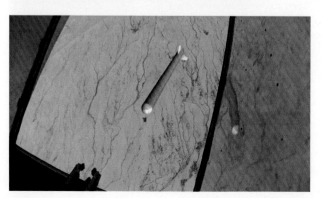

Ballistic dart leaving the aircraft.

The landing site for a ballistic dart that did not work.

Cluster testing over Tucson. At over 100,000 feet, one balloon is popping and causing the other to rupture.

A hydrogen-filled balloon being blown up in the desert outside Wilcox, Arizona to assess the feasibility of using hydrogen with latex balloons.

The bizarre crater created by the failed ballistic dart. There was virtually no debris at the impact site. The wooden fins were found in the disturbed dirt behind the long cylinder, not scattered next to it.

Blikkies inside the hole made by the 10-foot-long ballistic dart after digging to find the back, buried several feet underground.

Dr. John Straus and Rolfe Bode filling one of the countless latex balloons they would send to the stratosphere. (Photo by Volker Kern.)

CHAPTER 6

...

Chambers

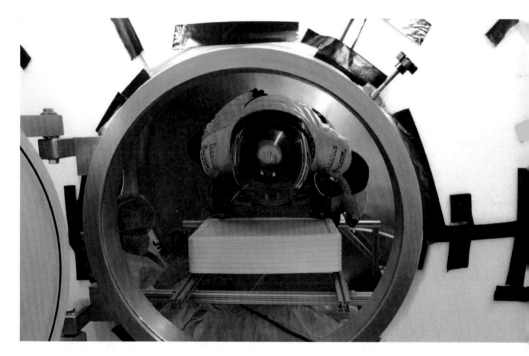

Engineers rely on an iterative trial and error process. Without a complete understanding of a system's functionality, an engineer can still build something. It will likely fail, and then the engineer observes whatever caused the failure, changes it, and tries again. And again. Unfortunately, this type of process can't be applied to things that go to the stratosphere. It's too expensive and too difficult.

Aerospace engineers are forced to approach problems in a completely different way than other engineers; they must analyze the system up one side and down the other, test it in as similar an environment as they can find, beating it up in every way they can, all without actually using it in the way it is intended to be used. This is all in the interest of being sure they are right before they start testing in the real application environment, because it only takes one or two trips out of the atmosphere before an entire budget is gone and the project is over before achieving its goal. This happens all the time in the space industry.

Our team was fond of testing; we wanted to be sure things worked. Our advisor Julian liked to quote his engineering friends at the Jet Propulsion Labs: "In God we trust. Everything else we test." When a team wants to be testing all the time, but the cold space vacuum they need to test isn't available, they seek creative ways to make a fake representation of the cold, faraway nothingness of space on the surface of the Earth. They use chambers.

March 2013: Manned System Checkout

On March 1, 2013, the first test with the entire system assembled was conducted. We had the suit upper assembly, or the torso, suspended from a steel gantry, and the suit pants laid out in the staging area. For more than a day and a half, we had been following hundreds of pages of procedures, all to prepare the suit for human occupation.

Because the suit is filled with oxygen, one of the major concerns is fire. A typical fire is an oxidation reaction when oxygen combines with hydrocarbon to create carbon dioxide and water. Once that reaction begins, its heat sustains it. When more oxygen is present, the reactions happen at a lower temperature and more things will react, not just the hydrocarbons that we typically think of as flammable. In pure oxygen at 3,000 psi even stainless steel is flammable. For this reason, all parts in the oxygen system are meticulously cleaned, after which they can't be touched, dropped, or, in some cases, even exposed to ambient dirty air without creating a dangerous fire hazard. Inconveniently, both the oil that the human hand naturally produces and lubricants used in the machining of nearly all the components in the system are highly flammable around oxygen. At one point during the build of the suit, astronaut Mark Kelly, who was visiting the facility, gave us a brief word of caution after a shakedown of the suit. He bluntly told us not to mess around when it comes to fires. They are nasty when they happen—and they do happen.

This test would be the first time the suit was essentially "turned on" with a person in it. In Houston, we had tested the oxygen system, but not the chestpack. For the past month we had been saying we were a week away from this test, but constant holdups during the very last pieces of the assembly process finally pushed management to "motivate" my team a bit more by sternly demanding a completion date and scheduling the test. The dates couldn't slide anymore; we would have to finish. The biggest problems were with the packaging of the suit components into the chestpack. With our "bring everything" philosophy, whereby everything Alan needs for his entire mission is physically strapped to him, we were pushed to pack a very complex engineering system (over 1,000 parts) into a tiny space attached to a soft suit and interfacing with an awkwardly shaped human being. (Not that Alan's shape is especially awkward—everyone's is.) We struggled to find anything we could minimize to save space and weight. As the days up to the checkout rolled past, we whittled away the remaining space conflicts with small alterations so everything could be squeezed in. Management upped the odds and invited a review team to oversee the test: flight surgeons, astronauts, and life-support experts.

Five days before the scheduled test, we had abandoned every effort that wasn't directly related to getting ready for the test. Bulging oxygen lines that restricted the shell from closing needed to be replaced. New ones were created after dozens of hours of design, and then when they didn't work, another iteration was made. Review and machining went on around the clock. Three days before the test, the review team of dignitaries started to arrive. There was a large team of advisors for everything, and while they were extremely knowledgeable (and in general really cool people with wild histories of daring adventure), they were peskily underfoot as the team pushed to prepare for the test. As the last couple days closed in, we realized we were not going to finish in time.

We started negotiating with management in front of a 15-person audience about whether to move into the test with a partially completed suit or send everyone home. It was decided we would make some alterations to get around the remaining fit problem, that overlarge piece of the fluid loop, and press on with the test. We built special standoffs to hold the shell further away from the fluid lines during the test. The hardware to attach them arrived the day before we were to begin. Management continued its full-court press and we arrived at the office as the sun was coming up to install the parts and suspend the suit for this maiden occupation.

Alongside this mad rush to get the suit together was a completely separate effort to build and integrate the room that would be home to most of our testing at our facilities in Tucson. The test director, Rolfe Bode, a stubby, feisty test engineer who had previously worked in the spacecraft testing lands of NASA and at the University of Arizona, was in a continuing war with me over personnel. We both wanted all the technicians working on our projects, and it seemed that every day we had the same exchange: "The room's not gonna be ready for this test if all the technicians keep being occupied with the suit." "There isn't going to be anything to test if we don't get this suit built." Rolfe always said what he meant. He loved his job and led the builds of tons of test equipment from the start of the program to the end. He was fueled by home-roasted coffee during the day and, if his test equipment worked, whiskey in the long evenings.

When the foundation for our first test chamber was poured, we team members wrote our names in the concrete to leave our mark as the StratEx team. While the rest of us were making cutesy handprints, someone wrote "the frankenfreezer" in the wet cement. The testing chamber, referred to as a freezer because it was highly insulated and equipped with a liquid nitrogen injection system to cool it far below freezing temps, took on that name for good. The last required tasks to have the room usable for tests were completed hours before we moved the bright white suit into it.

This was our first opportunity to figure out how long the whole process of preparing the suit for use would take. Including the preflight checks, tests, and walkthroughs, we were estimating it was going to take about four hours to get the suit ready to put on, and then another five or six hours to actually put it on. In order to vet those times and get some practice, we went through everything, start to finish. First we examined every connection in the system, running several functional tests of the avionics to show that the computers were responding and then pressurizing and checking that the suit didn't leak and that the oxygen system was functional. Much of the suit tubing assemblies had been constructed by a technician named Ernie Arispe, a jokester who was becoming a crucial part of the team. He built the final version of the plumbing system for the suit.

The process began. With all the reviewers present, three hours of preflight briefings were conducted. We talked and talked on various tangents about what we were trying to accomplish and how we would do it. Finally, we were cleared to begin. Because we were so far behind on time, and because we were required to finish this "test safety readiness review" before starting the procedures, we went into the session without testing anything; none of the equipment had ever been turned on together. We also would be trying all of our procedures for the first time on a stage in front of 15 of the world's leading experts in spacesuits, astronautics, ballooning, and general adventure in the sky.

The arduous session played out as expected: it was a complete mess. The first day, with the team of reviewers standing watch, we finally hooked the newly completed ground carts to the suit and pressurized the fluid loop. We waited for a moment, listening to the light whir of the pumps, admiring our accomplishment, until we noticed a steady stream of pink fluid leaking from the bottom of the suit. This would be the first of several leaks. Multiple fittings hadn't been properly tightened and were spewing thermal fluid. We quickly went back in and tightened the joints, double-checking the rest (and noting the need for more scrutiny). The slow drip from the bottom of the suit continued.

Ernie and I would spend the next several hours lying on our backs under the suit in order to replace the heating element, which was leaking at a weld. Fortunately, we had a spare on hand. Our advisors strolled around asking questions and munching snacks.

When we finished, we continued with what would become our preflight checklist, what we called "phase zero."

With new oxygen lines in place, our chestpack was close to fitting together. The only remaining issue was a grenade-shaped fluid component responsible for managing changes in fluid volume. A relatively large cluster of fittings was supporting it because the proper fitting was on back order from the manufacturer. Until that fitting came in, we wouldn't be able to get the shell on. We contemplated doing the checkout without the shell but decided that would be too risky; if any tubes or wires were exposed they could get yanked and put Alan at risk. We had to find a way to get that shell on so we could start the test, a test that was supposed to now be almost done. The review team was getting antsy. We ordered standoff sleeves to raise the internal ribs and allow the shell to sit higher and miss the problematic component. As we were installing those standoffs, we saw that this half-baked plan wasn't going to work. Because of the geometry of the shell curled back behind the oxygen tanks, the standoffs would suck the shell into a collision with the tanks. It wouldn't fit. We would normally have checked for that sort of thing, but this time we had rushed right on to buying the parts to make deadline.

I had personally spent dozens of hours designing, redesigning, and negotiating the build of our aerodynamic chestpack casing. A little part of me died when we carried it into our machine shop and, without measuring or marking, pushed it through a band saw to remove the cups that hugged the tanks on the back of the shell. With the shell chopped in two, the front part would now fit over the equipment. We could run our test.

The point of this test was to put a person into the complete suit for the first time and seal it off from the outside world. The show was on the road.

We stammered through tens of pages of checklists that had been poured from our imaginations into writing over the past few weeks. Every other step was nonsensical when real life met paper. I slyly disregarded our orders from the least-connected member of the executive team, who was demanding that we follow the procedures directly and verbatim. It would have been impossible and I wasn't about to slog through another meeting about it. Red ink poured onto the pages as we powered through the preparations, changing the procedures in real time to keep the wrenches turning.

With tired, drying eyes, we got our shell onto the suit and checked the final box on the preflight checklists.

The following morning we came in before the sun rose to get the suit ready for Alan. We were following the flight suit-up procedures (which we had just written) as if we were going to strap Alan to a balloon and send him to space that day. We would go through our "pre-chill" procedures, getting Alan cold ahead of time so he wouldn't get too hot in his over-insulated spacesuit. We would get him into the suit and run through functional checks of all the components. That would be followed by a process where we had Alan breathe in many different ways so we could start to quantify how much oxygen he would consume while wearing the suit. Lastly, we would lay Alan down on tumbling mats and practice our very first extractions.

Alan put on his undergarments in a little office crammed with stacks of spare parts and equipment. The undergarments consisted of regular Under Armor long underwear, then a liquid thermal garment originally designed to be used in bomb-disposal suits. All was covered by a modified thick wet suit. Alan sat in the parts room while we turned our equipment on, creating Christmas trees of winking lights emanating from computers, sensors, displays, and status LEDs.

As we called Alan out to the freezer room, the frankenfreezer, to enter his suit, the feeling of apprehension was universal. So much personal, creative thought had gone into this system, now being used for the first time.

Spacesuits are airtight. They are sealed with metal lugs that can't be opened in any way other than their intended method, and they are connected directly to tanks of air compressed to pressures that could quickly destroy a person. An overpressure event will leave a person crushed and a lack of airflow will suffocate them. There were, of course, safeguards in place and fallbacks to those safeguards. However, that didn't make it any less real that we were about to seal a person in a pressure-holding airtight space that had never been tried before, and we didn't know exactly what was going to happen. Alan donned the spacesuit pants in his room and walked out joking with the other advisors. He stepped into the frankenfeezer to put on his suit.

We marched through preparation checklists. Then we worked Alan's legs through the loops of the parachute container and pulled it up, then clicked the chest strap clips and belly band into place. Soon enough I was standing in front of the suit, Alan behind it, with people holding up the two arms and Blikkies holding the inner helmet. We counted down from three and Alan ducked down for his maiden occupation. He squeaked through the yellow rubber, fighting the wet suit's grip, which made disturbing squawking noises. His head popped through the neck dam. Step one complete. Alan leaned against the retaining straps in his spacesuit, looking calm, cool, and collected.

The suit technicians closed the suit up easily. The seals were just like the ones they used on other suits. Alan was all bagged up except his head. It was time to turn on the oxygen and close him in.

We opened the oxygen tanks. With the helmet off, the oxygen regulators were attempting to maintain a pressure across the open neck dam, blasting oxygen into the room. When we closed the helmet, the noise would stop. The flow rates were right. The tube sizes and lengths were correctly calculated, such that the resistance in the plumbing fit within the tight margins. The tubes were large enough to accommodate heavy breathing but small enough to stop the suit from decompressing if a tube were to fail. Turning the brand-new machine on like this was really only possible with a person inside to drive the sinusoidal flow through the system. There were uncertainties about what exactly was going to happen when we locked the helmet down.

We all readied ourselves for the closing. Ryan would push it down and snap the latch. Zane and I stood behind the tanks with our fingers on the switches. I counted down from three, and the latches closed. Oxygen blasted out the spray bar in front of Alan's face just as we expected, making a loud hissing noise while a thumbs-up went to Ryan and the helmet was pushed down into the metal helmet receiver. When the helmet hit the seal, the hissing stopped and all went calm. Ryan fussed with the latch for just a second, but then it clicked; Alan was sealed in. I flashed a thumbs-up sign in front of his face, intensely anxious to confirm that he could breathe. Alan returned the thumbs-up. We listened to the regulators clicking on, then the exhalation valve flapping open. The mechanical sounds of breathing were an audible affirmation. Ryan opened up the comm line and they started talking.

The next stage of the process was perhaps the most important. We would remove all the ground support. With the go-ahead from Alan and mission control, we separated two ground cooling lines, a ground power line, and then the two oxygen lines. With a push and a click, Alan was truly isolated.

In that moment something incredible was gained for the team. Alan was not in our atmosphere anymore. He was totally alone in his space. There were 7 billion people on the planet, all connected to an ecosystem that Alan at that point was not part of. Sight was his only link to planet Earth. Then the ground lines clicked back in. Test over. He was again connected to our world.

For the next couple of hours we cycled through pages of procedures, checking every piece of the system. We turned the heating system on and off, cycled the displays, switched between comm systems, and pushed Alan to reach for components on the suit and determine his limits. We were a timid team, though, and he was very much in charge. We stopped when he stopped. Our pilot was also our funder, founder, and leader. We were wary of the new machine and wouldn't yet push any limits.

The checks were clunky. Alan couldn't reach the valves. He couldn't get the glove heaters turned on. He couldn't reach the toggle to control temperature or voice communication. The suit needed a lot of work. We would learn the hard way to stop pretending things worked when they didn't.

As we walked through the last of the reach-and-move exercises, Alan moved his face and managed to knock his facemask loose inside his helmet. The facemask flopped off and hung inside the larger over-bubble dangling from one side of the inner helmet. This was a code yellow, but our eyes widened and heartrates quickened like it was a hard code red.

We had calculated the carbon dioxide washout rates without a facemask, and we knew the environment would slowly go toxic. The carbon dioxide that Alan was exhaling was mixing with the pure oxygen in the helmet and then migrating into the lower half of the suit as a mixed substance. The inside of the facemask was still exposed to the helmet, which would rise in pressure when Alan exhaled so things would still flow, just as a mixture. The CO_2 levels would slowly rise, and breath by breath Alan would get more of his own exhaled CO_2 until at some point symptoms of CO_2 poisoning would set in. We aborted the test, and quickly.

We depressurized the suit using the suit controller on the side of the suit and broke the seal on the helmet. Alan inhaled some air that wasn't dosed with his backwash. He was fine. Small as the unclipped facemask issue was, it scared us enough that we called the test. In the coming hours we would all pack up and go home.

While we packed up and updated procedures, crowds of reviewers roamed around, congratulating us on a test that was only a mild success. I understood then that the advisors knew how this worked. The review team had experienced the same thing in their own careers and they fully understood the situation. They weren't pretending that the test had achieved its stated success criteria. They were congratulating progress. We were clearly on the way to a real live system. For the first time, Alan had hung in complete isolation a few inches above a concrete pad in an insulated room in the southern part of Tucson, Arizona.

Late March 2013: Unmanned Vacuum Chamber Testing

In late March 2013, the suit began its resurrection for the second time after it was completely taken to pieces. This time, the details were scrutinized even further; no stone was left unturned as we prepared to assemble some components for what we hoped would be the last time. One problem we found was with the main suit pass-through, the point where oxygen and water enter the suit from the equipment module where they are processed and stored. This main suit pass-through happened to end up right in the center of the chest, and it leaked. It was underneath everything in the system, so we had to pull everything apart to fix it. As we reassembled it all, we took a new level of care to avoid leaks by leak-testing all the components with helium. Helium consists of small, highly energetic particles, and because it is easy to detect with a mass spectrometer it is ideal for finding leaks. We tested everything at 80 to 90 psi, a greater pressure than the low-pressure fluid required.

We also went to great lengths to rigorously "qualify" our electrical components, writing a 40-page electrical connections manual and creating test samples for every type of action we would make, including cutting, stripping, and crimping. This caused another overhaul of the system as we reworked every electrical connection, dismantling and reassembling with painfully slow documentation.

On April 9, 2013, I worked through a sunny Sunday on completing the avionics box lid, the last component to complete before the suit was ready to prep for testing. Two days later, we buttoned up the aeroshell, the plastic shell that covered the guts of the suit. We flipped the suit over onto its chest and rolled it over to a big, round, steel vacuum chamber where it would slide in to take its first journey into the thin traces of upper atmospheric pressure.

Because vacuum chambers are kept meticulously clean so not to contaminate the emptiness during testing, anyone going inside the chamber has to wear what's known as a bunny suit. Bunny suits, as the name implies, make one look like a bunny. The all-white plastic suit is clean far beyond what the eye can see and is accessorized by blue booties, gloves, hair bonnet, and in my case a beard cover. I put on the bunny suit to make all the required connections to the suit. We connected water lines through a sealed chamber pass-through, added a cable to connect to an antenna for our communications link, and installed a rat's nest of over a dozen thermocouples to monitor all the temperatures of various components.

The purpose of the vacuum chamber test was to make sure things didn't get too hot. The vacuum of empty space is like a down blanket. During our last buildup of the suit, the inside ends of the thermocouples were taped over anything that could create heat. They reached deep into the chest of the suit, so as to measure the heat of the flight computer and data-acquisition board. We also wanted to verify the performance of the fluid system's ability to regulate temperatures in the thermal weirdness of a vacuum.

In the morning, the connections were made and checked. By midday, we were closing the giant steel doors and briefing the team on emergency procedures. Our lanky, meticulous lab technician was at the helm while we began the simulated ascent. The giant doors of the vacuum chamber were held shut while we turned the pump on, then they sucked down against the steel ring from the pressure difference. Only pressure was holding the doors shut. The technician began to pull the chamber toward vacuum.

To simulate a body floating upward toward space, we built a graph in the computer showing us where the pressure in the chamber should be at any given time during the mission. On the same graph, we plotted the actual pressure inside the chamber. The technician then stared with drying eyes at the computer screen, clocking a manual valve to make the actual curve match the mission curve. When our line got below the mission line, we opened the valve to let the vacuum pump remove more air. When our line got above the mission line, we paused the pump and waited for the mission line to twitch upward and meet our line. Slowly, we simulated creeping toward space. We also had attached the altimeter we were planning to use for the mission to the suit. An altimeter measures altitude by measuring air pressure, so we could watch the altimeter through the tiny glass window to see where in the atmosphere it thought it was.

The chamber leveled off at about 110,000 feet. It had been built to simulate the vacuum of deep black space, but because we were dumping a steady stream of oxygen into the chamber from a standard leak that was built into the suit to represent human breathing, the pump could only pull enough oxygen away at that low pressure to simulate something around 100,000 feet, which was lower than our target altitude of 135,000 feet. We could have used a bigger pump, but we decided it wouldn't affect the results so saved the money, remembering that 99% of the Earth's atmosphere is below 100,000 feet.

The suit has an emergency valve that won't let the pressure fall beneath 3.5 psi. As the pressure inside the chamber reached that point, the suit started to inflate. As the chamber then approached a vacuum, the suit continued to pressurize until the differential pressure was 3.5 psi. The test was a success.

In our second test we pressurized the suit with the doors of the tank open and then sealed it up and took it back to 110,000 feet in the chamber. At this point we wanted to see what would happen if the suit popped a hole. We used a 0.25-inch diameter hole, about the size of a ballpoint pen. In spacesuit terms that is a massive hole. We did this by opening a valve on a line that passed from the suit to outside the chamber and then back in through sealed ports. We made the call to start the test and opened the valve.

Instantly, oxygen blasted out the hole and into the vacuum. The expanding oxygen was audible through an inch of solid steel. The suit pressure started to drop. If the pressure fell low enough to allow water to boil at the pilot's body temperature (known formally as the Armstrong line), the pilot's fluids would start to vaporize. Below that pressure, the gases in the pilot's blood would begin to come out of solution like a soda being opened. When those little bubbles reached the pilot's brain, it would quickly be game over.

In our system, however, the fail-safes worked exactly as expected. When the pressure reached the lowest tolerable, which was 3.3 psi, the regulators opened up and blasted oxygen from the high-pressure bottles and overpowered the leak. The rushing air would keep the pilot in a windy, loud, but temporarily safe suit just long enough to cut loose and plunge to thicker, safer air. We simulated that drop and reached the simulated ground with breathing gas to spare.

Finally, we performed a test to make sure the computer wouldn't get too hot when we powered the heaters through the frosty jet stream and into the vacuum above. We powered it all on high during our third simulated trip into 21 miles of thin air. Aside from one bad battery pack that caused some strange power outputs and made us switch to ground power, all went well. We sent the data to the number crunchers and pulled the suit from the chamber to prep for the first test with a pilot in a "non-livable environment." It was time for thermal testing. Negative 70 degrees Celsius for four hours in a room without air was next.

April 2013: Manned Thermal Testing I

Even though the vacuum chamber tests went amazingly well, we had a laundry list of things to fix. Sensor issues and finicky readouts, wobbly switches and stripped bolts all got onto the list of to-dos as we ripped the suit down for the fourth time, with the primary goal of changing some sensors that were buried deep in the tangle of life-support tubes. The whole system had several thousand parts packed into an incredibly tight space. Taking it apart felt like overhauling a car packed into a space the size of a coffin. We pulled it open with tender care and spent more than a week preparing to reassemble it with new working sensors. Alongside the suit overhaul, Zane led the build of a brand-new oxygen fill station for filling our oxygen tanks to a problematic high pressure of over 3,500 psi, higher than anything used in normal industry.

The next set of tests happened in two sessions. The first was a set of suit system checkouts that we didn't get to in the previous test. The second was a cold chamber test in which we filled a highly insulated room with liquid nitrogen in order to bring the temperature to stratospheric equivalents, with Alan inside the suit.

My team was in full swing, working around the clock to get the suit ready. We put in a fresh set of batteries so the suit would have several hours of unplugged use time, allowing us to run at least one three-hour test. The oxygen tanks went together without a problem, and we fastened together the shell covering the chaotic guts. With the insides contained, the suit looked organized and ready for manned testing.

We readied the suit yet again. The luster of working with the suit was beginning to wear off. For the first time we were not amped to touch and handle the shiny fabric. We weren't clamoring to be the ones to do things, and we weren't awed by its mystic power. Now it felt more like work, as we slogged through a 110-page procedure that we had been through dozens of times already. The whole idea with operations like this was to do it so many times that it was second nature, so many times that it was monotonous. The whole morning was devoted to checklists, line after line. Check the seal on the right glove, check the seal on left glove, turn the heaters on, turn them off. Four hours later, we were aching to get Alan in and buttoned up so we could move onto the real meat of the tests.

Our first order of business would be to finish our system checkouts at room temperature. We had intended to do these tests alongside our previous "manned system checkout" but were stopped short after the facemask came loose. The first test of the day was of extreme importance in the suit's ability to preserve a pilot in a living state. We were going to test the use of our purge valve (the valve that flows oxygen into the helmet) as an anti-suffocation valve, or a valve that Alan could breathe through. To do this, we had made a plan to close the helmet with this valve open, and then wait to turn on the oxygen. If the valve worked as intended, Alan would comfortably breathe through the little tube for five minutes, and then we would turn his oxygen on. This configuration was a bit chilling for me, because it was the exact one I had been in when I nearly suffocated in the suit. The difference was that the valve we should have opened during my episode (which was blocked off by a gauge we added) was the valve we were testing.

Alan emerged from his prep room in his blue, liquid-cooled long underwear and we dove right in: pants on, gloves on, helmet ready, check, check, check. We prepared to have Alan slide up under the suit's upper assembly by adjusting the height of the system on the gantry. Alan crouched below the yellow rubber womb and pressed upward. I pulled the neck dam wide around his head and he was in. We talked about the plan and all recited our roles. Alan would indicate a thumbs-up as long as he felt okay. If he felt like the valve was failing, but he was still fine, he would go thumbs-down. As always, if he felt he was in any sort of danger and the helmet needed to come off, he would swipe the air and the testing would be over.

We glanced at each other with newly excited eyes and I said, "Thumbs-up" so Alan would know it was time. He put his thumb in the air and we sealed the dome. We could instantly see the facemask suck in and the neck dam flip upward as the pressure in the helmet region reduced. He appeared to be breathing but it seemed like he was having difficulty. I was the only one who truly knew what he was feeling. His head was in a moderate vacuum and it was a fight to get at the air. We stared with tunneling focus at his erect thumb. It wasn't panicky or tense, but in less than a minute his thumbs-up went thumbs-down and we turned on the oxygen. It didn't mean much for the day, or the immediate future, but it did mean that the suit was not currently equipped to deal with the hazard of suffocation. Alan later took a moment to commiserate with me on the claustrophobic nervousness that accompanies rubber sucking your head and face like that. We both agreed that it is not fun.

Before Alan exited the suit, we quickly ran through all the routine reach and access exercises. We were working to make these tests more frequent so Alan could get enough training to locate the positions of things by habit. That left one more weird breathing exercise for the day.

The medical team had assembled. The leader of the medical crew was Dr. Jon Clark, a space medicine legend who had spent his long career as a flight surgeon. The team also included a younger MD who was an aspiring flight surgeon specializing in space medicine, and an EMT who at his day job spent his time racing to remote accident sites and dealing with various traumas. The whole medical team worked on the Red Bull Stratos project and so knew a bit about what they were signing up for. This also meant they were much less giddy than other folks who came on site for the first time; this was not new to them.

Dr. Clark came in to lead the breathing exercise portion of the testing; he had Alan breathe in different styles, such as short, fast panting or long, deep breaths. As he did so, we recorded oxygen depletion from the tanks. If Alan started depleting one of his tanks faster than the other, we would instruct him to move into a breathing style that worked the opposite tank harder. After 30 minutes of hyperventilation on pure oxygen, Alan must have felt ready to pass out, but he persevered. Successfully, we saw no difference in the draw on the right tank versus the left, meaning we wouldn't have to ask Alan to adjust his breathing during the flights.

Nobody caught the one significant mistake we made as the test finished up. One of the items in the test plan was to have Alan remove his own helmet, an essential portion of a mission because he could suffocate if his helmet stayed on while out of oxygen. Because we wanted to see the system response to the actual flight tank regulators for the breathing exercises, we were using onboard oxygen tanks (as opposed to large external tanks). So we didn't want to actually take the helmet off because too much of the oxygen in the internal tanks would be consumed when the helmet was removed. Instead, we had Alan simply go through the motions of taking the helmet off. When he went to access the helmet latch, he couldn't quite reach it but thought he could probably have done it if he had tried harder. We weren't convinced he was right, but because we were optimistically assuming there would be opportunities to test in the future, and because we were hot and tired and ready to move on, we let him slip by without actually taking off his helmet.

The testing continued through more human factors tests, and finally it came time to take to the ground for doffing exercises. We laid Alan down by lowering everything to a mat on the ground. Once on the ground, we realized, he became a flipped turtle incapable of doing almost anything.

He couldn't reach across his chest to access the flares we had stored for him, so those got removed. He couldn't access the pocket where his emergency GPS was located, so the "HELP" function could not be used. He also couldn't roll himself over, and would not be able to free a pinned arm to depressurize the suit or remove his helmet if he happened to land lying on it. In all reality, he couldn't do much of anything once on the ground.

In poor spirits, our tired crew walked through the motions of staging an emergency extraction. We then moved quickly to the real extraction and Alan enjoyed free, dry air after his sixth suit experience. We convened to debrief and prepared ourselves for what we had really gathered for: the thermal chamber testing.

The next day, I left at 6:20 a.m. for a bike ride through the pleasant streets of Tucson in time to arrive at the office for the pretest briefing, the suit-up, and our first thermal test. This test would be the first time the pilot would be in an "non-livable environment." Even though the suit was made exclusively to keep someone alive in an unlivable environment, all of our testing to date had been performed in a livable environment. The most dangerous part about every test we had performed thus far was the suit itself, with its serious suffocation risk and unnatural pressure cycles. We started our brief by reiterating that on this day the environment around the suit would very quickly kill any person who wasn't inside a highly specialized protective pressure vessel.

The test plan was to run through a full flight preparation, which includes a taxing pre-breathing protocol in which the pilot breathes pure oxygen for several hours to purge his blood of nitrogen, which is harmful at low pressure. We wouldn't actually be going to low pressures; this was just for practice. After flight prep, we would put Alan into the suit, close it up, and leave him alone in the chamber for a stationary journey to temperatures far below what naturally occur on Earth's surface.

We talked through the details and broke at 9 a.m. to start the long process of readying the suit. Alan began the suit-up process: he put on his man-bra life-support monitor, his diaper, his long underwear, his liquid thermal garment, and finally his neoprene rubber over layer. The desert sun approached midday while Alan started his pre-breathe. The oxygen lines weren't long enough to reach all the way into the air-conditioned building, so Alan had to do his pre-breathe outside under our work tents. We used our portable liquid ice pack cooling system to try to keep him at a good temp. As the pre-breathe, which was supposed to last four hours, continued, Dr. Clark convened the troops to talk about the hot sun and whether we should shorten the pre-breathe to keep things moving. The test would take four more hours after the pre-breathe was finished, so with the delays pushing the start to midday, we had to act swiftly to avoid the risk of any further holdups pushing our test against the approaching night. We cut the pre-breathe short. We readied the suit on the gantry inside the chamber.

Alan walked into the chamber with a black mask draping long hoses to the ground like the face antennas of an alien. The hoses connected to an oxygen tank and a gas analyzer measuring the amount of nitrogen in his exhaled breath. We got ready to have Alan make the move from the pre-breathe oxygen to the suit oxygen. It was critical for Alan to make this transition as quickly as possible to minimize breathing normal air, which was filled with potentially dangerous nitrogen.

We were testing this tricky process for the first time. We didn't waste a moment. Suit pants on, boots on, duck down, mask off, push into the suit upper half, inner helmet on, flight mask on, neck dam check, thumbs up from pilot, and break. I took a breath. I looked around the room for calm faces, shot a thumbs-up to Alan, got a thumbs-up back. We continued. We buckled the helmet down and flipped the switches that put him on onboard oxygen. Alan and I did one final communication check and then we were ready for the parachute pack. Blikkies stepped in and pulled on the pack. We locked the clips and the pack was good. Alan showed us another thumbs-up. I saw him calmly pop his ears by wiggling his jaw around as the suit inflated around him and his cocoon hardened up, pressing into the straps of the parachute rig and transforming the suit into the shell he would reside in. From there we could suspend him by the parachute pack in the flight's hanging orientation. He was lifted with a hoist and swung over the flight rigging assembly that would hold him at the "comfortable" 45-degree angle. We connected the straps and lowered the hoist to lay Alan into the lounge position. One final look and we were ready to go. Assuming we would have one last check of things, we pulled out and made space for the chamber team to add their final sensors.

Through all the commotion, the hot pre-breathe, and what we later learned was an extremely uncomfortable inner helmet (which had been altered prior to the test with new padding), Alan was visibly anxious to get things under way. The chamber team worked fast, but the communications from Alan got more pointed as the prep dragged on. He was clearly not in good spirits. Beads of sweat were forming on his head before we even closed the door to start the test.

Head sweat was one of our biggest enemies in this program. Every stratospheric skydive to date has had a problem with helmet fogging. We took a fresh approach to the fogging issue by adding our neck dam and pushing all of the pilot's exhalation below it. That way the only moisture in the helmet region is from head sweat, which we erroneously assumed would be negligible.

The chamber team finally finished adding the sensors they needed onto the outside of our suit. All was closed and the pilot was handed off to mission control.

The next half hour was tense. I was part of the "first responder" team that was posted next to the emergency door. We had what were called Emergency Life Support Air, or ELSA, systems with us that would allow us to enter the chamber before it had reached safe oxygen levels through the use of pressurized air to a bag we'd wear over our heads (going against everything my mother had taught me about putting plastic bags over my face).

The test began with open valves sending nitrogen roaring through the purging of excess gas that had built up in the lines. After the excess gas was purged, the room grew quiet, and light gray fog surrounded the bright white suit as the chamber temperature plummeted. Rolfe called out the temperatures of the chamber in 10-degree increments as they dropped from the mid-90s to a frosty negative 95 degrees Fahrenheit. We peered into the chamber. When Alan saw my face pop into the window, he would give me a comforting wave.

As the temperatures lowered and the frost built on the chamber walls, Rolfe and the test technicians noticed something unexpected happening with the equipment. While our pilot was reporting that he was staying hot, maybe even too hot, our equipment temperatures were falling and we began to worry that our pilot was going to overheat while the equipment froze. On the surface this didn't make much sense. We had intentionally designed the equipment so that it shared a thermal loop with the pilot. Basically, the thermal fluid lines ran around our pilot and then went to the equipment. That way the fluid loop could warm the equipment when it was cold and cool the equipment when it was hot, using our pilot as the heat sink in either direction. From this perspective, the numbers coming from the thermocouples didn't quite make sense—and appeared to be disagreeing with the months of scrupulous analysis we had performed on the system.

One sensor on the heat exchangers showed it was getting dangerously close to freezing. The heat exchangers housed both the high-pressure oxygen and low-pressure water. Frozen heat exchangers could be catastrophic. The expanding ice could break the sheets of metal that divided the oxygen from the water, mixing the systems and pressurizing the water loop to a far higher pressure than it is designed for. This would undoubtedly result in a rupture in the water lines, which would then lead to an oxygen leak, depleting the pilot's oxygen supply. The solution to the problem seemed simple. we needed to turn the heaters on to warm the fluid running through the heat exchangers. The problem was that Alan had gotten so hot during our long preparations, sitting inside his heavily insulated suit in the middle of a hot desert, that even though the water running around him was cold, he was still hot. His core temperature was being recorded from an ingestible pill.

His temps were topping 100 degrees Fahrenheit. We had to make a choice. Either we turned on the heaters and heated up our already hot pilot, or we killed the test to stop our heat exchangers from freezing. The heaters were turned on.

Hot got hotter for Alan as the cold water running around him heated up. Sweat ran down his face and water pooled in the low point of the helmet bubble as we watched the temperature readings on the equipment return to acceptable ranges. As the equipment returned to the 40 degrees we wanted, our pilot's core temperature stayed in the hundreds, at what a doctor would diagnose as a serious fever.

While we dealt with the temperature issues, Zane was manning the instrument readouts at the ground cart and noticed another serious issue developing. We were burning through oxygen at a rate far exceeding what we had planned for. We would be out of oxygen in a hasty hour and 40 minutes, more than two hours short of the intended duration of the test. We calculated burn rates over and over to try to pinpoint the problem, but every time we came to the same conclusion: even taking into account the pressure drop from the extreme cold, there was no way we were finishing this test—and we had no idea why.

All the problems came together at a critical moment as we approached the end of our oxygen. Equipment temperatures required that our hot pilot again be blasted with hot water. Two inches from Alan's skin, it was colder than anywhere on planet Earth, yet he was panting from heat exhaustion. The system had utterly over-performed when it came to its ability to retain heat. Meanwhile, there was a fairly simple temperature-control problem going on in the chamber that the test director wanted to fix: the temperatures across the vertical profile of the chamber were forming a gradient, making it much colder near the floor than near the ceiling. To fix this, Rolfe wanted to turn on one of the huge fans, intended to simulate the freefall portion of the profile, and stir things up. One of the two fans was turned on without consulting my team, and we immediately saw a bizarre fall in heat exchanger temperature. The scene livened again as my team yelled to shut the fan off, as we were again at risk of freezing our heat exchanger.

It took several yells to get the fan turned off, but the heat exchanger temperature had fallen below freezing. It wasn't clear if the water in it had frozen, but we knew the test would have to be cut short. The heaters were turned on yet again to stabilize the temperatures while our pilot continued to bake in his plastic oven. The team huddled in to discuss the situation and what we could do to get as much data as possible from our now highly abbreviated test. The agreement was made to simulate the dive itself, during which we would blast the fans and push everything into extreme cold yet again, so we could at least show that the equipment could handle the drop. Then we would quit and go to debrief.

It was communicated to Alan that we would be cranking up the wind for an abbreviated dive simulation before opening the doors to let the room thaw out. We kept a close eye on our equipment, which was teetering near freezing, and cranked on the fans. The roar overcame the ambient noise of the surrounding area. I watched intently through the tiny window at Alan being blown by fierce winds at extremely low temperatures in a room that contained no breathable air. In surprisingly good spirits, Alan brought his arms into the wind stream like he was skydiving. The temperatures appeared to be declining, but slowly enough that during the couple minutes of simulated freefall we would not, yet again, risk freezing our equipment. After a few minutes the fans paused, and the test director yelled for the technicians to open the doors. The test was over.

I opened one door and a tech opposite me opened the other. White nitrogen smoke billowed out the doors into the parking lot, and the fans roared back to life to force oxygen back into the room so the crew could enter with air to breathe. After 20 seconds or so, I dipped my oxygen sensor into the room and it stayed silent, meaning breathable atmosphere had been restored. Rolfe yelled, "All clear!" and the four members of the pressure suit assembly team filed in to document the situation and get our brave pilot back to the warm, breathable world.

For every one picture we needed we took seven. We captured a frosty suit, a sweaty pilot, a completely fogged-over helmet bubble, two access doors mistakenly left open, and a leaky purge valve hissing oxygen away. While this test was an incredible learning experience, it became clear within seconds that the team had pretty well botched it. Alan came out in an easy slip, and we convened for a four-hour debrief to list our failures and outline the parameters by which we would try that test again.

Our first mistake was obvious: the access panel on the chestpack was left wide open. I was supposed to close the access panel upon leaving the chamber. I hadn't. The open door exposed the heat exchanger to the freezing environment of the chamber. This was especially pronounced when the fan was blowing air right at it. It was easy to see that the temperatures that were strangely reading so low on the heat exchanger were being read by a sensor that was in the chamber, not protected by the suit as it should have been. We definitely had not frozen our heat exchanger, but at the same time it was disheartening to realize our very expensive test had been partially thwarted by a very simple mistake. We also had the obvious problem of a partially open purge valve, another simple mistake. We had inadvertently left open a valve, depleting oxygen much faster than planned. In response to those issues, it was decided to make a closeout checklist, a very standard thing in aviation and aerospace. This test emphasized something we already knew, the unquestionable importance of an age-old invention: the checklist.

Realizing these obvious mistakes answered a couple of the major questions with our test, but we still didn't know why our pilot got so hot. We determined that the main issue was that Alan started the test at a dangerously hot level, so when we turned on the heaters to keep the equipment warm, we continued to heat up the already-hot pilot. The simple answer was to get a more powerful chiller and keep Alan cooler before the test, but that was much easier said than done. It also wasn't clear whether we had over-insulated the suit in general. If there was too much insulation in the suit, it would mean we would have to remove layers to keep Alan away from heat exhaustion while running our heaters. The problem was attacked on both fronts. Overnight, Sebastian and Zane built a new chiller using a copper coil and an ice bath. It was modeled after what is known in beer brewing as a wort chiller. In fact, the hardware itself came from a personal beer-brewing setup in Sebastian's garage. The suit techs also removed thick neoprene insulating layers that Alan had been wearing.

We still had to deal with helmet fogging, which meant dealing with head sweat. We ran numbers to try to pinpoint just how much a normal head sweats, which of course varies from subject to subject. Alan was a very fit guy who claimed he didn't sweat much, but as would be expected with a core temperature near fever levels, a helmet that was killing him, and a long, hard day of testing, he was sweating profusely during this test, producing what was ultimately a sizeable pool of moisture in the helmet and enough liquid to create a dense layer of fog when the bubble fell to sub-arctic temperatures and the suit interior stayed hot and moist.

We decided to keep Alan cool through all the suit preparation, mold the helmet foam to better fit his head, and insulate the metal helmet ring of the suit so that the double-layer bubble could be more effective without the exterior cold creeping around the edge of the metal seal and cooling the inner bubble.

The second test would be different from the first. In order to keep the duration shorter, we would take a conservative approach to temperature but shorten the length of the run. Instead of going to the coldest temperature, which only occurs relatively low in the atmosphere, after which temperatures would climb back up across the span of several hours, the chamber would drop to the coldest temperature and hold it for 30 minutes. This would stress the hardware to the max in regard to temperature without taking up all the time that a slow warming would take. The downside, of course, is that it would not be the same as the mission anymore. It violated the "test as you fly" rule. We also would be hooking into ground oxygen lines to avoid running out of oxygen mid-test with our now-depleted suit.

In our haste, we accepted this approach, flawed though it was. That was the last detail noted at the debrief. The team broke away into the night to try to sleep for a few hours before going into the freezer again for the second try.

We were back at it before the sun came up. Ernie and I were preparing the suit when the pre-test talks started. As the checkouts labored forward, we found ourselves once again with too many things to do and not enough time.

We called the mission control group to ready the pilot, and once more Alan was waiting while the hardware teams worked out details. All of our thermocouples were reading too low for no identifiable reason. We combed out a two-inch spinal cord of tiny wires trying to figure out what was going on. Rolfe had us run control points by dipping the sensor leads into ice baths that should read exactly 32 degrees Fahrenheit, and then checking the human temperature that should read very close to 98.6. Through that process, the technicians were able to apply the offsets in the computer and keep moving. Two hours went, by with Alan sitting partially dressed just like the day before. Luckily, this time he was in an air-conditioned room with his liquid-cooled undergarment on, so he was staying comfortable.

The team was getting more used to the procedures, and by skipping the pre-breathe and combining some steps, our crew got the suit ready to use in a matter of just a couple of hours and got Alan into it in another 40 minutes or so. As was done the previous day, we suspended the suit in a 45-degree position. He was almost giddy; we hadn't realized just how badly the old helmet padding was crushing his head. The new cooling system appeared to be working wonders as well; his core temperature was at about 97 degrees. The thermocouple cord was laid out and ready. The team ran through our brand-new closeout checklist and turned the chamber over to Rolfe to connect all the thermocouples and close the doors. We were far more prepared and less anxious in general now that we'd seen the chamber work. The thermocouples came together smoothly, and data came streaming in on dozens of channels, painting a colorful coded picture of the world inside the chamber. After the thermocouples were connected, Zane checked my work on the closeout checklist. The final approval was radioed to mission control, and the huge freezer doors were swung shut to begin the test.

The process began again, and it was much like the day before—but this time, our pilot was staying calm and free of sweat. As the room plunged deep into the negative temperatures, with all of our access doors closed and valves properly shut, everything was going beautifully. The equipment approached freezing temps, and our pilot was ready for some heat: we kicked on the automated heating system, which brought the temperature right back where we wanted it.

Then Alan needed some hand heat. The liquid thermal garment doesn't include the hands; they have an independent heating system that is activated by a button on the back of the glove. By the time Alan asked to activate the heaters, the temperatures in the chamber were as cold as they would ever get.

At temperatures this cold, normal equipment simply stops working. Everything plastic turns to rock, rubber turns to plastic, and fabric gets stiff and slippery to the point where nylon parachute straps would let go in their friction buckles if we didn't sew them down. Alan felt his fingers stiffening up in the cold and moved his hand to push the button to turn on the heater. He did it on the first heater first try. The second heater was on the side of the system where there was a toggle to activate the radios to talk to mission control. Something about the placement of the button was making it difficult to turn on the heater. Perhaps because he was grabbing a metal stick (the toggle for the radio) and squishing up the insulation in the glove while the fingers on that hand kept getting colder, he was failing to activate the glove heater. Minutes went by and he still couldn't get the heater to turn on. There was a camera near the heater that was blocking his view, and he asked permission to rip the camera off. I gave the thumbs-up and in a quick push he ripped off the GoPro camera that captured his face and continued to try to activate the switch. We watched through the window as he tried over and over again to get the heater turned on while his hand was reportedly going numb and potentially approaching irreparable damage.

Meanwhile, our test was approaching its end. The only worrisome temperatures were the suit temperatures around his legs, which were approaching the chamber temp of negative 90 degrees Fahrenheit. This troubled the suit techs because they thought the rubbery inner suit material might crack, causing the suit to depressurize. Alan's legs inside the suit were plenty warm, but the outside of the suit legs were extremely cold. The communication radios were also too cold, reading just below their rated temperature of negative 30 degrees. Almost on cue, when the radio reached 10 degrees below its rated temperature, it turned off. We lost communication with Alan. The team huddled quickly to decide how we would close the test. The last item on the agenda was the freefall profile, where we blast Alan with the giant fans to simulate the fiercely cold descent. That was by far the most intense part of the mission from a thermal standpoint. To do it without communication was a risk. We didn't know how bad the cold hand was, and the last thing we needed was frostbite. Without the freefall profile, however, it would be hard to say whether we'd gotten our required data points.

Mid-debate, behind the freezer, the other first responder on post next to the window saw Alan swipe his arm through the air side to side, signaling an emergency evacuation. We didn't wait a second. I yelled, "Evac, evac, evac!" and the team jumped to action.

Two technicians sprinted behind the chamber to shut the nitrogen valves and stop the cooling. I shouted, "Doors!" and opened my door. Ernie pulled open the opposite door, and dense white frozen nitrogen gas poured around our legs. My oxygen sensor started beeping to indicate that there was not sufficient oxygen to breathe in the chamber. Ernie rushed to turn on the fans to blast out the nitrogen. They roared to life. In a moment of mad confusion, against the force of the blowing air the huge fan stack fell backwards into the back wall. The floor had deformed so much from the extreme cold that the panels had tilted. When the fans fell, the plating on the interior of one bent inward and the huge blades started bashing against the sheet metal on every turn. Several people yelled, "Fans off!" and Ernie killed the fans.

I stood in that panicked and chaotic moment holding my oxygen sensor inside the chamber, waiting desperately for the oxygen to reach breathable levels so we could get to Alan. I turned to the other tech to ask if he thought we should go in on the emergency life-support packs until the oxygen remixed with the stagnant nitrogen that filled the freezing chamber. Right as we started reaching back to suit up and enter the toxic chamber with bags of air over our heads, the sensor stopped beeping. I shouted, "Clear!" and we flooded in to pull off the helmet.

I immediately depressurized the suit and panic struck again. The sensors were reading like there was still pressure in the suit. We jumped around in confusion trying to troubleshoot the problem. Every few seconds I flashed a thumbs-up toAlan and he would flash one back. It appeared he was fine, but we had to get the suit off.

The suit techs concluded that after the strenuous test, the pressure sensor was failing and the suit was depressurized. We decided to open the suit even though the sensor said there was still pressure in it. Ryan suggested we release a glove instead of the helmet so that if there was still pressure, it would cause the smaller, softer glove to launch off instead of the hard, heavy helmet. The glove came off easily, indicating that the sensor was reading incorrectly and the helmet could be removed. Everyone was relieved when the helmet came off and we saw Alan's smiling face. He was okay. We pulled off the suit as fast as we could and took hundreds of pictures we would use over the course of the next few hours, as we slowly determined whether we had conducted a successful test.

That test left me feeling sick and on the verge of collapse. We were all mentally and physically exhausted. The team gathered and started to talk about whether the test was successful enough to check the box for a completed thermal test. If we determined it wasn't successful, we'd have to delay and test again in the chamber.

The debrief was weird. An airplane jump was scheduled in two days, and we needed to call the test a success in order do it. Yet there was an elephant in the room. The test wasn't finished; it had been aborted and ended in an emergency evacuation. Additionally, the evacuation occurred because our glove heaters, radios, and ultimately our entire basic sensor package had failed. In that room we convinced ourselves that this is how these things go; tests were about learning. We had learned what we needed to learn. We knew the suit could be thermally equipped to take on the mission. We left the meeting in record time with a general thumbs-up. We began tearing down the testing equipment and packing it up for the trip to Coolidge, Arizona, where, for the first time, Alan would climb into in the reconstructed suit and jump from an airplane while wearing it.

I skipped dinner to sleep for 12 hours before meeting Blikkies early the following day to break down equipment and start packing the trucks. Within 48 hours I would be driving a box truck filled to the ceiling with equipment across the empty Arizona desert, thinking about pushing Alan, and the suit, into the wild blue from the back of a military training aircraft at 14,000 feet.

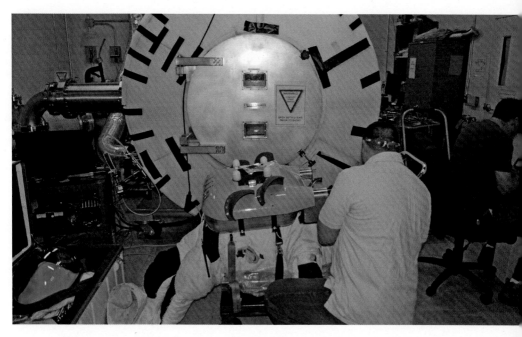

Testing crew outside the vacuum chamber before unmanned vacuum testing of the suit at the Paragon headquarters in Tucson. (Photo by Volker Kern.)

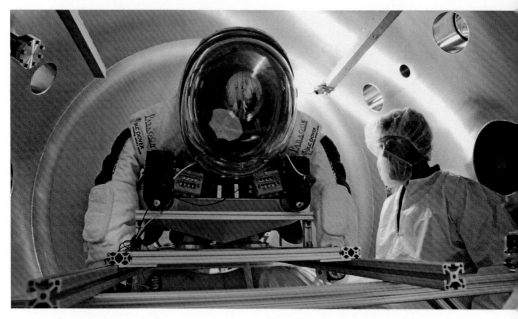

Preparing the suit for vacuum testing inside the vacuum chamber. (Photo by Volker Kern.)

Alan Eustace hanging inside the cold chamber preparing for thermal testing. (Photo by Volker Kern.)

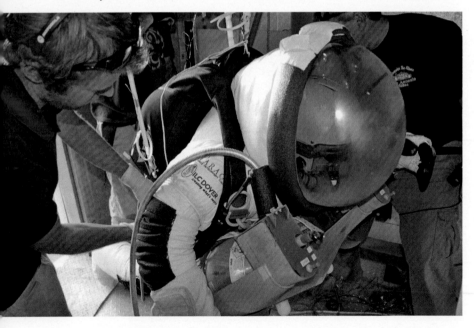

Alan hangs in the cold chamber with a frosty helmet after the first cold test of the program fails. (Photo by Volker Kern.)

The "Frankenfreezer": a home-built liquid nitrogen freezer system capable of creating a stratospheric temperature profile down to below -100 degrees F at the Paragon headquarters in Tucson. (Photo by Volker Kern.)

Sebastian, John, and support personnel in the makeshift mission control room across the parking lot from our cold chamber during mission preparations.

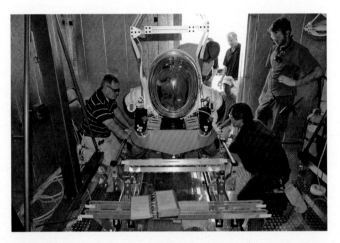

Utilizing some extra time to check launch equipment in the cold chamber before testing.

A hot and tired aeronaut after a chamber run. In Alan's first chamber run an access panel was left open. The suit heaters were run full blast to keep the equipment warm despite Alan's body temperatures being characteristic of a high fever.

CHAPTER 7

...

Skydiving

Skydiving is a raw defiance of millions of years of evolutionary hardwiring. In the invention of airplane flight, humans mimicked the function of birds, even creating aircrafts that looked like them. There is no similar natural analogy for skydiving. Exiting an aircraft tens of thousands of feet above the ground defies some of the most basic of human instincts and does so on the understanding that if the engineered equipment doesn't work, the jumper dies.

Skydivers deploy a tiny device at high speed that raises tens of feet above their heads and spreads out. During the deployment process, the parachute changes surface area by a factor of a thousand. A parachute typically weighs 2% as much as whatever it is slowing down. Terminal velocity for a person in freefall is usually over 100 miles per hour. During parachute deployment, a skydiver will slow from the speed of freefall to the speed of a neighborhood ice cream truck in about three seconds.

While apparently madness, skydiving gives humans intimate access to the sky. In a unique position to mix work with pleasure, I decided during my first year on the StratEx program to learn to skydive alongside some of the most knowledgeable parachutists on Earth.

My first skydive would happen with two instructors holding me on either side by handles attached to my jumpsuit. We got on the plane behind the roaring prop, inhaling the distinct smell of skydiving airplane exhaust blown from the roaring engines of what I considered a rickety plane. The door was a rattling Plexiglas panel with a rubber flap at the top that had to be folded under by the person who closes it.

My body was trying to convince me not to jump. My heart was beating so hard I could feel it in my hands. I enlisted a trick I had learned in altitude chamber testing: repeatedly counting down from 20, skipping the number 17. I had failed this test in the chamber when I became oxygen deprived. I knew that as long as I could do it, I was all right.

Researchers have strapped monitoring systems onto people jumping out of planes to analyze their breathing and heart rates, and in general a person's heart rate steadily climbs as the plane's altitude increases, peaking while they are standing on the door frame looking out at the world below. This was my experience.

The moment a jumper leaves the door of an airplane, their vitals stabilize to normal levels. Before the jump happens, the brain tries to stop it, but once it's a done deal, chaos shifts to clarity. The brain knows it has lost the battle and it resets.

As I stepped up to the door, 18,000 feet above sea level, I decided to quit. I looked at the instructor, ready to yell my decision over the sound of a roaring jet engine, but he mistook the glance for a ready signal. Panic continued to mount as the instructors shook my jumpsuit, signaling that we were about to go. My whole being filled with a sense of chaos and uncertainty in myself. They pulled me back into the cabin for a split second to gain momentum, then pushed me into the air. My brain on fire, I let go of the bar above the door and slipped into cool blue serenity. Air rushed around my body at 100 miles per hour while an endless landscape of the Colorado Rocky Mountains spread out before me.

Our trio neared the Earth, plunging 1,000 feet every five seconds. My blood pressure slowly rose as I neared the next event, the parachute pull. Less logically this time, my brain appeared again to be bargaining to keep me where I was instead of undergoing a dangerous change. My brilliant engineer mind couldn't understand that if I stayed in the state I was in I would die. The needle on my altimeter dipped below 6,000 feet, and it was time to pull out the hacky and release the parachute. Parachute instructors like to joke to students about not "going the extra mile" before pulling—at the end of that mile, you'll be on the ground.

Stiff with panic, I reached back for the hacky. I grabbed and threw. The pull didn't feel right, and nothing happened. I was still in freefall. I reached again and felt the same lumpy object I had been attempting to grab and throw but felt only resistance. Something was wrong. My hand was constrained. Was it stuck? I wriggled and yanked, accumulating enough adrenaline to rip nylon straps apart. Then the two instructors shot past me and out of sight while a parachute bloomed into a giant flying wing above me. I piloted my first canopy flight to a tumbling landing on a grassy field beside the airport.

On the ground I learned that I had grabbed the instructor's hand instead of the hacky that pulled the parachute. After my two attempts to throw her hand into the air, she tried guiding my hand onto the hacky. When I started flopping around in the air, she pulled the parachute for me. Surprisingly, they called the experience a pass. I would move onto my next drops despite the fact that the instructor had to intervene to pull my parachute.

I continued instructor-led courses for the better part of a year, slowly progressing from jumping with multiple instructors to jumping alone, trying new maneuvers and improving my skills with each skydive. I took more courses: I was hung from the ceiling in a jumpsuit, I lay on a cart pretending to skydive, I exited hollowed-out airplane fuselages, I jumped into swimming pools wearing a parachute, and through the onslaught of new information I jabbered with wild-eyed excitement. After each training session, I would take my new skills to the sky. I exited the plane in different ways, intentionally tumbled and recovered, pulled the parachute lower, left the plane lower, and jumped in groups, working parachute skills until I felt comfortable in freefall and could land on my feet most of the time.

During the training jumps, I repeatedly questioned whether what I was doing was madness. During a canopy course in the middle of the training, I had to intentionally collapse my parachute and let it come back open, increasing the risk of line malfunction. The instructor told me and my fellow students that if we got to 2,500 feet and there wasn't a good parachute overhead yet, we simply cut away and used the reserve. He repeated, "That's why you have two parachutes."

I started jumping more regularly, doing several jumps in Florida with the StratEx parachute designers, who taught me the deepest details of what makes parachutes work—or not. Their lessons included stories of gruesome deaths. During one jump with Blikkies, I first felt the incredible sensation of truly flying. Blikkies left the airplane a couple seconds ahead of me, and I had to make myself into a diving wing to catch him. Turning like a fighter jet with its wings back, I blasted toward Blikkies at 150 miles an hour, while he ballooned up and slowed himself to give me a chance to catch up. Feeling the unreal sensation of unobstructed human flight, I rocketed sideways through the air toward the speck I was chasing, and after traveling miles across the cloud-pocked sky I met Blikkies with a locked-in smile and the deep satisfaction of having become a controlled wing.

As my skydiving campaign continued, I developed a coping method for when I was too scared to jump. I would picture myself in a quiet freefall, stretching my legs out slowly and taking in the infinitely vast space I occupied, nothing liquid or solid within miles of me in any direction, an experience that only lone skydivers know. When I pictured this very specific scene, I became calm and relaxed, and then I could jump.

As I chalked up more jumps, my fear of the experience subsided. There was a safe way to fall through the sky. I had learned that people who had done it several thousands of times were still alive, more or less undamaged. It seemed like the most dangerous parts of the learning process were behind me. The beauty of the experience had captured me, and I was confident I could continue this pursuit safely; my teachers were the world's best. I would push more and more to be in airplanes and in the air whenever possible for the program. It wasn't the usual introduction to aviation. The craft I was piloting solo in the air was myself. It's an experience that will never leave me. One long, scary year after that first jump in the grip of two instructors, I received my license. I had become a skydiver.

Early May 2013: Bleeding Together in the Big Desert

The weather conditions required for a stratospheric jump are specific and they happen only twice a year: once in the spring and once in the fall. Alan and Taber had gotten the idea in their heads that we should make the spring window. We had to finish a host of tests in a matter of weeks, tests that historically took months to execute, tests that had to be performed perfectly in order to be called successful. The latter we had yet to experience. I assume direction was passed from Alan and Taber to Sebastian and then to me and the other hardware team leads. We hesitantly, skeptically complied.

The thermal testing had been scary. It was the first true trial of the team. It generally worked, or at least that's what we told ourselves. The suit had become more or less reliable. Slowly, we gained confidence that maybe the date we were shooting for could be possible. We built a plan and started running. We would pack up the gear and go to the central Arizona desert. Over farms and sand, we would knock out our required parachute tests in two days of grueling but rewarding airplane sessions.

The timelines for these tests were compressed to something miniscule compared to the scale of the program as a whole. The two thermal tests and the airplane jump test all took place within the span of just six days within a program operating on a timescale of years.

I had stumbled euphorically out of the thermal testing on the verge of physically shutting down. Without pause, we rented a U-Haul, both to move our small village of provisions and ground-support equipment and to provide us with a ramp, which we intended to scavenge off the truck to use to load our pilot into the tail of the aircraft. We scavenged the ramp because we didn't have time to build one, not to save money.

Tensions were high. With five days left until jump day, the onslaught of work at all hours was driving the team beyond their limits. Fixated on the upcoming date, we accumulated failures and fixes that skewed us further and further from our originally stated goals.

In our sprint, we ignored a critical issue. The folks who normally run the facility where we were jumping wouldn't be there during the week we needed to test; two of the jumpers were out with injuries, and a third was on vacation. A second parachute engineer who was slated to jump as a safety diver bailed the week before the jump for unknown reasons. We found ourselves with a makeshift team of instructors, none of whom were coaches for heavy drops at that facility. The support diver team we ended up with were exceptional jumpers, but they did not fit the mold of the original jump team. Blikkies was the only jumper from the originally planned team. To further destabilize the faltering plan, we learned that we might not have access to the facility's aircraft, which would force us to use a different aircraft from a neighboring skydiving facility. All our calculations—for cabin size and Alan's ability to exit the plane cleanly—had been done for the on-site aircraft. Thus, for a myriad of reasons, conditions were far less than ideal, but we decided to jump anyway because we were dead set on our weather window. We would prop our tired eyes open and get through this one more test.

We discussed the issue of fatigue regularly. On the one hand, sleep-deprived people should not perform physically demanding, life-critical tasks. On the other hand, there was a pervasive unspoken understanding that fatigue simply comes with the territory of doing this type of thing, and we would just have to power through it.

We didn't know how fast Alan would fall. We had run numbers, but they couldn't be trusted; we didn't know the angles at which the suit would fly or the suit drag coefficient. If we didn't know how fast Alan would fall through the air, the skydivers wouldn't know how fast to fall in order to accompany him. We needed three skydivers capable of falling at a range of speeds to jump with Alan.

One of the test jumpers was Derek, the instructor from the wind tunnel who was also a champion freeflyer. Derek would be our fast-fall diver. He would point himself on his head in a tight, slick jumpsuit and maintain acute control of his position and speed at rates probably up to around 200 miles per hour. At the other extreme was an engineer from the parachute company who would wear a squirrel suit with flaps of fabric connecting his arms to his torso and holding his legs webbed together. He had honed his skills as a cameraman for skydiving teams and could control his speed and remain stable at speeds as low as 70 miles per hour, using his special suit to catch air. In the middle was Blikkies, who would wear a normal jumpsuit and fall at around 120 miles per hour.

The night before the jump, we unloaded the trucks and set up for suit preparation. We returned the following morning at 6 a.m. and went straight into preparing the suit. We pulled out the checklists and started the preflight checks. All the valves were checked and the electronics cycled through all their expected functions. Right near the beginning of the checks, as we started to power on the oxygen tanks, reading off the pressures on the display panels, the whole suit shut down unexpectedly. We turned it back on. The motors turned off again, the displays shut down, and we had no idea why.

We rebooted the suit. The system came back on but with the displays showing their initialization values, not the real values. Within a few seconds, the displays all froze up again. We rebooted several times more, but the suit displays refused to work. It was becoming apparent that we had missed something critical in our sprint to try to make this weather window. I remembered someone having asked how the suit was working after the thermal test, and the realization dawned that this was the first time the suit had been activated since coming out of a chamber with negative 95-degree temperatures icing everything over. Dan, the avionics lead, was immediately dispatched from Tucson ferrying two spare display panel circuit boards. We would do the replacement right there in the hangar. Sometime between Dan leaving Tucson and arriving with the new boards, someone suggested that the system wasn't fully rebooting because we weren't leaving it off long enough. Sure enough, after we turned it off and left it off for a couple minutes so the capacitors could discharge and the chips reset, when we turned it back on it worked beautifully. The new boards arrived and Dan stuck around for the evening.

We had decided in another rush that we would have Alan get into the pressure suit inside the airplane so that we didn't have to move the heavy suit. The original plan was to have Alan walk from the hangar to the plane after suiting up, but nobody had ever really tried walking in the suit with all the equipment hooked to it.

The skydivers drilled Alan on how they would exit the plane and fly, while the suit team minus Blikkies continued through all the preflight checklists. That occupied the rest of the day. After the final preflight check, it was dark.

After a short night, we were again driving through the cotton farms between our hotel and the drop site, anticipating the steps we'd take to get the suit ready for its very first jump from an aircraft. Upon arriving, we pulled out our plastic tubs and opened up our checklists. We were starting our third manned suit-up in a week.

Around noon we were ready to start putting the suit onto Alan. The Sherpa aircraft that would ferry us into the sky arrived and parked on the tarmac outside the hangar. This, luckily, was the larger aircraft we had planned to use. The plane was right on time, but we were not. The morning dragged on. Slowly, we got highly tentative go-aheads from the relevant leads. Alan put the suit pants on. We mounted the suit's upper half to the floor of the airplane and Alan practiced getting into it. A crowd had formed: a film crew, a still-camera crew, and about 10 random bystanders watched us huddle around the tail of the airplane as Alan lay down and crawled through the tunnel of the suit's upper half.

Alan got through the tunnel of suit fabric just fine, and we were able to button up the gloves, pants, and finally the helmet. Alan was sealed into the suit lying on the floor of the aircraft that would bring him to altitude. We pressurized the suit in the plane on ground oxygen, checking the last few preparation checkboxes. Everything worked. We were pulling the equipment when the wind gusted up. Alan lay on the aircraft floor while the wind battered the plane wall and shook the boxy frame of the huge aircraft. When the gusts peaked at 20 miles per hour, we called it for the day. The pilots agreed, telling us the winds were too strong even for the airplane to fly, and the weather didn't look likely to get any better. We chalked up the day's activities as practice. We learned while packing down that the large Sherpa aircraft would not be available for future jumps, so we would have to contract the smaller Skyvan aircraft from the neighboring facility.

We began helping Alan out of the suit while he lay on the airplane floor. We popped the plastic helmet bubble off and removed his inner helmet, giving him fresh, clean outside air to breathe. The waist ring came off next, along with the gloves. As Alan prepped to pull out of the suit backwards, I reached into the head region, pushing my fingers around the rubber neck dam that sealed Alan's head away from his body. Alan scooted out of the suit, and as I stretched the neck dam to pull it over his face, it loosened up and turned to butter, ripping right down the middle. The rubber skirt hung from the suit in torn strips. My heart sank. Ryan and the suit techs breathed hard, letting their dismay show for just a moment before they commanded their resolute demeanor and methodically suggested options for repairing the neck dam so we could continue the following day. More work to do. Alan and I made the 13-minute trip to Tucson in his plane and retrieved the spare neck dams from company headquarters.

Blikkies provided his traditional sausages and coolers of beer. We didn't know, as we sat drinking beer in the hangar on the eve of a very intense first jump, that our pride in ourselves was hubris.

Well into the night, Ryan and the technicians performed surgery on the suit, opening up the neck ring and pulling out equipment clusters to access the necessary bolts to replace the thin rubber neck dam. It all came apart and went back together over the span of a few hours.

Later that evening, eating and wandering about the cavernous hangar, I was looking at the radio communications setup with the flight director and Dr. Jon Clark, the flight surgeon. I made the very naive comment that it was surprising how easy it was to set up the radios to do long-distance communication. Dr. Clark, with more scars than most and an intense understanding of space systems, responded with a bite. He said that we ought to do a long-distance radio test, implying that we actually had no idea if our radios worked at long distances, and maybe further implying that they probably didn't. He then said something that resonated deeply with me: "You haven't bled enough. You're going to be running around the desert looking for Alan without comms." Then he softened the reprimand by adding, "But then you'll find religion." The implication was that we (probably mostly me) needed to grow up a bit and realize that we weren't at band camp; we were in the desert preparing to throw a human out of an airplane in a pressurized spacesuit.

Dr. Clark was completely right. We were children, and the following day we would eat our ill- preparedness in a terrifying way. I think there are only a couple people who really grasped how under-prepared we were on that evening, and how lucky we were when things went the way they did. He could see that we were dancing on the edge of a dark pit, but he also knew we needed to first make mistakes, fall in a bit, and then claw our way back out before we would truly understand what we needed to do to accomplish this project without anyone dying.

At 5 a.m. we were munching the hotel breakfast of bland cereal, bananas. and yogurt, thinking that today was the day we would throw a man in a spacesuit out of an airplane for the first time. Because of the aircraft scheduling conflict, we were going to be loading Alan into the smaller Skyvan aircraft. It was yet another last-minute change that would get less thought than it deserved.

The only important difference we saw between the Sherpa and the Skyvan was that the new airplane didn't normally fly from that airfield and didn't have the right tools to restart its engines away from its home, so it would be leaving the engines on while we hurried to load up. Instead of suiting Alan up on the plane as we had done the day before, we would put Alan into the suit inside the hangar and walk him to the plane, a process that one day earlier we had doubted we could do.

We suspended the suit in our usual fashion from the gantry that we had brought with us from Tucson. We plugged in and started the ground cooling system. Alan put on the familiar long underwear and liquid thermal garment running to the auxiliary cooling box. He waited for the thumbs-up from the suit team for the start of the donning process. The exceptionally loud Skyvan bumbled down the runway and pulled into position outside the hangar. We signaled Alan to come over and get into his suit.

We got Alan into the suit but had some trouble putting the gloves on. I shoved my nearly anatomically identical hands into the gloves to index the fingers, pushing around like I was fixing a ski glove turned inside out from a too-hasty removal. With the gloves cleared, Zane mashed through the 20-some pages of checklists while I worked with the suit techs to close the bubble and get our pilot onto oxygen. Blikkies pulled on the parachute pack. We signaled the all clear and Alan, with 280 pounds of equipment on his back and six sets of hands supporting him, began to shuffle toward the roaring plane 60 feet away.

We were a slow seven-man mob trying to move 450 pounds of bulky weight, our 12 work boots and two spacesuit boots tangling and tripping us. We set Alan's big spacesuited butt against the tailgate of the aircraft and lifted him aboard like a heavy plank being tipped into a pickup truck. We paused for the heartwarming thumbs-up from the spaceman. We rotated him and swung his legs underneath him so he was lying on the chestpack with his head facing out the giant open door at the back of the airplane. The engines roared on, and a crowd of a dozen or so people, including the documentary film crew, stood at the rear of the plane getting bathed in jet exhaust while we did the final checks. Sebastian yelled, "The displays are off!"

I looked over the suit shoulder and sure enough, the displays were dark. We were puzzled for a split second then realized that we had not powered on the flight switch before leaving ground power. Yes, we'd forgotten to turn the thing on. We pulled Alan to his knees, opened the access panel, and flipped the switch. The displays sprang to life, showing ample oxygen and good suit pressure. We were good for flight.

As Alan lay back down on the floor of the plane, I put on a parachute pack so that I could move around the plane freely once we climbed above 2,000 feet. The three safety divers stretched their torsos back and forth with their hands in the air, preparing for what would certainly be a memorable jump in their parachuting careers.

I was finishing the check when Sebastian hollered up to us in the plane, his hands cupped around his mouth. We barely heard him over the sound of the engines. "You don't have a GPS fix!" The GPS was inside a metal box when the system was powered on, so it could not see the sky to acquire a signal. The data link will not update without a GPS signal. Our flight rules said that we could fly without a data link, so although we hesitated, we proceeded without it. The spectators were shooed away. We sent straps around the suit handles and cinched them, tethering Alan to the floor. Within a minute the engines feathered into forward motion toward the runway.

The airplane was off the runway in seconds, powering up in true skydiving fashion. I remembered the view from our dart tests months before. I sat on the bench watching Alan, who was attached to the floor facedown with criss-crossing straps. It was impossible not to think about Alan, or any one of us, simply tumbling right out the back of the plane. The suit technician riding with us wore a grin that stretched his face. "This is cool," he squeezed out, giddy, as the Earth fell away out the huge door and we climbed fast and hard. At 2,000 feet everyone with a parachute on their back (which was everyone except the suit technician and the documentary cameraman) started unstrapping the suit and preparing for the shove-out. We got our thumbs-up from Alan to pressurize and turned the knob to bring the suit to full pressure. It all went smoothly and we got our third thumbs-up of the morning at full pressure as the plane reached 10,000 feet above ground. I took out my Bible-sized flight manual, already open to the final checklist. The suit tech sat opposite me over the suit and we hollered a litany back and forth, verifying that each item on the checklist was good.

I shouted, "Dual suit control set to pressurized position!"

Tech yelled, "Pressurized!"

"Oxygen tanks set to on position!"

"On!"

"Ground-support panels closed!"

"Closed!"

"Lock pins set!"

"Set!"

"Display panel on!"

"On!"

"Oxygen pressure above 1,525 psi!"

"2,080!"

I gave the final shout. "Suit team clear!"

I let the parachute team know Alan was in their hands and sat down near the cameraman filming the three parachutists from the front of the plane. Everyone was tense. The three parachutists pulled Alan to his knees and scooched him up. They yelled, "Mat!" and we scrambled to pull the squishy gym mat out from beneath Alan so the parachute team could set him on the floor. He was scooted back about a foot from the door. I checked the oxygen levels one more time. He was still over 2,000 psi, which was plenty, so I gave a thumbs-ups to the parachute team. Alan was on his knees, ready to keel forward in the ultimate trust fall. He had to be closer to the door, but without a platform behind the door to pull from, they just weren't able to scooch his knees to the edge of the tailgate. The parachute crew huddled. A yellow light came on in the back of the plane, indicating we were three minutes away from the landing zone.

The green light came on and the parachutists looked at each other with one last sober glance. Blikkies poked his head out to verify that we were in fact over the grassy landing pad. They grabbed Alan and rocked him forward to indicate "Ready!" then pulled him back for a "Set" and pushed him toward the door.

The first safety diver, the fast one, leapt into the space behind the plane just before Alan tumbled out. Alan tipped forward from his knees, angling over center and accelerating as Blikkies and the safety divers pushed on the back of the parachute to launch him past the metal lip at the bottom of the door. Alan's body rotated off the tailgate, straightening out just before his back was parallel to the aircraft floor. The bottom of the plastic chestpack collided with the aircraft floor, bashing plastic against metal and raking off two of the three communications antennas that stuck out of the bottom of the pack. One of the antennas was sheared off so cleanly that it was left sitting on the inside of the airplane cabin, wires and all. Blikkies and the other safety diver leapt into the air behind Alan to track his progress.

Alan flipped out the back of the plane with his head curling under the system in the start of a front flip. The stabilizing parachute was inside a small canvas bag that was connected to the back of the plane so that as Alan fell away the parachute would pull out of the bag. Less than a second after Alan rolled out, the stabilizing drogue parachute pulled out of the static bag as it was supposed to, and the little drogue snapped to life with a loud whap! followed by a fabric whip of the little bag against the airplane wall.

I watched from the tailgate as the team blasted away into space toward the awaiting airport three miles beneath us. As the drogue set in and started pulling up on the center of the parachute pack, the three safety divers swooped around the suit and formed a perfect formation on three sides of Alan, with Blikkies staring at his masked face from just a few feet away. The GoPro camera attached to Blikkies' helmet would capture his reflection in Alan's helmet bubble.

From my perspective up in the plane, Alan seemed in control as he plummeted away. I saw the safety divers catch up with him and hold steady at his side. I stared with a painful fix on a shrinking white dot: the drogue chute falling toward the Earth at over 100 miles per hour. Panic shook my gate, awaiting entrance. Alan would be freefalling for almost a minute, and I started counting the seconds so I would know exactly when to allow myself the onset of fear. If it took too long, it would mean he had to use his reserve parachute at 2,200 feet. With a wave of relief, I watched the white dot morph into a bigger orange dot and glimpsed a white stripe. The main parachute. That meant he hadn't been forced to use the emergency reserve. From where we were in the sky everything seemed okay.

I leapt to my feet and pumped the air, yelling, "The main parachute is out!" The cameraman yelled back, "Say it again!" This time I looked into the camera: "The main deployed!"

It was a happy ride down. We hopped from the plane, gathered our gear, and drove to the landing zone, ready for high-fives and back-pummeling. We pulled up and saw people calmly packing parachutes. When I saw an orange one, I hollered in euphoria, "He's on the lawn, he's down!" Then I realized that there were far too few cars and people there. As we got even closer, I saw the lawn held only two parachutists. The orange parachute belonged to one of them. Confusion set in.

"Where is Alan?" I asked one of the parachutists, and he looked back in confusion. "He went out that way," he said, pointing across the desert. "Is he okay?" I asked, and the parachutist looked confused again. "I don't know," he said, finally realizing that we had no idea what had happened. What had happened was disaster.

The near-flip set in motion by the collision between the chestpack and the airplane had caused Alan to rock back and forth as he descended to the ground at 125 miles per hour. He wobbled up and down in a teeter-totter motion. He started turning. The safety divers remained in their formation, rotating in space to maintain their left, right, and front positions. Their arms and legs twitched and shuddered as they tuned their speeds to match that of the heavy suit and stabilizing parachute system. The diver with the slow-moving suit arched his back hard and sucked his legs toward his butt to counteract the slowing effect of the fabric flaps between his limbs and his torso and increase his freefall speed. The safety diver in the tight, fast jumpsuit fell with his elbows out and legs extended, his feet pointing toward space to maximize his surface area. Blikkies fell naturally, opened up in a classic skydiving pose, palms forward, knees bent at a right angle. They matched the speed of the system, remaining within feet of Alan at all times.

Alan extended an arm of the suit into the air to try to stop the turn, but instead the turn accelerated. The evidence from the wind tunnel seemed to be holding true. In intense moments people revert back to their instincts. Alan forgot that his altered center of gravity in the spacesuit would require him to reverse his responses, so he kept his arm out and spun faster. The safety divers had to intervene. The fast diver swooped in and expertly pushed a hand against Alan's spinning leg, executing a perfect bump two miles off the ground. The spinning stopped. The system blasted down and things were again stable.

Alan attempted once more to control his fall. He pushed an arm into the air again, and again the system spun toward the extended arm. In the midst of what I'm sure was pretty serious confusion about why the skydiving skills he had developed over hundreds of past jumps weren't coming into play, the freefall was over. It was pull time.

At 7,000 feet off the ground, Blikkies showed Alan a straight finger pointing sideways, the signal that says, "Pull your parachute." As Alan and his attending formation slowly turned in a circle, he reached to the side of his chestpack, grasped the handle, and pulled. No parachute slithered out above the divers' heads. In developing the pack, we had worked out a pull method whereby the arm first pulls out, then up. Alan wasn't doing that. I had been in the suit when we developed the method. This was required to get enough stroke to release the parachute. People can imagine how paralyzing it must be to pull the handle and feel nothing. Nobody wants to find out from experience.

There were handles on each side of the suit for releasing the parachute. Alan had first pulled the handle on the right side of the chestpack; he had one more option to get the main parachute out before changing to the reserve system. The reserve parachute would open faster, more violently, and, in this particular scenario, out past the stabilizing parachute, which would present an entanglement hazard to the reserve as it flew by. Alan reached with his left hand for the other handle and pulled it. Still no parachute. The safety divers knew that if they didn't get a parachute out before 2,200 feet off the ground, an automatic opening device would fire and launch the reserve parachute out with just enough time to stop Alan from colliding with the Earth at full speed. Should Alan manage to get the main parachute pulled at an altitude too close to that 2,200-foot mark, there was a chance that the automatic opener would spit out the reserve parachute at the same time the main parachute was extracting, dangerously leaving two parachutes competing for space above Alan's head.

Blikkies made sure that wouldn't happen. With a few thousand feet to spare, he pulled his arms behind him and dove headfirst at the suit. He smacked into Alan mid-hurtle and grabbed the exposed cable between the plastic pull handle and the start of the steel housing that guides the cable to the pin that pulls out of the pack. Blikkies couldn't grab the handle itself because it was locked firmly in Alan's gloved hand. Clutching the bare pull cord in his hand, Blikkies arched back away from the suit, letting the huge force of the rushing air rip him away from Alan. As Blikkies flipped back away from Alan, his foot got shoved into the plastic pocket where the parachute pull handle was previously tucked, and the quarter-inch-thick carbon-filled nylon handle cover shattered around his foot. It is amazing that his foot didn't shatter in the process, though it wasn't undamaged. Alan's parachute finally bloomed above his head.

The safety divers continued to hurtle toward the ground ahead of Alan, pulling their own parachutes at lower altitudes. Everything had deployed correctly. He was flying under a perfectly good parachute. Only Alan knew what happened next.

It was time to depressurize his suit. This would give him near-normal mobility so he could reach up to grab the parachute steering toggles stowed above his head. He needed to turn a knob located near his right hip three counterclockwise revolutions to depressurize the suit. He couldn't find it. Spacesuit gloves are seven layers thick and filled with air, rendering normal dexterity nonexistent. We had not practiced enough, and it also seemed a strap might have shifted around during the deployment process and caught on the depressurization knob. Whatever the reason, Alan could not depressurize the suit. He continued to fly toward the open desert, moving at over 30 miles an hour away from the safety crews on the ground one mile beneath and a half mile behind him.

If the depressurization knob didn't work, as in this scenario, the backup plan was for Alan to reach up and grab the parachute handles in the pressurized suit. It would be uncomfortable, but he would at least be able to steer himself to the landing site. When he reached up, the parachute straps locked against the suit shoulder bearings and prevented his arms from extending upwards to reach the stowed handles. He just couldn't reach them in the pressurized suit. It was yet another scary deficiency in suit design, a product of a green team that simply hadn't checked everything they should have.

Alan was heading for wide-open nothingness. The safety divers, under tiny parachutes, were likely already on the ground. With the communications antennas sheared off, the ground crews could not track the suit and Alan couldn't hear us. We later learned that Alan's transmit function was working all along, but because he couldn't hear the team, he didn't know that so he quit using it.

Alan flew over the desert, untrackable, out of control, and quickly getting out of range of the ground crews, who were not equipped for a chase across the open desert. He was sealed from normal air with a finite oxygen supply and would suffocate when that ran out.

Alan met the ground about two miles away from the airport. As he approached, he was heading straight for a massive saguaro cactus. In a last-ditch effort, he leaned as hard as he could in an attempt to alter the course of the suit just enough to miss the cactus. He succeeded.

Modern parachutes are made to land in a "flare." The diver pulls down on the steering toggles to lean the tail of the wing-shaped parachute back. Forward speed is transformed into lift as the airfoil slows down and stops descending, setting its user on the ground lightly. Without access to the toggles, Alan could not flare. He collided with the ground, moving forward at over 30 miles an hour and descending at over 10 miles per hour. His feet clipped the hard, dry dirt and he slammed onto the chestpack which housed his vital life-support equipment. The suit flipped forward until the system was acrobatically poised with the feet 45 degrees in the air. He slid on his helmet across the flat, dry clay, burning a skid mark into the plastic. Alan came to a stop on the desert floor in his busted but still-pressurized suit, hoping that the ground crews could find him before his oxygen ran out.

Alan's antennas had sheared off. His GPS location was unknown. He was incommunicado. There were backup independent trackers on the suit, but their signals were being output to a screen in an empty trailer at the other side of the airfield. The last thing the crews on the ground could tell was that he couldn't control the canopy, so nobody knew if he was injured, unconscious, or worse. The team had made no provisions to deal with the current situation.

Our amateurish status as a team was obvious in the chaos. I was the only design team member with any skydiving experience at all, and the others were asking why the safety parachutists had set themselves down on the grass at the airport while the pilot was so clearly headed for the horizon. They didn't realize that the safety jumpers were on tiny sport parachutes that fell thousands of feet per minute faster than the suit's giant parachute and that they would plummet thousands of feet below Alan before they pulled their parachutes and slowed, reaching the ground much sooner than he would.

Several radio calls to Alan went unanswered, including signals to Alan to respond with physical motion like a turn. The huge orange parachute could be seen from miles away though binoculars. Alan never turned. The team started shifting into disaster mode. Cars scurried into the desert attempting to follow his trail. Blikkies kicked the communications engineer out of the passenger seat of one of the chase trucks in a frenzy.

Alan should have had about an hour's worth of oxygen in the suit, but the desert is big, and finding something in it can take hours. The flight director used his aviation radio to send an SOS call to any active pilots in the area. In a surprising stroke of luck, a helicopter pilot in the middle of a training run responded immediately. The helicopter had seen the parachute heading into the desert and knew roughly where it must be. The instructor took over the helicopter, headed immediately in the direction he had seen the parachute go, and was there in seconds. The helicopter hovered over Alan's dirty spacesuit so the ground crews could see where to head. The cars sped across the open desert until they hit an impassible wash. People jumped out and sprinted. They found our pilot at the end of a 20-foot skid mark. The crew pulled his helmet off, shut down the tanks, and extracted him.

Given the events of the 27 minutes since the plane left the ground, Alan was remarkably chipper and, unlike the suit, completely undamaged. The ground crew collected the suit, pilot, and a few pictures before heading to the highway to take the long way back to the planned landing zone, where I milled nervously with the rest of the team in the yawning open door of the C-130 hangar from which we had so confidently staged this chaos.

The team was stunned into shock. Alan was almost giddy. We watched the videos from the cameras on the safety divers' heads and painfully understood the root causes of each of our issues. A strap had indeed moved during the parachute deployment and covered the depressurization valve. It sunk in that we had let Alan fly completely unpracticed in activating the valve. In fact, he had never once turned it unassisted before he attempted it under parachute. Because the suit was supposed to be unpressurized when he reached for the parachute handles, we had only tested that motion in the unpressurized scenario.

The suit was banged up. We found the comm system earpiece ripped out of the helmet. It was never fully understood whether the damaged earpiece or the broken antenna caused the lack of communication, or if it was a combination of the two. The air hose running from the facemask to the exhaust valve under the neck dam was torn and bashed up. It might have been circulating some amount of CO_2 back into the helmet, which would have eventually poisoned Alan. The chestpack shell was cracked in half from the ground collision. Blikkies' foot had ripped off the handle guard. The helmet was irreparably wrecked.

Coolidge Failures by Altitude

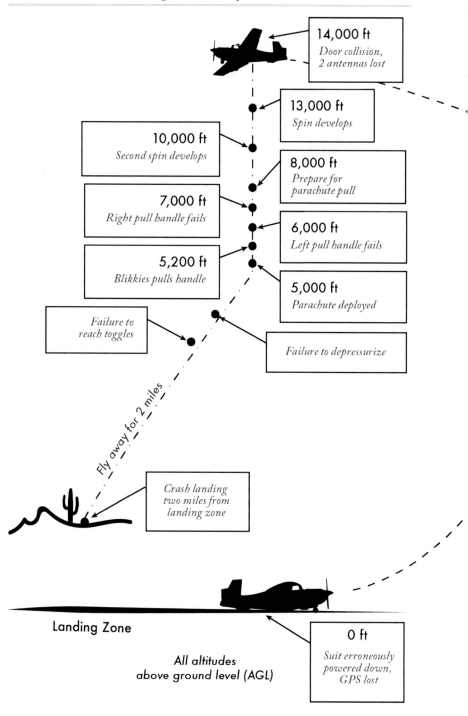

14,000 ft
*Door collision,
2 antennas lost*

13,000 ft
Spin develops

10,000 ft
Second spin develops

8,000 ft
*Prepare for
parachute pull*

7,000 ft
Right pull handle fails

6,000 ft
Left pull handle fails

5,200 ft
Blikkies pulls handle

5,000 ft
Parachute deployed

*Failure to
reach toggles*

Failure to depressurize

Fly away for 2 miles

*Crash landing
two miles from
landing zone*

Landing Zone

0 ft
*Suit erroneously
powered down,
GPS lost*

**All altitudes
above ground level (AGL)**

We discovered one more failure as we dissected the system and interviewed Alan about his journey, and it was perhaps the scariest. The neck dam, which is the seal that keeps the head region of the suit isolated from the body, the one we had just replaced, was ripped again. This time the neck dam had pulled away from the bolts in the ring around the head. Oxygen can rush through a hole like this, quickly blasting away the oxygen supply. Depending on when the rip happened, the tanks may have been draining oxygen into the suit. Alan could have been tens of minutes from the start of the same type of mechanistic suffocation I had experienced a few months earlier. A few key factors, including a random helicopter and an incredibly motivated chase team, may have saved his life.

The following day, as expected, an executive team initiated the beginnings of another "safety stand-down." Three days later, in the Tucson conference room with all the top executives of the company, I found myself a part of the short list of decision-makers on the future of what was now the company's biggest project. I was there because the suit I was responsible for, which was supposed to protect a man I had grown to admire and deeply respect, had almost killed him.

May 2013: Safety Stand-Down II

Throughout the safety stand-down, I started to think about what motivates people. Is it better to be satisfied by small things or by big things? If one is content with small things, perhaps one will always be happy, but maybe won't achieve greatness. If one is satisfied only with big things, one might become great, but will also be much more susceptible to failure, much more likely to die suffocating in a heated spacesuit in a hot desert. Different people had different views on how close we actually got to true disaster on that jump in Coolidge, Arizona, but regardless of opinions, it was now painfully clear that Alan really could die before this was all over.

Alan hugged me in the hangar after the crash, alive and well. No one doubted that the risks of this program were clear to him now, and everyone wanted to know how he reacted. My mom wanted to know if he was angry with us. He wasn't, but it was nonetheless a reasonable question; the thing we had made didn't work right. Other people wanted to know if he was thinking about pulling the plug. My girlfriend had a three-word response to my struggle: "Shut it down." We didn't.

As we debriefed in two full days of meetings, I felt changed in ways I couldn't articulate. We pulled apart the gritty details of what had gone wrong and why, and discussed how we would move forward. The executives made every effort not to point fingers of blame, but there were inescapable conclusions. The whole team, from management allowing the schedule to get unrealistically compressed to the design team overlooking details with high consequences of failure, had been careless. Nobody denied that these were mistakes that could have cost a life. The thick chunk of blame we were supposed to avoid was distributed thinly across the entire program, spreading all the way to the top, where even the sages were faulted for trickling down a virus that touched us all. A veil of confidence had been pulled over our eyes by fast-talking geniuses who easily convinced us to give them what they wanted.

Alan wasn't at the meetings. I don't know how much he considered himself responsible for the incident. He either minimized the seriousness of the crash or didn't fully understand the technical details of what had happened, because he mostly didn't address the issue at all. Taber seemed to accept his fair share of responsibility for pushing us to test with an unfinished system, though he wasn't very vocal in that regard. It was also clear he believed the team leads should have halted the effort if they had thought they weren't ready.

The consensus and stated conclusion of the review was that a constellation of mostly programmatic failures led to our incident. We went too fast. We didn't train Alan enough. We didn't train the crew enough. Most of all, had we not compromised on the completion of some of our stated mandatory tests, we might have caught the design flaws that came to a head on that day. The flaws themselves were simple, although their consequences were near catastrophic. Alan couldn't activate the parachute rip cord or depressurize his suit. He couldn't reach the parachute steering toggles or take his own helmet off.

After reviewing the oxygen data and talking with Alan, we learned that the hole in the neck dam had not opened up a flow of oxygen. Maybe the tear had happened while Alan was coming out of the suit, or maybe it was small enough that the flow was negligible. The late news didn't make much difference, though; the scare was over either way.

It became clearer just how much this project had consumed my own life. My girlfriend broke up with me, citing transgressions like spending only four days a month at home, extreme distraction, exhaustion, and no indication that this would change in the coming months. There was a sense building amongst everyone that we were "all in" on this, gambling together with the highest stakes there were.

Ultimately, Taber would convince Alan that we had to take a major step back. We would redo the tests we had skimped on and add new ones. We would try for the weather window in the fall of that year, 2013. It was clearly a hard pill for Alan and his family to swallow. He took weeks to respond to the new proposal to add lots of money and several months to the program. It felt like money was the smaller part of the discussion. His family was focused on the now-apparent risk of the program.

Nobody left the program over the incident. Instead, on that day in the desert, our team became closer in a profound way. It was the same intense camaraderie I had experienced in the cabin of skydiving airplanes right before people start jumping out. I have never left an airplane at altitude without first sliding my hand across the hands of the people around me, and then bumping fists in an embrace of acceptance and empathy. When you come to terms with something so momentous as leaping from an airplane, everyone is related. The more experienced jumpers become the parents and the others their children. I think it's because a mind poised at the edge of panic strives to embrace all relationships. Considerations without immediate purpose fall away, and the only evident purpose for human relationships becomes care. On that day our team grew together in ways that only the team could understand.

I thought back to Dr. Clark's foreshadowing talk 15 hours earlier. He had said that we would be running through the desert without comms, terrified, and that then we would get religion. If "religion" is embracing all the things we don't understand, he couldn't have been more right.

Safety divers leap out after Alan in the suit as he plunges toward the ground in his first airplane jump attempt in Coolidge.

Alan attempting to deploy his parachute. The parachute handle is partially pulled, but the parachute is not deploying. Shortly after this moment the safety divers will intervene by grabbing an attachment cable to release the parachute.

Alan skydiving in the suit in his first jump.

Alan's crash-landing site in the desert outside Coolidge. This picture was taken from the cell phone of the helicopter pilot who found him.

Skid marks showing Alan's crash landing in Coolidge.

CHAPTER 8

...

Ups and Downs

We had a lull during our redesign process on the suit team. We went back to working 40 hours a week for a while. I took a vacation. Life seemed almost normal as I spent time with friends in New York. On my fourth day in the city, after going out every night, sleeping in late, and forgetting about work, the holiday screeched to halt. An upcoming test in Roswell, New Mexico, was pushed forward by a week due to a good weather window. I was summoned to come and observe the stand-up of a large balloon envelope and size up some interfacing concerns so I could further plan the suit preparation. My long nights with good friends had to give way to early mornings of entanglement in the stratospheric testing process.

The program had changed my life and my responses to it. Things that used to shock me simply didn't anymore. I had become hard to startle and felt neutral about the bumps of normal life. As I rushed to change planes at the Denver airport, behind schedule as usual, my phone alarm went off. There was a tornado warning in the area. I silenced the distraction and boarded the tram to the terminal. On the way to my gate, I ran past a herd of people piled against the bathrooms and into a totally empty terminal. I did note the strange emptiness of a place that usually bustled, but kept running down the 100-foot-wide hallway. A security guard yelled, "Sir!" I stopped, turned around. "Your flight's not taking off. Get in the shelter!"

Along with hundreds of people who had been pulled out of bathrooms and aboveground shelters, I was ushered five stories underground to the guts of Denver International Airport as a tornado approached the hundreds of empty airplanes stuck to their metal square walkways. I sat against a concrete pole in the underbelly of the airport, watching people taking pictures with their phones and reflecting on why I hadn't realized that empty airport terminals and multitudes of people trying to cram into bathrooms wasn't normal.

My life was unique and I felt privileged to live it, but one could argue that I wasn't entirely sane, that I was losing touch with reality. I was impatient to get out of the shelter and get the show on the road. The tornado passed within a quarter mile of the airport and moved on without incident. My flight was half an hour late, landing in Roswell in time for me to make the night briefing.

June 2013: 70K Balloon Stand-Up

In Roswell we were going to do what was referred to as a "stand-up" of a plastic balloon. A stand-up is simply the act of raising a balloon by filling it with helium exactly as it would be done for a mission. The only difference between a stand-up and a launch is that at the end of a launch the balloon is let go, and at the end of a stand-up the helium is vented from a manhole-sized valve at the apex of the balloon and it is allowed to fall back to the ground.

Polyethylene high-altitude balloons are hard to launch for a single reason: they are huge. Laid out on the ground at launch, our balloon would be over 400 feet long. The balloon itself is composed of many acres of plastic sheets meticulously joined by heat sealing and reinforced by the load tapes that carry the weight of the payload. At full altitude it would expand to occupy 11 million cubic feet of space; a normal city block filled with 25-story buildings could fit inside the balloon. We were opting to launch in a way never done before, using a modified front-end loader and a static release point to get the balloon standing before we attached our human payload and released it to the heavens.

Large balloons are launched in a way that is either "dynamic" or "static." In a static launch, the balloon is attached to the payload, erected while tethered to the ground, and then released. If the winds are too high with respect to the payload size, the payload will drag across the ground for some distance before starting to fly.

In a dynamic launch, the payload is suspended from a vehicle, such as a crane, that can drive. The balloon is held down by a spool while it is filled and straining to float up. Just before launch, the balloon is released from the spool, and while the balloon floats up and leans into the wind, the vehicle drives toward it. The idea is to get the payload right under the balloon, which initially leans into the wind, arching in a wide parabola. At the last second, before the balloon starts yanking on the vehicle, with the payload directly below the crest of the balloon, the vehicle lets go. That payload will fly straight up, instead of swinging sideways and potentially striking ground as it begins its journey up.

Our method of launching was a combination of the two methods adapted from a Japanese system in which the balloon is erected on the ground, fixed by a giant roller as in a static launch. The payload is on a cart, or "sedan," so that as the balloon lists over at release, the sedan will roll the payload into the wind until the balloon lifts up and pulls the payload off the sedan and up into the air.

Most of the team was asleep when I arrived in Roswell. They had been doing dry runs of the stand-up in the middle of the night for several days. Between 9 and 10 p.m., as I took a swim in the hotel pool, folks started to come to life. We drove to the airport, where our launches would take place in a caravan with authorized airport drivers at the wheel, stopping at the security gate to punch our codes and enter the active international airport grounds. We headed for the growing StratEx City, which housed a mission control trailer, a large warehouse-like structure we called the "tin shed," and an array of heavy equipment, communications trailers, outhouses, and chase vehicles that would get us through the mission. This was my first trip to Roswell. It was exhilarating to see what the project had become. Our four-person team had grown to an army maintaining a permanent presence at an active airport, operating millions of dollars' worth of equipment. We were really doing this.

We filtered into a preflight briefing at midnight. The meteorologist team consisted of an off-site representative named Don Day, who fed us the dates and times of our weather window, and one on-site meteorologist who was monitoring real-time conditions. Don ran a small consulting business called Dayweather, and we had been told by multiple people that for big helium balloons he was the best there was. He did the meteorology for Red Bull Stratos and had worked with NASA on several occasions for their big balloon launches.

The desert Southwest is meteorologically the calmest place in the US, but it is still a needle-hunt to find a weather window for inflating a balloon most of the year. Conditions have to perfect. A dirigible was flown to 400 feet with wind monitors outfitted underneath it to report winds through the full balloon profile. Winds had to be below seven miles per hour if we were to stand up the balloon. It was breezy outside, too breezy for ballooning, but Don assured us that right after sunrise the winds would drop to around four miles per hour and we would have our window. The on-site meteorologist was scrambling around with a tiny wind meter hanging around his neck, finding little pockets of wind and constantly reporting changes and gusting values. The two meteorologists worked together to correlate the existing wind profiles with the predictions to hone in on when the window would hit.

The stand-up started with the placement of the launch platen, a 4,000-pound steel plate that anchors the balloon to the runway without physically penetrating the concrete. We wanted to point the balloon lying into the wind at launch without running out of runway, so we had to be able to launch from whatever position made that possible on any given day. We were using a section of an abandoned runway that had been converted into an aircraft boneyard. Companies like to store their dead airplanes in the desert because it's dry and nothing rusts. The part of the runway not covered in old aircraft was a roughly 1,000-foot by 300-foot section used frequently by balloonists. Red Bull had used the same stretch of runway to launch their much larger Stratos balloon. For the stand-up, the platen was set to the west so the uninflated balloon could lie with the crest pointing to the east where the winds, which were moving from east to west, would fold the balloon against a drum as it lifted. This kept the balloon away from the heavy equipment holding the drum.

A heavy-duty boom forklift (which we called the "boom lift vehicle," or BLV, because we were too proud to call it a forklift) set the giant launch platen into place. The platen was further weighted with heavy concrete barriers to prevent horizontal motion. On an actual launch, the BLV would then transition over to the suit team and carry the pilot, hanging from a cable, to the launch site.

The StratEx Equipment Fleet

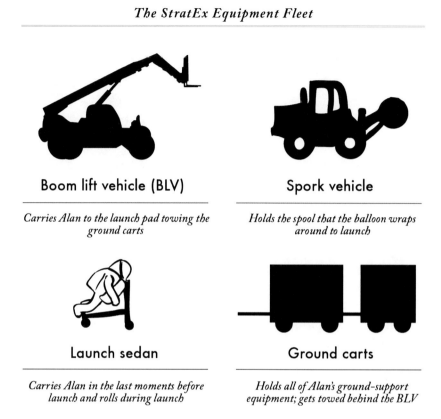

Boom lift vehicle (BLV)

Carries Alan to the launch pad towing the ground carts

Spork vehicle

Holds the spool that the balloon wraps around to launch

Launch sedan

Carries Alan in the last moments before launch and rolls during launch

Ground carts

Holds all of Alan's ground-support equipment; gets towed behind the BLV

The balloon we were standing up had been purchased from the Tata Institute of Fundamental Research in India, the same institution that would make all of our balloons. This balloon was originally manufactured for our expert and Senior Balloon Advisor, Julian Nott, a pioneer in the world of ballooning with an impressively long career.

Julian was the epitome of an adventurer braving the sky. His hair stood up on end when he had ideas and his aviator glasses added the scientific and engineering element to his aeronautic adventurer persona. He was tall and remarkably energetic, even after a lifetime of hard-hitting balloon landings across continents and in oceans. He crossed the English Channel in an experimental hybrid balloon in 1981. He has set 79 world ballooning records. He built the first hot air balloon ever to have a pressurized cabin and used it to set the world altitude record for a hot air balloon: and it now sits permanently in the Smithsonian Air & Space Museum at Dulles Airport.

Julian had intended to take the balloon we were testing on a long duration flight but changed his plans. Dropping deadweight ballast is the traditional method used for gaining altitude on long-distance balloon journeys. Julian, however, invented a novel method of venting and filling a balloon with reserve helium carried in cryogenic tanks. Patented by Julian, this made for a far lighter system than anyone else had ever used. It was designed to carry a heavy payload around 36,000 feet, and fly in the core of the jet stream, as demanding a place as there is for a balloon. The capsule and its two pilots weighed two and a half tons. Because of the long mission and difficult conditions the balloon was designed for, it was also tough, with 4 layers of plastic and extensive load tapes. Fumbling first timers like us would have a hard time ripping it.

The balloon rode the quarter mile from the tin shed to the launch pad in the back of a burly pickup truck. The box was opened with a crowbar under the supervision of the launch director, who had flown in from India to guide the event. The layout began. Foot soldiers scrambled to turn on the floodlights that surrounded the runway. They meticulously cleaned the dirty runway surface to prevent some sharp little rock from ruining our day.

Using Don's prediction about the direction of the wind at launch, the balloon team laid canvas ground cloths onto the runway where the balloon and fill tubes would go. Those canvas cloths were about six feet wide and ran the length of the balloon. In addition, two long canvas arms to hold the balloon's fill tubes were extended toward the sewer main–sized helium diffusers waiting to blast helium from a tanker further down the runway. Then the launch platen was set down in the place where the balloon would be held once it was standing. The heavy concrete barriers to prevent the platen from sliding sideways were attached to it.

After a final confirmation from Don about the predicted wind direction, the pickup inched forward while two people fed the bright pink sleeve holding the balloon onto the canvas runway. They let it out until they found the crown valve. The valve marked the crest of the balloon. It was carefully extracted from the tube and set on the ground.

All that was left to do was to find and extract the helium fill tubes, ready the vehicles, and wait hopefully for ideal wind conditions at sunrise. The launch director guided two of the launch crew on a dig through the pink plastic in search of the fill lines, which appeared at the exact location the director said they would be. They cut open the pink cover to extract the tubes and laid them out on smaller canvas sheets. The canvas flapped in the rising night wind. We all shifted our attention to Don to see if we would be lifting a balloon that day, or packing up the gear for another shot on a less windy morning. Don was confident that the rising winds would fall to nothing right as the sun broke the horizon. We were less sure. We paced around uselessly, occasionally tending to the fabric lifting up at intervals across the lengths of the long runways.

Dawn was breaking as a hazy light reflected across the endless desert, and the calm settled in. As the sun nicked the eastern skyline, all flags fell. Every person on the flight line found a kick in their step at the accuracy of the meteorological witchcraft. The machines roared to life and we prepared to stand up this plastic monster in what we were promised would be a one-hour calm.

The spork vehicle approached the top of the balloon, ready to thread it, inside the long stream of plastic, under the drum that extended off the body of the spork. About a quarter of the balloon would be threaded under the drum and then laid back over the rest of the balloon. The balloon had to be threaded far enough that fill tubes went past the drum, so that when the bazooka-style diffusers from the 3,000-psi helium truck blasted helium through the hundreds of feet of ultra-high-pressure lines, the bubble would rise over the front-end loader and tighten up against the drum. The tricky part about this stage was the heavy crown valve that resided at the top of the balloon. Normally we would also constrain the top of the balloon with what is called a "launch collar." Because the team was new to the process, and this balloon wasn't flying, the launch crew wouldn't use a launch collar even though it would be required for real flights.

Launch Setup

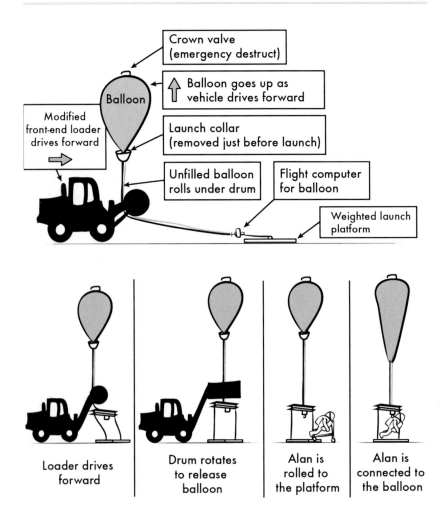

The heavy crown valve could be opened remotely from a ground station via communication link. It could be used to vent the balloon down out of the sky if needed, or to deflate it on the ground. We would be using the valve to take the balloon down after the test. Three people held the valve so the balloon material wouldn't scrape the ground during the early part of the fill. The signal was given to start the fill. There was no turning back.

The diffuser's valves were slowly opened. Flowing helium roared. Across the two-foot diffuser, pressure dropped from 3,000 psi to atmospheric pressure, expanding in volume by over 200 times, violently shaking the nozzle. The balloon bubble bulged and rippled as the diffuser operators opened the valves further. The three men supporting the big crown valve at the top of the balloon were no longer keeping the valve up off the ground but struggling to hold it down. They wrestled to keep their boots off the fragile balloon fabric on the ground while the massive upward force of the expanding helium tried to pull them into the air. Just at the panic moment, when we all thought they would be lifted up with the top of the balloon, the director gave the signal to let it go. They did, and the heavy metal valve slipped gracefully to the top of the balloon as it blossomed above the spork vehicle into the rising sun.

Immediately, we had our first unpracticed phenomenon. The standing balloon began to twist. The Indian launch director yelled, "Go!" to the fill team, who stared, confused, as the turning balloon threatened to strangle the fill lines and cause them to pressurize and pop. Our inexperience was painfully obvious. The director gave more precise hand motions, and we all realized that the fillers needed to run with the twist so that the lines continued straight to the balloon. As they both started running a long lap around the balloon, holding their shoulder-strapped diffusers, the black high-pressure lines started catching on the concrete barriers anchoring the launch platen against horizontal motion.

For the first time, I actually had something to do. I sprinted to the barrier closest to me and cleared the line. I stayed on the line, pulling it around as the fillers circled with the twisting balloon to keep the lines from kinking and popping. Luckily, the balloon was twisting back and forth more than moving in circles, making it possible to keep it clear. Then, as quickly as the racing had begun, the calculated helium volume read by the gauges on the tanker had been met. The launch director called for the valves to close. The fill was over.

The spork vehicle was signaled to drive toward the launch platen. The tension on the plastic rolled the drum as the vehicle moved forward. The vehicle crept to its destination. About 10 feet before reaching the platen, the spork's drum was lifted up by the front-end loader's hydraulic system so it wouldn't strike the balloon's metal anchor lines. The full balloon was now straight up and held directly by the anchors to the launch platen. The drum arms held the drum out in front of the balloon, caging the balloon base. The launch director called to release the drum. At the pull of a handle, the two-foot-diameter drum swung free, uncaging the balloon. The spork vehicle backed away. We had successfully completed the first ever balloon stand-up of this kind.

The tall, lanky lollipop swayed hundreds of feet in the air. We enjoyed our success for a full three minutes, then it was time to take it down. A command issued through the communication computer linked to the balloon equipment module under the balloon opened the valve. Plastic flapped violently and went limp, flopping into the wind while a scramble of excited engineers strained to catch the crown valve before the expensive piece of hardware crashed onto the concrete. The plastic flailed harder.

While the helium blasted from the top of the balloon, the team circled the giant valve and caught it. The flailing balloon plastic could grab someone and suck them into a suffocating embrace if a sheet got over them. Immediately Don, the meteorologist, sawed out the valve, leaving a huge hole for the helium to vent through. (These balloons can't be reused.) I was behind the hole and enjoyed a blast of cold helium just long enough to realize that there was no oxygen in that helium wind, and I should move. We stood away from the dangerous turbulent plastic sea and stood by as the last waves of helium cleared out.

The sun was fully up now. Exhaustion crept over me. The last time I had slept was in New York. We picked up the site, repacked the balloon carcass, folded canvas, and stowed lights. It seemed like an endless list of physically demanding tasks in the wake of such excitement. We filed back to the trailer to congratulate ourselves in a post-test brief. The management offered kudos and the boss's credit card so we could go celebrate. I debated hard about whether to go to bed. I knew I was wearing a thousand-yard stare, but this team had just stood up a massive balloon in a way that had never been done before. The day was theirs and it would be wrong not to celebrate with them.

The day was a riot. After cocktails on the patio at Pepper's, we circulated through nearly all of Roswell's drinking establishments. A herd of people, average age 45, visibly smashed on a weekday morning—we got some looks. We must not have cared because we kept on going. Our early-morning cocktail ritual would eventually become well known in the tight-knit town of Roswell.

Our quality director and one of the technicians settled some grudges the old-fashioned way with a wrestle on the floor of a bar. We were asked to leave. We crossed the street for burgers. As the sun faded to afternoon, I paused, three sheets to the wind, to count the hours since I'd slept: 36.

But instead of going to bed we went to the Roswell alien museum, a monument to the alien conspiracies that the town is known for. We made yet another scene, taking selfies with all the aliens while the staff considered throwing us out. We slipped back to the hotel, where most the team finally went to bed. I headed to Applebee's with the only project member within 10 years of my age and had a final drink to toast the momentous night and day. In the morning, I'd drive three hours to the airport to head to Houston for design implementations. I was back. We were back. The show was on.

August 2013: Manned Thermal Test II

The successful balloon stand-up had been an enormous morale booster for a frazzled team and a nervous group of executives. It was a win. We had moved past a milestone, something not so easily said for the suit systems. So far that team had had two runs and two aborts.

We had planned from the start that we would do one each of a series of environmental tests to prove out the systems. Cold-case testing subjected the system to extreme freezing. Hot-case testing cooked the components in a vacuum. Manned-case testing put the entire system, including the pilot, in a space-like vacuum to vet it as a whole. Budgets, schedules, and personal lives, not to mention expectations, were all built around doing these tests once each.

As the Arizona temperature climbed into the hundreds in August 2013, we assembled the teams and a truckload of new hardware to bring the system, with a pilot, into the cold chamber, the frankenfreezer, for the second round of testing. This would be Alan's third trip into the chamber. By the end of the tests, our one and only suit would have seen over 50 hours of use. The system had never spent more than 40 minutes in the chamber at one time through the initial testing, testing we foolishly once called complete.

After Alan's crash we rethought our philosophy about when to call a test complete. On our first test, the official reason that we bailed was that a hatch we left open let the equipment get too cold. The second, highly abbreviated test was aborted when both radios froze and Alan couldn't get his glove heaters turned on. In each case, because we felt compelled to test before a window of opportunity closed, we considered the test complete and moved forward. We recognized that we hadn't really checked all of the boxes.

After a test, the team would scatter, and we'd reconvene weeks later to go again. It was time for another round. We had a window of five days before vacations and executive obligations would end the effort for a while.

We prepped the suit inside the chamber. It went faster than ever, and for the first time none of us were dazzled by the suit and its unique processes. Things were becoming routine. We knew the 100-page procedure to ready the suit for a person nearly by heart, but slogged through the list checkbox by checkbox as we were supposed to. The suit went together without event. After five hours of preparation, we had screwed in the last bolt.

The last checkbox before leaving reminded us to plug in the radio chargers so the voice communication system would charge overnight. I plugged in while the others packed boxes. Where there was supposed to be a solid red light on the charger, I saw flashing orange. On the label I saw that flashing orange meant "waiting to charge." Something about the battery was preventing the radios from charging.

After we froze our last radios, we had created a special insulating diaper for the bottom of our equipment module and installed brand-new ones. Now those new radios didn't want to charge and we didn't know why. The hours ticked on as the blistering hot afternoon edged toward our 4 a.m. start time and we disassembled the covers over and over again, trying to figure out why our radios wouldn't charge. We made phone calls to everyone who had touched the units. We plugged the old units into the chargers. We tried plugging handheld units into the chargers, still with no success. We took the chargers apart. We took the radios apart. We pulled out hair and snapped at each other in mounting frustration. Finally, we took the whole cover assembly inside to do more electronics investigations with our electromagnetic interference bench. Before we tried anything, the units started charging. It turned out that it was simply too hot outside. Four hours late, with three days to our final run, we left the radios to charge inside in the air-conditioning and went home to try to get some sleep before the early-morning test.

When morning came, we were back at it. The first signs of dawn broke while we held pre-test briefings and prepared to get things moving. I had returned in the night to verify that the radios had successfully charged, and they had, but since we left them inside, away from the heat, they needed to be installed before the test started, and in less time than usually allotted for it. We mounted the radios and performed the very last step of the initial preparation stage, a communications test. We fired up the radios. I put on the helmet and spoke. "Suit one, this is pilot for comm check."

My own voice echoed my last word back, blaring it louder and louder, "check, checK, cheCK, chECK, cHECK, CHECK!" I scrambled to pull the helmet off and escape the ear-piercing blast. This had happened before, the voice-activated radio picking up the signal from the transmitting radio and amplifying it as it bounced back and forth. We thought we had fixed it by putting the radios on different frequencies. We dove into another troubleshooting session.

We removed the covers over and over again, programmed the radios to reset the frequencies, pulled up old documents to try to pinpoint the problem. But nothing would fix it. While looking into the equipment module, adjusting the settings, we saw that the channel knob was brushing against one of the oxygen tanks. We pulled the covers yet again and saw another face slapper: each time we installed the cover with the radio on it, the tank pressed on the radio and changed the channel. In a wildly frustrating coincidence, it changed it so that the two radios were now using the same channel, causing the feedback.

We reinstalled the radio so that it was further from the tank. When we went to comm check after installing I couldn't believe it. The problem wasn't fixed. How could some other malfunction be the one causing that problem? There was no way that the channel changing was a coincidental, unrelated factor alongside some other problem which was the true cause of the failure. I peered inside the cover and saw that the radio hadn't touched the tank. We were stumped. As the time rolled toward midday and our seventh hour of troubleshooting, we pulled the covers yet again. I don't know how it happened, but the channel was again pushed over to the wrong setting. We changed it back. It worked like a charm ever after.

After the extended preflight procedures, Alan was anxious to do something. He had been sitting for eight hours liquid cooled in his thermal garments and under strict supervision by the doctors in the prep area. We sent him steady updates every 20 minutes, telling him that we were half an hour away. The sun was directly overhead and the outside temperature was in the hundreds, exactly what we wanted to avoid. Alan was rushed to the chamber to avoid getting hot on the trip out. Any perspiration made the helmet susceptible to fogging. We got him suited and sealed in record time. We all took a deep breath while Alan did his pilot radio check. We used the cryptic, rigid radio language we were learning so as to avoid confusions over the radio.

"Suit one, this is pilot for comm check."

"Pilot, this is suit one. I've got you loud and clear, how me?"

"I've got you loud and clear."

We had good communication. Time to go. The test team applied the web of thermocouples that fed real-time temperature data to a program which compared the array of temperatures to a profile calculated ahead of time. A virtual instrument that required lots of computing power to function would use those values to command the opening and closing of valves. The valves controlled the rate at which liquid nitrogen poured through the nozzles into the soon-to-be oxygen-free, unearthly cold room. We would also use the temperature data to validate our test.

Ryan, the lead suit technician, passed control to mission control, signifying that the test had begun. Liquid nitrogen began flowing. Almost immediately, the situation deteriorated.

Just minutes after starting to inject liquid nitrogen, the test team called a hold. I was on the first responder team, staring hard through the chamber window at Alan in the suit, and had no clue why we had stopped injecting. Sebastian let us know that the hot desert day, combined with the heavy processing the computers were doing, was overheating them and they were turning themselves off. Ernie, the technician who had taken the lead in operating this chamber, and the test team sprang to life, lifting computers up onto wooden blocks and piling ice from the break room underneath them. They scavenged computer fans from the R&D lab to blow the cold air from the ice piles at the base of the computers. Rolfe talked to Sebastian, who released the hold. The computers came back to life in their new cool breeze, but remained intermittent. In a bold and tense move, Rolfe commanded the chamber technician to start injecting liquid nitrogen despite the highly sporadic temperature reports from the patchy computers. When the computers cycled off to stay cool, Rolfe would lose the profile.

In an impressive last effort, as the computers failed in the heat, Ernie tried to determine the liquid nitrogen injection rates manually. The doors were opened for a brief period while he went into the chamber and hooked a thermocouple to a voltmeter on the outside, stringing the wire through the hole with our antenna cables. Inferring temperatures from the voltage readout, Ernie started injecting liquid nitrogen again, working the temperature of the chamber down toward the profile with his hand on a manual liquid nitrogen valve and his eyes on a voltmeter. He was hitting the profile accurately, but it was all for naught.

While we were all wrapped up in the mini-victory of overcoming the overheating computers and the spectacle of Ernie controlling the roaring liquid nitrogen system by hand, Sebastian radioed from mission control to inform us that the heater circuit of the avionics system was malfunctioning. If the chamber got much colder our pilot would start to freeze. We would have to hold yet again.

The only change to the system since the diagnostic tests had been the addition of two cameras that we were testing in the cold. The avionics team was speculating that the new cameras were dragging down the voltages of the flight control board, dropping the voltages so low that the whole system was at risk of shutting off. For the second time, we opened the doors and let the icy nitrogen pour out. This time I went in. My oxygen sensor was barely at the edge of acceptable levels while I lay on the frosted steel floor and unplugged the two cameras so we could analyze whether they were the cause of the problem.

We didn't need the cameras for the test, so we closed the doors and prepared to start again. Meanwhile, the computer ice-blowing system had been much improved and we were able to use the original computer-controlled system. The actual profile looked pretty ugly, showing two sharp rises in temperature from where we opened the doors to the blazing Tucson day, and the switch from computer to manual control. The cameras hadn't been the source of the problem. As soon as we turned on the heaters, the voltages dropped so quickly that the system threatened to shut all major components off. We were out of ideas and the day had worn itself out. The abort was called. We were zero for three. With doors open, we drained the chamber and pulled out our pilot. Only 40 minutes of the three-and-a-half-hour test had been completed.

We discussed what to do. We had our pilot and our suit technicians for two more days. If we missed that window, it would be weeks before we could finish the test, but we had no idea what had gone wrong. The decision was that myself and Dan, the avionics lead, would work into the night.

We tore apart the suit that night looking for signs of troubled power systems. The problem looked a lot like one we'd seen before in our vacuum testing. When one of the battery packs fails, the load on the other packs increases and creates problems. When the heater is working hard, the load goes up so much that the capability of the remaining batteries is exceeded and the overall voltage starts to fall. Our best shot at figuring this thing out was to check all the battery packs and see if we'd had a short that had knocked one out. We were able to get the guts of the suit spilled onto the clean lab benches in the few hours leading into the night. To our disappointment, the packs all checked out fine. It wasn't a shorted-out battery. We went home to try to get a little sleep.

In the wee hours of the next morning, we started to dig further, asking questions, peering at things, turning screws. And pounding the linoleum. About halfway through the morning, we found the problem. It was more embarrassing than usual: the batteries were just dead. In a previous test we had intentionally run them all the way out to verify their total capacity. The suit batteries weren't rechargeable. The order to change the batteries had gotten lost. We had to suck it up and tell the Vice President of Knowledge at Google that he had just sat through a failed test because we didn't change the batteries.

We installed new batteries for a test the following morning, our very last chance. Alan didn't jump down our throats for the taxing and expensive day lost to an avoidable screw-up. We prepped the suit with the daylight dimming. Suit technicians installed new batteries. We performed oxygen checks. Dozens of bored advisors watched. Radio checks, good. Data checks, good. Suit suspended, shell back on, covers back on. Close up. Go home.

My feet hurt and I was nauseous from the nonstop work. I walked to the hotel for a few hours of sleep, then came back in the dark at 1 a.m. We hoped to avoid overheating the equipment by starting in the middle of the night.

We were ready to suit Alan up around 4 a.m., and the computers were nice and cool. We briefly became the well-oiled machine we desperately wanted to be. We walked Alan out to the chamber in the cool darkness. We suited him up, popping his head through the neck dam and closing the helmet. The suit team tagged out and the test team slipped in, silently, with purpose. The thermocouples were all labeled and the technicians plugged them in. Rolfe read back the room temperatures as they appeared on his screen. The suit team walked through a final checklist and we closed the doors.

The stream of icy nitrogen immediately condensed the vapor in the air, making beautiful plumes. Every few minutes a voice called across the radio with a new temperature.

"50 degrees."

"Passing freezing, 30 degrees."

"15 degrees."

"Crossing into negative temperatures."

"Negative 20."

"Negative 40."

In order to avoid the freeze-out we had gone through previously, we had decided never to let the chamber get colder than the average atmospheric temperature at the altitude we were simulating. As the chamber approached its lowest temperatures, the test crew switched control modes. We normally would use the temperature of the suit surface, as read from a thermocouple stuck to it, to control the temperatures in the chamber. However, for this period they started reading the temperature of the chamber itself. This new control profile indicated that the room had reached the targeted temperature floor of negative 70 degrees Fahrenheit.

"Starting into chamber warming."

The room would begin to warm and there were no issues to note. Alan appeared to be getting a bit cold, and started working his arms up and down to warm up, but that was not a big concern with the chamber warming.

The word "warming" gives a false impression. It is true that negative 50 degrees is warmer than negative 60, but they are both absurdly cold. I paced in front of the door, peeking in every now and again at Alan flapping his arms and playing around with the controls while he waited. It appeared we were heading for a success—nothing was breaking and nothing was turning off.

50 minutes into the test, we were well past the coldest part of the profile, and our guard was down. The call from mission control to Rolfe, the test director, was casual. The warning light for suit pressure had come on. Rolfe wasn't at his chair. Sebastian, the program manager, passed a radio to me. Suit pressures were reading high. Over the span of the next 40 seconds they read higher, and then much higher. With no warning and for no discernible reason, the suit pressure was actually approaching its emergency release pressure. I yelled, "Abort!" for the fourth time.

We ripped open the doors and, shaking with confusion, held our oxygen sensors into the doorway while giant fans blasted arctic nitrogen over our wrists. Five oxygen sensor alarms chirped their warnings in unison as the chamber drained an hour and fifteen minutes early. When the sensors quieted, I walked in.

I threw a thumbs-up into the frosted helmet bubble and got a quick thumbs-up back. Alan was fine. I turned the valve at Alan's hip and drained the suit. The suit seemed to be depressurizing, but the readings didn't fall back to zero. I grabbed the suit arm, and sure enough, it still had pressure, even though the valve was open and the controller fully turned off.

The pressures in a suit generate huge forces at the seals, often preventing them from opening. We spent a few minutes discussing how best to break the pressure manually, and decided to try to remove a glove. With a smaller area than the helmet, it would take less effort to break the seal. Right then the pressure fell to zero. We verified it with a squeeze to the suit arm and popped the helmet.

We hurried through the suit-doffing and hustled inside for a briefing. Dan scrambled to plot the data. It showed the pressure profile of the suit flaring upwards and peaking around the point where the emergency release valve was set to blow. Later we would find out that it had blown. The abort had been necessary. Our suit had a major problem, one that would take more than a few hours to fix. We packed up and the team scattered.

September 2013: Long-Distance Communications Testing I

Our original proposal had stated we would fly our final voyage and pop the champagne in December 2012. It was now September 2013. Two years deep, we potentially had more work left than we'd originally proposed for the entire project. I found myself confusing days with weeks and weeks with months, writing the wrong year on test reports. We were all tired. Risks loomed heavier. Even the executives were at a loss for options. We were becoming weathered soldiers in a losing war against disappointment.

We moved the team to Roswell to prepare for a sequence of tests to prove the compatibility of all the radio signals.

Personally, I was struggling to repair my relationship with the woman I had lost back in Denver and wanted nothing more than to go home. I wasn't sure anymore why we were doing this, what the world would gain, or who would care if we succeeded or failed. The anticipated glamour was dulled by Red Bull's successful mega jump a year prior. Felix Baumgartner had already broken the 50-year-old altitude record and become the first person to break the sound barrier outside of a vehicle. I didn't know that anyone was even going to understand the difference. Yet, although I didn't exactly know why, I resolved not to quit.

Alan was unavailable for the first few days in Roswell, so I would be wearing the suit for the upcoming communications tests.

On this trip, the team started the long process of transforming the airport grounds to an operational hub for the design, build, and launch of stratospheric hardware. A host of updates would mandate an almost-permanent presence on the airfield. The site already included a mission control trailer, a VIP trailer where we all had desks, two large generators, an outhouse farm, and what we called the "tin shed". The most substantial updates would be to the tin shed.

The shed was constructed as part of Walker Air Force Base in the first half of the 20th century and so at its core it was old. Various upgrades, including some made by the Red Bull Stratos crew, made the building a bit more accommodating. It now had a power distribution system and a center for on-site medical attention. Because the ancient shed was filled with holes and dirt and rodents, we couldn't have the suit in it. We renovated the room next to the medical room, building an uncertified clean room to house our suit in preflight operations. We also constructed a huge clean tent, a monster temporary building within a building. It had two rooms. One room was a pre-breathe tent with a recliner, temporary carpeting, and inspirational posters on the walls. The other was large enough to be entered by a crane, the BLV that would extract Alan once he was suited up. The ceiling of the pilot prep tent reached more than 20 feet up, coming within eight inches of the lights hanging from the old ceiling of the tin shed. We would store the suit in the clean room where we could work on it if needed. We would remove it to the tent and hang it from a gantry when someone was going to wear it.

For the communications test, we would suit a person up in the clean tent, and move the suit to the flight line under the BLV. This test was not only the first time we would beam our signals to a faraway place, it was also the first time that we would be hauling around a live human occupant under the crane.

The number of communications signals swarming around the suit system was daunting. 11 signals communicated with satellites in orbit, one signal bounced to air traffic control, and nine signals linked the system in the sky to the ground, for a total of 21 wireless communication links. When the real mission occurred, that number would jump to 48 individual radio frequency wireless links as two helicopters and one ground vehicle joined the party. We needed to prove compatibility of all the different signals and make sure the transmissions didn't slip themselves into each other and scramble. Adding the BLV transport of the suit to the mix made the test an even bigger undertaking.

Communication Signals

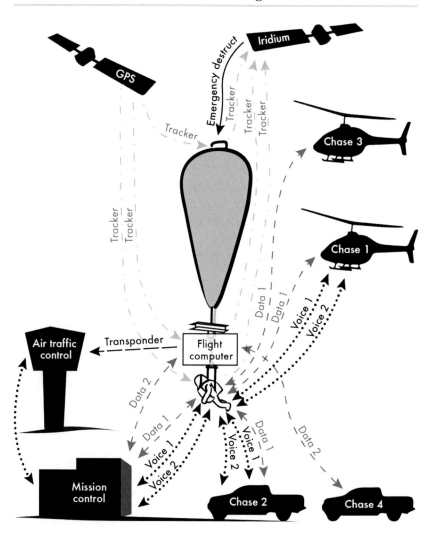

As we finalized our test plans, it became clear that our executive team back in Arizona didn't know what we were doing, which caused a near boiling-over of the political cauldron. We had put together a full plan for the test, including excruciating detail on how our test subject was to be transported to the flight line. That method was rejected out of hand by the executive team claiming that transporting a person under an industrial crane (a reach forklift with a lifting hook) was just too janky. The executives who were supposed to be our guiding force clearly hadn't been paying attention. The BLV transport method had been cooked up the previous season and had been described in excruciating detail in several documents with those executives' signatures of approval all over them. Maybe they hadn't read the details closely enough to understand them. Maybe they hadn't read the documents at all.

The executives had mistakenly assumed that the crane transport system was for this test alone. In meetings fraught with tension, we explained that disapproving this method would require more than a redesign of our test. It would mean a redesign of our whole launch-day system. We would be tossing out literal tons of designed, built, and acquired hardware, including the now-customized BLV.

The final compromise was that we could proceed with our method, but only after coming up with redundant safety systems to get a test subject in peril off of the BLV in the event that it failed.

These conversations hit me personally. I was the test subject. We were supposed to race through a bunch of extra work, diverting from a plan we had built with care and detail to appease a band of detached executives who clearly had almost no understanding of what we were doing. There was an unsettling mentality developing that a lot of what we were about to do didn't actually make much sense, but was done to quiet the executive voices that were by far the least informed voices involved. If we altered the plan now and something didn't work right, I was the guinea pig who would take the knife.

I fought hard against deviating from the well-thought-out plan. I wanted to tell the executive team to back off. I contemplated refusing to do the test, but the outcome of that path would be to bring Alan into the shit storm. We'd have to tell him why he needed to fly out. That was the last thing I wanted. Besides, I had willingly volunteered, even pushed, to become the test subject. I had to accept the position and everything that came along with it.

Finally, the holdouts caved and agreed to a new plan involving a lowered boom height on the BLV and a different emergency plan involving a pickup truck and a system to cut straps and drop the suit into the bed of a truck in the event of an emergency. We also would bring in a scissor lift as a potential emergency method for retrieving the suit from a high position. We would spend a day on the tarmac drilling all the emergency scenarios. In the end, the solution was admittedly safer than our simpler approach of trusting the BLV to function correctly. We moved into our training tired and agitated.

Zane and I spent a day drilling the process of attaching and hauling the suit to the tarmac using a 55-gallon water bucket as the stand-in for the suit. (Humans in spacesuits are pretty similar to buckets of water.) We taped the oxygen and water lines to the side of the bucket to simulate the hook-up. We repeated the exercise until we had every detail right and knew exactly what we would do at each step. Zane reviewed the higher details of leading the process as well, because once the rest of the crew arrived, he would be in charge while I was locked in the suit.

The team was splintering. Ernie, the now deeply involved technician, had become our spork vehicle driver. He all but quit in an epic blowout, swearing up a storm and condemning the operations director. The chase director Dave Jourdan stepped into the office to let him know we were all outside listening, which was only met with more swearing and the angry parties all storming out of the office. There were genuine difficulties with the operations director, but the blowout was unjustified. Warily, we limped forward.

Nearly the entire team was involved in the test. The drills were intended to end by midday so we could get some sleep and come back early the following day to start well before sunrise.

Everyone positioned themselves and Zane readied the ground carts that get towed by the BLV. The ground carts hold supplemental oxygen, a cooling system, and auxiliary power. They were just used as a prop during the water bucket tests but would be a vital part of the communications test because they would supply me with oxygen, power, and thermal fluid to keep me cool. We readied the water bucket.

Flight Train Setup

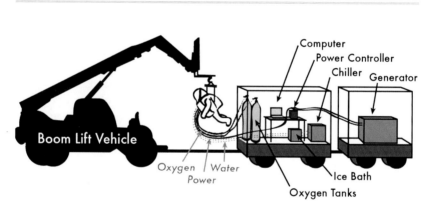

The vehicle approached the water bucket and picked it up from a strap looped through the plastic handles. It distorted and pulled together at the top under the weight of the water, spotlighting the home-cooked nature of our testing, which was already being so scrutinized. Zane attached the ground cart to the BLV using a tow system we had designed, and the crane pulled out of the tent, out of the World War II shed, and into the sunlight, heading toward the tarmac.

The BLV was remarkably smooth. The full bucket of water didn't lose a drop while traversing the dirt road from the shed to the abandoned runway surface where we would run the drills. I walked in silence, taking care not to detract from Zane's practice as leader of the team, while the crane made the slow 20-minute drive. Two trucks inched along behind us.

We spent a while determining the positioning of the BLV, which was important; its giant boom would block the radio signals. We found the bearing to the spot on the mountain where the communications trailer would sit and marked the ground with the ideal position of the vehicle. We walked through the process of removing the ground water lines from the suit, setting the suit down on the launch sedan, grabbing up the balloon equipment module with the crane, then lifting the suit up under that to put everything in its flight-like configuration. After that, as the heat of the day was coming on, we began the long, hot process of drilling the emergency procedures that had been established in the recent decree from the executives.

If we found ourselves in an emergency situation and the BLV spontaneously refused to start, we would back a truck under the suit, cut the rear two of the three straps so the suit would swing forward, and then cut the final strap, sending the whole thing to fall into the truck: wham! The truck bed was not padded. I imagined the chestpack crumpling. We determined the final suspension height based on the reach of the tallest team member (Sebastian), who would have to cut the highest strap.

We started by drilling the scenarios in which the BLV did work correctly. John would lift the water bucket simulating the suit and then someone would yell something like "FIRE, FIRE, FIRE!" (We always repeated emergency calls three times to distinguish them from general conversation.) We would respond according to procedures: lower the boom, open the hose valve, grab the fire extinguishers, etc. That was followed by the more intense "broken crane" scenario, where an emergency would be called and John would fling his hands in the air indicating that the BLV was not starting. At that point Dan would throw the pickup in reverse, position it under the water bucket, and the three designated cutters would pretend to slice through the straps form which the suit dangled. The drills went on and on.

This was the type of situation that amplified into a mess of opinions. It was far too detailed, and every detail fanned into an infinity of permutations of possible circumstances. The sun blared down. I badly wanted to step in and stop the banter, but this was Zane's drill. In this exercise I would be locked up in the suit, communicating only by radio to Ryan, who would be next to the suit, and to the trailer far away. As the afternoon rolled in, the drills finally came to a close, but not without one final argument about whether we had trained enough. Our dry runs hadn't come off all that smoothly. The cranky crew needed sleep.

By the following morning, the angst had lifted. We were excited to get the suit into the desert sunrise for the first time.

We went through the normal briefing, and I went into the shed with the suit. The setup was slow. Zane wasn't used to leading the team. We had to hold and wait for the communications trailer to get situated on the mountain about 70 miles to the east of Roswell.

The trailer needed to be sufficiently far away to stress the signal, but could not be physically blocked. The Earth's curvature mandated that the trailer site be at a higher altitude than the suit. We had found the location for the communications trailer by combining detailed Google Earth terrain investigations with information from a bike ride I had taken a week before. We needed a place at least 50 miles away with no obstructions in the line of sight to the airport. I remembered a broad switchback with a big shoulder on the edge of the mountain I had ridden up, and Google Earth showed a broad corner that had good line of sight to the airport.

When Sebastian and the communications team lead arrived at the switchback indicated by Google Maps, it didn't resemble the one I had described. That one seemed to be two switchbacks down the mountain and likely did not have good line of sight. This spot was a tight hairpin switchback with no shoulder. The road was a path to a ski area that wasn't operating. Assuming no one would come by, the team put the hazards on and left the communications trailer full of expensive equipment parked in the middle of the road for the entire day. Once it was set up, we received the final clearance to finish putting on the suit.

I entered the suit with very real anxiety about being picked up by a crane (much of which I had designed) being used for the first time and being ferried to an abandoned runway where I would be set down and then re-hung in order to talk to the gang on the mountain.

I put on the undergarments, including the diaper, because this time I didn't know how long I'd be in the suit. The test was supposed to be a simple run-through of each of the systems, but it was the first test of this type and we all suspected things would take a while. We had reviewed the oxygen toxicity requirements; at our one-and-a-third pressure near the ground in the suit with pure oxygen running in, the doctors were willing to allow five hours of continuous pressurized time in the suit.

I ducked into the hanging suit and entered my private atmosphere. The rest of the suit-up was slow and tedious as Zane scrutinized the procedures and followed every step in the exact order written. Our one change was to replace the helmet with a "not for flight" tinted bubble because Ryan was worried that in a helmet bubble made for the cold stratosphere, my head would cook in the desert sun. Bubble locked down, pants latched, gloves pulled on, everything into flight configuration. We wanted to gain as much experience as possible through the exercise. Within minutes, I could feel the pressure points beginning to eat into me.

I hung in the suit staring at the inside of the zip-up door for almost an hour. Normally my morning would have been harried by tasks: checking and rechecking, fixing and breaking. That day I just lay in the suit. I flipped back and forth between the peaceful feeling of being suspended in the air in a one-of-a-kind spacesuit and the terrifying feeling of testing hundreds of components all at once. Scariest of all was the knowledge that the things we thought of before the test were rarely the things that nailed us. I didn't even know what things to be scared of.

The outer door opened, lighting up the door of the tent, letting me know it would soon be time to ride the crane. I couldn't do anything but watch. The inner door unzipped, revealing the dead grassy fields of Roswell International Air Center. Fear washed over me. The BLV was coming to snatch me up. Zane guided the driver in. All I could do was lie there and stare. I knew exactly what was supposed to happen, but had no idea what it would feel like. With the crane halfway through the door to the big tin shed, the driver stopped with the wheels about a car length away from me. Zane directed the driver to extend the boom over my head, then had him lower the boom until a strap could be looped through the hook on the BLV.

I stared at the driver as the boom lifted me up. The room swayed. Almost immediately, I rotated a few degrees and Ryan caught me from continuing to spin. Zane continued to give directions to the driver, raising me up higher so they could connect the ground carts. They moved me around like they were dealing with a dummy hanging from the crane: swing 90 degrees this way to get a hose unhooked from the foot, tilt it forward to set the pin on the ground carts. They treated me like a rigid test mass. No need to ask for permission to move it and shift it around as needed. It was the same way I treated Alan.

The ground carts were latched; it was time to move out. To exit the shed, the BLV would drive down a ramp and then back onto flat ground. When the wheels were angled down, the extended boom would lift. Then, when the wheels were back to flat, the boom would lean back down. The motion was such that in the upturn, the boom would hit the door on the way out and then on the downstroke drop me onto the beam that hooked the ground carts on the crane. This required Zane to guide the driver through raising and lowering the boom to keep me level.

The sensations were all new and extraordinary. Suspended in a spacesuit jostling about under a boom and being raised and lowered gave me the sensation of flying. I immediately felt the urge to vomit. The panic of the sensation overwhelmed the sensation itself. I played the whole scene out in my mind step by step, processing what I thought would happen were I to barf in this suit.

Step 1: Get on the radio to tell Ryan I think I'm going to barf.

Step 2: Crane lurches to a stop.

Step 3: Mission control freaks out, safety calls an abort.

Step 4: As the driver lowers me to a reachable level, commence step 5.

Step 5: Barf.

Step 6: I open the purge valve, which pushes whatever is in the face-mask out the valve to outside.

Step 7: Suit Techs depressurize the suit.

Step 8: Nasty puke shoots out of the purge valve and bits of my morning bagel get stuck in the small tube.

Step 9: I hack on my puke, pushing most the rest of it out of the larger exhalation valves onto my back in the lower half of the suit.

Step 10: Ryan gets the helmet off and grabs at the nylon webbing pull cord to separate the facemask from my face.

Step 11: Mask comes off, dumping a pile of vomit onto the head seal closure. Test over.

Step 12: Out of embarrassment, I execute gross cleanup alone.

Step 13: I never get to wear that spacesuit again, because I am from that point on known to be a puker.

The thought of that process got me through to the moment when the crane was flat on the ground. I stopped going up and down and twisting around. Nausea, fear, and confusion gave way to serenity and euphoria. Pre-dawn clouds illuminated bright orange. While everyone else scurried through their checklists and squinted at spec sheets, I watched the sun rise over a shimmering sea of junked commercial jetliners.

The drive to the test site took about 20 minutes. The plan was to set me down onto the launch sedan to wait for the BLV to bring the balloon equipment module. After that, the BLV would retrieve me and hook me to the balloon equipment module, configuring the system exactly as it would be for flight. Then it would be time to start talking to the trailer in the middle of the road up on the mountain.

Ryan and Zane removed the ground cooling lines and power cord that stuck off of the front of the suit so it could be lowered into the launch sedan without crushing them.

I saw the launch sedan travel toward me with the launch crew at the helm. The sedan arrived beneath the dangling suit and the BLV driver lowered me into it. The sedan had four receptacles that grabbed four knobs on the front of the suit to hold the suit in place. During launch, the suit would pull the sedan along underneath it until the balloon lifted the suit up and away as it started rising. That day, without a balloon, the sedan was merely a handy tool to hold the suit. The driver slowly lowered me while Jacob guided the suit down into the receptacles. The suit locked in, and I felt the loop on the crane unhook.

The crew pushed me back over to the spot underneath the balloon equipment module now dangling from the BLV. I stared at the faint outline of the distant mountain where the communications trailer was parked. I felt the rustle of things happening over my back while the crew attached the flight hook to the balloon equipment module and then I was hoisted into the air again.

My cooling lines and power were reconnected. I felt like a robot getting serviced. They raised me a few feet. The highly scientific method of determining how high we should raise the suit was to drive the pickup truck under it and then continue to raise it up until Sebastian could just barely reach the lower structural straps he would cut in case of an emergency. Dan backed the truck up. Sebastian was up on the mountain with the communications trailer, so Blikkies stood on the edge of the bed while the driver raised me up. When the suit was in position, Blikkies got down, the truck drove forward, and I was alone, hanging over the old airfield, a place where I'd stay for quite some time.

Our longest suit runs to date had been about four hours. NASA did 8-hour sessions in their suits, but those were generally in zero gravity or neutral buoyancy environments. We had heard stories of astronauts going as long as four hours in the Russian Socol suits. Those four-hour, full-gravity tests were fabled to be miserable.

It's hard to describe what is so exhausting and hard about being in a spacesuit. The pressure and pure oxygen wear at you. Your body knows its environment is somehow wrong, and that slowly but persistently creates a situation that is deeply draining. Hour after hour of pressure points and itches, the facemask denting your face, and the neck dam lightly choking you add up to agony.

For the first hour and a half of the test, I waited. The team was clearly troubleshooting something, probably working back and forth through the other signals trying to isolate an interference. It wasn't my place to inquire what they were doing, so I didn't. Sometime around two hours in, they had me start counting off into the radios, and it became apparent to me that there were all sorts of problems.

To add to the aggravations, my first contact with the outside consisted of intermittent blurts of noise recognizable as a human voice scrambled into aggressive barks. The volume was too high, but I had no way to turn it down. Bits of sawed-up words pierced my ears in no apparent pattern.

Ryan jumped on the radio from close by and to my huge relief it worked. Because he talks more softly than the flight director, the sounds were at a bearable volume. He asked me what I had heard. "Loud aggravating jumbles of sounds, none of which I can distinguish." We tried again. Nothing but messy garble.

The next 45 minutes were occupied with what was clearly some heavy troubleshooting of the radio signals. The team on the mountain could talk to the other radios as long as those radios were at least a few dozen feet away from the suit. This pointed squarely at an interference issue with some piece of communication equipment that was on the suit. Every time they tried to communicate with me, I got a jumbled mess. They could hear me but I couldn't hear them. We started counting down from 10 to isolate when the signal was cutting out. When they did that, I tended to get about one out of three numbers in succession. "Ten . . . seven . . . fo——— . . . ———oo, one . . ."

Several people were trying to isolate what was going on, and it wasn't good. As I hung there, about half an hour into our radio session, knowing nothing about what was happening on the hill, I finally got a crystal-clear signal, full 10 count. I was ecstatic: "Got the full 10 count, loud and clear," then I shot back my own 10 count. I would find out later that for that test they had muted the signal on the main data transmitter, which happened to transmit every two seconds. The countdown test had indicated that the main data feed was interfering with the voice radios, blocking the voice signal every time the suit transmitted over the main data link. This was a non-starter. The clear signal that made me ecstatic told them that we were hosed for the near future.

They switched over to the voice-activated radio and we went through the same exercises for what was dragging into a painfully long suit run. We went through 10 counts and attempted talking while the flight director's loud voice blasted into my ears in short, painfully incoherent bursts. During these exercises Zane had started reviewing oxygen toxicity limits from the doctors because the day was looking like it could hit those limits. Zane pulled up an email from the doctors that spelled out some specific situations. It seemed like it would still be okay to stay pressurized for up to six hours.

They went back into troubleshooting. They attached different antennas to the system, turned me around in circles, cycled through turning each of the instruments off and watching what happened to the interferences. Nothing helped; the two most important radio signals directly interfered with each other. We had a broken ship.

Between each new attempt, a good 20 minutes would go by when I did nothing but hang in the desert sun. The launch team and I played rock, paper, scissors; everyone on the team took selfie portraits with the hanging suit. At one point I spotted something on the ground. "Hey, Ryan!"

"Quiet! Clear the chatter; something's up in the suit! Okay, copy, what's the problem?"

"Nothing. I see a toad."

"A what? What's he saying? What's wrong? Everyone clear the radios!"

"Sorry, it's just a toad."

"A toad?"

"Yeah, a toad right there." I pointed clumsily at the toad from my spacesuit. Nobody thought it was funny.

Something about the situation, perhaps the pure oxygen, was making me sleepy. Keeping my eyes open became another chore while the sun circled round and the team filled up what had become the longest suit run we'd done to date. We were working up on six hours in the suit, five of them pressurized, and a full eight hours since I had started putting the thing on. I was parched from several hours of bone-dry oxygen and no water. We had removed the drink bag.

The doctors had authorized one more hour of pressurized time. Ryan asked me how I was doing. I said I was good to go until the final limit, but he heard the pain in my voice. The slow prodding that comes with the territory had beaten me down. Ryan made the call to pull me out.

By then Sebastian had concluded that our system was wrecked anyway. They could troubleshoot all day long to hone in on the specifics, but we weren't going to fix this in the next hour. He agreed with the call.

The driver of the BLV fired it up and lowered me to the ground. They flipped open the helmet. The first breath of normal air felt incredible. This test was and would remain the longest time a person would spend in that suit. The facemask had dug deep trenches into my cheeks that felt scarily permanent. I was pulled, like a fetus, out of the suit and onto the concrete.

I lay on the cracked tarmac dripping from my gross, sweat-saturated long underwear while I was debriefed on what I already knew. We had failed again, and this time it was a big one. This was the tail end of a long string of exercises culminating in a team-wide realization that we hadn't completed a single system-level suit test yet. Not one. In the entire program.

This was perhaps our darkest hour. We were looking at true failure. Maybe it was time to accept that we had taken on a task filled with too many elements we knew nothing about, naively entering a tunnel with no end, a bunch of bumbling idiots pretending to understand things we didn't. I truly wondered if this was the end.

We drank that night. I drank to the deliciousness of real air, while the rest of the team drank to more screw-ups and the ever-diminishing chance that our bastard suit would ever see the backlit black of the stratosphere.

The "spork vehicle" used to stand up balloons. (Photo by Julian Nott.)

Patrick Pasadilla positions a directional antenna on top of our communications trailer in the mountains outside Roswell. (Photo by Dave Jourdan.)

Jacob Dang filling his first balloon. The balloon is wrapped around the spork drum. After fill, the balloon will be let up by the spork vehicle driving forward.

The 70K balloon fully erect after the team's first static stand. (Photo by Julian Nott.)

A beautiful sunrise behind the 70K balloon as it deflates.

The suit hanging from a crane at Roswell International Air Center preparing for long-distance communications testing. In the testing, the suit will transfer data and voice communications back and forth to a trailer parked on a mountain 70 miles away.

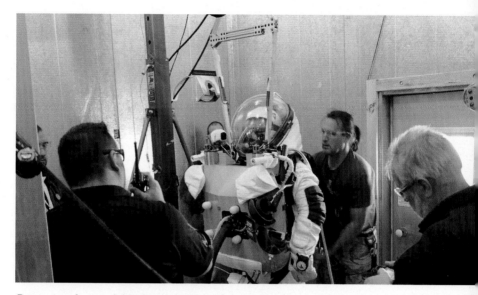

Preparing for our fifth thermal test, which was finally successful. (Photo by Julian Nott.)

Looking down on the mountain test site. This location is 70 miles from the airport where the suit is hanging from a crane. This location was chosen because it has a clear line of sight to the airport.

*The communications test site viewed as
a reflection off the suit helmet.*

*Our communications engineer Ryan Osborne working on
the communications trailer. This trailer was hauled to the
mountaintop test site for testing. (Photo by Dave Jourdan.)*

CHAPTER 9

...

To the Desert

Alan's perseverance was infused with an otherworldly optimism. This is a quality I've seen in all the leaders I've interacted with, but never so robustly and acutely as it existed in Alan. Taber is that way, too. Over the months of this program, they both deeply inspired and ragingly frustrated me. To them, everything was easy, simple. There is no space in their brains for difficulty. They are blind to overwhelming levels of work and setbacks. This renders them incapable of fearing defeat or noticing the barriers that restrict most people from taking on great things.

Not only do people with this quality fail to realize how difficult a project is at the outset, every setback infuses them with a desire to push harder. The more intractable a problem seems, the more they enjoy it, like a dragon feeding on its attackers. Adversity emboldens their spirit; it makes the challenge more worthy of their time. If you ever find yourself with a personal reason to want someone like Alan to quit an endeavor, don't try to dissuade them by telling them it will be hard—try to convince them it will be easy, and hope they don't bother.

We came out of the latest tests beaten and broken. Several members of the team were yet again considering whether the familial neglect and sense of failure were worth it. Alan, on the other hand, was at the peak of his excitement as the opportunities to solve hard problems abounded. His love of challenge reinfected us. The quitters had quit, and the rest were staying in until the day he would be at our feet in the sand inhaling hot desert air after a trip home from the wild black yonder.

In the summer of 2013, just prior to our chamber sessions, we traveled to Roswell for the suit team's longest stint yet. This trip would include chase training, then simulation of our upcoming dummy drop, followed by a record-setting stratospheric flight by the lovely Ida, the iron dummy assembly.

July 2013: Chase Training

Observers could have mistaken our chase training for wild backcountry romping. We had to get proficient at chasing signals, equipment, and Alan through the desert. To do that, we dangled little flight computers from latex weather balloons, sent them to the stratosphere, and tracked them from big pickup trucks with ground stations. When the balloons cut the payload down, we sped through the sand around old oil wells and through barbed wire fences until we got to our little orange parachute and foam computer cooler. One training had occurred before I arrived. The chase team had got themselves under the computer while it was still in the air, 70 miles from where it launched.

The basic goal of chase was simple: be at the place where Alan lands when he lands. The logistics associated with that task were staggering. Alan would take off from the Roswell airport and rise into various wind layers that would take the balloon in any number of directions at speeds up to 150 miles per hour. We treated the chase like any other engineering system. We assumed that anything, including the crew, could fail, and the system needed to be able to sustain any one failure and complete its job of getting to Alan within five minutes of landing in case he needed assistance. The chase plan showed the true complexity of what this would entail.

We would use three different types of chase asset: trucks, helicopters, and small aircraft. Trucks couldn't always access abort locations and might not reach the landing sites if high winds carried Alan too fast. So the trucks were backed up by helicopters. The first helicopter, given the call sign Chase 1, would make a team with another helicopter, Chase 3. These two helicopters would fly beneath a fixed-wing aircraft called Chase 5 carrying a support skydiver. Chase 2 and Chase 4 were trucks that would drive the balloon path. The trucks would also clean up the balloons.

As soon as Alan took off, the chase would start. The ground crews preparing and executing the launch would all become the chase crew as soon as he left the ground. First, we would all pile into trucks and wait for Alan to leave the airport grounds; inside the fences it was faster to drive a truck to Alan in the case of an abort then it would be to a fly a helicopter to him. Once Alan flew past the airport fence, some of the folks in the trucks would jump out and get in the helicopters. The helicopters would split duties, one flying under Alan to cover an abort, the other heading straight for the projected landing site. A mobile fuel station would be set up along the expected track of the balloon. Helicopters could refuel during flight by dipping down to the station. If the abort helicopter had to refuel, the landing site helicopter would move in to cover the abort during the refuel. The trucks would mirror the operation of the helicopters on the ground, one covering an abort and the other going straight for the landing site.

In addition to the trucks and helicopters, Blikkies would be at 10,000 feet in a small skydiving plane circling beneath the balloon waiting for release.

The Chase 1 helicopter would double as a mobile mission control with a data and voice communication link to Alan, so that if the balloon flew out of range of the main mission control trailer, the helicopter crew could perform critical mission control functions, such as releasing Alan from the balloon. There was also a mobile mission control in one of the trucks capable of those same functions. A modem in Alan's chestpack would beam his location to the FAA through a special transponder, telling them his location, and they would clear the air around him for safe passage.

A cluster of vehicles would tag along. A medevac helicopter, call sign Med, would stage near the fuel station and stand by for emergencies. A helicopter with a Cineflex camera mounted on the front, call sign TV, would film, sticking with the Chase 1 helicopter through to landing. The ground trucks would be accompanied by a Roswell EMT crew in a Suburban and the Roswell Fire Department. We'd have a total of nine vehicles, five in the air and four on the ground. That was the plan.

Our initial chase exercises, however, would be nowhere near as glamorous as our grand plan. We would start with trucks and try to figure out just how hard it was to find something we had sent to the stratosphere and back. I showed up at the tin shed for my first day of chase training, ready to send a latex balloon to the stratosphere and then go find it.

We laid the balloon out on a tarp outside the tin shed and set the box containing a flight computer next to it under the supervision of a communications engineer and technician. The computer established its link with the mission control computers as we blasted hydrogen through the loud valve into the balloon envelope. I stood around watching, because it was neat to see and I had nothing else to do. They hooked a scale ordinarily used to measure the weight of fish to the bottom of the balloon and held it upside down to measure how hard the balloon was pulling up as it filled. When it pulled hard enough, it would be time to attach the payload. The balloon was the size of a small bathroom when the tech started curbing the flow. The release mechanism on the computer box was opened via a remote command from mission control, so it could be attached to the balloon base, and then locked back up the same way.

The tech asked if I'd ever launched a balloon and I shook my head. He said, "Then you get to launch this one." I was excited. You need to have the brain of a nerd to get revved up about this type of thing. I do and I did. To launch a latex balloon in a calm wind, you simply let go of it. The only challenge is to make sure it doesn't hit you in the face. He handed me the computer box. I could feel it pulling toward the heavens. I held it awkwardly at arm's length with my head arched back while they verified the ground station links. I was sure I looked like a little kid holding some slimy creature that I didn't want to drop, but was also mildly afraid of. The comm tech said, "Okay, let it go." So I let it go. Away it went, into the sky.

We watched it briefly, then headed for the trucks to start our chase. I was in Chase 1, which covers aborts, riding in a truck that was standing in for the helicopter that would be used for the real launch. Blikkies started a new tradition of playing a recording of the sound of a helicopter taking off when we set out in the truck, because he wanted to get the feel right. After bragging to each other about how fast we were going to peel out for the chase, we turned on our hazards and rolled slowly away, abiding strictly to the airport's 15 miles per hour speed limit. (Good rapport with airport officials was critical.) At the airport gate we stepped on it. We raced to establish a position under the balloon while it climbed to altitude. Meanwhile, Chase 2 raced to the prospective landing site.

Chase 1 sped out on the highway heading northeast out of town, and within 20 minutes we were beneath the balloon. The road kept us just far enough to its side to stay out of the radio shadow that existed directly beneath the computer's monopole antennas. These are the same type of antenna as those sticking out of radio-controlled car controllers and ordinary walkie-talkies. The signal radiates out from the side, creating a blackout shadow that projects down in a cone from the tip. The higher the balloon gets, the bigger the radio shadow beneath it gets.

We got a little ahead of the balloon and stopped at a rest area, stepping out of the truck to watch the balloon rise to 50,000 feet. Spotting a balloon in the sky 10 miles up and five miles away is a bit like looking for a tiny screw on a clean shop floor. It seems impossible that you don't see it. You know where it's supposed to be, but you stare and stare and don't see it. Then you spot it and you can't believe you couldn't see it before. Blikkies shared some tricks honed over years of spotting parachutes and helped us all find it. Then we hopped back into the truck and made our move into the Roswell oil country between the two county roads. The other truck was tearing around the long way. They would drive an extra 50 miles to avoid the deep sands we were heading into and circle around to meet the balloon where it was supposed to land. In order to stay close for the potential abort (in this case, a premature pop), we would take on the dirty desert.

The first road was smooth and straight. Our truck could handle most terrain, but terrain was not the enemy, fences were. The land is covered with fences and gates dividing the territory between its respective owners. Only in a lifesaving situation would we be instructed to tromp over fences or gates. If we did so cavalierly, we'd quickly lose our welcome with the local community—and that could cost us our ability to fly.

We tracked our progress on three maps. One was satellite imagery, showing the landscape in its actual form, and one was a state-published map showing all the roads and our current location. The third was a map that held the secondary GPS signals. Knowing which map to use at any given time and which roads to trust was an art form. Some lines on the map look like roads but aren't more than a strip of grass with a fence through it. Some areas don't show anything at all, but hold a wonderfully defined road. Most are a mix of the two. We zigzagged through the landscape, turning around over and over again, then flying at 60 miles per hour down dirt cutouts to gain back our lost ground. The dot moved gently overhead while we tore across the scrub in persistent pursuit. Halfway through the excursion, we drove through about half a mile of nonexistent road, only to be stopped by barbed wire. We delicately flexed it down, drove over it, and found our road. We drove over one flexible oil line (this one made to be driven over) and landed just short of the other county road, where Chase 2 had been sitting for the last 20 minutes. Within minutes we got the signal that the computer was being released. We stepped on it again, racing toward the blip as Chase 2 came into sight just ahead.

When a payload is released from a balloon, it descends through the same wind profile as on the ascent, only faster. Our attention jumped between prediction software telling us where the flight computer was supposed to be and the map showing real-time locations, honing in on where we thought it would land. At around 40,000 feet, the flight computer's secondary tracking system sprang to life and right then we saw it. It was an orange dot—and we were heading right for it.

Our predictions refined over and over as we crept down the back road at 35 miles per hour, matching the parachute speeds and staring at the orange dot dropping from the sky. The parachute looked to veer away from the road at the last minute. We darted over a set of railroad tracks and onto ranch land. Seeing it falling fast toward us, I jumped out, while the trucks went through the gate. I sprinted along the railroad tracks, staying right underneath the parachute. It seemed like it would drift through the wind and fall right in my hands, but quickly I realized its pace was faster than mine. The trucks tore alongside the ranch fence, staying ahead of it while I pumped along the railroad tracks, losing ground.

The mission was more or less over at this point; we had succeeded. If that had been Alan, we'd clearly have reached him within five minutes. Now the chase goals shifted. Specifically, I had to touch the payload first, ahead of Joe Levy, an engineer on the launch team who was riding in Chase 2 intending to do the same thing. Suddenly, the test was about who had supreme dominance as a chase artist. Joe was athletic, close to my age, and a fierce competitor. He had wanted to be a tennis pro. Instead he became an aerospace engineer, staunchly devoted to the project and logging more time in Roswell than anyone else in the program. He and I ran together most mornings through the pecan farms that surrounded the city and became close friends. At that moment, however, we were not on the same team.

When the payload was about 50 feet off the ground, the trucks screeched to a halt. Joe and Blikkies sprang out of their vehicles with no misconception about what was going on. We were in perfect position for the contest, each about 100 feet away. I was tired from the quarter-mile sprint along the tracks. Joe had a barbed wire fence in his way. The computer touched down on the slope next to the tracks. Joe hopped the fence, shot over the tracks, and touched the parachute. He won by 15 feet.

Competition aside, we had reached the computer within a few seconds of it touching the ground after a full-length mission in the stratosphere. We damn near caught the thing out of the sky. It was a big success and a big step in gaining the confidence we needed to trust that the chase teams would find Alan right away, before there was any chance of things going bad. With the disappointment of earlier failures all but faded away, we looked ahead to a practice run and then a big show with Ida, the iron dummy assembly that would take the next ride to the stratosphere.

Flashback to October 2012: Felix Baumgartner

On an otherwise normal day in October 2012, while I geared up to jump from a plane tucked against the Rocky Mountains in Longmont, Colorado, I was glued to a TV in an airport hangar watching Felix Baumgartner leap from a pressurized capsule over 128,000 feet off the ground for the start of a wildly impressive skydive that would capture the world's attention. That day Felix became the highest balloonist of all time and then completed the longest and fastest freefall to date. He broke the sound barrier with nothing between him and the sonic air but a frail little spacesuit. It was a momentous feat, matched only by its incredible media draw. I wanted to be on his team that day. I did a skydive to celebrate their achievement.

We hadn't known if Red Bull Stratos was aware of us, but if they were they didn't seem to care much. We were one of a handful of crazy groups trying to do this type of thing. How were they to know whether we were any more credible than the rest? We worked along on our merry way and they worked along on theirs, until their day of triumph, when they stopped. Their mission was over. Nothing would have changed for us as a result of the Red Bull Stratos jump if it weren't for the fact that during his plunge, Felix rotated on his back and entered a classic, horrifying flat spin, whirling like a top and coming within seconds of activating his emergency drogue system before all his blood whirled out to his head and feet, with disastrous results. The stabilizing drogue parachute, however, would have yanked him back to safety at an unhealthy proximity to the sound barrier.

Crossing the sound barrier in a stratospheric plunge carries some unknowns. The speed of sound depends on the temperature of the air the sound is traveling through. It is about 768 miles per hour at room temperature, and slower at lower temperatures. In the stratosphere, where it's very cold, the speed of sound may get as low 690 miles per hour. There are actually two sonic crossings to worry about, one where the diver goes through the sound barrier from low speed to high speed and then again when they cross through from high speed to low. In powered vehicles the sonic crossing from low speed to high is generally more problematic, but the air surrounding jets typically isn't changing density during the process. In freefall, the second crossing, from high speed to low, is the scarier one because air densities are higher closer to the Earth.

At substantial air density, the behavior of flying vehicles can completely change. The atmospheric drag of a vehicle will drastically increase near the sound barrier, slowing it down more and more as it gets closer, which I'm sure contributes to why it's referred to as a "barrier." In early test flights it seemed like a type of impenetrable wall that pushed back on the aircraft. In addition to drastic changes in drag force on a body, the control characteristics of vehicles, presumably including humans, changes. In extreme cases the controls can be reversed, so that when a pilot pulls the stick right, the plane rolls left. Because the air density at the time a stratospheric skydiver encounters the sound barrier is so low, it was hoped that control problems would be blunted or muted. Trying not to move much is probably the best strategy a stratospheric skydiver can employ for crossing the sound barrier. Aside from control issues, other claims that more drastic things (like the exploding heads and catastrophic booms discussed before Felix's jump) would happen to a person as they crossed the sound barrier were thought by the experts to be unfounded. Felix's flight proved this.

Felix Baumgartner, despite lots of training, a world-class team, and the fact that he was a professional skydiver and base jumper, was not able to avoid the flat spin. Prior to his jump, some wrote off the potential for a flat spin as myth and some preached it to be a recipe for certain death for anyone who went that high. He didn't die. In fact, he didn't even set off his backup. But he had spun, despite a huge effort to avoid it.

From the outset of the program, we had been testing a system that would allow Alan to fly untethered in his custom spacesuit. We tested our system in a wind tunnel. We ballistic-tested drogue parachutes for opening at high speeds and felt we had built a system that would support freefall without any type of stabilizer. The drogue parachute was intended as a backup, only to be used in case a spin developed. That all changed when Felix cartwheeled sideways through the sky over central New Mexico. I watched it live.

Felix's spin caused us to rethink our position on stratospheric stability. We were told that Felix worked out compulsively several hours a day in preparation for his jump. It appeared the flat spin was real, and probably more real for us than Felix. We intended to go higher, our suit was bulkier, and Alan was in his late 50s. We had seen signs of this type of spin forming in both the wind tunnel and the Coolidge skydive. We couldn't ignore it anymore.

From this realization, along with steady prodding by Dr. Clark, we would refocus on trying to stabilize Alan all the way from the balloon to the ground, eliminating the chance of the dreaded flat spin.

Return to Present, Late July 2013: The SAEBER

Stabilizing a falling body from the stratosphere is a difficult business. The main problem we came across over and over again was one of timing. Stratospheric freefalls include a bizarre sort of pause at their beginning, when an aeronaut will feel like they are floating in space. This same thing happens low in the atmosphere too, when someone parachutes out of a hot-air balloon. High in the atmosphere, however, this period is unique because it is exceptionally long; when one is diving from the top of the stratosphere, they will enjoy over 20 seconds of relative weightlessness as they accelerate to incredible speeds through an absence of air or any force to counteract that of gravity.

That floating is bad for stabilizing parachutes. Parachutes have long lines that can tangle with other things if they aren't properly tensioned. Rushing air, something not available at the top of the stratosphere, usually provides that tension. Throughout all that floating, the parachute would be free to wrap around its user, potentially hitching over itself and becoming useless while at the same time incapacitating the pilot. In our system, the drogue parachute was also used as our main parachute extraction device. Using the drogue as the extraction chute for the main allowed for the system to be simpler, with one fewer parachute, and also provided huge extraction forces, making for a more reliable extraction. This did mean, however, that if the drogue were demobilized, we would also lose our main parachute. In an even worse and more frightening scenario, if the drogue bridle were to hitch over the reserve container in a zero gravity float, it would render both the reserve and main parachutes unusable in a single action, leaving the adventurer to impact the Earth at full speed.

This problem was not new. It had come up during every stratospheric mission we knew of, and several solutions had been attempted, with marginal results. In his mission to the middle regions of the stratosphere, Joseph Kittinger used a timer to ensure that he would have gained some air speed to pull the stabilizing parachute away from him before it launched. In one of his missions, the timer accidentally started early, deploying the parachute while he was still floating. The parachute wrapped around his neck while he floated in relative zero gravity. Thanks to the suit he was wearing he wasn't strangled, but he was left without a functioning stabilizer and spun at incredible rates— he blacked out and was saved only by the automatic opening of the parachute system, luckily landing without brain damage.

I learned in a phone call with a former member of a French team that they had attempted to solve the problem using a system that would accomplish the same thing as the timer, with a long tether attached between the pilot and the balloon which paid out, maintaining tension by continually tearing a light seam called "rip-stitch." After the diver had fallen a certain distance, the tether would pull out the stabilizing parachute. That team never made it to manned high-altitude drops, but they did do an anthropomorphic dummy drop in which the tether froze up and broke before pulling out the parachute, leaving the dummy to spin at outlandish rates that could have killed a pilot. The relative zero gravity floating that came at the beginning of stratospheric freefall turned out to be a lion in the bushes, waiting to seize parachute lines and hook them onto grabby equipment with frightening results.

Our team took a new approach to the problem. Some type of timing system, whether it's an actual timer or a long tether, seemed dangerous. None of the previous versions had worked, and we were running into problems with the math. By the time a system is going fast enough to effectively keep a stabilizing parachute off a stratospheric diver, some models showed that the very thin air would still be rushing by fast enough to rip the parachute apart when it opened. Other models said it wouldn't open at all. A major part of the problem was that the models simply couldn't accurately find the deployment window. To top that off, a timer system doesn't mesh with aborts. Each jump altitude would have a unique timer setting, so if some issue caused us to end the mission on the way up, Alan would be moving through thicker air than anticipated and could end up with a shredded drogue at the end of his bridle line.

We started from scratch. After months of math and tests and research, we decided to deploy a stabilizing parachute from the instant Alan left the balloon. Instead of messing around with timers or tethers, we would solve the entanglement problem physically, with a rigid bridle.

With that decision behind us, we started brainstorming and prototyping, using the familiar process of attacking the problem from all sides, hunting down every idea that held promise, and hurling stones at it until we either killed it or found it strong enough to survive. After deciding we would somehow make the bridle stiff to keep it away from Alan, we set to work. Since Alan couldn't ride to the stratosphere with a 13-foot bridle attached to the parachute pack, we had to figure out how to send him up with a small package that could deploy into a rigid bridle when he was released from the balloon. We bent carbon fiber rods into little coils. They shattered, spraying splinters across our office building. We bent phenolic rods into little clusters and cut them free to spring across our parking lot. We analyzed tapered-design fishing rods, which produced nearly uniform bending resistance to a remote load (the fish). Finally, we found our match, an elegantly simple solution suggested by the manager at the parachute company and spurred into existence by Blikkies. It was a modern carbon fiber invention called a deployable boom, or a "split tube," basically a really massive carbon fiber tape measure. I wrote an email to my boss presenting the tube, which started as a small coil that unspooled and erected itself, becoming long and hard. We called it the Bridle Orienting Non-tangle Ejecting Rod. My boss didn't like the acronym. So we renamed it the Stiff Anti-Entanglement Bridle Ejecting Rod, the SAEBER.

The SAEBER would coil up on a spool mounted above Alan for his ride up to altitude. When he released, his weight would pull the SAEBER off its spool, and it would go from being a little coiled-up block to a fully formed, remarkably rigid tube that would hold his stabilizing parachute away from him when there was no airflow to do it for him.

SAEBER and Parachute Expansion

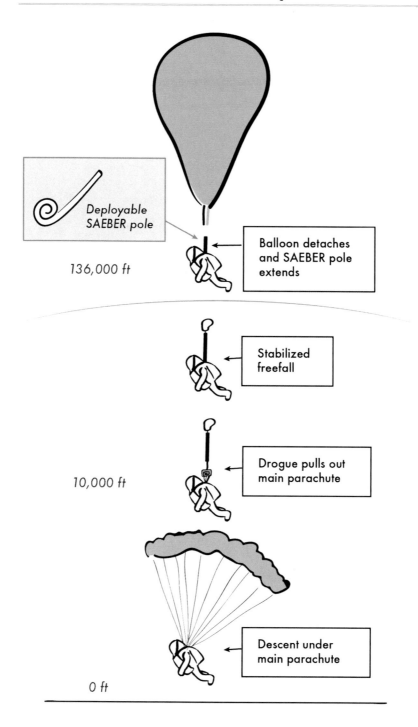

Deployable SAEBER pole

136,000 ft

Balloon detaches and SAEBER pole extends

Stabilized freefall

10,000 ft

Drogue pulls out main parachute

Descent under main parachute

0 ft

I went to Florida and spent a week in the parachute labs testing the idea in every way we could think of. We built bench-top deployment spools and deployed the split tubes, watching them erect themselves in the aisles between sewing machines. We fit the tubes with parachutes, carried bags of sand to the balconies of rigging lofts, and dropped the assemblies so see if the system would deploy as we hoped. Blikkies and another engineer took a split tube to 13,000 feet, strapped themselves together, and jumped. Blikkies deployed a parachute high in the sky and then his companion unhooked from his chest and fell away, pulling a SAEBER off a spool in the process. The thing deployed every time. When used in a stratospheric jump, it would erect a parachute the instant the system left the balloon, so that the parachute could inflate at whatever rate the thin air allowed instead of us shooting for some mathematically derived time. It seemed right, but there is no trust without testing. We would bring it to the stratosphere.

October 2013: Preparing for Unmanned One

The experiment we were preparing to do was given the boring name unmanned one, and it was our first run at sending something big to the stratosphere. The thing we would send was to be a denser version of our pilot. It was a steel dummy, an iron dummy assembly, nicknamed Ida.

The launch team was deep in debate about which balloon they would use for this big upcoming flight. Up to now, they had launched several small latex balloons, the kind that stretch to accommodate the expanding lift gas and are very manageable near the ground. They had also launched a couple of sounding balloons, which are long and delicate, but also generally easy to handle. Those balloons were also launched by hand. The only experience this crew had with big balloons that required heavy machinery for launch was our stand-up test. Not an impressive resume.

We only had two options for which balloon we would use for training. The balloon team had acquired the balloons we needed for the final record flights, and through some deals with the balloon provider had gotten a couple extra balloons for things like this, but we didn't pick the altitudes the balloons were designed to go to. For this session we had the choice of a 90,000-foot balloon or a 120,000-foot balloon. Both would be the biggest balloon the launch team had ever launched, and there would be no forgiveness at any step. They cost about as much as a modest home, and would be destroyed in the test. The debate was long. I was involved because the SAEBER system my team had created would be tested for the very first time in the environment it was designed for.

If the dummy was dropped from the higher-altitude balloon, it would break the sound barrier, which would show us if our device could keep Ida stable through a long-duration, high-speed journey and two sonic crossings. If something went wrong, we would have the winter to fix it. The argument for using the lower-altitude balloon was that the balloon team was green, and the lower-altitude balloon was about one-fourth the size of the big one. After weeks of talking brought us no closer to agreement, we asked Alan to make the call. It was his money—not to mention his life on the line. He said to take the risk and do the big one.

The launch team in Roswell had been setting up and exercising hard on their heavy-lift balloon-launching capabilities for a week before I got there. This launch would be one of the highest human simulator drops ever, performed from 120,000 feet, just short of 23 miles from the desert floor.

Roswell had two brief weather windows for launching stratospheric balloons. We had done the stand-up test during the spring window. We would test with Ida in the fall. We needed ground winds to be dead calm, less than four knots at the greatest gust. If ground winds were too high, the balloon's 700 pounds of lift and acres of fabric would twist and dip with the gusts in a very nasty dance. The slightest scrape with the ground would ruin it and scrub the test.

The atmospheric winds dictate where the payload will float during ascent and where it will land. For Roswell, there is a half circle of space about 100 miles in radius protruding to the east where landing is good. Landing to the west is bad. Rough terrain aggravates every difficulty with accessing payloads and downed balloons. Around the time of the good weather windows in Roswell, the high-altitude winds change direction and determine whether the flight will go east or west. Ideally, we would only test on days when those winds went east. If it's too cold, frost can form on the balloon and alter the lifting capacity. If it's too hot, thermals can form. Thermals can cause circular flows that can push the balloon back at the ground right after launch or suck the balloon up too fast. Further up in the flight, at the tropopause where temperatures bottom out, the temperature transition has to be mild so the gas doesn't cool too much and reduce the balloon's lift. Additionally, two layers of air moving in different directions on top of one another create shear layers that threaten the balloon. Meteorologists identify shear layers with sounding balloons. If a sounding balloon drastically changes direction during its ascent, this usually indicates that it encountered a shear. This would scrub the launch. The number of actual available days would be few, and there would be none after mid-November. If we couldn't launch in this window, we'd be in for a cold, disappointed winter. My team and I still needed spark after our long sequence of hard, frustrating failures.

To prepare for the big drop, we would spend a week doing dry runs and launching smaller balloons high above the Earth to practice, practice, practice before we would earn the go-ahead from management. This flight included some of the largest risks to the program of any yet because we were experimenting in active airspace. The airspace controllers were regularly involved and rightfully concerned about our ability to predict the path of the balloon and, most importantly, our ability to make it leave the sky when asked to. The system was planned to get to the maximum altitude, float around a bit to find a position away from inhabited areas, then drop the dummy under its new, untested parachutes.

Without the weight of the dummy, the balloon would shoot up fast and then either burst from the stress of such rapid upward motion or level out again much higher. If the balloon survived the surge, we would let it level off and float. From there we would use a pyrotechnic cutter which would cut a line holding the computer into its mounts and drop our avionics module, the 60-pound flight computer and frame. The module was tied to a balloon-destruct line, a nylon lanyard that was hundreds of feet long and ran from the avionics module into a stow bag holding a bunch of slack line which went into the balloon through a small hole at its base. The lanyard continued up inside the balloon to a round button heat-sealed into the balloon at the center of a panel designed to rip out. That special panel, if ripped out correctly, would to tear the balloon in half, releasing its helium instantly and sending it to the ground. It had no parachute. After the goring event, it would simply drop to Earth in a large pile that we would then come clean up with our trucks.

Balloon Destruct System

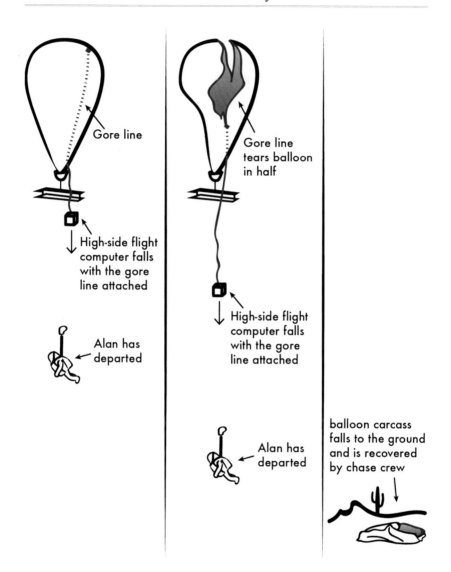

Gore line

Gore line
tears balloon
in half

High-side flight
computer falls
with the gore
line attached

High-side flight
computer falls
with the gore
line attached

Alan has
departed

Alan has
departed

balloon carcass
falls to the ground
and is recovered
by chase crew

Before dropping the avionics module, we would use the computer inside it to open up a large valve at the top of the balloon. If for some reason the rapid balloon destruct failed to work, the slower but also effective crown valve would vent the balloon and it would eventually come down. Using the crown valve to bring the balloon down was acceptable but highly undesirable. Depending on the size of the balloon, it could take hours to descend by the crown valve alone. Air traffic controllers could be routing airplanes around our experimental "keep-out" zone for a long time, compromising our good relationship with the agency. Ironically, we would have to open the crown valve, the backup, first because that was done with the flight computer. If the flight computer released, but the gore line deployment somehow failed, the computer would no longer be connected to the balloon and couldn't open the crown valve.

A failure of both the gore line destruct and the crown valve opening could mean the end of the program. Air traffic control would route traffic for hours until the balloon got so far away that our communications failed. They would continue to track the balloon via radar (when available) for what could be weeks while it bounced around the world at stratospheric heights, waiting to slowly drain and come back to Earth, blanketing something with a farm-sized sheet of polyethylene plastic. All the while, everyone would be hoping that the final resting place was a quiet plot somewhere, not the nose of a jetliner or an urban freeway.

The pressure suit team would support the big day by helping build up the dummy that would take the journey to space to represent our breathing, suited pilot. We would also practice suiting up our real pilot and carrying him to the launch pad under the BLV with the full suite of ground support equipment, keeping him on ground power and oxygen, all as test and training. Our preparation tasks would be relatively easy compared to those of the launch crew, who moved on the tarmac in a whirlwind of heavy equipment and a long list of mandatory training exercises.

October 2013: Sounding Balloon Chase

Four days ahead of what appeared to be our weather window, we started the sleep shift, going to bed earlier and waking up earlier each day, aiming to wake up at 11 p.m., the time that launch operations would commence.

Three days prior to the actual launch, we set up for our final dry run, actually more of a moist run. We planned to run the full operation, but launch a 100-foot sounding balloon to simulate our 400-foot heavy balloon. Soon after the sounding balloon went up, we would send a chain of payloads under a second, latex balloon, including both a radio repeater (a device to make walkie-talkies work over longer distances) and a simple version of our flight computer. The first balloon was just to practice launching. That second balloon launch would give the chase team something to chase. The repeater would keep us connected during the flight, and the flight computer would stand in for our pilot. We would also do a suit team run. We would prep and carry out a big bucket of water and bring it to the launch pad, just as if it was the suit with Alan inside.

The suit team met in the lobby of the Holiday Inn Express at 12:30 a.m. to depart to the airport, where our official pilot-preparation sequence would start at 1:40 (we started slightly later than the launch team.) Our seven-person team now had its own black Suburban. It was a cheery morning, and spirits were high. Today's run felt more like play than work. We had to carry a bucket down a runway with a crane (the BLV), watch a sounding balloon launch into the stratosphere, then four-wheel through the desert chasing a blip on a map. Easy.

The launch team was in full swing when we arrived, and we were probably a somewhat annoying bunch as we lolled around sipping coffee and watching them scramble to ready their system in time for the morning send-off of the sounding balloon. At 1:40 a.m., we started casually running through the checklists in the tin shed, pretending to perform each step on our lightless, beepless bucket, making calls to mission control indicating each step as "simulated" so they knew not to expect any responses from the electronics.

We did perform an actual pre-breathe on our team doctor, Alex Garbino. Alex was a PhD, MD, and a flight surgeon in training. He knew the process well and made it easy. He sat in the recliner we had purchased specifically for comfortable pre-breathing while we monitored his exhalation stream for blood nitrogen all the way down to fractions of a percent. When the pre-breathe ended, we simulated a full donning of the suit with Alex as our stand-in. Then I headed to the flight line to pick up the BLV to carry our bucket down what we had come to call Stratosphere Lane, the well-worn track from the tin shed to the abandoned runway.

We met our first little hiccup when the BLV was tied up at the flight line moving the jersey barricades that secure the heavy launch platen. We chalked it up to having a budget. Sometimes you have to wait if you only have one crane.

I had become the BLV driver. I'd worked construction in the summers during college and had gotten fairly experienced driving heavy equipment. Within 20 minutes, I was driving the BLV toward the bag of water in the suit-up environment. The tall, Broadway-style curtains parted to reveal the innards of our brightly lit space prep theater. The pilot-simulating bucket was hoisted into the air. The suit team connected the ground cart wires, oxygen lines, and water hoses to the bucket. They attached the tow bar to the front of the BLV, and we were ready to move.

Meanwhile, the balloon team laid out the canvas mats where they would spread the delicate plastic of the balloon in the expected direction of the wind. There had to be no chance for the filmy balloon to slip to the side of our spool vehicle and get caught between the spool and tractor arm. A breeze that didn't behave according to prediction could scrub the launch.

It was cold. Temperatures hovered around freezing, a shock for the Tucson teams, most of whom didn't have jackets. Worse than the discomfort, the cold created what Don called drainages, cold air dropping into washes and creating unpredictable variations in wind direction near the ground.

The suit team parade crawled silently down Stratosphere Lane in the numbing cold: BLV, water bucket, seven-man crew, and two-cart train. We rounded the corner onto the runway and faded to a stop. I called in to the flight director that the suit team's simulation was complete. We had delivered the water bucket to the runway incident-free. With 20 minutes yet to go until launch, we had time to return it all back to the shed so that Ryan and I could be available for the chase simulation starting immediately after the launch.

The 100-foot plastic envelope was spooled around the massive drum projecting from the front of the modified front-end loader. Joe took the single fill line hanging from the top of the balloon and wrapped it around a helium diffuser, taping it into a seal at the back.

The calculations used to fill the balloon this particular time were slightly different from what was normally done. Because the weather instrument that was being launched under the balloon (basically a dead weight to simulate a payload) was so light, the launch team's free-lift calculations wouldn't quite apply. Joe opened the valve and the familiar helium bubble became visible at the crown. Then a deliberation started up among the launch crew. We didn't know why. As the balloon began creeping up, the team tied off the fill line. It rose up and hovered above the spool. The balloon reached its full height above the spool.

Two things were clear from afar while watching the bubble rise. One was that the wind was not going in the same direction the spork vehicle was facing. At 20 or so degrees off, it would have been a deal-breaker for a bigger balloon, threatening to tangle it in the machinery that was supposed to be behind it. The balloon seemed to bob and bounce more than I'd expected, drifting and fading like a plastic shopping bag dancing in the corner of an alley. It almost looked like it was on the verge of falling out of the sky. As the spork vehicle crept forward, letting the fabric out over the drum, the technicians had to intervene and grab the plastic before it could jump its way off the spool and fall into the space between the arm and the drum. Joe pulled open the spool, freeing the bouncy balloon even more. The launch team watched this drifty behavior for a while and then decided the helium calculations must have been off, so they needed to recapture the balloon and put in more helium. This system was definitely not one that would make it to the stratosphere.

The spork vehicle crawled back to the balloon and recaptured it by swinging the drum back into place around the now standing but floppy 100-foot-high plastic lollipop. The spork backed up, pulling the balloon down, stopping just before it would have started to suck helium around the drum. The fill line had been knotted off and was flinging around in the wind. The launch team started playing grab-the-fill-line like it was a game, but quickly settled back to seriousness and rigged a ladder so they could reach it. They cut away the knot on the fill line and held the plastic tight around the nozzle. With gloved hands, they sent more helium pouring in. The leading balloon expert grabbed the balloon and helped guide it straight up from the spool, while the spork vehicle backed away. They let it free. Rising, it traced a perfect asymptotic curve pointing directly toward space, looking stout.

The spork and the fancy fill calculations were just for practice. We'd never see the balloon again. It was sliding toward Mexico where some farmer would find it when it came down from 130,000 feet. The farmer might see a little weather instrument drifting down under a cheap little parachute. It would have clearly marked disposal instructions, including icons that showed it was biodegradable. It would be trash.

Right after the launch of the sounding balloon, it was time to put something we could chase in the sky. The chase trucks booted up their tracking software and mounted their roof antennas while a small team, including myself, hauled hydrogen tanks onto the asphalt and started filling another latex balloon. This one was smaller and stretchier and would carry a radio repeater and a flight computer to 70,000 feet and drift around so we could practice chasing it through oil country south of Roswell near the town of Artesia, where Don said it would go.

Federal regulations allowed us to launch two six-pound payloads under the same balloon as long as they were separated by at least 50 feet. The balloon was capped off when full and two folks spaced themselves out along the 50 feet of line holding the payloads together. One person held the package of electronics tied to the balloon directly under it. The other person stood with the radio repeater 50 feet away. The electronics were turned on, link status achieved and verified with mission control, and the balloon was let go, jumping into the air with the computer, a relatively light load. As soon as they let go, the person holding the radio repeater ran across the field toward the balloon, keeping the line taut so the sensitive electronics equipment wouldn't be rattled by the jerk of a tightening line. The repeater was let go perfectly, and the package lifted peacefully away.

We always stared at the balloons for a while when they started up. It's hard not to. As we cleaned up, I could feel the sense of pride that had built up among us. Few have the privilege to send things to space under any circumstance, and we were doing it in fields by hand for practice. We hit the cars for the chase.

Blikkies and I were following the repeater in Chase 1, a truck that was simulating a helicopter. Blikkies played his helicopter noises. We ducked under an imaginary rotor as we piled in.

Mission control stayed in contact through the radios while we cruised the road toward Artesia. We had our mark, a blip on a map. The balloon hit the jet stream and started to move at highway speeds 40,000 feet above us. Chase 1 was responsible for aborts, so in our simulation we tried to stay as close to the balloon as possible. We'd dash onto little county roads and zigzag through dirt near the balloon. If it popped we'd be right there. Any number of things could send our pilot into a plummeting abort, and we'd need to get to him within the few minutes it would take him to reach the ground.

As the balloon reached its float altitude, mission control, unbeknownst to us, muted the radio signal on the balloon. Both trucks went blind. We pulled over and scanned the sky for the tiny white dot. A trained eye like Blikkies' could see the little speck all the way into the darkness of space. I was getting much better at it, too. We located it straight above and watched carefully. It didn't appear to be moving at all. A real malfunction then cut the radio repeater out, and we lost all communication. Only a gargle of nonsense came through the radios. We resorted to cell phones.

After we called mission control, they turned our tracking signal back on. We had a blip on the map to chase. The stratospheric winds were all but nonexistent. The balloon was creeping at four miles per hour and entering its float, leveling off in the stratosphere. We got the call that mission control was ready to start cutting down the payloads.

First, mission control would signal and release the repeater, which would come down under its own parachute. Then, shortly after, as the flight computer rocketed up under the now unweighted balloon, the second cut-away would be quick, lest the upward surge stress and pop the nylon of the balloon, now paper thin in the coldest part of the atmosphere.

Our location data was coming from the flight computer. The repeater didn't have the same live tracking signal that the computer did, only a ground-based tracker that turned on low to the ground. So we switched our map displays to show the predicted landing site. As soon as the two payloads released, the computer and the repeater would be drifting along different trajectories. We got the word that the repeater was away, one bird in the sky. Shortly after, the computer was free.

We were late. At 30,000, feet, the trackers on the repeater came alive. We were several miles away and it was dropping fast. We bounced the rented trucks across the deserted roads. We wanted to pass the test, and I was in a grudge match against Joe in Chase 2. We had four different maps on four computers navigating which roads were actually roads, and which of them were open. The GPS feed told us the repeater was tracking west, and just our luck, the road we were on wasn't going to connect to the one we needed. We veered the long way around, cleared the corner, and the GPS locations stopped changing. It was on the ground. We split the difference on the several feeds and maps and screeched to a halt next to a little oil depot hut by a fence. We raced on foot across the field and over a barbed wire fence, scanning for an orange canopy and a white repeater box. A few hundred feet from where we'd stopped in the truck, we spotted our target.

We texted the other truck that we were going to go for the flight computer as well, thinking we could score the greatest glory: both payloads. But Chase 2 chimed in that they had already found it and were heading back to Artesia, where we'd meet up and drive the hour or so back to Roswell. We had recovered the two payloads in 18 minutes.

Next was the debrief, and a tired, hot discussion about how the dry run had gone. We had proved what we needed to prove, but there were some major hiccups. The balloon stand-up left a lot to be desired. The helium calculations were off. Moving the envelope by hand would not be possible with a full-size balloon. The chase teams had lost communication, forcing us to rely on cryptic text messages to communicate, like teenagers on prom night.

The message from upstairs: we would go for a major balloon launch in two days, but it wouldn't be to 120,000 feet. We would launch the much smaller, but still impressive and highly demanding 90,000-foot balloon. It would be one of the highest human simulator drops ever performed and would open our eyes wide to the madness that loomed. For now, we needed sleep and mental regeneration. In two days we would suit up, fly again, chase again, and drop a dummy from remarkable heights.

Late October 2013: 93,000-Foot Dummy Flight

It was the day before we were to drop Ida, a rest day. The communications engineer, Jacob, and I were struggling to keep our eyes open and rig a secondary hot-wire remote cutting system to Ida. Ideally, a pyrotechnic cutter was to sever a tie, letting Ida loose. If that system failed, Ida would go down with the balloon. This wouldn't threaten the program, but without a test of the SAEBER drogue system, the program would be delayed until we could make another test launch.

For this backup cut-down, we wrapped a special wire around the retainer strap connecting Ida to the balloon. The wire was composed of a metal called nichrome, able to withstand extreme heat without melting. If necessary, we would be able to short-circuit the battery packs with that wire, which would then melt through the retainer strap and release the dummy. The kit to build the wire assembly had arrived just that morning. Late in the afternoon, I found myself groggily racing to a hardware store in the Suburban to buy a nine-dollar wire-crimping tool. In the web-like desert sunset, we tested the assembly in the parking lot by stretching a length of the retainer strap material between two sawhorses, tensioning it with a dangling wrench. I looped the wire over the cord while Jacob set up the ground station computers and turned on the mission control transmitters. Mission control would signal Ida's computer to power up the hot wire and melt the line.

Jacob and I trained our cell phone cameras on the stretched wire while Jacob counted down to mission control for the cut. At zero, the wire browned, then glowed red hot. The strap melted and the wrench clattered to the asphalt. We cleaned up and went to the hotel for a nap before operations started at 11 p.m.

Alan was there to go through a full rehearsal of the launch alongside the balloon. We'd start with the pre-breathe, suit him up, then send in the BLV to bring him and the life-support train to the launch site. The only difference between the process we would execute and a manned flight would be that Ida would be hooked to the balloon, leaving Alan behind dangling from the hoist inside his spacesuit, watching his stunt double sail to the stratosphere.

An hour ahead of the pre-breathe, about 30 people, most of whom had active roles in the launch, mingled in the VIP trailer munching cardboard pastry like we were a skydiving club. The suit was already suspended from the yellow gantry in the pilot-preparation tent. We had finished our phase zero suit preparations two days prior. The suit team had a secondary mission today, but it was an important one. We wanted to vet out conflicts with the launch team and see how good we were at having the pilot ready at the same time the balloon was. Alan would watch the launch from inside the suit, with the goal of exposing potential flaws in our preflight sequences and experiencing the brutal six hours he could spend hanging in the trying suit. He could practice staying calm.

The all-white interior was lit with ultra-bright LED lights mounted to the top of the towering yellow gantry. Alan was surrounded by the medical team, people so enthused about space medicine that they were working for free, and insatiable for details about the program, pilot, and suit. We shooed them away so we could get Alan into his life-monitor belt, long underwear, liquid thermal garment, and movie villain mask. The pre-breathing mask would provide pre-breathing oxygen, preflight water, a microphone to shoot the shit with the med guys, and a sampling port to monitor the nitrogen content in his exhalation stream.

We hustled around his recliner with our checklists, turning knobs and valves, watching lights go on and off, and maintaining a steady dry conversation with mission control. From this point on, we would be identified in radio communications by our call sign, PSA, which stood for pressure suit assembly.

"Engineer, this is PSA."

"PSA, engineer. Go ahead."

"Note a nominal unit attach. Connecting ground power."

"Roger that. Continue with ground power operations."

"System power switch being moved to on position. Removing ground power. Standing by for confirmation of voltage drop."

"Roger that. Engineer can confirm voltage drop."

"Roger that. Going back on ground power. Standing by for confirmation of voltage rise."

"Engineer confirm voltage rise."

"Roger that. End of test."

The only checkout issue was a GPS signal re-radiator that failed to turn on. After some troubleshooting, we found the wall plug was no good, which sounds trivial, but under the exact wrong set of circumstances, a bad wall plug could abort the mission. We fixed it and charged forward.

As the clocks neared 3 a.m., we were getting ready to put Alan in the suit. Outside on the runway, the launch crew had the lights on and the canvas mats down and were preparing to lay the huge balloon onto the mats. While the launch team carefully laid out the acres of balloon, they also meticulously checked the balloon equipment module systems that would actuate both the primary payload cut-down and the balloon-destruct sequence. The balloon-destruct sequence was critical. If the balloon failed to destroy itself when told to do so and disrupted global air traffic, the US Federal Aviation Administration would certainly review whether we were a competent enough crew to operate heavy machinery in the high atmosphere above the United States of America. The team ran simulations on the ground, both opening the giant valve that would slowly start the balloon descent and testing the pyrotechnic cutter system. We asked the flight director for clearance to put Alan in the suit. The balloon team was on track. Clearance was granted.

Alan appeared collected while we started pulling the covers off the suit's upper half, which was hanging from the gantry. We went through our checks with especially acute detail. We were carrying out a new protocol for the first time, putting the sealed helmet bubble on before the gloves and pants to reduce the time Alan would inhale nitrogen from the outside air. The entrance went quickly. Alan took only one breath as we slipped him through the rubber tunnel and closed the bubble. Blikkies adjusted the helmet, and we shot out our thumbs-up before the final latch locked, sealing him for the seventh time in his personal, privately owned atmosphere. We put on the parachutes and tilted him to the more comfortable 45-degree position where he would spend the rest of the morning. Communication checks were good. The heater system was working. We ordered in the BLV.

Alan now watched what I had seen during the long-distance communications test that sent me down the long bumpy road hanging from a boom in the suit. The pilot-prep tent opened on the morning light, silhouetting the BLV, a modified construction rough-terrain forklift that loomed into the sparkling clean tent to snatch him up. Zane and Ryan guided the beastly machine through the curtains, and I extended the boom over Alan. The machine didn't touch anything other than the loop above Alan's head to avoid contamination of the clean room. The boom lowered to within a few inches of the suit, Zane looped a strap over the giant hook, and then the suit lifted off the towering gantry and onto the boom. The ground cart train with Alan's ground oxygen and cooling water was attached to tow behind. I backed the BLV out of the tin shed at creeping speeds. The brakes on the lift moaned as the crane inched down the ramp and away from the building. The boom was raised, then lowered to keep Alan at the correct height above the tow package between the ground carts and the vehicle.

I dead-set my gaze on a point between the road and our safety walker, who was supposed to let me know if something went wrong with the BLV or anything trailing from it, and started down Stratosphere Lane in reverse, away from the tin shed. The balloon bubbled out of a huge crate onto the football-field-length canvas pad. A painful 20 minutes brought us the quarter mile to the launch site, where the suit simulation would end. We pulled to the side of the runway at a far corner of the pad, where there was no risk of any unforeseen mishap getting close to us. I shut down the lift, leaving Alan to wait, hanging in space. In 45 minutes a balloon would launch. We were fully ready to hook him to it, but we wouldn't. Our portion of the exercise had ended successfully.

The launch crew had laid the long crest out on the ground while first light peaked. They hugged and pulled the heavy plastic slug over the big drum of the spork vehicle, winding it back toward the launch platen, careful to leave the fill tubes exposed. Once the balloon was fully wound, the fill tubes were pulled out and the helium semi-truck readied for filling.

The poll went around the teams to gain clearance to start the fill. If the launch had to be aborted beyond this point, we wouldn't be able to reuse the balloon. Joe and Jacob readied the diffusers. They roared to life, stiffening the tubes and frosting their gloved hands. Instantly, the balloon crest plumped into a bubble. In a few minutes it was the size of a house. Two people held the crown valve until, just when it seemed they would be pulled off the ground, they let it go to bob and bounce above the spork vehicle as the last of the helium poured out of the freezing-cold diffusers.

The sunrise flared deep pink arms around the balloon envelope, penetrating the waving plastic. We stared in raw awe. Ida waited patiently on her launch sedan near the launch platen.

The spork driver crept the vehicle forward, reeling out the rest of the towering balloon envelope from the drum, keeping the plastic safe between the little lips on the drum until the drum raised up at the end of its journey to be unlatched above the balloon equipment module. This was the first time the driver had unwheeled a full-size envelope. The articulating steering of the vehicle made the movements awkward as the spork slowed over the launch platen. The plastic stood straight. The drum freed the balloon, which strained perfectly straight toward space in the absolute dead calm of morning. We had never seen a balloon stand perfectly straight. It was a beautiful success.

Joe pulled the cable that freed the drum to swing open like a door and uncage the balloon. The spork reversed away from the towering tight plastic reaching well into the morning sky. All that was left was to hook Ida up, pull the release, and track the hours of climb into the sky.

It was my job to hook Ida up, because in the real mission I would hook up Alan and do the final suit checkout before giving clearance to launch. A launch crewman left the balloon stalk to help me roll the launch sedan over a speed bump. Ida lurched slowly toward the launch platen.

One electrical connection and a single mechanical hook would connect Ida to the straining balloon. I reached up and pressed the connector into Ida's release mechanism and pushed the other end into the receptacle on the balloon equipment module. The lower release mechanisms flopped down with a snap. The straps that were supposed to connect the payload to the balloon fell in a wad on Ida's back. I stared in disbelief and sheer confusion. The extremely simple operation of plugging in one plug and hooking up one hook had failed. What the hell had just happened?

I grabbed the primary release mechanism, which flopped over in my hand. John pushed his way into the circle of inquisitive bystanders as I said, "It fired, the release fired." We had been seconds away from launching the balloon and leaving Ida behind on the launch pad.

This very disaster was not unprecedented. Colonel Joe Kittinger, the highest skydiver of all time before his record was broken by Felix Baumgartner, had seen two such failures. An aspiring French aeronaut lost his last mission to an antsy balloon that went flying without its lower half. These failures had always baffled me: how do you let that happen? That's why we had checklists. At least our balloon was still hooked to the launch platen.

We knew that it was possible for the energized part of the connector to touch the grounding wire while it was being inserted. If it grounded, it would fire the cutter. We had seen it happen in testing. We knew the system needed to be powered off while the connector was plugged in. Somehow, this particular item had slipped through the cracks. Its checkbox hadn't found its way into the many books of itemized flight procedures. Now our dummy wasn't hooked to our balloon anymore. Checklists don't do any good if they aren't perfect.

Blikkies, who had personally rigged the release system, flew into action. The balloon calmly twisted above our heads. We had five minutes to reset the release mechanisms on the pad before our launch window for the day ended. The airport had told us we needed to be off the runway by 7:30 a.m., after which the runway adjacent to ours would open and our apartment-complex-sized balloon had to be gone. It was 7:25.

The flight director counted down the minutes. I felt like I had just landed in a James Bond movie. It was easy enough to reset the releases, but we needed a new retention loop because the old one had been sliced through. The cutter was spent too. A silver jeep with Blikkies at the wheel took a hard corner onto the runway, and I jumped in to head for the spare parts inventories in the tin shed. We raised a rooster tail of dust down the quarter mile of Stratosphere Lane. With the seconds ticking by, we rifled through the spare parts, flinging parts and assemblies onto the ground in search of the silver cigarette-sized spare cutter and a spool of green and white cord. We screeched back down the lane with them, past Alan hanging bewildered in his spacesuit, to the base of the balloon as the flight director called the two-minute warning. I leapt from the jeep before it stopped next to the reclining dummy. I re-laced the lower release mechanisms while Blikkies ran a new loop around the main structural lift web. We laced a new cutter through the loop as the quality engineer performed the fastest quality control inspection in the history of the department, verifying the serial numbers and registration card for the cutter. One minute. Blikkies and I chased each other in a circle checking each other's work, making sure the three lower releases were correctly set and properly routed to the main release where the new cutter was installed over the fresh loop. All checked out.

We did what we should have done the first time around and killed the power to the balloon equipment module while we plugged in the cable. All good. The final seconds ticked away as mission control powered the system back on and verified the link. We had time for exactly one breath before John signaled Joe, who was standing by at the cable that would send the balloon on its climb. Blikkies and I exchanged sidelong glances of disbelief. Had we really done this? Had we missed anything?

John counted down from five as the launch crewman and I set up to push the balloon in the direction of the nonexistent wind if needed. John got to zero. Joe pulled the cord.

The mechanisms creaked, and Ida lurched up. The launch crewman and I both gave a little push forward, but Ida had already departed—up and up she went, silent and swift. The system started to spin. The balloon spun circles in the light, changing winds 100 feet above, then began to untwist. The motion could twist up our release mechanisms and dump Ida. After a few turns, the balloon righted itself. Nothing fell. The 20-some engineers peppered the flight line, necks kinked back as the plastic column lifted away toward the darkness of the stratosphere.

Chase teams quit gawking and sprang to their vehicles, setting out at 10 miles per hour down the airport road. With Alan still dangling from the crane at the corner of the runway, I didn't go with them. My day was almost over.

Underneath Alan, the suit team talked through the process of exiting the suit by laying it down on some mats on the ground and doing a "ground doffing" exercise. This would be practice for when we would do it somewhere out in the desert. We removed some antennas and lowered the suit onto the mats.

Alan tried to depressurize the suit. He found the knob, but in his exhaustion from all the time in the suit, he struggled considerably. In the end he wasn't really able to depressurize himself, making some old worries new again, but that wasn't what today was about. We helped him get the depress done. He was able to remove his own helmet, which restored our confidence somewhat. Alan was all smiles, glad to have that helmet off and knowing how that enormous rising balloon brought him that much closer to his own ride. We took off the gloves and the waist seal, unstuck his neck dam, held his arms, and yanked him out the back of that suit and onto the ground.

Four of us spent a languid hour tidying up the runway. I took the ground cart train back to the tin shed, then climbed into the BLV to move the jersey barricades and load up the canvas. While we went through this straightforward cleanup, a giant mass sped toward the heavens above us. Mission control was no doubt a frenzy of activity.

A truck came out with word that it was getting close to time to unleash Ida. We slipped into the back of the mission control trailer, and on the huge screens in front of us was the three-dimensional path of the balloon rising to the east out of Roswell. It had crossed the dangerous inversion layer at the top of the tropopause without trouble and was climbing through 80,000 feet at over 1,000 feet per minute, leaving the domain where only the highest of high-altitude airplanes could fly.

We were using slightly more helium than what is normal in our launches to accommodate our launch style, and were unsure before this launch what kind of effect it would have on ascent rate. It was rocketing up 40% faster than our calculations had predicted. This wasn't entirely unexpected and was actually a good thing. At that speed, our flight would go faster overall, consuming less oxygen, a commodity in short supply with our system.

Higher speeds also meant that in general the balloon would stay closer to Roswell because it would have less time to drift. Most importantly, it would pass faster through the dangerous jet stream where wind speeds between 60 to over 100 miles per hour are not an oddity. The speed added more stress to the balloon envelope, but this balloon was performing like a champion, no signs of failure, not even a flinch in its surprisingly linear ascent profile.

We were getting an intermittent live video feed from a camera looking at Ida, the same camera that would be looking at Alan. As the balloon leveled off, mission control contacted the FAA to inform them that a payload would soon be falling through a certain column of air east of New Mexico. The FAA would enforce an air traffic keep-out zone in the space where Ida would fly to ensure that aircraft encounters would not be a concern. We waited at float altitude for Ida to drift out of range of a county road. Then it was time.

The poll went round for clearance to release the payload. All go. The flight engineer armed the cutters, and a green light flashed on the screen to signal they were ready. At the click of a mouse, the signal was sent. The control panel indicated that the cutter had fired, and then the scratchy video feed scribbled empty space into the spot where Ida hung. She had departed the balloon. We threw up our hands and cheered. The simulator was in flight. The second part of our test was on.

With the heavy payload gone, the balloon shot back up toward the heavens in a stressful second climb that could rupture the fragile fully expanded envelope. Ida was plummeting in the opposite direction at speeds crossing 500 miles per hour.

Ida spent about nine seconds in a low-gravity-like environment at the beginning of her journey. This was not true low gravity; on the scale of gravity the Earth was still quite close. The near vacuum created an environment without air resistance, where things behaved as if they were in low gravity relative to one another.

This was the moment for the SAEBER test. The device had unraveled into a carbon fiber tube immediately upon leaving the balloon and done its job of preventing the drogue parachute line from entangling with the dummy during these nine seconds. At 10 seconds she started to feel the wind that filled the parachute and oriented her "chest" to Earth for the rest of her freefall. The wind started to pick up further as she crossed her maximum velocity of over 550 miles per hour. As air density increased, the wind became stronger and stronger until she entered the most dangerous part of the fall, the "max dynamic pressure," or Max Q, where the wind would feel the strongest as she decelerated from the stratospheric velocities she had achieved back to terminal velocity. At terminal velocity, she drifted in what would feel like a normal skydive across the last few miles of flight until, at 7,000 feet, a flight computer sensed the altitude and fall rate, and blasted out a reserve parachute that guided her to the ground at 15 miles per hour.

With Ida away, all that was left was the balloon cut-down. We tensed up for the opening of the huge crown valve, which would be followed by the destructive slashing of the balloon. In theory, the two methods were redundant; the valve would vent the balloon and take it down even if the more rapid destruct sequence didn't. The valve had to be opened first. The computer that opens the valve is the weight that rips open the balloon in the primary destruct. If the main destruct were initiated first and failed, the computer needed to signal the backup valve to open would be hurtling to the ground at Mach .7, trailing a stub of disconnected wire.

By the time the poll went out to issue the balloon destruct, the chase teams had spotted Ida's giant orange parachute.

The signal to open the giant crown valve was sent, and verification came back that it was open, and step one was complete. There was no sign of the balloon dropping, which was why opening the giant valve was a bring-down of last resort. It could take hours to vent millions of cubic feet of helium, even through the manhole sized hole` in the massive balloon. Once falling, the denser air would compress the helium and speed the venting process.

With the valve open, Dan armed the cutters, and when the green light flashed, he fired. We waited. The balloon, which was supposed to be crashing to the ground, stayed at altitude. Confusion set in. Mission control verified across several signals. The destruct had failed.

We stared in shock at the screens. The balloon continued to rise. We had a sensor verification that the crown valve was open, but until the balloon started to descend, we wouldn't be certain. The balloon technicians didn't seem very worried, but the rest of us stewed in our fear that we would be on the news in a few hours. Would we have to inform the authorities that our balloon was rogue and we'd soon lose the ability to track it?

I had nothing to do with the process, but the stress in the room was heavy. People started to discuss what they should do. The video feed had been turned off to alleviate interference with the transmit system during the cut-down. A debate began over whether there would be visual evidence that the crown valve had failed to open if we turned it back on. There was concern that doing so would drain the batteries, which needed to remain well charged in case the balloon needed to be tracked for hours.

There were too many cooks in the kitchen. Mission control needed calm to figure this out. The unnecessary members of the crew, even John, the balloon team lead, stepped out, a difficult thing to do with the outcome of the flight in question. We silently cleaned up the rest of the site, then peeked into the window at the back door of the trailer. The balloon was crossing 50,000 feet and falling fast. The valve had worked. It was coming down.

Alan wanted to try to catch up with the chase crew to hunt down the balloon, which was now several miles further north into the desert then we had expected. Sebastian gave us the okay to leave the site, and we tore off in the Suburban for a desert chase.

We had an idea where the balloon was at the start of the drop, which gave us a heading to start out on. We didn't have any of the tracking tools that the real chase cars did, but once the system passed through 40,000 feet, an Internet-based tracking system would come to life. Alan logged in with his phone. We scanned the sky in the general direction where we thought the balloon might be. Within a few minutes of each other, the trackers came alive and gave us a location. Knowing where to look, Alan spotted it. Finally, I did too: a long wisp of white fixed between the clouds. It wasn't falling fast enough to see it dropping. It appeared much larger than the little parachutes we had chased before, even though it was much farther away. It looked to be about 10 miles away, judging from the maps. We sped up.

We turned down a ranch road, bouncing deep into cattle and oil country, and got a cell phone call from mission control. The landowner where the balloon had fallen had seen it come down. He already knew about the test flight, and he'd called mission control to let them know he'd meet us and take us in. This meant Alan and I would be able to meet the chase teams and see the balloon with the first responders. We were eager to observe the failed balloon equipment module to see if we could find out what had gone wrong. We reversed our course and caught the county road back to a pull-out where the two chase trucks were parked, along with another pickup hauling a mule ATV: the rancher. The chase trucks had already dug in deep that morning. They were washed in dirt, and the front undercarriage of one was half ripped off, dragging under the front of the truck.

I jumped out and found Ida lying in the bed of the truck. Her aeroshell was smashed to pieces, which was not unexpected, but the SAEBER, the carbon fiber rod that was supposed to be on the stabilizer parachute attachment line, wasn't there.

"Where's the SAEBER?"

"It's gone."

"Where?"

"Check out the bridle line, it must have gotten twisted off."

Sure enough, the attachment line was twisted and bunched together in lumpy knots like a rubber band spun off a poster. Nobody yet knew what had happened between Ida's departure from the balloon and her landing under parachute, but we could tell it likely involved some spinning.

Alan took a minute to thank the rancher for guiding us in, and the rancher returned a slow nod and walked to his truck. It was time to go find the balloon.

We turned into a couple of dirt cutoffs before finding our path. The rancher had to determine not only which road would get us closest to the wreckage, but also which roads were most passable. We were getting used to the idea that hunting down gear in this type of terrain using a truck was way less about high-tech equipment and four-wheel drive than about knowing which roads are actually roads and where the fences and gates are. The rancher wove us through until we hit our first locked gate. He tried most the keys on a giant janitor's ring without luck before untying the barbed wire at the edge of the gate for us to drive around. During the slow, casual unwinding of the fence wires, we chatted up another rancher who had come onto the scene, and learned that he had been on the ground when Felix Baumgartner had completed his world-record jump a year earlier. Felix had landed on that very ranch. We drove on deeper, through gate after gate, as the roads got more rough and sandy. Partway through, the ranchers opted to switch to their mule ATV vehicle and charged ahead to try to spot the enormous field of plastic lying somewhere out in front of us. The computers said we were still miles away.

By now it was creeping into late afternoon. Waiting at another keyless gate while the ranchers took apart the fence, about a mile from where the computers said we would find the balloon, we downloaded the video footage stored on Ida onto the laptops in the back of the chase trucks and watched the amazingly beautiful sight of Ida separating from the balloon in the deep black of space. The SAEBER spool released beautifully and held the stabilization parachute away from Ida like a protective arm, stopping her from getting tangled. As Ida fell away, the balloon diminished to a speck in an instant. The curve of the Earth was magnificent. As Ida gently rotated, the video showed glimpses of the full Baja Peninsula popping in and out of view amongst the swirling clouds encasing the United States. The stabilization chute inflated right when we expected, pulling straight up and keeping Ida facing chest down. Then she really started turning.

The sun pulsed slowly in and out of view with each rotation. The gently curving Earth swung by at the bottom of the frame. Then it got faster. The sun popped in and out of view more rapidly. The scene wobbled back and forth in a potato-chipping motion as the spin increased and increased until the sun came and went like a strobe light. The centrifugal forces dominated, stopping the potato-chipping motion, and the visual blurred into a perfect, incredibly fast flat spin.

The ranchers got the gate off and we unglued ourselves from the screen to continue hunting. We were many miles and hours deep into rolling desert. Tufts of bushes topped sandy mounds. We drove down rougher and rougher roads until we hit another gate. The computers were saying we were close.

The ranchers took their mule off the road toward the blip and we waited again. I reapplied sunscreen.

Alan had arrived in Roswell the previous night at 10, showered, and headed straight to the airport. That meant he had woken up the previous morning and hadn't slept since. In those 30 sleepless hours, he'd flown a plane to Roswell, had the nitrogen removed from his blood, worn a spacesuit for four hours, then gone dune buggying across nowhere ranch land. Yet he decided he would trek into the desert to look for the envelope. The trucks were too slow, with all these gates to contend with. He took off, and we all glanced back and forth trying to decide if we should stop him. One of the med guys threw some water bottles into a backpack and charged off after him.

The ranchers came back through the brush and told us they had found the balloon. One of them indicated the two hikers, who had turned to look back from a couple hundred feet away. A smile cracked his leather face as he asked, "That the boss?" Someone said, "Yep."

We waved Alan back to the trucks. Under the ranchers' direction, we piled in the bed of a truck for the last run over the open ground. I saw a glisten in the desert as we crested a rise. I slapped the top of the cab. "I see it!" I yelled, and jumped out. I took a healthy sprint toward the shining field. Two people in the other truck leapt out, and the race was on. I was first to touch the monster, and then I just admired the spectacle around me. Two trucks made their way across the dunes toward a shiny football-field's worth of plastic that smothered all the local shrubbery.

We slowly documented every detail of the downed payload and balloon. We saw that the pyrotechnic cutter for the balloon destruct had fired correctly, but failed to slice all the way through the link. The balloon equipment module hung from a few strands of fiber trapped in the jaws of the tiny cutter, still fully connected to the module from which it was supposed to depart.

The chase team hacked up the balloon with stainless steel bread knives—with their serration, they chop faster than straight knives and don't clog like scissors. They stuffed the wads of plastic into the bed of the pickup and fastened them down with bungee webs. We put the (surprisingly unharmed) computer hardware into the cab. Alan and I climbed up on the plastic hummocks in the back for the trip to our Suburban.

With heads dropped back, we soaked in the relaxation of riding the spongy plastic pile back across the desert. We got to the Suburban and in a slow, drained effort, we backtracked out, crossing the same chain of old rusty gate after old rusty gate. Alan made it clear before heading out that we would be staying with the ranchers for as long as it took to repair every gate. At the first one, Alan called the ranchers over and asked, "You want to see the drop?" In an open field in the middle of nowhere, the ranchers watched in delight as the view from space whirled into a wild, strobing spin and ended under a bright parachute across the county road from their home.

After the final gate repair, we shook hands with the ranchers and Alan thanked them for devoting their afternoon to chasing plastic across the desert. They waved us off with the same gruff faces they had worn from the instant we met them. The chase was over, our day was over, Ida's record height fall was over, and our brief but rewarding and incredibly unique mini-friendship of circumstance with silent sturdy ranchers was over. Alan would climb into his plane and fly to some new challenge, and we would continue to clean up after this one.

We reviewed the videos into the night. The images spun through our heads. It dawned on us that we could have strapped Alan to that balloon. He would have made it to the stratosphere. But the spinning descent would likely have killed him.

Still, the world knew more about human freefall from space than it had the day before.

Early November 2013: Human Factors and Pilot Training I

In the midst of our woes from the flat spin, we also recognized the need to have Alan better trained in using his suit. The pressure suit team had to get through a pilot-training session where we showed that Alan could properly actuate all the required mechanisms. We also had to have another thermal test, then a manned vacuum test, an airplane jump, and a final dress rehearsal before we could consider a human stratospheric jump. That was a lot, but the list was finite. We were getting closer instead of further away. That alone made all the difference.

A week after the dizzying dummy drop, we were back in the tin shed at Roswell International Air Center for our pilot-training series with Alan. The training was organized around a long list of things Alan had to be able to do in the suit, such as depressurizing, reaching his parachute pull handles, working the parachute steering toggles, and taking his helmet off by himself.

Pilot Interface

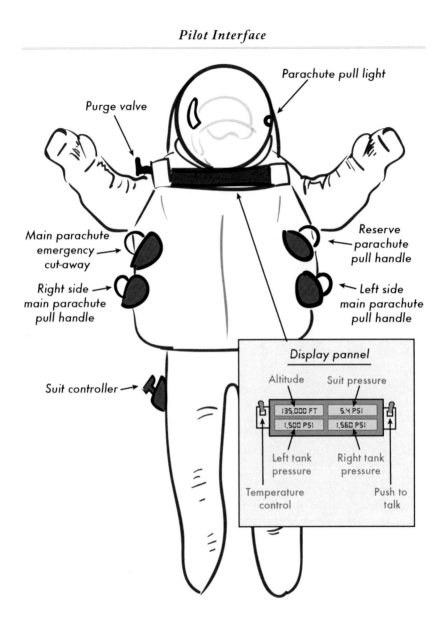

Our Roswell headquarters looked like a city abandoned in hurry. Tables were still scattered with bits of equipment people had been working on. Papers blew around the floor. We would do our training session and leave for the winter. All of the gear and parts would go back to Tucson to be staged for use in what we had started calling the "Arizona tour," a winter of testing in anticipation of manned jumps.

As had become our custom, the suit team arrived two days before Alan to prep the site, prep the suit, and be ready for an early-morning start to run our tests. This test was not particularly stressful for anyone except Alan. He would spend two grueling days rolling around on the tin shed floor doing the same things over and over again until there was no longer any concern about him working the machine that encapsulated his body.

We went through a partial phase zero checkout and early in the morning got the suit on him in record time. Tests like this had become so much easier. It wasn't scary now, it was just work.

Alan started by practicing taking the helmet off, a task that movies have made seem far easier than it is. Thousands of pounds press on a helmet when pressurized, so the small, lightweight lugs that hold them closed are strong and hard to activate. After the scary landing in Coolidge, we wanted to see Alan take that helmet off with no assistance in every conceivable scenario, a training exercise that clearly should have been done before that desert jump. For a good half hour, Alan did nothing but take the helmet off over and over again, in every position he could possibly land in. We became the sticklers we always should have been, strict about every item on the lists. With amazing proficiency, he learned to remove the helmet effortlessly every time, which was a major relief.

Exercising a pressurized spacesuit is a muscly, relentless battle. Astronauts spend hours a day in the gym leading up to their missions, and months in a suit practicing their exact tasks. Alan would be the fourth-oldest person ever to rise above 100,000 feet by any mechanism and by far the oldest person to enter the stratosphere by balloon. His predecessors in stratospheric skydiving were either middle-aged daredevils or air force kids. We were inclined to go easy on him given his age but were encouraged persistently by the doctors to do exactly the opposite. His age was an extra hurdle to overcome in this endeavor. He had to train longer and harder because of it. We started meticulously tracking his physical ability, a prospect that would make most people extremely uncomfortable. He was still months away from being physically ready, but he was making steady progress.

Inside the suit, movements that are within its normal envelope can be achieved robotically but readily. Other movements that are just slightly outside the range of motion of the suit can be accomplished, but only by flexing the strained, inflated fabric out of shape. The pilot has to exert a lot of force to do this. Alan was wearing the same basic style of suit the astronauts aboard the space station wore. It was made by the company that made the suits used on the space station and the suits that went to the moon—the most knowledgeable spacesuit manufacturers alive. No spacesuit existed that would be easier to manipulate than this one. But it would require work, training, and an able-bodied wearer to operate correctly.

After moving past the helmet exercises, an hour or so into the testing process, Alan was covered in sweat and visibly exhausted. We had yet to do the hardest exercise: suit depressurization. This was the first spacesuit ever designed to be depressurized by its user during a mission. After Alan was unable to manipulate the handle on the pressure controller during his plunge to the desert, we added a new, larger handle on top of the first one. These handles were mounted to each other like Russian nesting dolls. The updated handle was easier to manipulate than the original knob. For over a year we had been messing with that valve.

We had investigated the placement and shape of the hardware at nearly every suit session that had happened since we started the program. Alan had never really been able to work the valve. Several human factors milestones happened with me in the suit, when I had been able to successfully work the smaller knob. But I was a different person with a different body, and successes with me working the valve should not have been applied to Alan. The biggest root mistake in the events leading up to the crash we experienced in Coolidge can be attributed to falsely assuming Alan could work that valve without assistance from technicians. It was time to work through a training and evaluation of whether Alan could actually work the valve himself.

We knew off the bat that things weren't going to be easy. Alan projected an unwavering confidence in his ability to work the valve, but when we got the suit lying facedown on the ground, the position he would likely be in when he landed, he just couldn't do it. He would bat at the valve, trying to hit the knob with the metal ring between the glove and the wrist. Sometimes the valve would move forward and sometimes it would move backward. We rigged up a live video system so he could see what he was doing by connecting one of our cameras to a smartphone. It didn't help.

It was frightening to think that we had pushed Alan out of an airplane a few months earlier in that suit. The jump in Coolidge required him to depressurize the suit with that knob, both to be able to access his steering lines and to eventually access outside air. Not even in the calm of our peaceful tin shed, with the assistance of live video and his team coaching him on radios, could he open it.

We let Alan rest and tried some other exercises. We tried to hang Alan from the straps that connect the parachute to the suit so he could practice reaching up and grabbing and pulling the steering lines for the parachute. Had we tried this before the desert crash, we would have known it was not possible for Alan to reach the steering lines in that suit while hanging under a parachute. We reset the parachute risers for the training and soon saw that we couldn't do any hang tests at all because the parachute risers would get in the way of our ground oxygen lines. The test was quickly shaping up to be a dud.

While we experimented with the configuration of the oxygen lines, Alan had a rest and then decided to go back into his attempts to depressurize the suit, this time on his back, in the second most likely position he could end up in after skidding into a landing in the desert. When he was on his back, the parachute shoulder strap loosed up a bit, and he could get closer to the valve. He used his same method of brushing and batting at the valve, and this time it started to turn. After it turned a full rotation, letting some pressure out of the suit, it got easier. It looked like we were witnessing Alan's first successful in-suit depressurization. Strangely, though, the valve kept turning and turning when we thought it should have stopped. We took over. A little tug on the valve handle pulled the guts of the valve right out. We had broken it. Those valves cost as much as a new car, and take months to get. This was the second one we had broken. Worse, if the suit was still pressurized, we had an emergency. It wasn't, but we doffed the suit in grumpy spirits. We'd trashed our system once again.

Alan led a long discussion into the night. We faced the hard fact that he really wasn't able to actuate that valve himself, and that it kept breaking because it was not meant to be turned by a gloved hand. We couldn't do anything more. This test was over. Alan left a day early, and we loaded up the gear to go back to Tucson where we would initiate our second major architectural change in two weeks and try to figure out how to add an auxiliary depressurization valve that was easier to access and more robust than the pressure controller knob.

A year ago, we had officially checked the life-support pack into our computer system as a completed assembly. Since that first check-in, the assembly had been checked out and revised 124 times; this change would make 125. Maybe we weren't very good designers. Maybe we needed more oversight. Maybe we needed less. Most likely, we were learning what a lot of the more weathered advisors showed us by their complete lack of surprise at each of these changes and failures: this is just how these things go. This is why we test. We would fix it and then test it again.

*Blikkies drops
Louis Palomares
off his chest from
parachute flight
to test out the
SAEBER system in
flight for the first
time.*

*Looking up at the
SAEBER from
Louis's point of
view after the
SAEBER extends.*

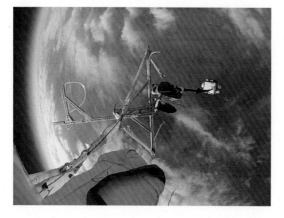

*The SAEBER deploys
perfectly the first
time it is used in the
stratosphere.*

The SAEBER fully extended, looking up from the dummy.

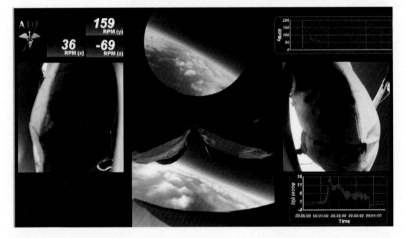

In our first dummy drop, the dummy spun at incredible rates. Our sensors maxed out and stopped logging at 16G of acceleration. The spin rates exceeded 180 rpm. This spin could have been fatal for a human.

Our first high-altitude dummy payload ascends on its way to 93,000 feet. (Photo by Dave Jourdan.)

Romping through the Roswell badlands in our chase trucks, looking for a transponder returning from a test flight to over 100,000 feet. (Photo by Dave Jourdan.)

Josh Hecht and Travis Palmer crawling under a barbed wire fence on a chase exercise. (Photo by Dave Jourdan.)

CHAPTER 10
...
A Suit Finally Working. The Arizona Tour

W e all knew what we were going to find up there in the stratosphere: a clawing vacuum that would suck the contents of a person's lungs out of their mouth, and then work to turn everything liquid in their body into gas before extracting that too. That vacant freezing air didn't seem like it could ever be called home by anyone. But going to space is supposed to be hard, right? Isn't that what makes it inspiring, a spark to the flame of human passion?

For better or worse, we humans have mostly conquered our planet. Old explorers sailing in rickety, uncomfortable vessels risked death and, the horrors of colonization aside, gave us access to the land I sit on now. Looking back, it seems so different, but was it? Most people probably thought traveling over the dark ocean on a smelly, wooden ship toward a target that so often featured disease and hardship was slow suicide. Exploration can change the world and its inhabitants, but not until well after it happens. Explorers unlock the world and universe.

The pioneers of Earth orbit and the Apollo program took trips in metal canisters the size of a Volkswagen for days on end with coin-toss odds of life or death. We forget, especially while constantly being reminded of the glory of the Apollo program, that one thing was universally true of all places we've explored above the Earth: there was nothing there when it was first found. The moon is a dead rock; low Earth orbit is a boiling vacuum. Since then the sky has been filled with satellites that connect us and guide us in ways we never could have imagined. Low Earth orbit has been permanently inhabited for years.

When charged with the difficulties of weighing a human life and finding my own position within the idea of "acceptable risk," I try not to worry about it. The important thing is that somebody get goose bumps when they think about staring at the curve of the Earth while clouds swirl below, seeing whole oceans in a single glance. Such people consider human exploration to be among our greatest accomplishments as a species. People can gaze at the moon and reflect, "I'm a human and humans went there." This is what makes me want to continue the quest, one that is not, has never been, and will never be without risk. That's what makes explorers great.

November 2013: Repairing and Testing the Broken Suit

We were making a pretty regular activity out of breaking our suit and then spending weeks fixing it. Now it had a big hole where the pressure controller was supposed to go. We spent the next month rethinking the depressurization system that Alan must be able to operate without breaking it. Ultimately, we realized that we needed two systems: one used by the suit team to pressurize and depressurize the suit, and a second, separate one that Alan would use to depressurize the suit during his descent. The pressure controller used by the suit team was too complex and fragile to survive Alan bashing it with his clumsy, pressurized gloves while dropping out of the sky.

The knob on the pressure controller sets the opening force of a differential pressure aneroid. This is basically a spring mechanism that opens when the force behind the spring, from the pressure, gets large enough. Turning the knob in one direction tightens the spring so that it takes more pressure to overcome, pressurizing the suit. The knob had a mechanical stop set at our suit pressure so that when the knob was turned all the way, the suit would pressurize the correct amount. For flight, the pressure controller is set to keep the pressure in the suit at 5.4 psi above the pressure outside. In a vacuum it would be 5.4 psi inside the suit. This is the pressure a person without a suit would experience at 25,000 feet. At that pressure the human body can survive in relative comfort as long as the person is breathing pure oxygen.

Turning the knob on the controller in the other direction reduced the opening force of the aneroid and lowered the pressure inside the suit. Team members on the ground would turn this knob to depressurize the suit. Of course, an astronaut would have to be out of their mind to depressurize the suit at high altitude, but decompression sickness and oxygen deprivation could sufficiently impair Alan's reason and awareness to make him do exactly that by mistake. Nobody knows why Nick Piantanida opened his helmet at 57,000 feet, but flight-induced mental impairment is a likely culprit. We had to guard against every conceivable (and inconceivable) operator error that could occur at 135,000 feet. Therefore, the differential pressure aneroid was plumbed in series with an absolute pressure aneroid.

An absolute pressure aneroid doesn't detect pressure difference. It closes when the absolute pressure outside the suit drops below a certain point. That pressure is set at 3.5 psi (intentionally slightly lower than the differential pressure aneroid so they don't compete), which is the pressure at 33,000 feet above sea level. This second valve would prevent air from flowing out of the suit when the pressure outside the suit was low enough. This made it impossible to fully depressurize the suit in a vacuum, even if an oxygen-starved pilot somehow thought it was a good idea to do so.

Knocking at this delicate system with fat, pressurized gloves was breaking it. Instead of trying to make the pressure controller more robust, we decided we had to have a second depressurization system for Alan to use from inside the suit.

We redesigned the chestpack to include a depressurization valve. We put a large valve made of thick stainless steel on it with a big plastic handle. We placed it high, in the most easily accessible and visible place on the chestpack. It was robust enough to withstand Alan's clumsy manipulations. A curvy white tube snaked out of one side of the valve to the bottom of the suit and a metal pass-through where it terminated at a hole. It was a simple, direct path for air to flow from the inside of the suit to the outside when the valve was opened. Because Alan would land in a dirty field somewhere, we covered the hole with a turret-shaped filter sticking off the valve so dirt couldn't get shoved up into the oxygen clean system on landing.

Intentionally making a hole in a spacesuit is risky. If the valve failed or the pilot mistakenly turned or bumped the knob at high altitude, the safeguards built into the pressure controller wouldn't prevent the oxygen inside the suit from escaping. Instead, we would rely on the oxygen system flooding the suit for that safeguard. Sizing the outlet tube was critical. If it was too big, the backfill system wouldn't be able to keep up with the leak and the suit would fail, losing pressure and exposing its occupant to vacuum. If the hole was too small, however, the pilot's breathing rate could turn out to be higher than the rate at which this hole dumps the oxygen out of the suit, so that the suit may never actually depressurize even when it is supposed to.

Previous testing had shown us that the hole could be no smaller than a quarter of an inch. That was the limit we had established for the maximum size of an accidental hole that the suit could withstand. We had tested this in the vacuum chamber the previous year. Oxygen would pour into the suit to backfill a hole if the outside pressure was less than the suit's backup control pressure of 3.5 psi, which occurred at 33,000 feet above sea level. If the hole was in the lower half of the suit, the pressure in the lower half of the suit would fall, sucking the oxygen from the helmet through the exhalation valve into the lower half of the suit. When the oxygen in the helmet was sucked below the neck dam, the pressure in the suit would fall, and an emergency pressure aneroid in the helmet regulator would open, flooding the system with new oxygen to backfill the leak. Above that altitude, opening the depressurization valve wouldn't do anything but make a lot of noise and waste a lot of oxygen. Below that altitude, we wanted the suit to depressurize, even though the pressure controller knob hadn't been opened.

So we had to know whether a quarter-inch hole was big enough, and how big was too big. I spent a week working through flow-rate equations for tube flow and running into our lab trying to get an idea if a quarter inch would do the trick. One afternoon I had the bright idea to just put a three-foot-long, quarter-inch plastic hose in my mouth and breathe through it to see if I passed out. I stood in the machine shop of our building, breathing through a tube, waving off curious technicians. My crude test was supported by the math. The tube would work, but there wasn't much room for error. We put together a two-stage test plan to put the problem to bed and ensure that Alan had a usable depressurization system.

We also took this opportunity to make two more upgrades to the suit: an anti-suffocation valve and modifications to the purge line so Alan could use it to breathe outside air if he was trapped in the suit on the ground without oxygen.

We didn't want to risk suffocating someone in our suit, ever. Left over from an older version was a fitting on the plate that separated the head section of the suit from the body section. It was originally used for a water-drinking tube that we had removed because of its bad tendency to dump water into the facemask and drown its user. We installed an anti-suffocation valve in that fitting. It would open to bring air up from the bottom half of the suit back to the top if the helmet should have lower pressure than the bottom of the suit. That air would be filled with waste and toxins, but it would buy the pilot some time.

Updated Demand-Regulated Architecture

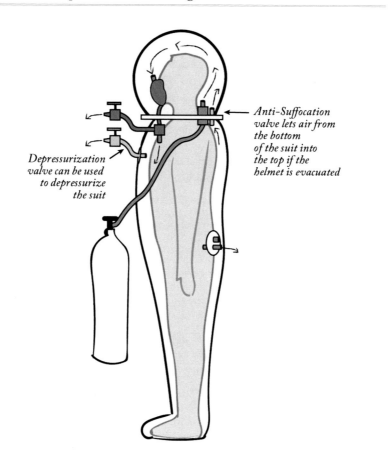

Depressurization valve can be used to depressurize the suit

Anti-Suffocation valve lets air from the bottom of the suit into the top if the helmet is evacuated

The second change was to avoid the dreaded scenario of Alan lying on the desert floor, out of oxygen, trapped in an airtight spacesuit while we were still looking for him. When the purge valve is opened, it connects the facemask to the outside. We wanted Alan to be able to open that valve if he was on the ground and out of air so he could breathe outside air through this tube, using it like a snorkel set, keeping himself alive indefinitely. Because this hole was plumbed to the helmet, the oxygen system would open up to backfill the hole directly as long as there was oxygen in the tanks.

All of these changes complicated the suit plumbing, making the pilot procedures to use that plumbing even more complicated.

Alan was instructed: When you open the parachute, depressurize the suit. If you can't depressurize the suit, steer yourself down in the pressurized suit. If you get to the ground and nobody is around, wait. If your oxygen starts to get low, try harder to depressurize the suit. If you can't get the suit depressurized, keep waiting. If you do get the suit depressurized and find yourself near the end of the oxygen supply, remove the helmet; with nobody there to close the oxygen tanks, they will loudly and somewhat dangerously drain. If you can't get the helmet off, open the purge valve to get some fresh air in the suit and wait. If the purge valve won't open, wait; when the air runs out, your breathing will reduce the pressure in the helmet and the anti-suffocation valve will let some nasty stale air up from the bottom of the suit, buying some time by trading the scary, quick suffocation for slower, smellier death by carbon dioxide poisoning. In all scenarios, if you are on the ground, hope someone gets there soon.

We would need to test this system. We bought the parts and Ryan came to Tucson for a week-long testing session where I offered my body to science for a series of nerve-racking, potentially air-deprived suit system tests. We started off with the new depressurization valve.

We knew that a quarter-inch hole would let air out slowly, possibly so slowly that the pilot's exhalations into the bottom of the suit would keep it pressurized. The team came up with a clever way to test that didn't require me to be inside.

We laid the suit on a table and sealed it up, except for the helmet. We set the pressure controller knob to the pressurized position and blocked the neck dam with a big plastic plug. The facemask hung off the suit. When we exhaled into the facemask, our exhalations went into the lower cavity of the suit. We wanted to see if this would leave the suit limp and deflated or cause it to gain pressure. If the suit gained too much pressure, we would activate the anti-suffocation valve to relieve the pressure in the lower half of the suit into the upper half, which in this case dumped it back out into the room.

We tested the shit out of it. I breathed into the suit. Ryan breathed into the suit. We used big hoses and small hoses, corner valves and straight valves. We took long deep breaths and fast short breaths. I even did sessions where I ran a mile down the streets of Tucson's south industrial district and sprinted through the front door past a confused front desk attendant and straight into the lab, where I strapped on the facemask and took heaving, panting breaths through the facemask into the suit's lower half. I found if I took a certain type of exaggerated deep breath, pushing out air as hard and as fast as possible, I could blow the suit up like a beach toy and activate the anti-suffocation valve. We decided that scenario was an over-exaggeration of the real application and ultimately disregarded it. The new depressurization valve test was a pass. I had to don the suit for the remainder of the tests.

We hung the suit up in our company high bay from an aluminum mini-gantry over a gymnastics mat with no fanfare. We were acting fast and getting it done. We would try all the new valves, including the anti-suffocation valve, which only comes open right before you start to suffocate. Scary.

I suited up. Ryan closed the helmet while Zane ran the ground cart. I took some breaths from my private atmosphere and began to generate the sweaty, carbon dioxide–filled stink below the neck dam, while still enjoying the pristine dry oxygen that existed above it.

By this point, the suit team was cohesive. All of us were present for all of the suit tests. Ryan and Mitch, our new suit technician, worked with the suit itself, while Blikkies was responsible for parachutes. Zane worked the ground carts and ran the team in my place if I went into the suit. In the first test I would open the purge line to see if it would allow enough air into the facemask to keep a pilot alive after the bottled air ran out. We did our normal thumbs-up sequence and Zane and Mitch turned off the tanks.

The suit went silent when the valves stopped the oxygen flow. I opened the purge line. I hung there, holding a thumbs-up at Ryan, hoping that I had opened a lifeline to the outside. I felt air trickle in, but it was only a trickle. Panic rose. I felt the rubber neck dam pulling up against my neck and the suit facemask digging against my face. I squirmed.

I wanted to be out of that suit. But I didn't want to bail. I had to keep that thumbs-up high so we could do our test. The rubber crept up further while I strained to suck air through a valve connected to four feet of skinny hose, knowing that if I didn't breathe slowly and calmly, everything I was feeling would amplify. It felt like I was sucking a marble up a rubber hose. With every breath, the rubber of the neck dam sucked harder against my neck and the facemask pressed further into my cheeks.

15 seconds into the test, I was ready to rip that rubber noose off of me. I kept my thumb up. Right as I was gripped by suffocation panic and about to go thumbs-down, I heard a poof! and instantly gulped the moist funk of the lower half of the suit. It wasn't pleasant but I wasn't suffocating. The anti-suffocation valve did exactly what it was supposed to do. Without enough air coming into the facemask, I continued to draw oxygen from the helmet until the pressure got low enough to open the anti-suffocation valve.

I didn't suffocate, but the purge valve didn't work. Had I been a pilot alone in the desert, I would still have been in danger of dying of carbon dioxide poisoning. Thumbs-down. Test over.

The team turned my oxygen on, filling the head of the suit with glorious pressure and clean oxygen. Ryan depressurized the suit and took the helmet off. I breathed the sweet desert air, rattled but fine. We'd chew on the results over the next few weeks. What we'd really learned was that we had to get to Alan fast, wherever he landed.

We still had to actually test the anti-suffocation valve. In some regards it was nice that the valve had unexpectedly opened during the purge valve test because at least for this test I now knew it worked. This test would be the same as the last one but shorter. With the purge valve closed, presumably the anti-suffocation valve would open that much faster. Once it opened, I was allowed, free of judgment and loss of spacesuit test subject macho points, to go thumbs-down. The test didn't require breathing sweat and carbon dioxide any longer than I had to.

Ryan closed me in again. With the purge valve closed, the vacuum in the head region formed much faster and firmer. The rubber tightened up just short of strangulation immediately. Sure enough, after just a couple futile breaths, a hot moist stream jetted up behind my head out of the anti-suffocation valve, creating a little vortex of oxygen, carbon dioxide, and body juice that I could theoretically breathe until I started into the violent process of CO2 poisoning. This test was a strange win. The suit could still kill someone, but not by making them suck vacuum.

Last up was the meat of the test, the depressurization valve. We knew that the hoses we had used were small enough that they would maintain the suit's pressure even if the valve ruptured or opened at the wrong time. Small hoses were our friends when we wanted pressure to stay in the suit and the enemy when we wanted it to leave. We had done multiple bench-top tests that indicated that the suit would just barely depressurize when that valve was opened. Now we had to verify it for real.

For the third and final time, Ryan closed me in. The suit's main pressure controller (the one that couldn't be reached inside the suit) was left open so the suit wouldn't start to pressurize until we were ready. For the first time ever, I would control the pressurization of the suit using the depressurization valve instead of Ryan pumping me up by turning the pressure controller knob. Regardless of which mechanism is closed, it is the user's exhalations that are actually inflating the suit.

It was actually quite comforting to control the pressurization process myself. Pressurizing a spacesuit like ours in a few quick turns of a knob was the pressure equivalent of diving an unpressurized aircraft from 25,000 feet to sea level. It felt like my head was going to explode. If for no other reason than to have the control to stop the increasing pressure when ears wouldn't pop, we decided from that moment that the suit occupant would control the pressurization.

This was another one of those moments where we didn't know exactly what was going to happen. Instead of closing a pressure controller designed to pressurize a spacesuit, we were just closing a gaping hole we had intentionally made in the suit. We were bypassing the mechanism that was actually made to pressurize the suit. We had done all the math and tested all we could. We had talked it through with the people who designed the pressure controller and all the responses were the same: "It should work," but with shrugs and hints of reservation. No pre-test guarantees. We tried it.

The suit came up to pressure just like it was supposed to. The display panel read 5.5 psi above the ambient pressure. I was at an absolute pressure well over the air pressure at sea level, equivalent to being several thousand feet below the surface of the oceans. The team gathered around the front of the suit in silent anticipation. Ryan came on the radio: "Ready when you are." The big plastic valve handle was in clear view, and it was completely painless and simple to turn. I turned it. A whoosh! swirled into the helmet. As air was leaving through our intentional hole, the suit started to depressurize. My ears popped and my guts expanded, gurgling around as the air inside me churned and moved while it took up more space. The process was stunted by my breathing, which was pulling new air into the suit when I inhaled, fighting the depressurization process. The whooshing and hissing slowed to a whistle. The display panels once again read atmospheric pressure. The suit had successfully depressurized. We had learned the hard way that in order for something to be just barely doable while hurtling at the Earth in a body cast, it had to be stupidly easy to do in a lab environment. Turning that valve was as simple as it gets. And it worked.

We repeated the test a few more times, trying to throw some curve balls at the system. I did my hard breathing test and long, slow breathing tests. It depressurized just as it was supposed to every time.

I lay on a gymnastics mat while they got the suit off me. High overhead, in the fluorescent-lit spacecraft assembly bay, hung a huge American flag, signaling the day's victory.

With another crisis behind us, we headed off for manned vacuum testing in the Arizona State University altitude chamber. We had tested the suit in a vacuum eight months ago, but Alan wasn't in it. This would be Alan's first time in a space vacuum.

December 2013: Manned Vacuum Chamber Testing

Hollywood loves killing people off in a vacuum. Sometimes people in a movie vacuum freeze instantly and bounce off a spacecraft hard as rock. Sometimes they explode, or their eyes bulge out of their heads while their veins burst through their skin. No doubt the movie industry employs sharp aerospace medicine experts, but our experts were the sharpest alive, and they painted a different picture of what happensm with the chilling directness only a doctor can deliver.

Our bodies are filled with blood that moves dissolved chemicals to our organs. Blood is mostly water, and our organs may or may not include cavities filled with air. The behavior of air and water in the presence of a vacuum are at the root of all the problems a human body will face in an environment with no air.

The first thing a person will experience in a vacuum is a severe form of "the bends," or decompression sickness. This is the well-known ailment that plagues scuba divers who rise up through water too quickly. Because Earth's atmosphere is mostly nitrogen, water on Earth is saturated with nitrogen. The higher the pressure, the more it will hold.

A person traveling up into the atmosphere will experience steady pressure decreases as the air thins. At around 14,000 feet, pilots are required to breathe pure oxygen. Above about 45,000 feet, serious health effects occur if a person is not inside a pressurized container. If the container ruptures, the air inside will rapidly escape, and the person will quickly experience the same pressure as in the environment outside. In the stratosphere, that pressure is essentially zero, a vacuum. The gas dissolved in their blood will fizz out of solution, for the same reasons carbon dioxide fizzes out of a soda when it's popped open. The average soda is pressurized at 30 psi, about twice the atmospheric pressure at the surface of the Earth. When the can is opened, the carbon dioxide comes out of solution and vents to the air. Human blood vessels can't vent the bubbles, so the bubbles combine into ever bigger ones inside the bloodstream. Depending on the pressure and the duration of exposure, the effects could be anything from the eerie tingling sensation of bugs crawling on skin to catastrophic damage to vital organs and a quick, terrifying death. In fact, the very first symptom people who lost suit pressure in a vacuum chamber reported was a bubbling, fizzy sensation on the tongue and grittiness in the eyes.

Oxygen in the blood doesn't behave the same way nitrogen does, and it doesn't fizz out when the pressure is reduced. Modern aviators defend against the bends by breathing pure oxygen for a length of time before their mission, so that there will be no nitrogen in their blood to bubble out. At low enough pressures, the bends will always occur, but once pressures get that low the bends are the least of the worries.

The next most catastrophic possibility is barotrauma. Barotrauma is what the makers of the movie Total Recall probably had in mind when they showed Arnold Schwarzenegger's eyes bulging out of his head when he took his helmet off on the surface of Mars.

Physics tells us that as the pressure of a gas decreases, its volume will get bigger. Think of how someone can blow gentle little bubbles out at the bottom of a pool where the weight of the water makes higher pressure the deeper you go. Those same bubbles grow in size as they rise, erupting to roil the surface. This is gas expansion at work. Just as the bubbles in the pool grow so fast, any air trapped inside your body will get bigger and want out quickly during a significant pressure drop.

There are only a few cavities of air in the human body, the lungs being the largest. There are also pockets of air behind the eyes and gas in the intestines. The ear-popping sensation experienced in airplane flight is caused by air expanding inside the body's pressure-sensing center, located in the inner ear. Exposed to a vacuum, air will ferociously expand or rupture those pockets, seeking wider expanses in the vastness of space. Expanding gas in the gut and ears can cause cramping or deafness, respectively. A full and closed-up bag of lungs suddenly exposed to a vacuum will explode. Astronauts are told to open their mouths in a potential vacuum exposure, and scuba divers are told to exhale as they ascend from the depths, in both cases to expel the expanding air. A person can survive barotrauma by opening their mouth, and once the gas has escaped, that concern will be over. The next several seconds will present a new problem, however: vapor gas ebullism.

As most dedicated cooks know, at higher altitudes, water boils at lower temperatures. With less force pushing down on the water, it takes less energy to uncage the molecules and send them aloft as steam. At sea level, water boils at 212 degrees Fahrenheit, at 6,000 feet up, it boils at 193 degrees Fahrenheit, and at 63,000 feet above ground, there is a layer known as Armstrong's line where water boils at 98.6 degrees Fahrenheit. If that temperature looks familiar, it should: that is the temperature of the human body.

Blood is mostly water. Anywhere above Armstrong's line, blood boils. If a person is exposed to a vacuum, the threat that eclipses all others is that of a person's blood becoming bubbles of steam blocking major arteries to vital organs. At the time of exposure, the largest bubbles will form in the largest cavities, starting in the heart and major arteries like the aorta. In about 12 seconds, the bubbles will arrive in the brain, cutting off blood supply to brain tissue. A person would have a few more seconds before the effects of ebullism set in, then a loss of useful consciousness and death. Left unattended, a person exposed to hard vacuum would likely be dead in less than a minute.

Unbeknownst to many, there is on record a case of someone being exposed to total vacuum in a chamber at Johnson Space Center in the 1960s. A hose came loose from a test subject's suit. He passed out within seconds. A fast-acting chamber team had the chamber back to pressure in seconds, and the test subject regained consciousness in a daze. Ultimately, he was fine. He reported feeling the water on his tongue bubble before he crashed backwards. A Russian Soyuz crew who were exposed to vacuum for a prolonged period of time were not so lucky. After their capsule experienced a failed valve that opened the capsule to vacuum during reentry, they passed quickly into their next life, perhaps closer to heaven than most at the time of death. Their bodies were recovered on the ground, exhibiting apparent signs of extreme hemorrhaging and ebullism.

An unflinching lecture explaining these phenomena was given by Dr. Clark in Phoenix a few days ahead of chamber testing at Arizona State University. Dr. Clark went through the list of dire possibilities with stern conviction, noting historical cases. He did not leave out the crew of the space shuttle Columbia, who likely lost their lives to vacuum exposure prior to or during the shuttle breakup. Dr. Clark was a NASA flight surgeon who had worked on that mission. His wife was among the astronauts aboard the vehicle.

In one day, Alan would enter a chamber with only his inches-wide suit between a vacuum and his delicate human body.

Despite our sense that we were true explorers of the unknown, most people either didn't know or didn't care that our program existed. Later, people would be surprised that we had been able to keep the project a secret for so long, but truth be told, there was nothing to it.

We barely felt like part of the company we worked for. I rarely darkened the door of our company's building or talked to my formal bosses, who stayed at Tucson at headquarters and rarely made the trip to wherever we were testing. We prioritized according to our goals. We made deals and solved problems. We had long quit worrying ourselves with what we were supposed to be doing and did the thing that made the most sense at any particular moment.

We made a deal with Arizona State University to use their high-altitude chamber. Without so much as a skeptical lecture, we received permission to test in a chamber that hadn't contained a person in years. We paid pennies on the dollar. Instead of spending months on the paperwork that would have been required to give us a shot at a NASA lab, we spent days convincing bored lab technicians to fire up an old chamber with our man inside.

The development of spacesuits and high-atmospheric suits was in full swing about halfway through the 20th century, when nearly all of today's spacesuit designs were taking their maiden runs in vacuum chambers. Today, there are only a few suit designs in regular use. They are made by three companies, one in Russia and two in the United States. The Russian one is Svesda, and they produce the spacewalking suit called the Sokol, as well as a launch entry and abort suit for their Soyuz, which carries three people at a time and rides to space aboard a massive, kerosene-powered rocket named Progress.

In the United States, spacesuits are manufactured by either ILC Dover or the David Clark Company. ILC Dover, where Ryan worked, makes the extra vehicular activity (EVA) suits for American astronauts, and David Clark makes the launch entry and abort suits that were used on board the space shuttle before it was decommissioned in 2012. Now US astronauts ride to the mostly American-built International Space Station on the Russian Soyuz wearing Russian suits, leaving the only American spacesuit actively manufactured for use in space right now the EVA suits used on American spacewalks. China has a functioning space station as well. They do go outside in what are more or less Svesda Sokol suits. The David Clark Company built the suit Felix Baumgartner was wearing in the Red Bull Stratos jump. All these suits were designed almost half a century ago. It was time for America, and the world, to test out a brand-new suit.

Very few spacesuit systems have been actually used in an operation. From what we understood, we had arrived at the point in development that inventers can't get past. There is a long list of suits that have made it through some portion of development testing (including at least six suits being created at this writing, in everything from multibillion-dollar contractor labs to people's living rooms). From what we could find in the public domain, this would be the first time a brand-new suit design would be brought to vacuum with a human inside in over 30 years. The team assembled in Phoenix for what we would call Manned Altitude Chamber Testing I.

The chamber was perfect for us. It was officially managed by a university but in reality wasn't managed by anyone at all. When we first went to examine the facilities and lay out where we would stage our little city of equipment, it became apparent that we would have total freedom in executing our tests.

There were two chambers at the facility, one of them used for running classes on hypoxia for pilots. In those classes they have a group of students enter the chamber and begin to breathe pure oxygen. Operators pump out air until the pressure is the same as at 25,000 feet. Then the oxygen is taken away so they feel what it's like to get slow and stupid from lack of oxygen. This is a standard part of pilot training.

The lab had a second, separate chamber. This smaller chamber was a holdover from when that part of the college was an Air Force base. The facility had seen some risky testing involving explosively decompressing chambers from aircraft pressure to 70,000 feet so U2 spy plane pilots could feel what it was like to have a cockpit lose pressure on a spy flight far above the normal skies. Those days were long gone. Since then, the smaller chamber that we would be using had mostly stood idle. We would be the first group in the 60-year history of the lab to max out either chamber with a person inside.

Vacuum Chamber

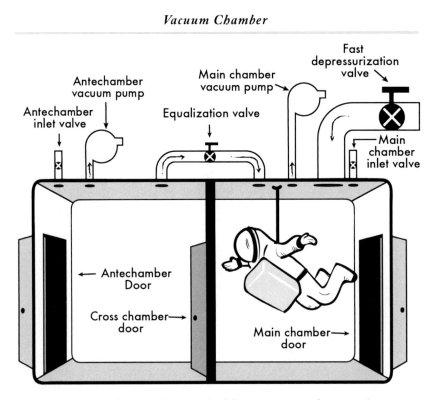

An aerospace physiologist who had been contracted to watch over us didn't flinch at our plans. He seemed eager to add us to his collection of war stories, which he related nonstop through 12-hour days for the solid week we were there. Some of them seemed like they could have been true, and all were recounted with passion. His tales wove through our setting up of the webs of tubes and wires that would make up our system. He was assisted by an ex-chamber manager who knew the machines well but no longer worked for the chamber crew. One stoned-looking kid ran the controls on the student chamber regularly. He was always available and seemed to be able to control the chamber with his bleary eyes closed. We had a team.

The suit team, along with Rolfe, the testing lead, arrived ahead of the rest of the crew to start the long preparations. The scrappy nature of this test was apparent. Modern space people would call the approach "commercial" to distinguish it from the strict government processes followed by NASA. It wasn't the prettiest chamber on the planet, but despite outward appearances, the team was highly diligent and knew everything there was to know about the machines. We appreciated having the freedom to tailor the safety procedures to exactly fit our test. This definitely wasn't NASA. The bathroom nearest the chamber was the designated bathroom stop for the local campus busses, so we shared our bathroom with a never-ending stream of bus drivers, all ducking eye contact with us, on break from their route. A slicker, more formal chamber would have cost two orders of magnitude more. A chamber isn't much besides a big sealed metal box hooked to pumps. This one worked, and we were glad to be there.

We had a special mini-gantry for hanging Alan in his suit. The chamber was small, so there were only a couple of inches of clearance on each side of the suit. Blikkies built a special holding strap for hanging the suit from the gantry. Overall, the tight space was tricky but workable.

In two days we had effected our habitual transformation. The room was customized from floor to ceiling with our ground-support equipment. A little techno-city of tubes, wires, tanks, racks, and computers would support our spacesuit. We surfaced the chamber and the space behind the doors with special mats to help reduce the risk of damaging things in contact with the ground, and installed a mat in the main chamber room where Alan would hang. We ran the data transmission system through a wire to the outside of the chamber, where it would be less likely to interfere with the voice communications. Mitch, with almost a decade of experience operating chambers at NASA, shored up the chamber itself, chasing down all the incipient leaks.

Mitch Sweeney was a man of few words. Most of his career had been spent working for the test chambers at Johnson Space Center cramming prima donna astronauts into spacesuits prior to routine but no doubt hair-raising rides in NASA vacuum chambers. If he'd had his way, he would be a mixed martial arts fighter, but the universe didn't agree and instead he had to settle for testing spacesuits and then later building them. He was the best. After NASA, he moved across the street to ILC Dover, and that's how he ended up on our team. Mitch could build anything, and as an operator he had mastered the singular focus that the rest of the team was just coming to understand. During these tests, he would shine. After these tests, he would be a permanent member of the suit team.

The chamber we would use had three submarine-looking thigh-thick steel doors, two for entry and exit on each side, and one in the center that divided the space into a main chamber and an antechamber. A massive fast depressurization valve equalized pressure from the main chamber to the outside. An equalization valve connected the main chamber to the antechamber. Electrical wires spaghettied to all the monitoring equipment. The fact that these dusty rooms hadn't been used in decades made Mitch relish the challenge. He closed the doors and raised the altitude of the chamber leak by leak and valve by valve to a good flight altitude. Each repair bumped it up a few thousand more feet until he achieved a stabilization pressure above 90,000 feet, well above Armstrong's line and more than sufficient for our test.

The thought of a suit breach during the flight was terrifying. Ryan had worked on lots of suits that were used in spacewalks, where a suit breach could have even worse consequences than what we feared. We fed on his confidence that the suit envelope he and his colleagues had designed would maintain its integrity. Nevertheless, we set up all provisions for a speedy abort and tested each of them several times until each person knew exactly what they would do in every second following an abort.

We would take the antechamber up to some altitude in between the main chamber altitude and the ground altitude and use it to stagger a descent in two stages. This would help minimize Alan's risk if his suit depressurized and we had to abort. In the first stage, the two chambers would be equalized, dropping tens of thousands of feet in seconds but avoiding the last few thousand feet where the pressure rises fast enough for barotrauma to wreck his ears. By making one quick drop from ultra-high altitudes to something in the middle, the chamber would drop below Armstrong's line fast enough that the pilot's blood would reliquefy quickly, thereby avoiding the most pressing threat of an ebullism. Then we could move through the final altitudes more slowly to let the ears adjust without any blowouts. Sometimes in chambers like these, a team of technicians would actually ride in the antechamber to get to the pilot that much sooner in an emergency. We saw that as an extra risk to a new set of people, further complicating an already complex situation. We would stage emergency crews outside the doors who could rush in if needed as soon as the chamber pressure got to ground and the doors could be opened.

We considered four categories of abort. In a category 1 abort, we'd bring the chamber back to ground altitude at a slow rate, emulating a normal two-stage decent that took tens of minutes and posed no risks to Alan from a pressure-shock standpoint. Category 2 was a single-stage descent that skipped the simulated parachute ride, letting Alan fake-freefall to the ground. The last two categories were loud controlled valve-blow chamber equalizations between the antechamber at 8,000 feet and the main chamber, which could be anywhere from 8,000 to 90,000 feet. There were very few situations in which we would blow the chambers, but we practiced them like they were going to happen and readied every person for the worst. A major suit breach would trigger a level-4 abort, our worst-case scenario in which Alan would be exposed to a vacuum. We would blow the chamber equalization valve and take him straight down to survivable atmospheres. If he then looked unconscious and we had reason to believe an ebullism had occurred, we'd throw the remaining valves open and within 20 seconds, air from the room would dump in, taking the room back to ground pressures in less than one minute. Then we'd sprint in to pull our pilot out of the box. For the first time, aborting a test itself had the potential for serious medical consequences, in addition to any in the conditions that had necessitated the abort. We didn't expect an abort, yet we hadn't had a major test without an aborted first attempt. They were caused by minor technical issues, but they were still aborts. It would be a tense day.

Test preparations tended to become more complex during their last few days. People have a way of shoving uncomfortable details to the corners of their minds to maintain a state of optimism. Those details then float to the surface at the last minute, morphing a 10-person team into a 24-person crew working into the dark every night to scrape together the last million pieces needed to construct the test. We re-designated John, normally the "launch" director, as our "lunch" director, the one who would make sure we all had food throughout the days, starting at 5 a.m., with no breaks.

As Mitch sealed up the chamber, concern arose over whether the suit's venting into the chamber would overpower the pumps and keep us near the ground. Without any experience with this type of suit, the chamber folks had no idea if the suit's dumping oxygen, especially during our purge test, where we would intentionally introduce a hole in the suit to clear the helmet, would take out their pumps. Because the chamber was leaky and the pumps' old factory ratings were all but useless, we would need a real-life test that dumped into the box so we could see if the pumps would pull it out. We developed a last-minute test.

Norman, the project engineer, and I ran calculations to figure out what size hole would match Alan's breathing rate, which is the same as the rate that the suit dumps gas. We would then drill a hole that size in one of the chamber pass-through ports, normally used to connect test equipment outside the chamber, and let air rushing through it from outside the chamber to represent Alan's exhalations, forcing air out of the suit and into the chamber to challenge the pumps.

New concerns also arose about our ability to get Alan into the suit in the cramped chamber, so we added last-minute dry runs where I was hoisted up in the suit to make sure everything fit. We also ran a test with Alan to ensure we hadn't missed any problems specific to his anatomy.

Two days before the test, we finished building the pass-through cluster that registered the pressure in the chamber on our monitors. We drew the chamber down over and over again so we could refine our programs to control the chamber pressure to a specific profile. It wasn't easy. A technician in southern Arizona worked to clean up the code while Rolfe paced around in a near panic. One of a thousand tiny issues was always threatening to derail the huge test. As the day trailed off, the suit team set up the suit systems, and I put on the underlayers to go into the suit and get hoisted up into the chamber so we could see how the suit-hanging process worked.

I dressed in the family bathroom rather than the men's to avoid modeling the long underwear for the bus drivers. In the chamber, I got down on my knees so Ryan and the crew could push my head through the rubber tunnel on the floor and help me work my arms up into the sticky little arm holes.

Ryan pulled the rubber neck dam up over my head and helped me lie back onto the equipment pack. The crew laced the newly constructed hold web over the bar that I would hang from, and with my head tilting back, Mitch and Blikkies shimmied me up, one side of the suit at a time, while Ryan hoisted the straps up in the front, raising the suit, and me, inch by inch. The crew got me fully into the air, resting at a 45-degree angle within the confines of the little chamber, which was not much bigger than the suit. The helmet was off today, so the suit wasn't pressurized. The full 200 pounds of the suit system pulled against me in strange ways and dug into my arms. My hands fell asleep while we casually discussed details of hoisting the suit into position on the day of the test. By the time they helped me down, I didn't have any sensation past my elbows.

With most of a day to spare, we waited out our Sunday at the local skydiving center to show Ryan what a drop zone was like. I did a jump for fun. On the way back to the hotel, we stopped by the chamber to pad the cells with some new foam Mitch had picked up. While we taped up the floors, the rest of the crew trickled in, along with Alan and Sebastian and a squad of doctors: one state-licensed physician from the local ER, Dr. Clark to oversee the med staff, our regular suit team doctor Alex, the aerospace medical doctor responsible for on-site diagnostics of pressure-related incidents, and the chamber's aerospace physiologist: a total of five doctors on site and full provisions for a medevac to the nearest hyperbaric chamber, along with the fire department and local hospital ready to receive. We'd start at 7 in the morning with emergency abort drills, several chilling briefings about what could go wrong, and one more dry run of the suit, this time with Alan inside.

Sebastian opened the roles briefing: "The inside of those chambers will be beyond deadly 24 hours from now . . ." and turned it over to me. 24 of us would be admitted into the test room. Each had a specific role that was not to be deviated from. In an emergency we'd abort the test, get inside the chamber, get the helmet off, and pass Alan off to the medical team.

Next followed Dr. Clark's skin-tightening lecture on what happens to the human body when exposed to the low pressures of a space vacuum. He showed us slides of bubbles moving through blood vessels and lung tissue pocked with exploded alveoli. We got the point. Alan said it made him want to go home. He didn't.

The hardest part about the evening testing was trying to control 24 engineers in the presence of an incredibly fascinating machine that creates a fully isolated human environment in the deep silence of space vacuum. Firefighters came to look at the suit to learn how they would get it off if they needed to. EMTs checked out chamber access. University staff with a newfound interest in a program with a spacesuit floated past, poking their heads inside in hopes of an invitation to enter. We ignored them.

The room went quiet as we prepared to blow the valve on the antechamber to show everyone what a category 3 or category 4 abort would look like. The pumps engaged with a sharp sucking noise as the chamber climbed to altitude. With the chamber at full altitude, Sebastian called, "Abort! Category 4!" (He was supposed to yell it three times, but he only yelled it once.) The chamber operators snapped to action. The chamber tech pulled a giant red handle dangling above the control panel, and an entire room's worth of air shot through a massive pipe at the speed of sound, filling the evacuated chamber. The interior door banged open and the chambers equalized. The knife valves normally used to drain the chamber were thrown open, allowing air in from both the larger chamber and the room where we stood, bringing the last bit of space in the small chamber back to ground pressure. With two final bangs, the main exterior doors flapped open when there was no longer a suction to hold them closed. Ryan ran in with the main aerospace doctor and me on his heels to simulate pulling off Alan's helmet. The doctor would diagnose the situation and signal to Ryan and me as to whether the suit team should rush in and pull Alan out of the suit, or he would administer aid right away. The scenario took just over 40 seconds. That's how long it would take us to get Alan to a safe breathable atmosphere if our worst fears became real.

Most everyone scattered. Alan stayed with the suit team to get hoisted up. He changed into his flight undergarments. We tested out some new gear to make the suit easier to put on: some Teflon leggings and straps that laced through the arms for pulling. Getting in was easy. Alan pulled on the straps and wiggled into the top half of the suit while Ryan and I guided his head over the oxygen spray bar so he wouldn't smash his lip on it. The long test would begin the following morning, in 16 hours.

Alan made us confident in our ability to get him into the suit in the small area. Rolfe and I connected the plate with our little hole in it to do our one pending test before we could tell the advisors we were truly ready to run.

Once the plate was sealed onto the exhaust-pipe-sized pass-through, the chamber operator threw the valves to the vacuum pumps fully open and closed off the valves to outside air so that the chamber would suck down in a hurry. In 10 minutes we settled out at 90,000 feet. The hole test showed that Alan's breathing into the chamber would not significantly change the final chamber altitude. Our final checkbox, with 13 hours to go. We headed to the hotel to eat, sleep, and prepare ourselves mentally for the first new-suit vacuum test the world had seen in decades.

Trying to guess the outcome of a development test like this was like guessing the winner of a footrace on an ice rink: knowing the fastest runner on dry land matters, but not as much as you'd think. Many say, "Hope for the best; plan for the worst." We said, "Plan for the worst; run the test."

It was becoming a tradition for the teams to eat together before big tests to get our heads together and into the game. I wondered how we blended in with the 4 a.m. sea of faces at Denny's the next morning, two hours ahead of the chamber meeting at 6. The other faces looked worn out. I wondered which people were up early and which were finishing out the night. Our faces probably looked blank, with traces of fear and excitement.

There were too many people and too much chitchat at the briefing. We started seven minutes late. We cared about things like that now. We'd come a long way since our first tests, which started weeks late and ended minutes later. Alan put on his flight undergarments (including the diaper this time, and the ingestible core body temperature pill). He sat calmly in his metal folding chair, beyond complaint, his demeanor belying the terror of what he approached.

At 6:37 Alan began to breathe pure oxygen and would continue to do so for two hours. This was the first time pre-breathing would be a necessity. The problem of nitrogen fizzing up in his blood was not theoretical today.

The pre-breathe was textbook. Everything was in place. We moved when we were supposed to move and stayed put when we were supposed to stay put. Beyond the light annoyances of too many people in too small a room, everything was humming as the morning progressed. Checkboxes were checked. Valves were turned.

Two hours into the preparation, we moved Alan into the suit, where he would finish the pre-breathe. Even though we weren't going to need another two hours in the suit (time that would normally be used to scoop Alan onto the lift that would move him to the launch pad), we followed the flight timelines. We wanted to maximize our exposure to the actual processes and locate any minor crisscross of detail that could lie at the root of a spiral to disaster. Obsessive routine was our weapon of force.

We got Alan into his pants. The new slips for guiding in the legs worked; the amount of grunting was significantly reduced. We got his boots on. In order to thread Alan's head and torso into the upper half of the suit, he would have to disconnect from the pre-breathing apparatus. The math said that the fact that he would be breathing nitrogen-saturated air mattered. Once in the suit, he would be hooked back up to the pre-breathing system to purge the inhaled nitrogen from his blood.

We notified Sebastian in mission control, just a few feet away, and received clearance for a pre-breathe break. Mitch lined up on the right side of the suit with Zane on the left. Zane would hold the mask and time the break, while Ryan guided Alan's head into place and put on the flight mask.

"Flight, this is PSA requesting clearance to don the pressure suit. Be advised of imminent pre-breathe break during suit donning."

We counted to three. Alan took off his pre-breathe mask, pulling nitrogen-filled air into his lungs for the first time in two and a half hours. Zane took the mask and Alan crouched to push his head through the familiar tunnel of rubbery bladder. Alan grabbed the new nylon guide straps Mitch had made, and Ryan pulled him through. The flight helmet went on quickly, and then in seconds we were sealing the bubble. The helmet latched, and the ground oxygen lines attached. In the amount of time it takes to tie your shoes, we had put on the top half of the suit and gotten Alan back on oxygen.

Buttoning up the rest of the suit felt casual. The left glove took some wiggling to get clicked into place. The rest was smooth. We clicked the leg garments into the upper half. Closed the helmet. Alan was locked away. Blikkies grabbed the parachute pack, threaded his limbs through the cramped spaces around the suit, and installed the pack, shimmying his arms into crevasses, snapping clips.

I turned the dial on the pressure controller to start bringing the suit up to pressure. Alan's inhalations pulled oxygen from the tanks; his exhalations pressurized the suit. The suit legs shifted, growing subtly wider. After a few turns and a nod from our pilot, the controller was all the way closed. We waited for the suit to pressurize, pressed the partially stiffened fabric over and over, but something was wrong. The suit wasn't going to pressure. We opened the controller to depressurize the suit, closed it again, and tried to troubleshoot why the suit refused to take on full pressure. Once Alan was hanging from the gantry, we would have gauges telling us the suit pressure, but at this particular moment, Alan was lying on the ground on top of the access panel, so the system was powered down. We didn't have to know the exact pressure to know that it was it was less than full.

We weren't particularly rushed. We had lots of time because we weren't carrying out the process of driving Alan to the launch site. Still, the minutes flew by quickly. Something was stopping the suit from getting all the way up. If the pressure control was faulty, or even questionable, it would be the end of our test, and another hold for the program. We'd have to wait weeks for the controller to come back. We were stumped.

We started checking seals to see if there was a huge unseen leak causing the pressure to stay down. I held my oxygen detector next to the left glove that had given us a problem earlier, and sure enough, it beeped. We pulled the glove and there it was, clear as day: a seal had been pulled out while we were putting the glove on, probably from a piece of fabric getting trapped inside.

The blown seal was unnerving, but still a minor issue. We had the time. Ryan and Mitch could replace that seal in minutes. and we'd be back in action. Through the whole event Alan was on the radio with Ryan talking through what was going on. His vitals stayed solid: heart rate, breathing rate, body temperature all read like he was watching a particularly dull romantic comedy. The new seal went in and the glove went on like butter. We tested the seal and it was good. I turned the knob and straightaway the suit took on pressure. It climbed up to full pressure, where Alan flashed a thumbs-up from inside his shell, his home for the next four hours.

We hoisted the suit up close to the gantry beam. The rigid suit tilted easily into place above the steel floor of the chamber. We still had plenty of time to go before the call for doors closed. With the suit in place, we could power the system on, hook up the suit cooling system, and go through the final checkout items. We had run the data transmission system through a wire outside the chamber where it would be less likely to interfere with the voice communications. We tested all the communication, and the transmissions were crystal clear. The heating system worked as expected; the sensors were all reading nominal. All systems go. Spirits were high and tense. Alan said he was going to take a nap.

Ryan had promised Alan that he could sleep for half an hour before being alerted for the test. With time to spare, Alan again showed an unimaginable calm as he decided to nap while the team cycled through taking pictures of him in the suit inside the chamber waiting for the doors to close.

Ryan held his post. Alan wanted the time to calm and clear his head. I ate a bagel in the 1970s snack room, and there, facing a row of cabinets, tried to tame my own thought process into a simple, singular focus.

The minutes rolled off until we were close enough to start the preparation process. I tucked under the suit to pull the ground power cable. We notified mission control. We spoke on headsets with CIA-style earpieces. We followed strict radio protocols. We spoke only when the procedures indicated we should speak or to report an unexpected event. I used my call sign PSA (pressure suit assembly) while Sebastian, the flight director, used the call sign flight.

"Flight, this is PSA, requesting permission to move to flight power."

"PSA, this is flight, proceed."

Before closing the doors, we would pull the ground power and the ground oxygen and check the sensor responses one last time. The ground power cable, which we had just received permission to remove, came off. We notified mission control. We were ready for oxygen disconnect. Mitch and I got into position next to the suit on either side, ready to pull the ground oxygen. We notified mission control and counted three. Disconnected. Alan was on his own supply.

As we worked our way awkwardly out to the chamber door, Mitch gave a startle. He held up a wire. I squinted to figure out what I was looking at. It was the coaxial cable that was supposed to be going to the data antenna port. In normal operation, a data antenna would connect directly to the port. Because the chamber is a big steel box, we had opted to wire the radio antennas outside so they wouldn't be in a faraday cage with all the other signals. In the tight shuffle around the suit, Mitch had stepped on the cable and pulled the fragile wire apart. Without the antenna, the high-powered amplifier that supplies the heightened signal to the antenna was pushing hard against nothing and would overheat if we let it. I dropped to the ground, reached under the equipment pack, flipped the switch, and powered the system down. We were minutes before the door closed. Alan's displays went black. His heart rate showed he was still calm.

I rushed up to consult with Sebastian about what to do as we rolled past the scheduled time to doors closed. Sebastian calmed me down, reminding me that the protocols called for 15 minutes of oxygen use on the ground. We decided to bypass the cable and attach the antenna directly to the port on the suit. We would have to try our luck with radio interference instead of jumping into the longer process of repairing the cable while sucking down our flight oxygen. Once the antenna was attached, we powered the system on. Within seconds we had reestablished communications with the hardware and executed a simple communications test: Alan was asked to count to 10 over the radio. If the signals were interfering intermittently, numbers in the count would go missing. All 24 of us sat dead silent listening to Alan count, waiting to hear the missing number that never came. The signals weren't interfering. With just a few minutes lost, we were ready to close the doors. Ryan executed his symbolic radio pass-off, handing the pilot over to mission control, who would guide him through the rest of his low-pressure journey to a silence found only in that chamber and in the darkness of space.

We marked the time and called doors closed. Mitch closed the far door at his post and I closed the interior door, exchanging a final glance with Alan. I backed out of the antechamber and closed the outer door, setting the locks so the chamber could start sucking down. In an instant the profile programs were started. We had begun our journey.

Everyone was in the place they were assigned to stand. Behind the chamber was the suit team doctor, who also ran the ground carts when Zane was in mission control (which he was). Blikkies was in charge of the parachute system, which in this test consisted mostly of putting it on and taking it off. Mitch was responsible for monitoring the suit equipment at the back of the chamber. On the side of the chamber was the state-licensed surgeon along with Rolfe. At the front were Ryan and I for suit matters, and the primary doctor in charge of diagnosing Alan in the event of an emergency. On the other side of the chamber were the control panels, where Norman stood with the two chamber operators (one responsible for the main chamber and the other in control of the antechamber) and the crew chief for the chamber team. At the front of the room by the main door was mission control, with a communications tech, Sebastian as flight director,

Zane monitoring suit systems, Dan monitoring avionics, and Dr. Clark heading up the medical staff. Finally, at the door was a group of spectators, including John, our launch/lunch director, Taber, and Alan's pilot, all there to watch. The whole crew was attentive, silent, communicating only when necessary and holding a steady eye on our precious cargo.

The radios were set to speaker so the room could hear the transmissions between Sebastian and Alan. We marked the altitude calls as the pressure began to drop. A wrist altimeter came to life. A light on the helmet began to blink, indicating pressures that simulated rising altitude. We stared at it as it went up and up: 10,000 feet, then 25,000 feet, higher. Alan checked his onboard altimeters with the chamber-monitoring equipment to verify they were staying close to one another. Taped inside the chamber door where Alan could see it was a color chart with lots of colored squares surrounded by gray. If Alan went hypoxic, the red boxes should start to look gray, and the lines between the boxes and the border would blend. Sebastian would occasionally ask Alan if he could still see the boxes; he always could.

A boring test is a good test. The lack of surprise in the slow rise to altitude in that chamber was a testament to our maturity as a suit team and as a program. Proof we were getting close to being ready for our big day. Sebastian called out the important altitudes. At 45,000 feet we left the altitudes considered safe for unsuited travel, then at 63,000 feet we crossed Armstrong's line and it was official: we were the first known new suit to reach the deadly vacuum above Armstrong's line since the cold war era. Sebastian kept Alan busy with arm exercises to verify suit mobility, pull handle checks, and reading his hypoxia chart. Alan retained a meditative calm through the test, consuming less oxygen than he ever had in any previous test. (Typically, people breathe harder when they are nervous.) His heart rate never accelerated past benign calm. As the altitude cleared above anything airplanes can reach, the chamber leveled off. We would simulate the remainder of the climb to full altitude simply by waiting. The difference in pressure between where we were and the deepest deep space was fractions of a fraction compared with full sea level pressure. Our suit was working, first try, in the desperate emptiness of vacuum.

We waited out the last hour with building giddy happiness as we saw the systems all working and normal. In the last minutes of the run, we had to complete a final test of the purge valve. At full altitude Alan could need it—if he vomited into his facemask, for instance—so we would test it before starting the simulated freefall. This part of the test was again unnerving. The doctors were alerted, knowing we were about to intentionally create a hole in the suit in a vacuum. When Alan opened the purge valve, the oxygen from the helmet region was supposed to rush out into the chamber. To replace the oxygen that was rushing away, the regulator supplying air to the helmet each time the pilot breathed would open up and send air from the tanks in at the same rate as air rushed out. To Alan this would feel like a loud wind flying past his face. The chamber crew would see a drop in chamber altitude, while the suit team hoped to see no change at all.

Alan began by cracking the valve to make sure he had good control of its function. Then he turned it fully open. Nothing unexpected happened. Alan counted to five, as directed by Sebastian, and then closed the valve. A collective sigh of relief mixed with a palpable sense of excitement. The descent began, simulating the jump elevations. As the case would be in the actual jump, the elevation plummeted right off the bat. At the start of the fall, the suit would accelerate to a speed faster than the proverbial speeding bullet, with altitude peeling off the altimeters fast. In a few breaths we were back below Armstrong's line, where a major catastrophe wouldn't be all that catastrophic.

The altitude burned away. Sebastian called out the readings. Soon we fell below 45,000 feet, where people not wearing suits can safely go. The pressure simulated the long, harrowing fall. When Alan's suit altimeter passed the mark where he would pull his parachute, he reached for a simulated handle and executed the pull. The descent slowed again, simulating the parachute being fully open. Now the altimeter showed a slow, peaceful fall under canopy. The team let go their first cheer of the day. Alan was down in safe air. There was nothing left that could go drastically wrong.

Alan called to mission control that he would depressurize the suit. He reached up and turned the brand-new depressurization knob. For the first time Alan performed the operation himself. The air hissed out of the suit and his pressure equalized with the now-safe atmosphere around him. The team had their second cheer, initiated by Zane, when mission control reported that the suit had depressurized, a win that lifted a load off the minds of the whole team. At last, Alan could depressurize his own suit.

The altitude continued to drop. The two chambers equalized and the center door swung open. Now Alan could see the shining faces of the suit team poised at the outer window, prepared to race in as soon as the pressure in the chamber equalized with the room outside. When the big doors to the room swung open, we rushed in. The test was over. For the first time in the program, the first time in two years of sometimes bitterly frustrating offshoots and testing miffs, we had gotten one right, a nearly flawless test, just in time.

The thermal mitts we were trying out had half fallen off, so Alan couldn't quite manipulate the latch to remove the helmet. Knowing the gloves were going to be better fastened in the permanent version, we didn't let that faze us. Ryan took the helmet off, and we proceeded to lower the suit down and extract the victorious pilot—who had lived to fly again.

Post-test briefings were the easiest they had ever been. We talked a bit about the gloves and some cramping Alan had felt, but they were all small issues. Accomplishments: we passed our test. Failures: none to note. The leaders of the group all took a moment to praise the nature of our collective achievement. Two individuals were particularly responsible for this success.

Two years prior, Ryan Lee had been informed that his company was to build a self-contained spacesuit for some crazy rich man who wanted to use it to jump from the stratosphere. He and his close colleagues designed it, piece by piece, fabric and rubber square by fabric and rubber square, test by test. On that day, as Alan walked out of the chamber, Ryan's success was apparent. He had played a central role in the design of a suit that would work in the aggressive, deadly vacuum of space. Quietly, he told us this was the greatest day of his career.

The other man of the moment was Alan himself. The months prior to this test had been trying and arduous. People were worried about how much oxygen Alan had sucked down in every previous test, generating fears that we might not have enough oxygen to finish a mission. A dread had been rising over Alan's repeated failure to depressurize the suit himself, especially the time this failure led to a crash landing in the desert without steering control. We were already worried about how he would react under the intense conditions of a hostile vacuum around him. We worried whether anxiety would raise his breathing rates and overturn his ability to make the suit go limp. Those concerns evaporated that day. Alan showed that he would have enough oxygen to do the mission twice. He had stayed perfectly calm through every second of the test, even the parts when he didn't have to. When the fairy tale parachute shot above his head, he depressurized the suit cleanly.

We had plenty of time to clean up the chamber. It was early afternoon. Per usual, we started tests at 5 in the morning to allow plenty of time for mistakes, malfunctions, and delays. Instead of being hours late, as we had been with past tests, we were a mere seven minutes late this time. When the cleanup was finished, we went straight to a brewery, where we downed beer after beer in celebration beneath a winter sky, the sky Alan would be exploring soon.

January 2014: Manned Thermal Test III

The team was on a journey into the unknown. It was a journey undertaken through our actions: rebuilding our suit over and over again, learning what the thermally accommodating upper stratosphere just beyond the thermally devastating upper troposphere really was, inch by inch in chambers, again and again. The test ahead of us would be our third session in a cold box in a hot desert. Including multiple runs per session, it would be the fifth individual test run. Long ago there was a time when we thought we would test in a cold chamber only once.

This was the second time we felt the airy high of success and the smell of our final voyage. We were constantly reminded by the executive team that as tests finish up and teams like this get close, it becomes tempting to sprint for the finish line. This is when it's easiest to forget a detail that could cost something big. In failure we were lectured; in success we were lectured. At the dawn of a new year, well into the second year since the first conversations about this mission and just under two years since its official start, we had just one more environmental test to finish. The thermal chamber test.

Each of the first four thermal tests had been aborted before it was complete. The first test was lost when we found our pilot was boiling and our equipment was freezing. Alan had overheated in an overly insulated suit on an absurdly hot day, while at the same time we had left an access panel on the support pack hanging open and allowed frigid air to shoot inside. Just before the equipment started to freeze, we called the session off. Test 2 was lost to cold. Alan couldn't get his glove heaters turned on, and rather than sacrifice his hands to science we sacrificed the test. At that point we were down to communicating with hand signals through glass, both our radios having succumbed to the cold. (Luckily, the "abort" hand signal doesn't require much dexterity.) Test 3 was an early abort from heater cutouts, eventually attributed to bad batteries. Test 4 was the morale-shattering suit overpressure event caused by an iced-up suit pressure controller. We were approaching test five with a suit we'd updated to cover every previous failure and an iron resolve to knock this test home.

If the thermal test passed, the suit team would go into high gear again. After a simple communications test, we would return to airplane jumping, facing a host of new demons and the challenges of the desert. The completion of environmental testing would mark the true end of what had turned out to be a very long design process.

We had returned home to our frankenfreezer in the back parking lot of the company headquarters in Tucson. The thermal chamber was set up by the chamber crew days before the teams started to arrive. The outhouse-sized tank of liquid nitrogen was refilled and the ground stations collected to get ready for the test.

Ryan and Mitch flew into town to start our phase zero operation and install all of the new thermal covers on the chestpack and over the pressure controller. These would hopefully be the reason this test passed where others had failed. We had a smooth routine now, all the way down to finding hotels and scheduling advisors. The processes felt easy, too easy, perhaps. The advisors didn't like to see us so relaxed; they thought we needed pressure to be forced to pay attention. Maybe we did, but it felt easy anyway.

We worked through the phase zero steps in the normal fashion, no faster than the previous times, but better. Better because we missed fewer steps. Better because we knew where everything was. Instead of spending time fixing physical things, we spent time on fixing the method, refining ourselves as a team.

Esteban had replaced the main batteries in the system weeks before we got there, so the job was even easier. After half a day, the new thermal covers were on, making the whole suit a shiny white. We needed Alan to stay warm without the surface of the suit overheating. A black cover layer outside the presence of a regulating atmosphere would make the suit surface hot enough to melt. So we chose white, the least absorptive of the available colors and the same color chosen by spacewalkers of the past few decades. The fabric we used was laced with glistening fibers to make it more reflective. With the heating effect of sunlight reduced, we needed to insulate the suit more to retain the reliable heat generated by human metabolism in the cold parts of the atmosphere. As the design process continued, all our components became white.

After being rigged into the chamber, the suit was again dripping with thermocouple wires flowing like old-man hairs toward the ground. We also added a watch to the suit. In pretty stark contrast to my personal sense of excitement when I was in the suit, it was becoming apparent that Alan was often very bored. It seemed like his biggest concern hanging in a chamber near dead vacuum was knowing the time. We found him an aviator's watch rated to work in a near vacuum and at arctic temperatures. We weren't going to test it, nor would the mission rely on it for any reason, but he would have a watch.

To begin the test, I would do an integration testing session in the suit to make sure that our many modifications worked in concert, and that the changes hadn't introduced a new, unanticipated problem. We would run the suit through all of its functions without heating the chamber. We especially wanted to know if some modifications Mitch and Ryan had made to the gloves worked. We also wanted to re-rig the suspension system better. In the last thermal test, Alan's feet were touching the ground where the liquid nitrogen pooled, making for dangerously cold temperatures near his toes.

Blikkies rolled into town the next day to rig with us and get me into the chamber for the integration tests. The suit had accomplished its phase zero testing. Over the course of a full day, we had checked every one of the several hundred preparation boxes to make sure the suit was safe for use. It was.

Our astronaut advisor Ed Lu suggested that a person had to spend dozens of hours—from him and others we'd heard 32—in a pressure suit before starting to feel natural in it. I was closing in on his number with great anticipation. I followed careful preparations before going into the suit. For two days prior to a suit session, I ate a special diet, didn't drink alcohol, and kept a strict sleep schedule. It was beginning to feel less strange to have it on. Alan had spent a similar amount of time in the suit. Motions were becoming routine. Our heart rates had leveled out, suggesting that we had fewer moments of panic when we wondered if something in the suit had failed. I used to spend my time thinking about whether the oxygen had been turned on, or if a hot feeling indicated a malfunctioning cooling system. I was better at telling when the rising discomfort was just a confined brain sending panic signals to its conscious self.

Spacesuits, with their combination of sensory deprivation and over-stimulation, make it hard to diagnose things that are simply commonplace in everyday life. It was strangely very difficult to differentiate sensations. Sometimes I thought I was very cold when in reality the sensors would say I was very hot. The confusions and oddities of wearing this spacesuit subsided slowly, use by use. I think the advice was right: after 32 hours, one could feel normal in a spacesuit. Alan was on track to make that number by the time he would wear the suit for the real ride.

We set up on a cool winter day in the desert Southwest to do our integration testing. If all went well, we would do the integration run in the evening before the actual tests. We slowly got prepared in the frankenfreezer. Because the freezer had all the equipment to hold the suit, we often used it for testing at normal temperatures. In those cases, it was functionally just a small room with a convenient gantry. We got there as the sun started to fade toward the horizon. I stepped inside the freezer to put on the long underwear that went inside the liquid-filled thermal garment with its network of tubing wrapping my body like vines around a statue.

While I was occupied inside the suit, Zane operated as the lead for the pressure suit team, executing the steps in his meticulous, matter-of-fact manner. The lead holds the checklists, instructs people when to perform the requested actions, and makes all the radio calls to mission control. I put on the pants. Ryan and Mitch laced the boots up and started the ground cart checkout. Once the ground cart was ready, I hobbled under the hanging suit's upper half. In our refined three-minute swoop, I ducked under the torso portion of the suit and pushed through the fabric for my 15th time.

The long snaky oxygen lines and thick insulated water lines were hooked up. Within a few more minutes the helmet was sealed. Once again, I was separate from everyone else in the room, hanging in pure silence while a room around me bustled with the activity of clicking lines and turning valves. It felt like one of those scenes in a movie where the people around a subject begin to move at super-fast speeds while the subject stands perfectly still and the soundtrack falls to silence. In the suit, I had left the company of the people around me. I had also caught on that when inside a suit, it is better not to try to help with anything. It's not in my nature to stand idle but after working with Alan in the suit for so long now, I had realized that it's the opposite of assistance when you to try to help. You have too little connection with reality to be useful and too little sensory feedback not be clumsy about everything. Most of the time being a spacesuit test subject means sitting there and doing exactly what people tell you to do, which most of the time is nothing at all.

We had anticipated a 20-minute session where we got the suit pressurized, cycled through each of the things a pilot needs to do with their hands, including using our new valve to depressurize the suit. The last test was the biggest unknown: I would try to open the helmet wearing the new, thicker gloves. Once again, the testing took far longer than we originally planned.

I sat and watched in silence, the Darth Vader breathing noises filling my head in rhythmic repetitive calm. There was a problem with the length of the straps that would hold the suit up after it was reoriented into its flight position at 45 degrees. Almost half an hour went by while four people worked in concert to lower the suspension straps enough that they would reach, but not so much that Alan's feet would soak in a pool of liquid nitrogen. It was finally properly adjusted and I was being pulled into the air and then dropped back into the strap web that would hold me. Now it was time to perform.

Ryan called items from a checklist telling me what I needed to try to do with the new gloves on. I worked the push-to-talk toggle and cycled my temperature up and down. I grabbed the parachute pull handles, turned the purge valve, touched the depress valve, and gave Ryan the trusty thumbs-up after a couple cycles. Easy-peasy. All that suiting up for five minutes of hitting toggles, pulling handles, and opening valves. All that was left was to open the depress valve, empty the suit of air, and try to take my helmet off. The depress valve turned easily and the sonic hiss of air rushing out the hose filled the bubble. It cleared out and left me lying in a limp suit, angled over the frankenfreezer's steel floor.

With another thumbs-up, I reached for the latch to open the helmet. I grabbed it, but with the thicker gloves, things that I knew were features now felt like dull bumps. First I needed to push two small buttons at the same time to unseat the latch. Then the latch became a long lever that could be cranked forward to open the helmet. I found a technique that let me locate the buttons, and with the right pressure, managed to release it into my hand, grasp it, and pull it back to let the helmet come open. Oxygen blasted my face as the spray nozzle went full on in the helmet. Ryan pushed the bubble back over my head with the familiar clank and locked it up for another go. After two more successes, we were convinced the helmet could, theoretically, be removed by a thickly gloved hand. My test was done.

It took 15 minutes to transfer the suit back from its 45-degree orientation to the vertical orientation and get out. We packed up and secured the freezer. I got dressed. A text on my phone said that Alan and Julian had left the West Coast and were on their way to the chamber. In about 12 hours we would suit up Alan to hang in the unearthly cold for his fifth and hopefully final time.

There was a lingering sense that we were too confident. The executives repeated their usual warning that we were in danger of slacking off on the heels of our successful vacuum test. The checklists provided restraint. They left no room for the inevitable confidence and arrogance that come with success.

Morning was on us. We gathered casually for breakfast at around 6, targeting 7 a.m. for the pre-test briefings. Mitch and I arrived early to re-secure the suit shell that had been removed to charge the radio batteries. All was ready at 7 when the briefing began.

So many kinks had been ironed out. The chamber team knew what they had to do and had done it. There were no looming uncertainties about the outside temperature being too hot or how we had configured mission control. We were ready.

The familiar bustle consumed the next couple hours. The ground stations were set up, run through their pre-use checklists, moved into position, and rechecked. Pop-up tents with computer consoles to control the temperature profiles were erected and checked. The now well-used spinal cord of thermocouple wires was run through a pass-through in the chamber and splayed against the wall in a dendritic bloom of tendrils, each individually taped and ready to be hooked to its receptacle when the time came.

Around 9 Alan was given the message to suit up. For such a big test, Alan suited up with the med team. Two doctors did the undergarments with him and went through the preflight examination, where he could confidentially disclose any information that might make the test or flight unsafe for that particular day. If Alan had the runs or a nasty head cold, for example, he could simply let the doctors know. Even a few poor nights' sleep could scrub the test. They would fail him on his preflight exam without embarrassing disclosures to the whole team. No medical concerns stood in the way. The doctors cleared him for the test.

We were through the checklists and cheerily made the call for him to come out. The pants were laid out on the table, the boots beside them. The process began with no hesitation: pants on, boots on, cover layers down. Checkboxes: check, check, check. We followed every preflight procedure. We had printed out a new textbook-sized set of procedures, as we did for a major test. Each time a step was completed, a check mark was put next to the step in the procedure. At the end of the test, the sheets would be scanned into the computer as a record of the actual process.

"Mission control, this is PSA requesting permission to don the pressure suit."

"Permission granted, go ahead."

"Simulated pre-breathe break start, mask off."

Alan ducked down into the womb for his 15th time.

We trucked forward: helmet on, mask on, oxygen ready, bubble down, bubble locked, tanks on, oxygen on. (We didn't actually turn the oxygen on until after the bubble was sealed to conserve oxygen.) Alan was sealed into the silence. After the gloves and the waist ring, he was ready for the parachute. Left leg into the parachute leg loop, right leg, hoist parachute up to the shoulders, left arm, right arm, ready to clip, left clip, right clip, ready for handle locks. The handles resided on the chestpack and they routed to the pack, so we had to hook them up after the parachute was installed. Main deploy 1, main deploy 2, main cutaway, reserve deploy, and the parachute pack is on. We were ready to pressurize.

"Mission control, this is PSA requesting permission to pressurize."

"PSA, this is mission control, go ahead."

We signaled Alan thumbs-up. He responded in kind. Valves open, pressure rising, full pressure, pressure controller opens to stop the pressure from rising further.

The new, very important over-mitts were installed. These mitts went over the suit gloves to provide even more warmth. Mitch and Ryan put them on with the suit pressurized in order to make sure they were oriented properly while in their final shape. Alan practiced working the switches and grabbing the handles with the gloves on, while we hustled around him turning our levers and checking our boxes.

The one thing we had added as a result of my run in the suit was a quick check of Alan removing the helmet himself so that we could buy down the risk even further that something specific to his anatomy would restrict him from getting that helmet off. We had to pressurize the suit in order to get the gloves on, and the helmet won't come off unless the suit has no pressure. So we had to accept the annoying delay, depressurize the suit, try the helmet release, then re-pressurize the suit to continue with the test. It was one more chance for Alan to practice depressurizing the suit and experiment more with the new gloves. Without waiting (we'd grown to be less and less tolerant of waiting as the program progressed), we gave him the thumbs-up to pull the helmet off. He reached up, and a drawback of the new gloves was instantly visible, one the rest of the team had noticed with me the day before. As he groped for the buttons to unseat the latch and remove his helmet, the glove fabric bunched and wadded. He did it, though. The latch swung open and the helmet popped up into Ryan's hands. Ryan pushed the helmet right back down to reseat it. Alan gave it another go and off it came. It looked as though he could do it. Continue test.

We pressurized again, then swung the main attachment web in place to move Alan into the 45-degree hanging configuration where he'd be more comfortable and in a position more representative of the flight configuration. We lifted him into the air and dropped him down where he sank into the now-familiar angled resting position where he would stay for the foreseeable future.

It did become readily apparent leading up to the test that things were taking longer than our very hopeful and increasingly impatient minds wished. It was 10 in the morning; we were supposed to be in the middle of the cold test. Alan's feet were slightly scraping the ground, in danger of over-chilling in a pool of liquid nitrogen. I had my first aggravated snap while we were trying to manipulate the webbing to get them up. Mission control was pestering us about making Alan face the camera. I shot back a snarky "We can't turn him, is that clear?" on a radio broadcast to a dozen people. I quickly and bashfully proceeded to help turn and secure him so he was facing the camera. Long morning.

At almost that exact moment, Ryan took Alan's brand-new watch (which he was very excited about) off his wrist. We had discussed previously that to avoid our new watch failing in the chamber and altering something unexpected in the test, we would remove it. The watch was somewhat secret at that point. We wanted Alan to have his watch, but we didn't want to go through the rigmarole of qualifying it, so we were sneaking it in without testing, without promising him it would actually work, and without telling management about it. We'd just let him wear it on the real day. Unfortunately, the secrecy hadn't been properly conveyed to Alan, and with the whole project team listening to the radio conversation we tried not to be caught out. For reasons only Alan knows, he was really annoyed not to be able to check the time. We couldn't just say over the radio that he would have to do without it for these particular four hours lest a whole lot of bureaucratic panties get into a twist. So we made him suffer with no explanation. He didn't like it.

We all settled our simmering heads. Alan hung properly oriented in the suit. It was time to turn control over to the chamber team. With a newfound efficiency, they plugged each of the thermocouple cords leading from the suit, one by one, into the ends of the splay of cords taped to the wall and leading to the suit. As each sensor came alive, the tech outside the chamber would yell back the thermocouple number and the temperature it was reading to indicate it was active: "Thermocouple 37, 87 degrees."

As the chamber team finished up, I walked around the suit performing our final, most important checklist. I made sure everything was turned on, hooked up, and otherwise all ready for flight. Zane made the same lap behind me, putting a second pair of eyes on every critical piece of the puzzle. We stepped through the big heated doors into the midday sunlight, ready to start the fifth journey into the cold.

The chamber team walked through the last of their checks with the same remarkable fluidity with which we had prepared Alan. We were all feeling how much the team was operating as a unit. We caught the contrast with our first time in this chamber when, at this point in the process, we were in the machine shop hacking our components into pieces trying to make them fit around the shell. Now, less than 20 hours since Alan had touched his jet down at the airport, he was watching the last technician exit his chamber and close the door so he could experience an environment colder than almost any human, alive or dead, ever had.

The doors swung closed. The giant metal latch handles locked around their roller stops, engaging the thermal seals. Alan was truly alone in there. Now for the waiting.

We knew the drill. Two by the front door and two by the back, hoping we'd do nothing but wait. The math for determining stratospheric flight durations is easy because balloons tend to ascend at 1,000 feet per minute. We assumed a rise to 135,000 feet and a 15-minute float at the top. 150 minutes.

In actual flight, the balloon would rise through increasingly colder air until it reached the tropopause, around 65,000 feet. This would be the coldest part of Alan's flight and is functionally the coldest part of Earth's atmosphere for a person. After this point, the temperature of the atmosphere would start to rise and the suit surface would begin to warm. While rising through this part of the atmosphere, a second phenomenon starts to take effect; the thin atmospheric air stops being an effective heat-transfer media. The air getting warmer and the temperature of the air becoming less relevant combine to make the upper part of the stratosphere quite thermally accommodating to a person in a suit. With the upper troposphere and lower stratosphere being so cold and deep space being functionally hot, we knew there had to be a place in the middle where the temperatures were just right. Alan was going to find that place.

Temperature and Air Pressure at Altitude

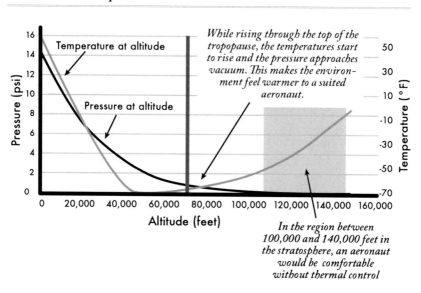

While rising through the top of the tropopause, the temperatures start to rise and the pressure approaches vacuum. This makes the environment feel warmer to a suited aeronaut.

Temperature at altitude

Pressure at altitude

In the region between 100,000 and 140,000 feet in the stratosphere, an aeronaut would be comfortable without thermal control

Our test flight profile was built off a thermal analysis that attempted to keep the suit surface temperatures at what they were expected to be during flight. Because the analysis that produced the suit-surface temperature profile was very conservative on the cold side, the whole test was extremely conservative. Using this method would require chamber temperatures far below the suit-surface temperatures at the coldest part of the test. At about 70 minutes into the test, it would be more than negative 90 degrees Fahrenheit around Alan.

Perhaps it has become apparent that much of the work is done long before the test starts. The actual test is certainly stressful and tense, but a successful test is entirely uneventful and consists mostly of waiting. For Alan, a successful test would involve the usual discomfort and whatever effort it takes to report cold spots at the edges of his circulatory system where the heating fluids didn't reach. In addition, he had to endure not knowing what time it was.

The first minutes of the test were the most nerve-wracking. If something was wrong with the system (like us failing to change the main batteries, as had happened on a previous test), it would come out early. The beginning of this test ticked through smoothly. Every few minutes, Sebastian would relay the simulated altitude and temperature in the chamber to Alan. The temperatures fell sharply at the beginning of the profile, simulating the temperature drops known to anyone ascending to a high mountaintop. Next, the trip progressed through the Himalayan summit altitudes where no humans can go without specialized thermal gear. Leaving behind the

Himalayan altitudes, Alan entered an area seldom visited by humans not enclosed within an airplane, rocket, or balloon capsule.

By the time our simulation exited the altitudes where jetliners zoom, 45 minutes had passed and the chamber was clouded with liquid nitrogen vapor. The computers, hooked to the liquid nitrogen solenoid valves, continued to control the liquid nitrogen flow and hold the chamber temperature right on its mark as it plunged dozens of degrees below zero degrees Fahrenheit. This is where the temperatures moved into the second, tense part of the mission.

At around the altitude where we leave the realm of commercial aviation, the reliability of commercial products becomes the source of tension. Most products, even aviation products, will never be in an environment as cold as the upper troposphere. The difficulty of accessing that part of the sky makes it likely that most components have not been tested there. Our few tests would verify the compatibility of these products. Earlier tests had shown that our voice radio system and pressure controller failed in such cold. With new insulation, we hoped that they would work this time.

Alan communicated a request that he not be required to give a response to updates because grasping the metal knob to activate the speaker was too cold on his double-gloved hand. We waited in complete silence outside the frosted chamber doors as the stainless steel room reached its coldest temperature, about 150 degrees colder than where we were standing outside. We kept waiting and kept hoping that everything would continue to work.

A tense radio call to Alan that we were at the floor temperature was sent. We had learned the hard way in our previous test that reaching the lowest temperature didn't mean much. As the balloon crawled out of the tropopause, the temperatures would rise but painfully slowly, and the cold soak would keep sinking in. Every piece of exposed metal we were measuring was reading far below zero. There would be half an hour of squirming before the components would start to warm back up. At some point through the silence, Rolfe gave a radio update confirming that we were now further in the profile than any test had previously gotten.

There was still nothing to do but wait. A couple radio calls came from Alan telling us that his hands were cold. He was pulling his fingers out of the finger slots in the gloves and balling them up in the palm of the glove like I remember doing in winter as a kid. The minutes rolled off as we waited for something to crack. The low slope of the temperature graph from the deep negatives of the tropopause to the relatively balmy low negatives of the stratospheric vacuum was properly appreciated. As we crept up, the reports of cold hands continued. We knew our test was conservative, testing beyond the range of what we expected the mission to experience. All we wanted was to finish it.

Toward the end of the test, the temperature profile of the surface of the suit strangely departed from the temperature of the atmosphere. This was attributed to a quirk in how the predicting analysis was run. In order to produce a worst-case scenario, direct sunlight had been neglected (an assumption that would make test temperatures much lower than expected). The analysis did, however, retain reflected sunlight from the Earth. This meant that as the simulation sent the suit out of the blue sky and into the blackness of space at the beginning of the stratosphere, losing the effects of Earth-reflected sunlight, it sent the temperatures at the surface of the suit plummeting back deep into the negatives.

Knowing Alan had a potentially test-killing case of cold hands and that the neglect of direct sunlight was a wild exaggeration of the actual conditions, we met in mission control to discuss departing from the calculated chamber temperature profile and allowing the temperatures to rise to predicted atmospheric temperatures instead of trying to attain the predicted suit-surface temperatures, which seemed unnecessarily low. Just like that, we made it so. With the test three-quarters finished, we gave Rolfe the call to change the profile and follow the atmospheric temperatures instead of continuing to follow the lower suit-surface temperatures predicted by a model that disregarded sunlight.

At that call our hearts lightened. Once the temperatures began slipping back to recognizable terrestrial numbers, nothing could kill the test. As the minutes dropped off, we passed into the realm of a cold day in Fairbanks, then to the mountains of Montana, and back up into temperatures the test personnel had personally experienced, the negative teens, temperatures we knew Alan could survive just fine even without his suit.

The last part of our test was short and, unlike the peaceful extreme cold of space, was to be a loud intensity of super-cooled evaporated liquid nitrogen blasted at Alan through two fans stacked taller than a person. It would simulate a freefall back through the intense cold we'd spent hours riding through. The suit would accelerate to freefall speeds and experience the thickening atmosphere as wind.

There was little concern that the minutes-long freefall test wouldn't be completed. It was unlikely to compromise Alan's safety. The biggest thing of interest was whether the components would all be working after the freefall and, most importantly, whether the helmet fogged. The ultra-cold air would quickly send the surface of the plastic helmet bubble to a frigid glassy temperature, multiplying the effects that make a car windshield fog up if the defroster is turned off on a cold day. We had worked hard to keep all moisture out of the helmet; this part of the test would tell if we had succeeded.

To simulate the freefall, the test chamber crew turned on their massive cryogenic-grease-lubricated fans and opened all the liquid nitrogen nozzles full bore. After our simulated separation from the balloon, the temperatures would plummet back to those from the worst part of the flight in minutes, then rise away at the simulated entry into the troposphere. Because the temperatures wouldn't rise fast enough just by turning the nitrogen off, a choreographed yell dance would take place in which the test directors had the safety teams open the doors using wood spacer blocks to allow outside hot air to get sucked in through the fans and bring the temperatures up.

Alan was given the final call to prepare for descent and, like a good sport, he assumed the skydiving position and opened his eyes wide for a full frontal of vaporizing liquid nitrogen. Rolfe yelled for the start of the test, and the second fan swirled to life as the roaring expansive gas filled the chamber with a white condensate swirling viciously around Alan. As the temperatures fell back away from earthly norms, Alan moved his arms up and down, pretending to skydive through the clouds. This was the only part of the test when all the valves were open, and the roar of the rapidly expanding liquid plus the refrigerator-sized fans made the situation appropriately wild. White condensate made a thick barrier in front of the doors, and the visibility in the chamber dropped to near zero as we lost sight of the suit sitting right in front of the glass.

In what seemed like no time at all, the roaring stopped and Rolfe yelled to crack the doors small side (meaning to use the smallest orientation of the spacer). We unlatched the giant doors and in an instant the cold nitrogen vapor poured into the southwestern sky. The chamber was crystal clear, with a white frost coating everything except Alan's perfectly see-through helmet bubble. The last couple minutes of the test whizzed with the fans as more and more of the relatively piping-hot air was let in. Rolfe shouted commands, working to match the profile: "Long ways!" "Small side!" "Back to long ways!" to adjust the width of the slide holding the doors open. Mixing outside air with the freezing nitrogen was bringing the chamber back to outside temperature. There was no danger left in the test and truly nothing that could prevent us from finishing. The descent ended with a glorious "doors open" call, and we swung the barriers wide to let the fans finish clearing the suffocating nitrogen from the chamber. For the first time in our program's history, we weren't dancing impatiently at the door waiting for oxygen detectors to quit beeping so we could rush into the room and deal with a problem.

Everything was coated in white shiny crystals. The cool was accommodating. These were the moments we lived for in the project. Now, with two perfect tests in a row, the team was on a roll. In the cool breezy room, huge smiles darted in and of Alan's field of view as we scurried around, closing out checklists and readying the oxygen system for some helmet-doffing exercises.

We turned off the communications so we could lay the suit down in the position Alan was most likely to land and prepared to knock out the helmet work. Tired and cramped from hours in the suit, Alan was in the right state for the exercises. When Alan had to remove the dome on the real day, he would be blasted from hours of tension and minutes of continuous freefall. On the ground and with what were undoubtedly brutally tired arms, he reached to pry open the latch. Off came the helmet. A full evaluation, however, consisted of three successful removals, so against what I'm sure was Alan's every desire, we pushed the helmet back on and locked it down. He reached again, but this time, overcome by exhaustion, he couldn't fully depress the buttons through the bulky gloves. We turned him over and let him try again, but it was clear the fatigue went deep. One was all we would get that time.

We took that little hit to our morale right there at the glorious moment, opened the suit, and released Alan to his moment of sweet freedom. We agreed the helmet would need some work, but we weren't going to let that ruin our day. Off came the suit and out came the high-fives.

With only a couple of minor glitches, we had again won the day. Sweet, sweet progress. The satisfaction ran deep. The final environmental test was behind us. We were moving forward, skyward.

The team that executed the manned vacuum chamber testing posed for a photo after Alan successfully exited the chamber unharmed. This was the first manned vacuum chamber test to be performed on a new spacesuit design in over 30 years.

The suit is prepared for its final thermal test.

Ryan Lee and Mitch Sweeney, the suit guys, pose in front of the suit just before the vacuum chamber test started.

CHAPTER 11

...

Spun to Death

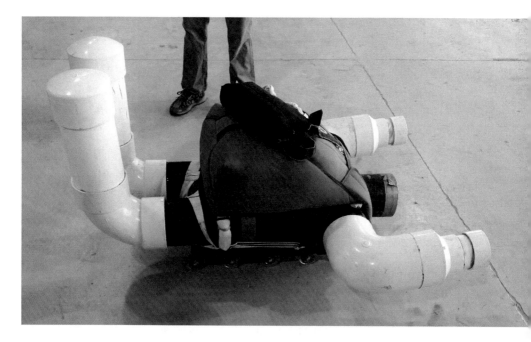

We started the spin testing with a passion reminiscent of an old version of ourselves, from before the grinding processes had chewed us up. We again saw the light at the end of the tunnel where our toils would finally pay off.

Dr. Clark had a big "I told you so" in store for us when we collectively admitted that the aggressive spin we saw in the dummy drop was not one the program could tolerate. He had been saying all along that flat spin was our biggest enemy and watched us shrug it off. We had been unable to see past the idea that a stabilization parachute was all we needed. It wasn't.

We finally accepted that whatever a human experienced in a stratospheric version of an atmospheric reentry was going to be different from what we expected from skydiving. It was possible that a pilot could reel around until the blood pressure at his brain rose to the point of hemorrhaging and permanent damage or death.

Conversations about the issue got heavy—and heated. Words like "fatal," "permanent," and the unsettling "acceptable risk" became commonplace once again. Each of us, and especially Alan, had to dig deep and ask, "Is the mission worth the danger?"

The threat posed by a stratospheric spin was our most challenging yet, and it took months to ultimately resolve it, through a process of deep analytic investigation, expert consultation, and eventually an architectural update to our parachute system. We hoped the effort would result in a stabilization system that worked without pilot input. It didn't have to be perfect, but it had to work to the extent that if Alan were unconscious, he could survive the flight.

February 2014: Airplane Dummy Drop Spin Testing I

The sun penetrated my fragile skin, already burned from the previous day spent roaming the empty desert. In front of me an extended-cab F-250 Super Duty truck was lodged in a wash, suspended between the front wheels and the tow hitch, which was dug in about a foot underground, holding the rear end of the truck up high. The spinning wheels whipped up sand so fine it felt like grains were tunneling through my pores. Alan's pilot, Richard, and Julian were out in the desert wasteland scavenging chunks of wood for a makeshift bridge to give the wheels something to grab, in order to get the heavy truck out of the dusty grave I had driven it into. At the start of the shoveling Richard, cheery but painfully old, had gently informed us that he was not able to help shovel because he'd had several hernias. We repeatedly urged him to stop carrying wood. The crew was running on three hours of sleep and some had just finished skydiving from 16,000 feet, chasing an iron dummy from the sky into the depths of the desert. We dug at the sand under the pounding sun, stacked and lodged branches under the wheels, and squinted against the gritty geysers spewing from the wheels of the truck each time they moved but it failed to.

Two days before this, we had come to the desert to verify an update to our stabilization parachute that would hopefully stop a falling suit from violently spinning its pilot to death. We were experimenting with changing the attachment point of the drogue so it was higher on the parachute pack, hanging the pilot at an angle when falling instead of holding him flat. Being held flat was bad for a lot of reasons that we didn't really learn until after we saw Ida spin at incredible rates from the start of the stratosphere.

The biggest issue with the old orientation was that when a pilot is held flat (chest to Earth), the largest surface areas are presented directly perpendicular to the air stream maximizing the responsive forces. In addition, the drogue parachute was fastened to the system very near its natural inertial spin axis, allowing a spin that would find stability at any rate.

Gymnasts spin the human body around some combination of its three principal inertial axes: a flip, a pirouette, or a cartwheel. When a person spins around one of those axes, the torques imparted on their body sum to zero. If a person tries to spin on some other axis (such as angled sideways), the forces of spinning would apply a load to their body which would try to stabilize, working its way back to one of those three principal axes. We hoped that by angling Alan, when the system tried to level out and attain a high spin rate, the drogue parachute wouldn't let it and the resulting forces would put an end to the forming spin. We also hoped an angled pilot would perform like a down-pointing airplane wing, driving Alan sideways across the sky and forming another dynamic that would hopefully counteract a spin once it started.

Inertial Axes of a Person

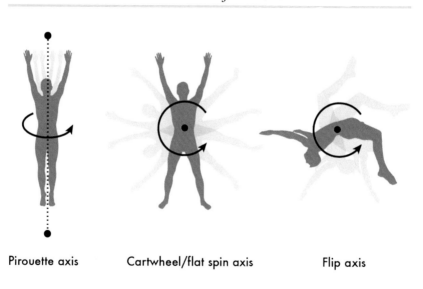

| Pirouette axis | Cartwheel/flat spin axis | Flip axis |

These were all theories, and rocky ones at best, based on dozens of pages of math and graphs about as reliable as a prediction about the winner of the next Super Bowl. They had a sound base in analytical knowledge and were much better than a blind guess, but they were still uncertain.

We outfitted Ida for these drops with a set of plastic limbs modeled roughly on the dimensions of the suit, hoping that Ida represented the suit when the pilot inside does nothing to steer it. This was a bit of a worst-case scenario, given that Alan would steer the suit. Some questioned hard whether Ida's drops really represented anything of value because there were so many departures from the realities of the actual situation, but ultimately we needed some way to understand fatal spin rates so we could prevent them. That dummy was what we had. Given the time and expense of high-altitude drops, or dangerously tossing Alan from a plane in the real suit, this seemed like the best way to work through the newly appreciated problem of high-altitude freefall spin, a subject we were becoming some of the world's experts on.

Blikkies was working in a frenzy, up at 4 a.m. day after day to build a brand-new parachute rig unlike any ever used. It would be state-of-the-art for high-altitude skydiving. The magnitude of the change was on par with other upending design changes that had swept the program over and over. Blikkies was starting from scratch, making a rig with the reserve parachute below the main parachute, 180 degrees different from the world standard in parachuting. This would accommodate our high attachment point without departing from the legacy architecture, in which the stabilization parachute is also used to extract the main parachute.

SAEBER and Parachute Architecture

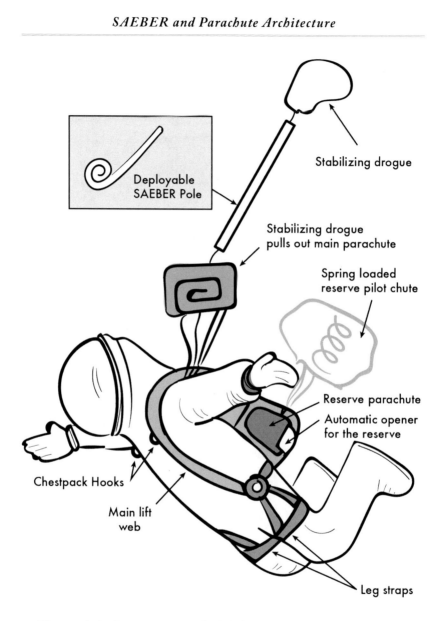

The week before we were scheduled to test the new rig by shoving it out of airplanes strapped to an iron dummy, I went to the parachute-manufacturing facility in Florida to rebuild the attachment rigging that held Alan to the balloon and help button up the new parachute system. I lived the life of Blikkies for a week, getting up in the dark and spending uncounted hours surrounded by huge racks of fabric above a warehouse where rows of people at sewing machines were making most of the world's parachute containers. I built a prototype of a new "spreader bar," the metal frame that held the straps between the balloon and Alan at the right position, out of aluminum. I hacked new parts on a two-hour cycle on the floor of the parachute factory in a little machine shop normally used to maintain the banks of sewing machines that make up the factory. If something between the parachute pack Blikkies was building and the rigging I was constructing didn't fit, we would split the difference on the dimensions, modify both components, and keep moving. On the final day, we proof-loaded the attachment rigging by draping piles of steel off a metal dummy (not Ida) strapped into the rig until the load was well above the expected weight. It held. We were done. I went home for two days before meeting in the central Arizona desert to strap the parachute pack to Ida and throw her from a plane.

The gear arrived at the main facilities two days before the drops, and I went to work, adding big steel plates to the front of Ida to represent the weight of our life-support pack, and big iron rails to hold rollerblade wheels that would help us push her out of the plane in a hurry.

The last of what I had to build were two sets of plastic limbs to glue to Ida. In a poignant parallel to the program itself, the drops would be a series of very quick, unimaginably enlightening moments that would end with Ida shattering herself against the ground. We would learn a lot in a very small amount of time, and then spend a comparative eternity rebuilding and digesting the wealth of information we'd just ingested before smashing our creation again. The limbs were high-pressure piping normally used in heavy industrial plumbing. We cut them to size and honed them out to slide over the nubs on Ida.

I was starting to grow fond of our stints in unattractive and sparsely populated corners of America. The nature of our program brought me to places I never would have gone otherwise. On the drive to the drop site, the cotton fields gave way to mustard-colored sand clumped at the edges of slicing ravines where thorny plants huddled, leaning over the occasional waterways, making formidable barriers that were easy enough to travel along but painfully difficult to cross. These were the same landscapes we had penetrated with our high-speed darts over a year before, landscapes so unwanted we had just left our refrigerator-weight concrete rods inserted into the ground forever, in an act the parachute team called "depositing minerals back into the Earth."

Joe was bringing an additional truck to support the crew for the recovery. We planned to do one drop in the morning following our arrival, then two the next day after Alan showed up with Julian and his pilot Richard. We figured we'd have to replace the plastic limbs after each landing and let the glue dry overnight, so the first day would be restricted to one flight. The next day we would do two drops, the second one without limbs. With data from both limb and no-limb drops, we could understand the effect limbs have on stability. We already had one high-altitude data set with a regrettably low-fidelity system and no limbs. These next three drops would be from low altitudes, two with limbs and one without, and using a stabilizing parachute attachment point at the shoulders instead of the standard low-altitude design with the attachment point at the lower back. We'd then try to thread a theoretical road through the incomplete data and our predictions for spin rates from high altitude, and see if we could reliably say how much spin our new and updated system might experience upon leaving the balloon in the stratosphere.

We had rented a skydiving tailgate plane from a nearby drop zone. Blikkies had gathered his traditional beer and meat and awaited our arrival. We worked into the darkness, building our units, surrounded by school-bus-sized aircraft parts and the quiet chill of the empty desert. The ramps were built, the limbs assembled, the meat grilled, the beer drunk, and by the late evening we were ready for sleep.

We drove to the drop zone in silence before the sun was up. We readied the system in the rising sun on the tarmac and donned jumpsuits and parachutes. Blikkies spotted our boxy tailgate airplane miles away, and we fastened a long strap over Ida's shoulders to help pull her on. The plane rolled off the runway toward us and spun a quick one-eighty in front of the hangar so that its gaping end was pointing at the hangar doors. Joe and I raced to prop ramps against the back of the plane. I hopped aboard, holding the long strap while Blikkies and Joe aligned Ida for the pull. With the three of us, it was remarkably easy to roll Ida, who weighed as much as a small motorcycle, up the waist-high ramps. Joe tossed the ramps on the pickup truck, and Blikkies and I strapped the plastic and steel adventurer to the floor so she wouldn't roll around. The pilot needed no more than a nod to trim the engines and start rolling away. Joe peeled off in the truck toward the drop site, where he'd watch Ida parachute down and get a first bearing on where she landed.

The view from the wide-open tailgate during takeoff still thrilled me. It went from a square shot of runway asphalt to a wide expanse of long ravines dividing the Earth like human veins. By the time we reached our target altitude, we'd be looking at a significant portion of the state, with both its major cities in view out of the open rectangle. I appreciated the accomplishment of lifting a heavy plane shaped like a storage container off the ground. I got my usual butterflies as the plane pitched back hard, and worried about how strong those straps were.

About halfway up, I got the signal from Blikkies to start preparing. Cameras were turned on and straps pulled off. I held Ida by her bent legs while Blikkies prepared the bag holding the static line connecting the drogue to the plane. The line would deploy the stabilization parachute. While I looked blankly out at the raw landscape below, Blikkies lay down on the tailgate per usual, with his head dipping off the back just inches from a ferocious air stream gushing an invisible explosion of twisting vortices behind the flying cube. He sprang up and walked back toward me, a signal to prepare. We wheeled Ida back toward the door, then Blikkies nodded. Push forward, pull back, then send Ida rolling out the door. She tipped back away from the plane slightly when the wheels dropped off the ledge, then we laid her chest onto the air stream rushing off the aircraft's belly. The exit was elegant and smooth, with the rollerblade wheels controlling the motion. The drogue parachute's static line snapped out of the bag and the stabilization parachute opened as Ida fell away. Blikkies walked to the edge, watched Ida descend for one breath, and hopped off the back of the aircraft after her, flipping head to Earth and then presenting his chest to the flow and disappearing behind the falling iron mannequin.

This time I lay down on the tailgate to watch them both rush away. The excitement of the moment drained as I watched Ida whirl downwards. For a full half minute she spun, and then she was too small to see. At the same time, the plane dove toward the landing site. My exhilaration quickly returned as the horizon pitched and the plane spiraled hard for the ground. Still stretched out on the tailgate of the massive door, I had to reassure myself I was wearing a parachute, although the force vector pointed firmly through the floor and I stayed put.

The aircraft flew nose to Earth, descending at nearly the same rate as the skydivers. As the plane approached the Earth, the pilot pulled up hard, leveling it out. It barreled just above the ground while we scanned the dirt. Joe and his truck were parked next to Ida. My radio lit up with Blikkies saying we were on top of him in the plane. I looked to the side window and there he was. I noted the heading from the access road to the landing site. It was time to land and go find them. I buckled in. The plane made the five-minute trip back to the airport and landed.

I stuffed the tie-down straps into the empty static line bag, gave the pilot my best attempt at a casual salute, hopped off the plane and into the truck, and tore out into the desert.

I radioed to Blikkies and Joe. Joe had been close enough to Blikkies that he sped off and retrieved him, and they were both waiting with Ida. They talked me through a romp across a spattering of small washes and one dismantled fence to where Ida lay on the ground, missing all of her delicate limbs and most of her wheels. Blikkies' talents continued to amaze me. Looking at the tiniest features miles below while moving at racecar speeds above stout shifting winds, he still managed to deploy Ida right on spot. She had landed just about half a mile from the split off of the dirt road to the drop area.

All in all, the drop was a great success. We videoed the landing site, high-fived, had some laughs, drank some Gatorade, and pulled the gorilla-weight dummy up the ramps and into the bed of a truck. Alan was set to arrive in just a few hours. We had to reset the system in time to dry before starting again the next day.

We arrived back at the airport to find a message from Alan that they were going to be late. We downloaded the videos from the drop and saw with a sinking disappointment that Ida had indeed continued to spin under her new, supposedly spin-proof system. The spin rates were drastically reduced from what the lower-altitude spinning had been in our previous drops, but nonetheless she twisted away. She spun peacefully like a merry-go-round instead of like a helicopter blade. This was hopeful, but no slam-dunk. As we watched the videos, I also got to witness for the first time what it looks like when something "goes in on line stretch," a technical term used to describe a type of usually fatal parachute incident in which a parachute opens too close to the ground to sufficiently slow the system before impacting. In this case we had intentionally set the controller low in altitude to avoid Ida drifting out of the drop area. The footage was nonetheless chilling; I couldn't help but picture a parachute I was wearing barely reaching an open state before the dull thud and then the little bunny hop that occurs when something hits the ground at highway speeds. We raised the opening height slightly to better preserve our dumb friend's static figure.

Returning to the hangar, we pulled out the tools and got to it right there on the tarmac. We joked and worked. I pounded away the bits of leftover glue with a mini sledgehammer and glued on new limbs with tacky amber-colored adhesive. Blikkies repacked the parachutes and repaired the damaged webbing where our added plates had started to cut through the main lift webs going over Ida's shoulders. We replaced Ida's wheels and axles amid continual calls from Alan's pilot Richard that they would be more and more late. We left them a car at the airport and headed home.

As midnight rolled around, Alan called to say they were in a mess of delays with his airplane. They needed a part to fix a problem with the landing gear and had been flying place to place trying to locate it. They were somewhere in the northwest and the problem still wasn't fixed. They would fly to a repair shop in Arizona with the landing gear down and then drive to us that night. Alan refused to push back the testing, so we stuck with the plan to ship out around 6 a.m. It was becoming ordinary that Alan would pack more than a normal human could accomplish into his schedule and somehow stay the course, blasting through incredibly demanding, life-critical tasks with sticky-eyed exhaustion.

We gathered in the pre-dawn morning with the full crew on call. Joe had returned to his desk in Tucson, and Sebastian had arrived to replace him behind the wheel of the second chase truck, this time with Richard and Julian tagging along for the romping. The previous day had been considered a sort of prep drop where we made sure everything was functional before

Alan got there to join us. We would repeat yesterday's drop. If all went well, we'd follow it with the third and final drop, that one without the limbs.

Experimental aviation is an activity that can involve a lot of waiting, and my antsy self had a steep learning curve for that skill. We exchanged mindless banter on the tarmac until the fat bumblebee of the skydiving plane sent its distinctive hum from the desert horizon to let us know we would be rolling soon.

We readied the planks to roll Ida on the plane and tied a strap around her arms for pulling her straight up the ramps. The plane swung across the weedy taxiways back to the tarmac where we waited. Without a word, the ramps went up, Ida went up, and we straightened her out with her head facing toward the pilots. We were ready in seconds. The opposite of waiting.

With a smack on the bulkhead to signal the cockpit, the plane fired up. Alan, Blikkies, and I buckled in for our trip while Sebastian gathered the planks into the truck to head for the drop site. We had a multi-pronged plan for finding the unit on the ground fast. The first prong is support divers. Alan and Blikkies dive with Ida to get midair footage of the stabilization chute and its ability to stall the spinning. They then back away and pull their parachutes well above Ida's computer-activated parachute deployment. On these particular jumps, Ida was using the reserve parachute because it was set up for the computer-activated deployment. That deployment utilized what's called a free-bag, which means the reserve extraction chute and deployment bag float away after deployment.

After all the parachutes were out, the two divers would separate, one heading for the landing site of the dummy and the other toward the smaller extraction parachute. On the ground, they could radio their location to Sebastian, the second prong, watching from below, getting a heading on each of their directions from the edge of the drop site. The third prong would be me in the airplane, scanning the ground to locate Sebastian and the landed jumpers. By looking to the surrounding roads, I would establish headings for Sebastian and me to find the jumpers in the mosaic of triangles between the washes. Finally, as a bonus, if the GPS locators strapped to Ida had survived the drop, we would pull up the coordinates and mark a position on digital maps for backup.

The world shrank away out the gaping square tailgate, like an aerial image on a computer screen being zoomed out. We sat in silence as the plane rose. I was learning the subtle motions and noises of an aircraft. I could feel the engines pull back and the wings level when the plane got over the landing area. Over the drop zone, I could easily recognize the water tank that marked our ultimate target. We turned on all the cameras and unstrapped Ida. Alan's excitement shone through his groggy sleeplessness. Blikkies and I were calm and ready. I held Ida's legs as the green light flashed. Alan stood ready at her head while Blikkies lay on the tailgate staring through miles of space to a point on the ground where we would try to land her. Blikkies popped up and pointed out the tailgate. We all lined up behind Ida's head. Blikkies yelled, "Ready!" and we pushed Ida forward on her wheels. At "Set!" we pulled her back toward our chests. "Go!" We pushed hard, running with her as she thumped forward and slipped feet-first into the air stream. She settled back, head up, laying into the rushing air like a kayak held by the nose against a smooth river flow.

The bag that held the static line snapped back at the plane, and the orange drogue parachute inflated into a taut ball as Ida fell away. Alan and Blikkies stepped off the tailgate, flipping head to Earth, and shrank behind the orange ball against the tan veiny backdrop. I lay on the tailgate watching them drift away, disappointment mounting as Ida again twisted away in a confusing static twirl that I didn't think was possible before watching it happen. As the plane made its first slow turn, I saw the parachutes open and sprang up.

I gathered the static bag off the floor, stuffed in Ida's straps, and buckled in for the descent as the plane twisted over itself into a rolling dive toward the ground. We burned away the drop altitude. When we leveled out, I stood up again and went near the bulkhead, watching the ground rush toward us, then spin away as we flattened into a low-altitude search pattern trying to spot the jumpers. On the second pass, we spotted their bright parachutes draped on the ground just as we got Blikkes on the radio.

The pilot appeared to have a policy that if circumstances allowed, it was mandatory to buzz the jumpers. With Alan in his sights, he dipped lower and lower until I felt a moment of worry, thinking for sure the props were going to clip a cactus. Alan stood, parachute in hand, staring directly at us. I don't know if it was determination, awe, or fatigue, but he didn't budge. I could make out his staring eyes as we skimmed over his head, rustling his parachutes in the prop wash before the pilot pulled up to flip around and set up a pass, readying a more traditional flyover that would draw a line from the pilots to the trucks. This would give Sebastian a heading on where the jumpers were. I buckled back up and we went back to set her down. I pulled up my headings on the remote trackers and headed for Sebastian at the skirt of the drop zone.

Sebastian waited with Julian and Alan's pilot in the truck as I bounced up the rough dirt road. We passed with a nod and collaborated on the radios to let Sebastian lead the charge into the desert. This time the jumpers were much deeper into the desolation of the drop area. According to the trackers, we were a few miles away as the crow flies, and we knew the basic direction from the flyovers. At the start there was a track to follow, but soon enough it turned hard away from our mark and we rocketed out across the empty wasteland. We held it at 40 miles per hour across perfectly flat hardened sand until the washes on either side of us converged. Then we bickered over the best way to proceed and crept into a deep scar, raking the sides of the truck with the surrounding thorny vegetation.

We got to the worst of the washes right around the time we spotted the jumpers. The colorful canopies lay 200 feet away on the other side of a scar in the open dirt the size of a semi. Alan and Blikkies pushed through the wall of thorns to greet us. If it had only been the two of them, we would have packed up and gone, but there was no way we could drag Ida 200 feet through the sand across the bottom of a wash lined with ultra-fine silt. By our estimations, a good running start would barrel the front wheels through the silt, and once they grabbed on the far side, we could snowplow through the thorn bushes and blast out the other side. Some estimations are wrong.

Because this was a move of the fast and destructive variety, everyone took positions to watch. I got in the truck and punched it. The front end plunged steep off the edge, raising a plume of dust. The truck plowed through the silt, but just as the front wheels caught the hard dirt on the far side and started to climb, it slammed to a halt with an ominous creak of metal. Our calculations had failed to account for the actual length of an extended-cab long-bed truck. Side to side, the bottom of the wash was just short of the truck's length. The trailer hitch had smashed itself deep into the rocky dirt, and the back wheels were spinning free a few inches above the bone-dry silt.

For hours we applied our never-say-never problem-solving methods, taking turns hacking at the rock-hard dirt with a shovel from the truck. We dug the dirt out from under the hitch to drop the back end of the truck in attempts to change our intractable geometry problem into one we could solve. The bed finally dropped. With the hitch finally free, I blasted a run for the other bank, failing to take into account the forward momentum required to clear the silt. The truck lost altitude until the running boards settled just above the powdery dirt. I got out, and we all stared at what looked to be the final resting place of our monster truck.

Blikkies and Sebastian took off in the other truck to find another way around. In a best-case scenario they could yank the truck from the other side. We hoped the worst-case scenario would be to extract Ida and come back the next day with heavier machinery to extract the truck, rather than inter it. The rest of us kept digging, jacking, and digging again, while we tried to convince Richard that he didn't need to help.

The sun beat on, and finally the other truck arrived on Ida's side of the wash. We were mentally ready and physically prepared: sticks under wheels, hitch free of the ground. Blikkies tied the trucks together using heavy-duty tie-down straps. Alan made an off-hand comment about how maybe somebody else should drive this time, which I hoped was a joke, but I noted that his laugh was a little forced when I caught his eye. I was both legitimately annoyed (could he have done better?) and pleased that our friendship had grown close enough to include bickering. I got in the cab. We still had another drop to do before nightfall.

With a smoky blast of silt and exhaust, the yellow straps birthed the truck through the thorn forest and out onto terra firma where Ida lay. We loaded up and went back to the hangars on the route that Sebastian and Blikkies found around the wash. The sun was lowering in the sky. I still needed another drop without the limbs to work out final correlations, gauge the connections between all the variables, and predict how the suit would perform in a high-altitude drop. The team was tired, maybe tired of me and my desire to keep working on a drop that Blikkies had already called too "mathy." With grumbles all around, they agreed to reset for one more drop, this time without limbs.

Alan seemed especially done for. He had spent the entire night trying to sort out a busted airplane, and the day had filled up from pre-dawn hours with the heavy lifting of Ida, a skydive, and an hours-long episode digging out a stuck truck. We were all more or less toast, but Alan, for the first time in our project, looked to be reaching the end of his string.

He saddled up, though. If there was one more drop to do, he would do it. We had an unspoken agreement that pushing Alan was good. He was tougher than any of us, but he had to be, and then some. In a perverse fashion, this particular situation was one rare occasion where we could allow ourselves to enjoy someone getting battered. Alan was older than anyone who had tried this type of drop in the past, and not all of them had made it. We all knew that he would never allow himself to give up. He wouldn't be the one to say stop.

We arrived back at the hangars with crusted eyeballs. The reset was our fastest yet. I bashed off what was left of Ida's limbs and fixed the bent-up wheels. Blikkies repacked the parachutes. The video cards were cleared so new pictures could be taken.

The bumblebee aircraft soared into sight, landed, and presented its rear to us with an already-open door. We were dragging ass pulling Ida up the ramps. The rush to beat the closing day fought against our will to curl up and sleep. Sebastian again headed for the holding area in the truck, leaving Julian and Richard at the hangar. Blikkies and I would push Ida out. Alan and Blikkies would jump. We were a smooth, tired team.

The lowering sun threatened a post-sunset recovery. We crept to altitude without comment on the shadows fading into the quilt-work below us.

Everything happened like it was supposed to. We arrived at the target altitude, turned on the cameras, unstrapped the beat-up iron dummy, and waited. Blikkes called the spot. We pushed forward on "Ready!" pulled back on "Set!" and on "Go!" launched the iron skydiver into the air.

I lay on the tailgate and, as I dejectedly expected, the limbless Ida appeared to drift lazily in slow mellow circles, suggesting that the presence of limbs made the solid body spin more. That would mean that the high-altitude drop we had already performed gave us an underestimate of the spin we could expect from a limbed dummy. I wouldn't know the whole story until we landed, but it appeared that the day would close with dog-tired head scratches and no conclusions.

I landed with the plane. The white smoke that curls behind the big open door as the wheels hit the ground amused me no more. It was dusk.

I drove the truck in the cooling air down the empty roads and met Sebastian's truck at the turnoff. He had seen the parachutes come down, so he took the lead in the chase. Dipping through one of the endless washes, the dangling plastic skirt on the front of my truck ripped off, leaving the two metal brackets hanging off the frame and making the truck look even more monstrous.

We arrived in ample light, with Alan and Blikkies sitting around Ida with punch-drunk smiles on their faces. "I told you we shouldn't have done another one!" Blikkies hollered as we pulled up. "The thing was fuckin' LAAAZZZYYY!" he howled, referring to the slow turn rate. That was bad news. The addition of limbs made the spinning problems worse; our high-altitude dummy tests were the opposite of good conservative engineering.

We loaded it up and drove out. No issues. Alan sat next to me in the truck. I knew he would fly out as soon as we got back and I wouldn't get my chance to talk about what this all meant. I asked him what he thought. He rolled his head toward me with the eyes of a drunken zombie and asked, "Can we talk about it at another time?"

If nothing else, we had finally found out that the tsunami named Alan Eustace had limits.

March 2014: Airplane Dummy Drop Spin Testing II

I was getting the feeling that we were part of something much bigger than ourselves, seeking to know what lies in places humans have not yet been. Alan's destination was too high for airplanes and too low for orbital rockets. Although the upper stratosphere has been traversed by hundreds of astronauts, they have only glimpsed it for fleeting seconds through sheets of fire, walled safely inside dense spacecraft structures. This was more than a rich man's stunt. Alan didn't lust for glory but for science, engineering, aviation, and the progress of humans as a species. He could have chosen to sit out the dirty, unglamorous desert-wash dummy drop. He didn't.

We thought we were close to a solution to the feared and fabled flat spin, but when we really ran the numbers, extrapolating the values found in Ida's flights, they still predicted outlandish spin rates and accelerations crossing the established limits for what a human could endure. There was no excitement in Alan's tired eyes as we left the Arizona proving grounds because we hadn't solved our problem yet.

We were becoming real experts at pushing human-shaped metal and plastic blobs out of the back of planes and finding them later on the desert floor. That motivated us to do it more until we had real answers.

Humans spinning out of control on descent from the stratosphere was no new problem. Colonel Joseph Kittinger had jumped from the stratosphere three times with the explicitly expressed goal of understanding how to safely return a human from those heights. The Air Force had dropped several dummies from great altitudes in attempts to understand how and why humans spin so hard up high. The only hard conclusion was that a freefall from high altitude without a stabilizing mechanism would go very badly. In other words, a system that could stabilize and safely bring a person down from very high altitudes didn't exist, and we were charged with creating it. A success would change aviation forever, allowing for a safe plan B in any scenario where a person found themselves that high in the atmosphere and under duress. Of course it was going to be difficult.

Parallel to the exploit of tossing the lovely fearless Ida from the tailgate of skydiving airplanes, I had been working on a long description of the mathematics of high-altitude spins.

We had already taken the lengthy advice of Air Force studies and the Stratos program by adding a stabilizer to our system, but that wasn't working either. There was more to this. The devil, as they say, is in the details.

Perhaps the most fundamental thing we learned in all these studies was that high-altitude flat spins are as much about spacesuits and long freefall times as they are about high speeds. Big numbers blow people's minds. Breaking the sound barrier blows people's minds. The reality, however, is that wearing a body cast and spending lots of time falling were showing up to be the biggest contributors to a falling aeronaut's troubles with spin. The high speeds and strange nature of air densities in the stratosphere played their part as well, and I tried to describe what we had learned in what was becoming a complex thesis on human high-altitude freefall spin.

The first lesson is one well known to aviators about equivalent speeds and true air speeds. Someone taking their first look at the dynamics of a falling body might conclude that it spins out of control because it is going 800 miles per hour. 800 miles per hour is incredibly fast. It would cause extreme reactions of the body to the air stream and maybe even make it spin.

When a body is falling fast in very thin air, one must consider its equivalent speed (similar to "indicated" speed, which is more widely used among pilots). Equivalent speed tells what speed at sea level would feel the same way, as opposed to measuring how fast the actual molecules are rushing past. Because of the low air density, equivalent speeds at high altitudes are far less than actual speeds, so one might think the general controllability of the falling body at high altitude could be determined by testing equivalent speeds at lower altitudes. But it's not that straightforward.

As a body falls from very high altitude, it gains speed faster than the atmosphere gets thicker, so a falling body's equivalent speeds increase rapidly partway through a drop from the stratosphere.

During the deceleration, there exists a period in which the equivalent air speeds are rising whereas the true air speeds are falling. The falling body is essentially experiencing a mini atmospheric reentry—it speeds up really fast, then runs into the atmosphere like a cliff jumper colliding with the surface of a lake, and has to slow down again. Was that causing the spinning?

The reality, even when looking deep into the complexities of equivalent speeds, is that the seemingly incredible velocities are not that outlandish in skydiving terms. The equivalent speeds reach something like 25% or 50% higher than what they are at terminal velocity low in the atmosphere, and while significant, this just isn't enough to explain why falling humans and anthropomorphic dummies experience enormous, potentially fatal spin rates. Modern skydivers do all sorts of crazy things, like turn on their heads and link together in big groups, which can send them flying at well over the equivalent speeds that send stratospheric jumpers into death-inducing flat spins. Something else must be going on.

True and Equivalent Air Speed for a Human Shape

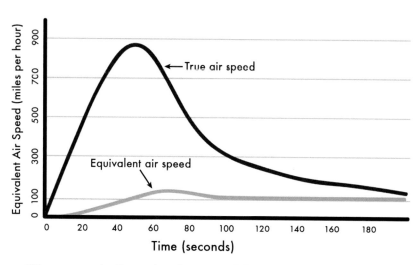

Classic Skydiving Arch Vs. Spacesuit

When we put it all together, it appeared that the most neglected element in discussions about flat spin was the spacesuit. Its rigidity bars the most fundamental element of skydiving posture: the arch. From the day a student first steps into a classroom learning how to skydive, the word "arch" will be repeated to them hundreds of times until they learn to relax and push the bush into the air stream. That is the nature of the arch—it is about relaxing into the air stream and making the human body into a sort of badminton birdie. That isn't allowed by most spacesuits.

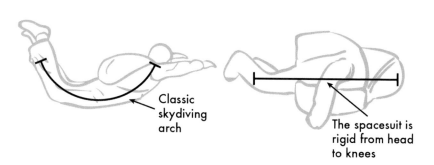

Furthermore, spacesuits restrict the movement of the arms and legs to very mechanical, unnatural motions that are limited to a few simple actions. Those actions are not sufficient for controlling the fall. Spacesuits, it turns out, really act more like rigid structures than humans do, so our work with Ida and the work done with dummies in the past was truly applicable.

Understanding this sort of rigid-body theory on flat spins allowed us to approach the problem more mathematically. Our assumption that Alan's skydiving skills could be applied to the problems of flat spin was naive and would have to be abandoned. On the bright side, we had an opportunity to truly solve this problem and create a solution that would apply to all high-altitude voyagers. If we succeeded, the future users of our system wouldn't have to be highly experienced skydivers.

The grand conclusion was that three factors combine to cause severe spinning when a roughly human-shaped object falls from the stratosphere, none too much more important than the others. The first factor is the reality that spacesuits are rigid, robotic machines that don't allow experienced skydivers to execute their skydiving skills. The second factor is the long freefall time. Severe terminal spins take a long time to develop, while the short freefall times experienced by skydivers jumping from airplanes just aren't long enough for a spin to develop. Regular skydives take about one minute, while a fall from the upper stratosphere takes four and a half. An experienced skydiver could certainly stay stable in the air for four and a half minutes—they do it in wind tunnels all the time—but things change when the spacesuit is added to the equation. From low altitude, by the time a suited skydiver's spin could start getting really bad, a parachute stops it. Finally, the third factor, which we found to be no more important than the others but which seemed to be the focus of most other theories surrounding the flat spin, is extreme speeds. Of course, 820 miles per hour is really fast, especially since it's higher than the speed of sound.

Even though the equivalent speeds aren't nearly that high, they are still higher up high than they are down low. The equivalent speeds, in combination with the oddities that high true air speeds present, along with two crossings of the sound barrier (one from low speed to high and one from high speed to low) made what we referred to as the "stratospheric aerodynamic profile" so much different from that for low-altitude flight, that a pilot simply wouldn't be able to practice flying there before going there.

This had all been the result of this grand thesis of the flat spin I had been working on. It was a report on the woes that come with stratospheric reentry and the ferocious spins that can occur. This report covered everything we knew, including what we'd learned, and how we were fixing it. The upshot was that we had to address definitively why all the work of the past suggested that stabilizing the pilot with a drogue parachute would fix our issues, when it most certainly had not.

The original system was based largely on a widely used parachute system for tandem skydiving. That system put the attachment point for the drogue parachute right at the center of the pack, nearly perfectly in line with the system center of gravity. Late in the process, we absorbed the fact that one of the biggest reasons for that was to give tandem instructors more control, and put the instructor and student in the traditional skydiving position of chest to earth. We wanted less control. We wanted little or no response to inputs, so whatever a pilot did during the four minutes of freefall wouldn't start them spinning.

As the theoretical pages about our lessons and failings spewed forth, a couple of themes were developing. One was that we needed to go all the way with the drogue attachment. It needed to be as high on the suit as we could put it so Alan would hang at the steepest possible angle, as far from that dangerous flat spin axis as we could get him. The second was that we needed a bigger drogue. The more force the stabilizing chute took up, the less force would be exerted on Alan, and the slower the speeds would be for the whole system.

The work stated that stabilization in stratospheric freefalls was an absolute necessity as long as spacesuits were clunky and the laws of gravity couldn't be altered to get folks down more quickly. We were ready for changes and a new test. First, attach the stabilizer at the very top of the pack. Second, use a big drogue. Third, see if it worked. We knew what we had to do.

I wrote up proposals saying the right answer was to go straight back to the desert and drop Ida out of a plane three more times. We'd take it to the limit in all extremes, attaching the drogue at the very tip-top of the pack and use the largest drogue pattern Blikkes could find a design for. The proposals were accepted, and we got to it. I got all the parts on order for three more disposable dummy limb sets and headed for the desert. Blikkes supervised yet another revision to the parachute rig. Alan made plans to meet us in the desert again, and after two weeks of cutting and sewing, we went back to the same hot desert to execute familiar tests with new gear.

Apparently, Alan had had enough of digging trucks out of silty ravines. He helped us decide this would be a good time to test the potential use of helicopters to move things around by ordering us a helicopter. It would use a long-line sling to pick Ida up off the desert floor and bring her back to the airport after each drop. Recovering the dummy was the hardest part of these tests. Alan had the helicopter meet us at the airport.

We had learned a lot about rebuilding the dummy after each drop. Using a different, faster epoxy in a caulking gun, we could reattach the limbs more quickly, completing a full reset in a couple of hours so that we could keep up with the operation, now made speedy by the helicopter.

We planned out our day. There would be three loads. The first load would have two drops. We would send out both a 900-pound barrel dragging our new drogue to verify its structural ability to withstand a high-speed freefall, and then do the first dummy drop. For the first drop, we'd attach the larger drogue in a similar place as before. Blikkies had modified the attachment disk by cutting the top off and moving it a bit higher. If the system was stable with the disk and the larger drogue, we would go with that. The next drop would incorporate our highest attachment point, combining that with the use of the larger drogue, and then finally we would fly a long-bridle version combining every aspect we knew to try: bigger drogue, longer bridle, and higher attachment point.

It was only a few weeks after the previous drops that I flew to Tucson with the new updated equipment. I went there early to build a roller system for our half-ton bundle drop, the structural test of the new drogue, and to prepare the rest of the equipment. It was several days of hacking and grinding, nothing like what one may picture as "aerospace." No lab coats, no clipboards, and only occasional safety glasses. It was machine shop work, chopping plastic and metal in big chunks to make rough shapes which, once they fit together, were good enough.

This time we pre-built all the dummy limbs so all we would have to do is fasten them onto Ida for each flight. One machinist worked on the limbs while I created a heavy-duty steel cart to dump our half-ton barrel out of the plane. We used our usual rollerblade wheels to carry the cart and did the math. A fat rollerblader can easily weigh an eighth of a ton. Factoring in their whirly-dos and one-foot maneuvers, we figured a full set of rollerblade wheels could take a quarter ton, so we would use two sets for our half-ton dummy. If the wheels failed, it wasn't such a big deal. We didn't need them back. If the cart ended up looking like a metal bird's nest and the new rigging worked, we'd still be happy.

A 55-gallon oil drum was shipped in. I'd spend a Saturday filling it with concrete behind our office building while the older, duller engineers were home with their families. I bought concrete and rented a mixer and spent the day mixing concrete and dumping it with plastic buckets into the drum.

A very complex aerodynamic study, computational fluid dynamics model, and several empirical dummy tests were used to compute a predicted max drogue tension at the worst part of Alan's worst-case mission. Math was done to predict how hard the stabilizing parachute would pull on Alan as he fell. We multiplied that number by a safety factor to make sure math errors and variations between our calculations and the real-world situation didn't cause an error on the low side and make the test too gentle on the equipment, only to see it break in the actual situation. Then we used a new model to calculate bundle bridle tension (as opposed to pilot bridle tension) based on the mass of a 55-gallon-drum-shaped object with our new drogue behind it. At that point we could multiply the max anticipated pilot bridle tension in the actual flights by our safety factor, then figure out how heavy the barrel needed to be to make that tension. If that bundle didn't fail, we could be confident the real system wouldn't fail either. At the end of all this work, I had an answer: 22. That's how many inches of concrete I needed to pour into the barrel.

This was all necessary because we were changing the drogue parachute envelope, and using the drogue in a higher-force environment than its rating. Old data and existing ratings wouldn't help us. We had to create our own models and do our own test.

I set the concrete-filled drum on a pallet and left it to wait for Blikkies, who would help rig it up. Blikkies arrived a couple days before the drops to help hone out the limbs so they could be easily attached to the dummy and rig the bundle up. We spent the next work day with the annoying bustle of other workers and paranoid safety officers pacing around while we were carving PVC. Late into the night, we rigged the bundle with cargo netting and heavy-duty straps to hold it to its cart. Knowing it's generally not good to let half-ton barrels hit the ground at full speed, we also rigged a bigger parachute for the end of its flight.

The next day I finished getting things ready while Blikkies left for the proving grounds to meet Alan. Joe and I went up late that night. We unloaded the trucks into the hangar and pushed the payloads into the plane, which was already there waiting. Everything would be totally ready for a morning send off.

We arrived very early the next morning. As we started our morning work, the helicopter pilot rolled up to say hello. We had been worried about the pilot, afraid he wouldn't be willing to land in the desert and leave us chasing around in trucks again. Those worries were quickly alleviated. He was a stubby, tan Hispanic guy with an "I'll try anything" attitude about the situation. He was ready to land anywhere.

We wanted to get footage of the pilot sling-loading equipment to show the rest of the team, were trying to decide whether we wanted to sling-load equipment at the end of the final mission. The pilot let us zip-tie a GoPro camera to the skid so that we could see the payload from the chopper's point of view.

We all went into the briefing room before the drop. For the first time we had been assigned a "jumpmaster" to monitor our activities. I couldn't help but wonder whether this was because we were getting a little too fast and loose, dumping too many heavy objects willy-nilly from their expensive plane. Our jumpmaster was a tight-jumpsuit bro. It seemed there was confusion on both sides as to what he was actually supposed to be doing, but we went with it. It was most certainly in our best interest to smile and let this guy ride along.

Drop 1 would have two payloads, the half-ton bundle for structurally testing the drogue parachute, followed immediately by Ida. Both Alan and Blikkies would skydive. The payloads would go out relatively close to one another, and both jumpers would follow Ida until the parachutes were out.

Then Blikkies would steer to follow the bundle, and Alan would land with Ida.

We boarded the plane, and for the first time took off with the door closed. It was a much more controlled environment. So much for my usual entrancing climb. We didn't open the door until we got to altitude.

As we started to unstrap the bundle, I realized we hadn't practiced maneuvering it. The plane was pitched back and that thing weighed half a ton. We pulled the straps and neither the bundle nor I flew out of the plane. The three of us huddled around the back of the bundle ready to push it out, while the jumpmaster lay on the tailgate spotting the target landing site. He jumped up. We started to push. The locomotive was sluggish to get moving. It drifted toward the side of the plane, and I felt a wave of panic. It was fast and fluent. We threw our collective weight harder inside the turn radius. In the 10 feet to the door it managed to move over enough to miss the edge of the airplane and slip uneventfully into the air, skimming the airplane belly. It wasn't actually that close, but we couldn't have course-corrected with something that massive. Who knows what happens when a half-ton barrel of concrete bashes through the door threshold of a jump plane at altitude? If it's not dangerous, it is certainly expensive.

The drogue opened without a hitch, and I hopped back to push Ida out. We got the signal again and rocked Ida back and forth. I looked at Blikkies to give us the second nod. This would be quick. They needed to be close enough to the falling barrel that they could find it in the air to land with it and hook it to the helicopter. The nod came. Push forward "Ready!" pull back "Set!" push for the door "Go!" I stopped short of the door while the other two kept their pace right off the edge of the plane. All three hurtled toward the ground together.

I lay on the tailgate and watched the drogue snap to life. With the drogue fully open, Ida slowly spun her way down away from the plane. Not good. Blikkies and Alan watched in living detail as Ida spun toward the hard Earth. Both their parachutes came out at the right time. Blikkies would later report that as he was going after the round bundle parachute, which he was able to spot and land by, it looked strange to him as it headed for the ground, limping and folding like there wasn't any weight under it. He ended up in a downwind landing that resulted in a plume of dust and tumbling. When he reached the landing site of the round bundle parachute, he learned quickly that there was indeed nothing attached to it, the main parachute having completely separated from the bundle. Amazingly, every single one of the parachute lines had broken clean off, leaving the bundle to smash into the ground at a faster speed than most airplanes fly.

Our main parachute, which had completely failed, wasn't really part of the test. It was more of a precaution, sensible because a full-on bundle smash-up, exactly what happened, didn't seem like a good idea. The drogue was there, and in perfect shape. The test was a pass. Our wild man helicopter pilot wouldn't mind if the metal bar he would attach to for hauling out of there was now a question mark instead of a straight line. We likely wouldn't get our video footage back from the bundle camera, but that was okay—the perfectly healthy and intact drogue was all the evidence we needed for a good structural test.

Blikkies walked over to the bundle, which looked remarkably peaceful, shoved about a foot into the ground. The whole top that wasn't filled with concrete had buckled in on itself, and the quarter-inch-thick steel roller frame was a train wreck. Good thing we didn't need the wheels anymore.

Just before the bundle smash-up, Alan located the dummy in the sky and accompanied Ida into her landing. Not realizing that Blikkies had careened into the ground with a hard downwind landing, he landed in the same direction Blikkies had and also ate it hard into the ground. Both ended up dusty but fine. Ida was fine as well, except for losing most of her limbs and unfortunately once again being dizzy.

I landed with the plane. The helicopter pilot was already en route to haul the equipment back under the 100-foot sling line and drop it on the tarmac. He went to the bundle site first. Blikkies hooked a set of straps to the bundle frame. The helicopter set the hook on the ground to relieve the static charge. The pilot stared out of the window down at Blikkies and brought the hook, 100 feet away, into Blikkies' hands. He connected it to the payload. The helicopter pilot lifted up off the ground and flew the mangled bundle toward the airfield.

I got off of the airplane right as the bundle was becoming visible in the heat-waved distance. The chopper set the bundle down and remotely released the hook, leaving it in the middle of the tarmac. It was a good thing the airfield wasn't too busy. Any pilot who encountered it would not be happy. That was the first time I had any thoughts about what we were actually going to do with that barrel.

A few minutes after the barrel had set down, the helicopter was becoming audible again. It was visible in the distance, with the long, slightly arching line underneath it flying Ida toward us. She had lost all her limbs but one, an arm that waved at us as she descended toward the tarmac. The pilot set her down close to the giant hangar doors. Then the helicopter hovered at about 100 feet and released the static line from the top. It fell into a coiled pile on the ground beside Ida. The chopper then landed so I could get in and fly out to get Alan and Blikkies.

There was little reason for me to be in the helicopter, but I wasn't going to skip the chance. It was my first time in a helicopter that wasn't catering to tourists and my first time in the front seat where the ground is visible directly below through domed glass.

Helicopters are everything they are cracked up to be. The headsets, the cool pilots, the high speed near the ground, the ability to land anywhere, the noise, and the raw feeling of it all put my entire state of being into action-movie mode. The blinking shadows of the rotors strobed the cockpit. The blades spun faster and faster, and the whoosh-whoosh-whoosh blended into a roar. At the moment of liftoff, all of the body's sensors instantly report that there is no stable baseline, creating a feeling of floating. The stubby Latino pilot pulled the bird to about 100 feet in a pleasant thrilling hover, then punched it forward, screaming over desert washes and toward our stranded compadres.

Alan and Blikkies were together, parachutes in stuff sacks, wearing dusty smiles. They piled in the back and didn't comment on my face-ripping grin from the exhilaration of a real live helicopter operation. We were back at the hangar in minutes.

The process of getting the bundle, Ida, and the jumpers back to the tarmac, which used to take most of a day, had just taken about half an hour. We'd be ready for the next drop by early afternoon. On top of the fact that carrying the equipment with the helicopter shaved precious hours off the recovery process, we saw that finding things from overhead in a slow-moving chopper was wildly easier and more practical than finding them from trucks on the ground or from a high-flying fast airplane. The chopper took us back to the tarmac. Project engineer Norman Hahn, who had come to these tests from the home office in Denver, collected and reviewed all the video footage.

Around this time we were introduced to our new chase director, Dave Jourdan, who was eagerly assessing our helicopter compatibility during our first official use of helicopters as a recovery asset. Until then, chase had been the orphan of the program. We'd all put chase high on the list of importance, but for one reason or another it hadn't been given much attention. That was odd, considering that our scariest moment in the program so far was when we found ourselves not set up to find Alan in the open desert. He had been saved then by a random helicopter.

We had run through one other chase director and a handful of stand-ins up until that point. The first was an aerospace engineer who made some headway from our original chase practices of romping cowboy-style across open fields in trucks. He fell victim to layoffs at our parent company, and we moved into a long stretch during which a handful of people passed the job around, trying not to stay there long enough to get pinned to the daunting, complex, and very much life-critical responsibility. Dave was proposed somewhere at the executive level as someone who could potentially take on the role through the rest of the project, and he stepped right up.

Dave was on the board of advisors at our parent company. His background was in the field of underwater discovery, a job oddly similar to aerospace chase and recovery; they are both all about finding things, some more urgently than others. He had scraped the bottom of deep oceans looking for everything from historical relics like Amelia Earhart's lost airplane the Electra to a sunken submarine filled with millions of dollars' worth of solid gold. Of modest stature, he wore a gray beard and a happy, determined look on his face as he tackled what seemed to some to be the black hole of our overall effort. In a matter of weeks, he took our chase operation from its state of infancy to something that could be considered one of the most advanced and efficient aerospace chase and recovery operations in the world. Under his tutelage, we graduated from Wild West romping in diesel trucks to fully legal, jet-fuel-burning helicopters professional enough to go into the spotlight when the time came.

I rolled Ida back though the hangar doors and smashed off all the little chunks of limbs left on her legs. Blikkies repacked the parachutes and set Ida up for the next drop configuration by securing the drogue bridle to her neck to simulate the highest possible attach point. The report came back from the chief engineer that Ida had spun at about 20 revolutions per minute, not much of an improvement from previous drops. We all hoped this next drop would be different.

The only remaining drop after that was a long bridle drop, which we really didn't want to be the only one that worked. The bridle (which is the long strap that connects the stabilizing parachute to the parachute pack) is the length it is for a very specific reason: it is as long as possible without being so long that the reserve parachute cannot deploy over the top of it. If it were longer, then in the event of a main parachute failure, the reserve could deploy with the drogue still out. Since the reserve lines would be longer than the distance from the pack to the top of the drogue, the drogue would fall between or behind the parachute lines instead of extending beyond the nose of the reserve canopy. This presented a higher risk of entanglement and failure of the entire parachute system.

I re-glued the limbs onto Ida's nubs and within an hour, using the new fast-setting epoxy, she looked like a real skydiver again. I went to help Blikkies put the freshly packed rig together. Richard had found some sandwiches. After spending the previous trip digging the trucks out of desert washes, he opted to stay out of the recoveries this time and was our new self-appointed lunch director. We refitted Ida's parachute pack and loaded her onto the plane. This time the situation required us to load the payloads hot with the engines running. Loading was relaxed; a huge ramp from the tail of the airplane lay on the ground and we rolled Ida up without our makeshift ramps, followed her on with straps, and tied her down. With very little time and equally little fanfare, we briefed on the plan and hopped into the plane.

We took to the air and rose slowly to altitude with the door closed. Boring. We unstrapped our Ida and with the usual rocking we booted her out. Alan and Blikkies jumped behind her and I lay on the tailgate to watch them all fall away.

To my deep satisfaction and enjoyment, for as far as I could see, Ida looked like a rock statue in the sky. She didn't so much as change heading throughout the entire time she was in view. We had done it.

I jumped up and pumped my fist. With no one to share my excitement, I yelled to the staid jumpmaster, "It worked! It wasn't spinning!" He looked back with a blank face and a slight grin that said, "Neat story, kid." Blikkies and Alan would later tell me they watched her all the way to the time they pulled their chutes: Ida was solid as a rock. Toward the end of the drop, she turned slightly (after I had lost sight), but it appeared to be a result of the drogue spinning up and turning the payload, not the product of a dysfunctional system. We just might have solved the long-feared problem of flat spin in a pressure suit. We would still need to extrapolate the results to higher altitudes, but zero extrapolates to zero. Obviously, there were countless loose ends, like repeatability and dummy-human similarity, but we still took that day. We had done it.

I jumped out of the plane, ecstatic, to tell Norman that Ida had been steady for as long I could see her. The chopper was making its way back to the tarmac with Ida dangling under it. The helicopter set her down, then landed. This time Norman jumped in with me to ride out to get the jumpers.

Alan and Blikkies were waiting together again with their chutes packed up. We snatched them up and took off without even letting the rotors slow down. We were joyous. Blikkies and Alan reported remarkably stable, not-turny flight and a generally well-behaved dummy. We decided our final drop would still be a go. We would knock it off the list for the sake of completeness, but as far as we were concerned, we had finished what we had gone to the desert to do.

Both of Ida's legs were gone and both arms made it. I rebuilt her. While Blikkies was still repacking parachutes, Alan and I learned that we could deposit the destroyed half-ton bundle in a local nearby dump. The helicopter could carry it there for us. That was a task that might have occupied the entire next morning, figuring out how to get 1,000 pounds of mangled metal and concrete into a truck and unload it at a landfill. It would take the helicopter a mere 15 minutes. The chopper pilot readied the static line and got airborne, hovering above us. We hooked the giant flight hook onto the crushed bundle and stepped back while it was lifted steadily into the air. True to his fashion, Alan tore the giant map of the airport off the wall to take with us in the truck, so we would be able to find the dump. We got there in time to hear the spinning chopper coming in over us with the bundle hanging below. We stood in complete awe as the chopper set the 1,000-pound crushed metal mess between the two of us. We reached out without moving our feet even a little, and unhooked it.

The chopper headed back to the tarmac, and we stripped anything that might be of value to us off the bundle, mostly just the cargo net that we used to bring the bundle over. When pulling the wheels off, I commented that everything was pretty screwed up and what was left was only worth a few bucks. Alan replied, "Money is no object." That was a phrase I'd only heard before in movies. Never had I expected to hear it in real life, even in this context, where it seemed to be so true. I tried to hide my surprise and we headed back toward the hangar.

The drop routine work was easy now, and soon enough, Ida was ready for her final flight. Norman had reviewed the footage and confirmed that the previous flight was a slam-dunk from all angles. One camera looked up at the drogue chute and verified that the minor turning could be attributed to a spinning drogue. She was not a spin-prone system, so the idle turning wouldn't develop into anything more severe. We had our answer. We headed to altitude, opened the door with tired eyes, and removed the straps for the last go. We pushed Ida out with her long bridle. Alan and Blikkies followed. I lay on the tailgate and watched her gently turn. It appeared our answer would be written in stone by the end of this flight. Under the harder, more complicated system, she turned more. There was no need to pursue the issue.

The flight characteristics of something with as wacky a shape as a human are crazy. The longer bridle should have pulled the drogue out of Ida's wake and generally made it more effective, but for whatever reason that didn't happen. That left questions for another day, another program. The results we needed were crystal clear.

Blikkies and Alan reported the same thing I saw. Ida landed as usual and also per usual arrived at the airport at about the same time I did. The chopper set her down and dropped the static line to coil beside her. Norman took shotgun this time, and I rode in the back of the helicopter. We landed in the thorny brush, snatched up the jumpers, and lifted back off.

We were exhausted and elated at the same time. We had a straightforward conclusion: a normal length bridle, a big drogue, and an attachment point at the very top of the pack would keep a suited person from spinning. Our sample size of one would certainly be cause for plenty of questions, but that was the nature of this business. Even if Alan turned around a little bit, the numbers promised that the spin rates would be small. We'd go back to our spreadsheets and math our way through it all again, but in our heads it was done.

Alan took off that day as usual, back to his packed-full life somewhere else. I bashed the remaining limbs off Ida to make her easier to move. Blikkies and I drank beer in the big old hangar into the night.

Pretty good day. We'd solved the flat spin problem.

Ida in her first set of dummy drops. She is intentionally angled at 45 degrees.

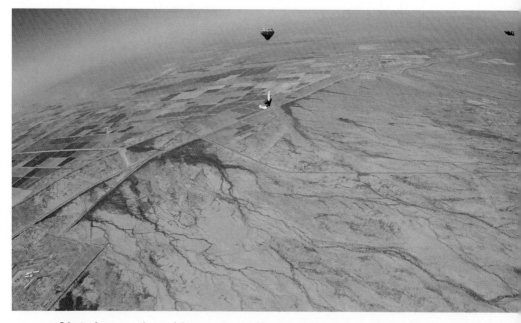

Ida in her second set of dummy drops. She is angled more steeply in this set of drops. This orientation ultimately produced the desired result—she did not spin at all.

Digging out a stuck truck in the central Arizona desert while retrieving our dummy after a test drop.

Cleaning up our busted dummy after she smashed into the ground. It was typical for the dummy's limbs to break off on impact.

Ida the iron dummy loaded into the back of a drop plane ready for testing.

The heroine Ida, our iron dummy assembly. This dummy was used in over 20 tests. She did eight skydives for the program, two of which were from the stratosphere, and sustained two high-speed ground impacts. (Photo by Julian Nott.)

CHAPTER 12

...

Failing to Communicate

You could say it was about freedom. Freedom in a very literal sense—like freedom to travel beyond the two-dimensional geography of planet Earth and freedom from the gravity that holds us all to our one earthy biosphere. Alan was a man of incredible means. He owned a fast jet, he was a pilot, and there was nothing on Earth stopping him from going anywhere at any time as long as that place was, in fact, on Earth. Maybe that's what drove him to go to the stratosphere.

Even the space station was relatively well traveled now. He was going to a place where no person had ever gone outside of a spacecraft. No one.

Our suit would float through a brand-new world and take Alan on a journey like no other.

The euphoria of the dummy drops gave way to mundane and irritating delays. We were then in the middle of what was, without a doubt, one of the most thorough human high-altitude freefall stability studies ever performed, yet the results were simultaneously comprehensive and marginal. Our slam-dunk test in the desert was just one test. There wasn't a whole lot more we could do. Although we felt we had solved the problem, there were no unshakable conclusions to draw. The math was incredibly flimsy.

March 2014: Losing Our Communications System

While we were absorbing the limitations of the conclusions of the spin studies, an unexpected and confusing political mess ensued which put a sudden, frustrating, and unnecessary halt to the program. It had to do with the communications equipment.

In our first communications test, we experienced and resolved a relatively minor problem when our voice radios interfered with the data communication equipment. Every two seconds, when the data system was transmitting, the voice radios cut out, making it nearly impossible to hear coherent sentences in the suit. I experienced this as a blatting of word fragments when I was hanging from the BLV in the suit during that test. We got past it by switching the transmit and receive frequencies on the equipment, essentially reversing the interference so that the radios interfered with the data stream instead of the data stream interfering with the radios. Unlike the data stream, the voice stream was intermittent. It consisted of occasional bursts and long gaps. People talking on the radios disrupted the data stream, but it could recover, so the radio interference with the data stream was acceptable for short durations.

After that solution was chosen, we sent the equipment to the communications company to update the hardware. With part of the equipment updated, the shit hit the fan. An irate email from the leader of the communications company informed us that we had violated the regulatory certification of the equipment. He clearly believed we had done something out of bounds in the equipment changes. We politely informed him that the update was performed by his company, not ours, and we relied on them to ensure compliance in that department. Besides that, the equipment hadn't yet been used, so no true violations had occurred. It became clear that the company was not well connected to itself and we had exposed an internal snafu—some employees were helping us along, others barely knew we existed, and some were vehemently opposed to what we were doing.

Coincidentally, the contract we had in place with that particular company had run out and negotiations were in process to renew it. In a near-comical festival of nonsense, the executives of both companies met and bickered over what had been done and what was to be done with this equipment. The interference problems were showcased as a testament to how amateur our communications equipment was. Our avionics team offered gentle reminders that the communications system was designed and vetted by their company, not ours. The wound was deepened when, confused as to how we managed to operate the equipment at all, the upper management of the communications company realized that a former employee of theirs was a full-time member of our team.

The relationship crumbled. Sending the hardware in for update amidst the stalled contract negotiations couldn't have been worse timing. The contract was never renewed, and the communications hardware was not returned. Even if the equipment had been returned, we would have had no licensed frequencies on which to run it. This left us with no communications equipment for our suit, which stopped all testing cold. The communications system was the brain of the suit and physically located at the heart of the chestpack. Nothing could even turn on without it. The balloon equipment used the communications system to track the balloon, monitor its health, and initiate the absolutely vital balloon-destruct sequence. Without that functionality, not even unmanned flights were possible.

A slow and deeply painful delay ensued while we were forced into a major redesign of a critical component just a couple months away from our plans to do the final flights. The whole team was dispirited. Successful completion of the project, which had seemed so near and concrete, was pushed into a vague, imagined future. Because the entire system was rendered dysfunctional by the revocation of the communications equipment, we couldn't even make progress on minor issues to try to dispel the gloom. We had hoped to attempt a launch in the spring weather window of 2014. That would not be possible after this incident.

There was a silver lining. Our avionics expert Dan McFatter stepped up and distinguished himself as a technical prodigy, working without rest for two and a half months until he had designed and tested a new long-distance communications system. The replacement turned out to be far superior to the previous system and redefined the state of the art for long-distance direct communication with stratospheric balloons.

In the meantime, unable to test anything that involved the suit, the balloon team refocused. By the second month into the development of our new communications system, the balloon group was averaging three flights a week to the stratosphere with a new platform. They used latex balloons that could fly without advanced tracking and destruct systems (latex balloons just pop when they get to their target altitude). Sending payloads to the fringes of space became commonplace for the test team. In flight after flight, components were tested in the near-vacuum and extreme temperatures which would be encountered in the final flight. They designed new equipment to replace antiquated filling and launching systems, improving upon decades of dated knowledge regarding what it took to send a payload to space.

We started launching more and more common materials and components and finding less and less correlation between a component's rating for use in space, and that component's ability to actually function under those extreme environmental conditions. We deepened our understanding of what caused parts to fail in the cold vacuum of the stratosphere, and we were able to apply that understanding directly instead of paying wild amounts of money to have someone else—who knew less than we did—do it for us. We started using many common components, sold for pennies, instead of shiny space parts that do the same thing less well with less testing behind them. We flew parts made of everything from aircraft aluminum to chunks of wood from hobby stores. We put household consumer electronics in high-vacuum bell jars, then floated them into the stratosphere. We were learning countless new things, charging ahead at a rate nobody would have ever thought possible in building brand-new space systems.

The push for using more common components had little to do with cost. We were operating with hardly any budgetary constraints at the time. The advantage of mass-manufactured common parts was simply that they could be procured quickly and in numbers large enough to rip them apart, see how they worked, and test them relentlessly until we could assure ourselves they would (or wouldn't) work in the stratosphere. The parts we bought were sold in such mass numbers that the manufacturer had virtually no interest in how their part was used or altered, helping us avoid touchy political relationships like the one that had just screwed us. It felt like we were birthing a new type of intensely effective development centered deeply on testing.

The sourness from the loss of a critical piece of our creation was rendered sweet by Dan's elegant replacement, which fixed the glitches of the old system. Within months of the bad news, Dan had the new system communicating across a broad swath of the country. By the third week of testing, the balloon launch crew had to drive for hours in the opposite direction of the communications team in order to stress the signal.

Personally, I was going stir crazy waiting to get back to work in the desert. I wanted the program to keep moving forward until it was done. Shaking off our lingering sense of apathy and disappointment, the team started migrating back to the hot, sandy center for our third long-distance communications test. I would fill the pilot role for the test, hanging from the BLV above the steaming tarmac and attempting to talk to a communications team in a mountaintop trailer 70 miles away.

Early June 2014: Long-Distance Communications Testing II

Calling this our third long-distance communications test was, for some, a bit of a stretch. Only once had an actual person hung above the tarmac in a spacesuit and attempted to stream data and voice communications to a faraway trailer bristling with antennas. The team had assembled a second time, but in the midst of mobilizing for the test, the communications system was suddenly and irrevocably withheld from us. We had no choice but to go home without even an attempt to establish communications between a spacesuit and a mountaintop. To my mind, a test is a test. That one failed because of political, not hardware, deficiencies.

We started our fourth great migration to the vacant Southwest. Over two days, the 15 or so people who would execute this signal transfer from desolation to desolation would straggle into town and stake out their territory in the Holiday Inn Express hotel extended-stay suites.

In this repeat of our original long-distance communications test, now using the new equipment, I hoped my ears would fill with the sweet sounds of crisp voices and not the head-rattling blatts of garbled noise I had experienced before. Even the best-case scenario would be a painful slog, however. I began to mentally prepare myself for another grueling run in the suit.

Our good luck began serendipitously when a communications tech and I took a long bike ride up the mountain pass to the ski area where the comm truck had been staged in the first test. It was a gorgeous, epic hill-climb for a cyclist, ascending thousands of vertical feet in just a few miles toward our prime long-distance communications site. I had located the original site while attempting to cycle to the summit of the same monster mountain, but I had been turned around by bad weather before the top. On this radiant, sunny day, the comm tech and I reached the summit and found an almost comical (because it was so perfect) parking lot and overlook one switchback past where the trailer had previously blocked the road with its hazards on for the other test. It was situated in exactly the correct place on the mountain. We had missed it because it was covered in clouds on the Google Map aerial images, making it invisible to us without a physical scouting trip.

We planned and gathered equipment with the intention of completing this test with three different payloads. We would test the communications equipment on each one. First would come the live suit. Then we would test out communications with our dummy assembly Ida. Finally, in a partial digression that would still give us some practice, we would squeeze in a test with a piece of equipment that was to be used with an entirely different project. (This one test was to be our only involvement with that project.)

We had fully abandoned our old avionics system and replaced it with a new version that literally sat in its place. It used the same bolt holes and physical mounting positions as the former, now-confiscated box. The only difference was that the suit system was now outfitted with a custom-designed, state-of-the-art long-distance communications system.

The new system did what is known as signal hopping and operated in publicly available frequency bands. Dan made us feel confident that it would not interfere with our radios. Everything was programmed to frequencies that were not owned by the old communications company. The chance of everything working was far better than before.

Ryan and Mitch came to the desert to meet us. This would be one of the first tests without Blikkies, leaving us to contend with the difficulties and intricacies of strapping on the parachute pack without someone from the parachute team physically on site.

We marched on toward test day. The bureaucracies raising concern about our rough-and-ready ways were more or less held at bay, since the test was a repeat of our earlier attempt which was, although a complete failure, safe. We spent the days before the test engaged in the typical monotonous successes and chaotic headaches of getting ready. We'd planned this test once before, so it didn't scare us. We ran through the normal phase zero checkouts to prepare the suit the few days ahead of time. A white shell on the front of the suit was having its maiden voyage, as well as new white knee- and elbow-pads. It looked to be near its final form. We were taking pride in the little things.

In contrast with our smooth suit-up efforts, drama was unfolding with the new communications system. Dan and the comm folks were running ground tests with the full systems active—and things looked bad. The few units that were built and available for the test were, one by one, ceasing to function. There was speculation that our new transmission array, with its higher-power transmitters and highly directional signals, was frying the receivers on the boards. This would be disastrous. If that was the case, we were in the process of wrecking all of our new comm boxes. Dan held out hope and kept testing late into the night. I helped by suspending a comm unit from the BLV near the airport exit to see how distance was affecting the strange signal drop-outs. Dan finally uncovered the failures. Multiple units were communicating at once in the new environment and data packets with the same names were confusing the systems. This problem was permanently and eminently solvable. Once again, confidence, determination, and work paid off. Crisis averted.

The night before the start of the comm test, Sebastian drove to the mountain for a long-distance pre-test of the comm system to verify for certain that the receivers hadn't been damaged from use at close range as had been previously suspected. His drive gnawed away at his night's sleep. After the chaos of scrambling to fix the communications equipment problems and executing a pre-test, our crew consisted of people who had been awake for nearly two days and would not be sleeping much before going through the dry run sequence and on to the test. As the test subject, I was allowed to sleep while most of this took place.

We had our usual dry run, spending the day prior to the test practicing the whole operation. The team knew the routine. The team practiced backing the truck up under the BLV and reaching to pretend to cut the tethers on the suit so it would fall into the padded truck bed if a suit situation arose and the BLV failed. I watched quietly, my normal role when I was to be the one in the suit. Zane methodically and matter-of-factly walked the paces.

Without much ado, we began the test. Per usual, we started long before dawn. Zane led the suit-up operation. We had decided, somewhat unfortunately as it turned out, that Blikkies could have a break and remain home in Florida because the test had nothing to do with parachutes. We experienced a rather scary moment where it became apparent that nobody on site and outside the suit was exactly sure how the release mechanisms assembled. Blikkies was the master of the release mechanisms and I was well versed in their assembly, but as the spacesuit was made ready to be taken away by the BLV, we learned that nobody else was.

While I dangled from the gantry about to be hoisted into the air from the release mechanism, I could just make out, through the double plastic head shell, debates and fiddling over the release mechanism. Finally, the crew took a cell phone picture of how the mechanism was rigged and showed it to me through the helmet so I could verify it was done right. It was a good thing they did. It was rigged inside out, with all the weight held by a cord too small to hold the system. The BLV would have probably dropped me, and the suit, onto the concrete. I walked them through the assembly of the releases from inside the suit, breathing my private oxygen supply and trying to maintain my mental readiness for the monotonous hours of hanging from a greasy crane over a cracked tarmac while crackling noise assaulted my ears.

As the crane inched backwards out of the wide, unzipped doorway of the clean tent inside the tin shed, the communications techs were setting up their giant ray-gun-like antennas on the beautiful mountain pass 70 miles away and a few thousand feet up.

Despite the problem with rigging the release mechanism, this hook-up and drive out was far less nerve-wracking for me than the first, reminding me how important it was that Alan get experience in every relevant environment. Practicing something once ahead of time makes the experience far more tolerable and less scary the second time around. Fear or nervousness at a critical moment can cause a fatal mistake, and you can't predict when those moments will come.

We got to the tarmac, just doing our jobs. Ryan and Zane walked next to the suit while John drove the crane. It was quiet and peaceful and normal and boring. We were regular people going about our day.

When I was over the mark, they removed my cooling lines and auxiliary power plug. I was set down on the launch sedan, so they wouldn't have to set me on the ground while the BLV grabbed the balloon equipment module. John picked up the balloon equipment module smoothly with the crane and drove it to where it hung over me. I was hooked up to the bottom of the balloon equipment module, and then the whole system, with me dangling from the suit at the bottom, was hoisted into the air. About halfway through the lift, my cooling lines were reconnected, along with the auxiliary power cable. The lift recommenced hoisting me to final height and swung me around to face the far-off mountain. I would dangle for up to seven hours, the doctor-mandated time limit for oxygen toxicity in this test.

Half an hour passed. I assumed they were performing all the comm checks they could without actually talking to me, such as making sure the new data system didn't crash into the GPS signals. These things take time. Questions from me would make them take longer. Sebastian's voice came on the line asking for a countdown from 10 on the push-to-talk radio. Unlike in the last test, his voice came through crystal clear. It was an incredible relief. I knew instantly that the interference problem was gone. I could see all my suit values displayed on the readouts, which meant that the data system was transmitting, and the voice signals were getting through. Dan the wizard had nailed it.

We walked through a few counts characterizing the quality, which stayed good. Sebastian had me switch over to the voice-activated radio, the backup system. Once again the signal was crystal clear. I got hoarse because I had to practically yell to activate the voice-activated system, making it apparent why we were only using it for backup.

The checks were meticulously thorough, but to my amazed surprise after what was probably an hour and a half of hanging, counting, and waiting, Sebastian signaled that they should let me down. The test was over. A complete and utter success. It all felt too brief. Unpunctuated by trouble. It was one of the only times in the program I was not that eager to get out of the suit. I had psyched myself for a long haul and instead I was coming down while it was still cool morning. The crane lowered me onto a set of thin mats laid onto the concrete at the test site.

Before removing the helmet, we took advantage of my suited-up state for more tests. I attempted, unsuccessfully, to pull the parachute handle. It bunched and shoved itself down into the handle guard, becoming unreachable. I kept struggling, but the outside crew soon recognized that I would not be able to grab the wadded handle with my gloved hand and cut the attempts.

The helmet came off after a couple tries. The thermal mittens made it tough, but it was doable. I slowly removed the bulky suit while John maneuvered the crane to grab Ida, our ever-willing and fearless dummy, for the second of three tests that would continue through the morning. The suit team retired to the tent for cleanup and basking in the uneventful success.

With Ida they would test the new communications box again. Ida was made of thick steel and so might block or alter the signals. That test was successful as well. There were a few small issues with interference, but nothing unexpected or unworkable. In every case, simple procedures circumvented the problems.

Our third payload was the tag-on where we tested the comm box yet again in the configuration specific to that system. It went just as smoothly. All the tests were clean. Everything talked like it was supposed to talk. It had become a theme for us that when we got what we wanted, it was anticlimactic. After working so hard and long against so many obstacles, it was difficult to get amped up about an extraordinary victory when it felt like just another day's work.

Clearing a final hurdle so calmly was sweet. First, a major test had failed. Next, human conflict destroyed an almost-working system. Finally, the system resurrected from the ashes was better than anything before. We would be getting bold again, striding toward the highest anthropomorphic dummy drop ever, and then the highest human balloon flight and freefall of all time.

Hanging in the StratEx pressure suit for the second time during a long-distance communications test.

Our communications trailer staged on the mountain for the third time to communicate with equipment at the airport below. (Photo by Dave Jourdan.)

The GPS track recorded during a communications test. On several tests we would fly over 100 miles from the main site to stress the communications signals.

Rolfe Bode holding a communications package that had just returned from a testing session in the stratosphere.

Launching a transponder test package from the Roswell tin shed. Photographer Dave Jourdan is watching the launch from a helicopter waiting to chase the balloon as it ascends. (Photo by Dave Jourdan.)

Long-distance communications testing from our BLV vehicle with a large payload.

CHAPTER 13

...

Big Balloons

L ife in the desert presented an intense duality. One part of it was
sweet beyond any aerospace engineer's imagination. We were building
a system for skydiving from the stratosphere and we had near-unlimited
money and resources to do it with. Unheard-of achievements required
unorthodox methods. We had helicopters, giant antenna arrays, and state-
of-the-art electronics. When we weren't in the thrall of this tinker's paradise,
we were miserable: stranded in a forgotten wasteland, far from home,
friends, and any semblance of normal life. Many of us resided for months
on end in hotel rooms in Roswell, New Mexico.

For every success we put under our belts, we had a failure to contend with. We were kept alive by the remainder of a chaotic extensive equation that barely but definitively tended toward positive values. Snapshots taken at any one moment might frame a mess or a masterpiece, while the whole widescreen movie would show a giant, cumbersome machine grinding in the general direction of its destination.

On top of the overwhelming difficulty of getting through the engineering, we were at that point more than ever playing town council. A substantial number of people required food, liquids, sanitation, transportation, and housing. We did all of this while careening toward our biggest balloon stand-up to date, followed by the record-high launch of a parafoil to the stratosphere and its autopilot flight down.

June 2014, Roswell, New Mexico: The World View Tycho Launch

The parafoil launch project called "World View" was a momentary diversion from the suit development. It was a totally different effort, spearheaded by the same leaders at the company leading the StratEx project. World View's dreamers envisioned a gondola to take paying customers to the edge of space, from where they would float down under a rectangular parachute called a parafoil. This effort was wiggled into our adventure for this one launch alone. The program we had been working on for the previous two years had been exclusively about one spacesuit and its one piloted flight to the edge of space. These two projects collided for this single launch because of several independently insignificant events.

Our company had gone through some lay-offs in the months prior to this launch, and one of our own, the spork vehicle driver, was among the casualties. The spork vehicle, a modified front-end loader critical to managing the balloon throughout the launch process, requires a uniquely trained driver. We had one test launch ahead of us, a dummy drop with Ida that would use our largest balloon, which we had exactly one of. So many variables could turn a launch into a disaster.

High-altitude balloons are sized for a specific altitude and a specific weight. The balloons rise while the helium in them expands until the balloon is full, at which point vents open and helium dumps out until it stops rising. This means the size of the balloon dictates what altitude it will go to. The balloons also had load tapes running longitudinally that held the weight of the payload. Those load tapes limited the amount of weight the balloon could hold. These two factors mean that balloons aren't always transferable from mission to mission. They have one specific altitude setting and a weight limit. Most importantly, they can only be used once—they are completely destroyed at the end of a mission.

Our balloon inventory was a hodgepodge. We had purchased seven balloons for the manned flights, one primary and one spare for each of three planned altitudes and one additional spare for the final 135,000-foot flight. Outside that set, we had a fairly random collection of additional balloons for testing that we had picked up in various deals, mostly with the Indian company Tata Institute of Fundamental Research. Most the balloons were made for other projects that for whatever reason didn't use them. All told, we had five balloons that weren't slated for manned flights and most went to different altitudes that may or may not have been suitable for any given test. We didn't want to risk ruining a balloon if our amateur driver made a mistake. Doing a stand-up for the World View team was an opportunity to give this driver needed experience.

The same leaders of the company working on our project were also in charge of World View, working on building the gondola with the parafoil. World View needed to do a launch to vet their parafoil systems, and it wasn't hard to strike a deal. We wanted a stand-up and they wanted a launch. If World View would make their test widget to the same size and shape of our suit system, they could hook it to our balloon and let it go. That also gave us a couple new valuable opportunities to chase the thing in some helicopters with real-live data.

During the mopping-up of the mess from our separation from the communications vendor, the people who weren't developing the new communications system were relatively free, and so for the first time in two years they could work on a different project than StratEx to help the gondola folks. We built up a big square box that was to represent a scaled-down version of the gondola, using home gym weights obtained from the Internet that helped the box mass to match the suit system mass. I built on my newly acquired high-altitude parachute system skills to figure out how to get a square parachute out over this contraption at very high altitudes.

The parachute vendor that was originally slated for the gondola project had also recently bailed, making everyone even sourer toward subcontractors and their tangled drama. The good news from that particular departure was that my crony Blikkies and his company, which had proved to be highly competent and drama-free, were able to step into this vacancy, putting me firmly into the mix for this test.

We hit the ground running. Blikkies did the concepts and the builds. I did the math. We quickly abandoned the former parachute company's plan to drop the high-altitude payload on a static cord that would pull the parachute out very close to the balloon, because we didn't want to worry if there was enough relative wind to be sure the parachute would actually open. We started work on using our newly invented SAEBER stiffened-bridle system, which activated upon releasing the payload, allowing it to fall far from the balloon into thicker air before opening the parachute. The SAEBER bridle allowed for the deployment of a stabilizer parachute right away, preventing the payload from tumbling while protecting it from being wrapped up by the stabilizer.

I was immersed in numbers, trying to predict the descent profile of the payload upon being cut away from the balloon. As usual, all of the math was in pursuit of a single number, this time, the number of seconds between payload separation from the balloon and parachute deployment. A timed pyrotechnic cutter would initiate a clock when the payload started to fall and would fire when that timer ran out, opening the deployment bag and letting the parachute out. We finished our design work, left the parachute folks to build the final rig, and migrated to the desert.

This time our little city was extra lively. Our tin shed crew was augmented by the crew that came with World View, which was headed by the loud Brit who ran our company, Jane Poynter, married to Taber, and not one to be trifled with.

The full launch team was on site preparing to send off their biggest balloon ever. I would help the parachute team rig the payload with our stiffener system. Another dozen onlookers from marketing, management, and the rest were there to collectively watch everything, ask too many questions, and touch too many things.

The event was to be used as a chase exercise for Alan's flight. We needed our chase procedures to be perfect by the time of his launch. We also needed to learn to work together with Dave, the new director for the chase operations. We began with a chase dry run.

We rigged a weather balloon with a communications package for a chase across the desert. The more staid executives had taken hold of the chase team and imposed new rules prohibiting off-roading during the chases except in the case of an emergency. Those of us who felt this was an unnecessary restriction had graduated to helicopters, so we didn't object.

The veteran balloon launcher filled a relatively small weather balloon in our rough hangar space. Per usual, they would give a newbie the uncomplicated task of letting go of the filled balloon. (Sebastian had taken to handing out Boy Scout weather balloon merit badges to anyone who launched a small balloon by letting go of it.) The balloon was filled and handed off. The first-timer was instructed to walk it outside and let it go. The winds were pretty high, so this would involve some walking around buildings to avoid a collision.

A little mob of managers and other members of the peanut gallery were standing outside the shed with excited looks on their faces as the Volkswagen-sized balloon emerged from the tin shed. When the turbulent wind outside the open hangar door hit the balloon, chaos ensued. Those of us who were familiar with balloon launches expected the balloon head to ripple and dance in the wind. Unsurprisingly, it folded over toward the ground. A wave of helpfulness passed through the onlookers, all of them eager to offer the suggestion that would rescue a situation that didn't need rescuing.

The balloon looked like a turbulent mess in the stout winds, but it was fine. It just needed to be walked around the buildings so it didn't careen into the side of one of them when released into the sky. Wind doesn't matter once a balloon starts to fly, but it makes things very strange right at the moment of launch. Somewhere in the confusion, the newbie balloon launcher froze and just stared at the violent bashing of the balloon through the invisible rapids. This type of balloon is launched with the parachute in line with the payload so the parachute will already be out if the balloon pops early and drops the payload, a detail that further alarmed the onlookers. As the balloon leaned over far enough for air to get up into the throat of the parachute, the parachute began to flap open on the ground. Despite the big flashing sheets of bright fabric, there was still no real problem. The newbie launcher just needed to walk the balloon to a place where there were no obstacles downwind. Someone from the crowd yelled, "Let it go!" and the frozen launcher woke up and listened. Letting go was very much the wrong thing to do.

Once free, the payload swung sideways like a clock pendulum directly into the air-conditioning unit affixed to the nearest building. After the wincing bash, it seemed like it would rotate sideways around the building and take to the sky. The payload swung hard in a parabola toward open space. The bottommost part of the launch train, hanging beneath the main load, was a dangling weather box the size of a thermos. As that little box turned the corner around the building, it swung under the arm of a light tower, whipping in a full loop and cleanly tying itself to the portable floodlight. The balloon lifted the top of the light tower right off the ground, dragging the base across the ground until it separated and fell. The head remained attached to the balloon. The balloon train, with its newly acquired caboose, cleared the building. The system was unpredictably heavy now.

At first the balloon lifted skyward like it was going to carry the whole light tower head right on into the stratosphere, but then the weight of the system prevailed and it came back down, smacking against the road leading to the runways. The system was tearing off at the speed of the wind, bashing the payload against the ground over and over again like a baby thumping a rattle against the floor. The balloon was heading off toward the airport terminal and a field of out-of-service airplanes with a jagged metal light tower head dangling off the bottom of it. I sprinted after it.

I reached the bouncing mess when it was about a football field away from the buildings, just as the small weather package beneath the main payload managed to untie itself from the rest of the balloon and leave the gnarly, now bashed-up light tower head behind on the ground. Somehow in all the shaking, the string had untied itself, leaving the main payload in an amazingly undamaged state. The balloon ascended peacefully away. We walked back toward the buildings, past the little-kid grins of the spectators, and jumped into the chase trucks. Nobody said too much. I assume someone cleaned up the light tower head.

We started driving. Our chase was uneventful. We hauled off across the open countryside to the east. This was our first time trying out chasing balloons without going off-road. Everyone who had ever driven a truck off-road had been removed from the drivers' seats. The trucks stayed together. We called ahead to landowners to let them know we would be entering their land. This was clearly a meander, not a chase. It was a good thing we had enlisted a team of helicopters for our mission, because the days of getting under a balloon payload with a truck were over. In a straightforward chase run, with the balloon eventually coming down within a mile of a major road, we ended up a full 45 minutes behind it. If that was Alan, he could have been dead by then. The trucks in this safety-centric chase plan were clearly reduced to picking up hardware well after it landed.

With the balloon payload already on the ground, we drove east and into a ranch. The trucks split up at a fork. For old time's sake, Joe and I prodded the careful driver to push it onto what one could call a road. Certainly it was a road for cows. We parked on the flatlands next to a watering hole and set out on a mile-long hike toward the foam box that lay somewhere in the wasteland in front of us. With Joe and me on the same team, there was no sense racing. In no time we had the stratospheric payload in hand, scrape marks from the AC unit still pressed into the side.

We went home to sleep it off for a few days before having a go at the real launch. When we returned, hardware work was in full swing, finalizing the payloads and preparing to lift the big box off the ground.

Once again, the little team got bigger as the day got closer. The operators of the guidance unit for the parafoil were on site from Canada working with the parachute crew tying up the final details of how the payload would release from a ground command, fall for a period of time under the stabilizing drogue parachute, then deploy the main parachute to guide the box to a preprogrammed landing site.

We had our weather window worked out by Don, but there were some complications. A small team convened in what felt like a rather secret meeting the day before the first day of the window during which we would try to launch. It was unveiled later that one of the many things making westerly trajectories unattractive are military operating areas (MOAs), which occasionally restrict airspace in certain regions. The MOAs would be active for the launch, but the team made a night-before-launch decision to continue, with a plan to float over the restricted areas at high altitude.

It was a brazen decision. It would require taking all the equipment to altitude for over twice as long as it had been tested for. This team was at the part of the project where they had to smash some grapes; they weren't endangering anything other than their own ability to succeed. Everything—from the equipment freezing or running out of power to the helicopters running out of fuel—would be a risk. We would press on with a drastically altered mission plan set in motion a dozen or so hours before the start.

We went to bed in the afternoon as we always did, and got up in the middle of the night to start the launch. The setup process was uneventful. The weather team went in before the rest of the crew to set up aerostats (flying blimp-shaped weather stations) and a balloon we called a pie ball to examine winds at various heights all the way to the altitude the balloon would reach. I was much less occupied during this launch than normal without a suit to tend to and because the hardware had its own team to manage it. I helped pack the stabilization chute and prepare the helicopter for our first chase attempts.

The helicopter would include one person from the parachute control system team who had the ability to set a beacon to change the landing location of the payload in case something didn't go as planned with the original trajectories. Joe would act as the navigator for our flight. I would monitor the payload using a remote telemetry package. I hoped to gain experience monitoring a system in flight and working the mission control software.

We had been working over the past days to improve the power system for the laptop, which was running a highly demanding mission control program and drinking batteries faster than one an hour. We would run the box on uninterrupted power using an inverter connected to the helicopter's 12-volt power source. All was ready early.

The team ran through the motions. The payload was brought out early so that the forklift would be free for the launch crew. The weather team launched a pathfinder balloon to get a closer look at the winds and weather conditions very high in the atmosphere. The pie ball balloons were tethered so they only found wind at one altitude relatively close to the ground. A pathfinder balloon floated through the atmosphere to examine winds all the way up until it popped at over 100,000 feet. That balloon, for unknown reasons, popped at an altitude lower than the ideal, leaving the meteorology team without a comprehensive picture of what was going on at the top of the stratosphere. Weather reports from other stations in the southwestern US still gave a decent idea of where the balloon would go, so things marched on.

Just after sunrise, the weather team provided the launch team with a final layout direction. The launch established several mini teams within the launch crew, each with its own procedures for completing their tasks, equipment inventories, and preparation. Team Diesel fired up the heavy equipment to set out the giant launch platen at the exact launch location, then placed concrete barriers to surround the platen and connect to it with heavy cables so it wouldn't move. Team Fill laid long canvas mats on the surface of the runway where the balloon would lie during the stand-up process. Two arms extended from the main layout mat, creating the surface where the balloon and its fill arms would lie. With the ground cloths down, a truck with the balloon box on the back would drive down the layout mat while paying out the balloon over a spinning bar, much like pulling tin foil from a roll.

The balloon was wrapped in a bright pink cover to keep it protected during the lay-down and preparation process. By the time the layout was done, a pink line stretched the length of a football field from the launch platen to the end of the mats where Team Diesel had staged the spork vehicle ready to guide the filled balloon into its standing position. Today the launch platen had ended up near the end of the abandoned runway with the fat pink line running in the best-guess wind direction for the launch moment.

The winds fluctuated as the morning rolled on, waxing and waning. It never felt like the wonderful launch morning we wanted. We were out of season. With the balloon laid out, the leaders met again to discuss the winds. The shaky table legs got shakier in what appeared to be a conclusion that they would go forward even though the conditions were outside the launch limits. The StratEx flight manual stated that the winds at the launch site that morning were too high. Our team wanted to gain the necessary experience for the spork vehicle driver, and it was apparently reasoned that higher winds made for a better, more stressing experience for the driver. As for World View, they seem to have decided to go forward with the operation because it was the only chance they had. Our past experience suggested that the launch would likely fail, but it was clear that everyone involved in decision-making thought it was an acceptable risk. I wasn't at the meetings. I made a case not to launch when I heard the conclusions afterwards, arguing that the extended mission duration and out-of-limits winds made for too many unknowns too close to launch time. It wasn't my call, though. The fill proceeded.

The fill lines were extracted from the plastic tube, laid down their own personal runways, and secured over the bazooka-style helium diffusers out of which helium would roar through the fill tubes and into the balloon head. The head of the balloon was doubled back over the spork vehicle drum. As the clouds above the horizon started to turn pink, the fill lines swelled to tubes. The sound of the gushing helium was loud enough to make the bystanders, a quarter-mile away, wince. The plastic tubes found a resonance and vibrated like the reed of an oboe. The noise intensified. As more and more helium poured into the head, the spork vehicle moved slowly forward, freeing more and more of the balloon to be filled.

As the balloon head grew, two people held down the massive crown valve atop the balloon to prevent it from lifting off the ground, waiting for the perfect moment to release it to ascend above the balloon. If it was released too early, it would fall back to the ground, banging against the concrete and possibly damaging itself or the fragile balloon. If they held on too long, it would drag them over the folded balloon surface and their boots could destroy the lower portions of the balloon still stretched along the ground. If they held on even longer, the helium would lift them right into the air.

The helium rushed into the massive, growing balloon head. Per usual, the tension grew with the size of the ball of helium inside the balloon. The two holders started to struggle, their feet dragging toward the folded balloon. Just as it looked like they would be lifted right off the ground, they got the signal to let it go and released it. The bubble of the balloon lifted up into the air. The big valve lagged behind the blooming plastic until the forces evened out and pushed the metal valve above the balloon body that was forming into an upside-down teardrop. The balloon was standing. The fill continued. Spurts of helium were shot into the standing tower through fits of yelling and hand waving. After 10 minutes of fine-tuning, John, the launch master, had dialed in on the target pressures. The balloon head was at its final size.

The spork vehicle inched forward to release some constricted balloon. For this launch we would use an additional piece of equipment called a balloon collar. The collar would be fastened with bungees around the balloon stalk, keeping it organized, tight, and pressurized such that the balloon head couldn't luff and spinnaker in the wind.

Half of Team Diesel accompanied the spork vehicle as it crept forward, allowing the head of the balloon to inch higher into the sky as the other Team Diesel member broke open the pink plastic sleeve in front of the vehicle. The plastic flowed around the drum as the balloon head rose up, arching further and further into the wind away from the vehicle.

The winds were stout and growing as the balloon rose. We were witnessing the chief difficulty of launching balloons. The head of the balloon was being blown a couple of school bus lengths in front of the spork vehicle. It was clear about halfway through the stand-up that the payload would need to travel a substantial distance sideways before being allowed to leave the ground, lest it drag or bounce.

Pendulum Arc of the Baloon Launch

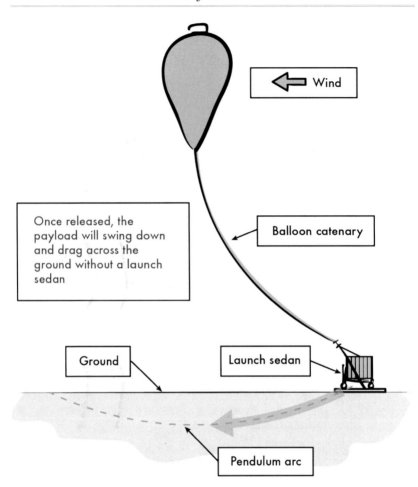

The spork vehicle ended its drive. The balloon head was traversing back and forth, listing away from the vehicle in a bizarrely mathematical-looking arc. The tube of wadded plastic extruding from the drum on the front of the spork was heavily angled out away from the vehicle. At the end of the drive, the vehicle would barely be able to swing the drum to free the remainder of the balloon because the balloon was leaning so far over and shifting off to one side. The drum was opened. The balloon head, pulled upward by the helium and simultaneously dragged by the wind, tugged on the main attachment webs holding it to the launch platen.

The call was made for the hook-up. The part of the exercise relevant to Alan's project was finished. The rest was in the hands of the World View team, who seemed determined to release the balloon come hell or high water.

The winds were almost triple the allowed limits for the StratEx program. The launch sedan holding the box was quickly moved to the launch point. The box was hooked to the base of the balloon, along with the one release cable. The winds were gusting so hard that the balloon was flattening the attachment rigging onto the top of the payload. The parachute engineer feared that the rubbing metal, which was supposed to remain above the system, would pull the trigger pins on the pyrotechnics. He ran in to hold the rigging up. Too much time was going by. The balloon needed to be either launched or deflated. The leaders ground through details of what was at risk launching in the wild winds. Within one minute, the decision to launch was made. Joe ripped the cord with two pushers standing ready to guide the payload. The turbulence in the air brought violence to the ground.

The tethers fell away, and we all watched with wincing squints as the mighty balloon yanked the payload right out of the pushers' hands. With no pushers to guide the sedan straight, and the sedan having only turning wheels in the back, the sedan quickly veered to the side like a shopping cart pushed from the front. The payload tumbled out. By our later estimations, the balloon head was almost half a football field ahead of the payload at this point, so the sedan survived only a tiny fraction of the long journey to liftoff. The payload lay on its side and with wild speed and fury, jammed its corner hard into the concrete, deforming the foam (which was intended for landings, not takeoffs). In a stroke of luck, the foam protected the fragile antennas buried beneath it. The cube raised a whirl of dust as it dragged on the concrete and then tilled a furrow into the grass before arcing without the tiniest sway into the air and starting its peaceful ascent to the stratosphere.

Everyone turned their heads sideways and breathed out, then passed around congratulatory handshakes for a "successful" launch. Now I had a role in the operation. We would hop around in the helicopter, chasing the balloon path and covering a theoretical abort. First the balloon would float to clear the military areas before cutting loose the payload for an attempted landing at a preprogrammed site. The parafoil could be steered by a machine pulling in and releasing the steering lines attached to the tail of the parafoil. Our data antenna was fastened to the built-in antenna of the helicopter. It communicated with the payload, giving us real-time location information and the option to actuate the secondary cut-down if the primary failed. Joe sat in the copilot seat with a handheld GPS to keep tabs on our location. I would track the payload's location. The third person rode along on the off chance we needed to set a beacon to redirect the landing.

The mission was running clean despite the payload pounding across the runway on takeoff. The pilot spun the rotors to take us to our first holding point. I played it cool. The loud engines roared to life. The racing shadows of the rotors blinked across the dash until the shadow became a disc. We did a communications check across the helicopter's internal radio system, and the pilot alerted the tower of our imminent ascent and departure to the east for a holding spot in the wide nothingness. We funneled out, watching the grass bend away like circular toppling dominos until we rose above the airport and flew away.

The farms passed below as we approached and passed the payload, also flying east in the low-altitude winds. Joe navigated us to the holding region, and the pilot found an open patch of long green grass where he could touch down. Within minutes of leaving the airport, we had lost radio communication with mission control, so our first touchdown would serve as a much-needed communications call to home base to find out what the balloon was doing and whether our plan would stick. Helicopters are too loud inside for cell phone calls. The grass flattened around us again as the pilot set the chopper down neatly in the peaceful field. The monster balloon was in perfect view, miles high nearly directly above us. It was taking on a rounder form as it floated toward a turnaround point where it would encounter the hard stratospheric winds pointing directly west. After making a full one-eighty, it would fly west for the remainder of its journey.

To the west of Roswell was a highly secretive, highly restricted missile range called White Sands. Unlike the MOAs, this missile range could not be crossed over at any altitude and was actively monitored by radar for intruders. The missile range was a blessing and a curse. It was a long, skinny range running from north to south about 100 miles west of Roswell. On the upside, it blocked commercial air traffic, making Roswell skies quiet and friendly to experimental missions like ours. On the downside, in the off-season all payloads flew west in the stratosphere and would enter the range.

The deep green field was calm. It felt equally like a privilege and an oddity to be in this field, cut off from human traffic by fences, long distances, and the absence of roads. We got an order from mission control to wait. We ate sandwiches from a cooler, drank Gatorade, and watched the sparkly orb float above us. We maintained constant contact on a conference line, listening to the trucks make their way on the sparse roads, heading in the opposite direction directly toward the predicted landing site.

As I sat with my back against the helicopter tail and an eye on the balloon, the call came through to move. The balloon had made its turn, crossed back over us, and was heading fast to the west, roughly an hour into its mission and halfway to its float altitude, already higher than the daily airplane traffic crisscrossing the country. We spun up the rotors and lifted out of the long green grass with an eye on all the telemetry that drew a bright green line across my computer screen, indicating where the balloon had been.

We flew beneath the balloon yet again for what was supposed to be one final staging point before heading to the hills in the east to try to see the landing. As soon as the helicopter touched down, I ran out, head ducked, to call into mission control. They ordered us to wait. We powered down. Within moments, with the balloon now far into the stratosphere, we were instructed to head west to the staging point. The telemetry was showing us the balloon had stopped rising.

We headed west. The desert west was described to us over and over as a cowboy country, a black hole that ate balloons, payloads, and people. The terrain gets vicious. Rising hills, rock outcroppings, and buttes hide lurking hazards and mission artifacts. The roads end just a few miles west of Roswell, leaving helicopters as the only vehicle for recovery. Communications cease to function out there. It was fabled by previous missions that even GPS and the sturdiest radio signals become unreliable in the no-man's-land we were flying into near the White Sands missile range.

As we approached our mark on the fringes of the badlands, the helicopter circled and hovered, looking for a spot where our cell phones got service and we could call mission control. We found a hilltop and powered down, this time with the bad news that our fuel was running low, low enough that we might not catch the landing and still have sufficient fuel to make it home. We were just learning about the limitations of helicopters and the criticality of fuel levels. The pilots were always careful to maintain enough fuel to get back to the nearest airfield with a healthy margin. The further a mission got from the airfield, the more fuel it consumed and the more fuel had to be held in reserve to get back. It was as if we ran out of fuel twice as fast as the helicopter actually burned it.

Mission control was likely now using the giant valve at the top of the balloon to bring the balloon down. Enough time had elapsed and distance covered that the balloon could drop down on the far side of the military operating areas. Once over the military areas, the balloon would release its payload and destroy itself before it could fly into the missile range and a potential world of bureaucratic pain. Cell phone service was patchy, but we got a call in. Adding to the fuel problems, our power system was not working as expected. A complex problem had arisen that caused the laptop to fail when plugged into the power source, so we were running on batteries. We only had two of them. The computer I was using was the secondary cut-down method for the payload and needed to keep working to maintain the backup release function. We would fly back to the airport to fuel the helicopter and pick up a pile of laptop batteries that were already being raided from every computer on site.

We flew fast, low to the ground where the air was thick. The farms of Roswell sped below us and we notified a now-tense air traffic controller that we were landing for fuel. After the fuel truck filled us up, we hopped from the fuel station to the grassy field outside mission control. A ducking figure raced to the helicopter holding a lunchbox-sized uninterrupted power source and a stack of nearly every laptop battery in our tech city. The rotors never stopped turning as the runner dropped off the batteries and ran away.

We would fly back to our previous location on the fringes of the western hills and wait again for final instructions.

After landing again on the rocky hilltop, the call was made. The balloon was racing over the western mountains at impressive speeds, over 70 miles an hour, still far above the bustle of normal air traffic. The crown valve was open and the balloon was slowly descending.

Not long after we left the launch site, it was clear that something was wrong. The mission control line was tense and busy. The trucks were being rerouted further to the west, and we too were going to get a new position deep into the sketchy hills between our current location and the missile range. There were several large mountains between us and the missile range, mountains too high for helicopters to cross.

The payload's guidance system was not capable of a real-time adjustment to its landing zone. If the drop location of the payload was out of range of the programmed landing zone, it would fly in a straight line toward the landing zone until it collided with whatever was in front of it when it ran out of altitude. Mission control was now worried that the straight line it would make toward its preprogrammed landing site would run it directly into the mountain range between the missile range and us. We got new instructions to fly to a location where a straight line to us would miss the mountains, and then call mission control. If things continued in their current way, mission control would instruct us to set our beacon, sending the payload to us, instead of on a straight-line course to its pre-set landing location.

We flew to our new spot as the balloon raced on toward the missile range. The pilot landed the helicopter at our mark, perhaps further from any sign of human habitation than I had ever been. Our cell phones, strangely, showed full signal, but when a call was attempted nothing happened. The balloon was rushing downwards, now approaching the altitude where the payload was intended to be released. The helicopter's back seat was alive with activity. We were swapping batteries into the laptop and constantly rebooting to keep the control software live. The altitude of the balloon leveled at the release point. Joe and I got out of the helicopter and ran to different hilltops in search of cell phone service, with no luck. With no cell service and the satellite phone still packed away, our third passenger was made useful; he jogged to the next hill and initiated the signal to set the beacon.

If everything worked, in a few minutes a big orange canopy would soar our way and we would scramble to get the helicopter clear of the landing site before the payload smashed into it. We rushed back to watch for the release of the payload on the computer. The altitude stayed remarkably stable as we stared at the numbers streaming in. Then it fell. The ascent rate turned hugely negative and we knew it was gone, perhaps on a collision course with the little hilltop where our silent third passenger had set his beacon.

For the first time since the World View team's arrival and preparations, skepticism about the beacon's ability to draw the payload formed. Our silent foreign guest in charge of the beacon was not confident it would work. Realizations and admissions tend to happen at the absolute last moment, when the truest realities of a situation can be appreciated in the actual environment. The beacon was meant to change the course of a payload dropped from an airplane toward a drop zone within eyeshot, not miles away and miles high. The unit was a movie-like giant black cube with an antenna and one button. The silent passenger was pushing the button.

Back in the helicopter, we stared at the computer screen. The numbers didn't update. The descent rates were still frozen at an astronomically high rate. If the payload leveled out under an open canopy, it should have stabilized and regained signal. It looked like the canopy had not opened, and the payload was plummeting. Then the descent rates stabilized, and the mission control program filled with numbers again. The signal was back. Our hearts briefly floated while we saw the tracking screen populate with dots that formed a line indicating a working open canopy. The team had just pulled off one of the highest parafoil openings in the history of parachuting.

With a fully working wing above the payload, we had time. I ripped open the satellite phone and tried to call mission control. The conference line was still hot. Our team was not aware, but the concerns of the payload colliding with the mountains had subsided. The winds had favorably pushed the balloon away from the track that would have put it behind the mountain. We no longer needed to set the beacon, but we didn't know that from inside the helicopter. In a mad scramble to miss a run into the missile range's restricted space, the payload had been dropped. The payload separation was followed by the flight computer drop, which ripped the balloon in half on its way down. From what mission control could tell, everything had started the journey toward Earth just in time.

The first words Sebastian said to me when the satellite phone was initiated were "Do not set the beacon."

I responded with a line-silencing "Negative, the beacon has already been set."

The truck with the other beacon had been on the way to a possible landing site, and mission control had opted, while we were out of touch, to set that beacon. Now both beacons had been set, and nobody really knew if either had worked, meaning that the 500-pound box could have been aiming at any of three possible locations.

It was most likely that neither of the beacons worked. The control system techs seemed to realize far too late in the process that the hardware had never been used at anywhere near the distances at which we were using it. The beacon system likely had too weak of a signal to actually reach the payload. There was some speculation that perhaps sending two beacon signals would have somehow scrambled up its computer, but that would have been unlikely. The beacon units were identical, so if the signals reached the payload, it should have just updated back and forth between the landing sites until finally choosing the last signal it received.

Not knowing if our beacon was set or not, I left the helicopter when the payload began to near the ground. We stared at the surrounding lightly clouded skies in search of a bright orange rectangle flying at our hilltop.

Energies were extremely high. I pictured in my mind a massive guided parafoil exploding through the surrounding clouds, whirling the white condensate behind it, and cranking a leaning turn into our mountain top while we ran. I pictured the canopy coming in long and wrapping its lines around the helicopter blades (though we had set the beacon what was decided to be a safe distance away), or some rolling, bashing combination of the two in which the canopy wrapped into the payload and went hurtling down a hill. None of those things happened.

The beacon was never set. The payload continued on a straight-line path toward the landing site programmed into it many hours before launch. Since the trajectories were off by tens of miles (actually not bad in ballooning terms), the payload would not make it to that landing site. If the payload didn't make it to a landing site, its preprogrammed landing elevation would certainly be wrong. The parafoil system wouldn't fire a flare to slow its motion for a landing, and the payload would eat dirt. That is exactly what happened.

In the final fleeting minutes of the descent, it became clear to mission control that the payload was not heading toward either beacon. The helicopter was given last-minute instructions to get airborne in an attempt to see the landing. In what was a serious anticlimax for our little team, the helicopter pilot informed us we again had too little fuel to continue. We headed toward the tin shed.

We flew in silence. The payload collided with the ground 30-some miles from our position in the badlands west of Roswell. My blood was racing at 1,000 miles per hour. I wanted to jump in the driver's seat and fly up to watch that canopy land. I wanted to go back in time and make the missing call that would have sent us to the landing site in the first place, like we were supposed to.

It would remain a minor point of contention whether I had followed my orders. Some would judge that in the heat of the moment and with a selfish desire to have the prized payload land near me, I had ordered our beacon to be set before attempting the satellite phone. Everything happened fast, and ultimately my actions had no impact on how the events of the day unfolded.

Nevertheless, I was nervous about the reactions I would meet when we got back.

The day was a success, especially given the starting circumstances, although I felt that my team and I had failed at our mission. That flight would help to restructure how our chase operations went, how we dealt with fuel, communications, and actions in the event that there were no orders. It was a worthwhile exercise. I tried to set aside emotions that waffled between excitement and a sense of failure. We had balloon hardware scattered across a formidable countryside that would need to be recovered.

We powered the helicopter down outside mission control. The site was electric with the feeling we had pulled off an incredible miracle. We had launched a payload in unheard-of winds, survived a bash with the runway, ascended to the upper stratosphere, dodged a maze of military operations and missile ranges at fantasy altitudes, and dropped a payload that flew a guided path toward a predetermined location. It was not elegant, but we had in fact done it, and the nay-sayers (who had included me at times) should have kept their mouths shut.

Mission control still buzzed with tense static, trying to direct trucks to payload, balloon, and equipment scattered across the desert. We needed to recover instruments, data loggers, and cameras. The teams were having particular trouble reaching the flight computer, which had landed far from any roads. As soon as we fueled up at mission control, we would fly out again, leaving Joe at the tin shed. John and I would search for the flight computer, which was only showing one working tracker instead of two. With GPS coordinates for the flight computer, balloon carcass, and release point programmed into our onboard computers, we flew toward the snaggle-toothed mountains.

The flight was long. The balloon had made its way across the state. We drained the better part of a tank of fuel just getting into the region where the drops had taken place. My eyes were glazing over as the adventure strung into its 17th hour. I was alert, but punchy. The hills looked gentler. We rolled over the pecan farms toward the bigger, more formidable mountains. The computer, which we thought had landed several miles from the payload, was somewhere in the lightly forested land beyond the rocky hilltops.

As we rounded the final hills toward the area where we had expected to find the payload, we spotted a white recovery truck parked on the road. We flew low over the bed of the truck, expecting to see the flight computer in the bed. Puzzled, we started circling the area looking for the red and blue canopy attached to the computer that would be draped somewhere in the trees. This was a different canopy than the one on the main experiment. It was a smaller round parachute responsible for bringing down the flight computer only. Instead of a parachute, we found four people hunting through the woods.

We landed the chopper and found the ground crew, one of whom was carrying a GPS tracker. The one working tracker had flown off the flight computer at some unknown point. We had accidentally flown a helicopter for an hour to the chase crew and a useless tracker. The flight computer was somewhere in the completely desolate area with no working trackers.

The ground recovery folks ducked down in the helicopter wind as we took off to fly the line to the balloon carcass, trying to puzzle together the pieces of information we had. The payload, with its active wing, had headed toward its programmed destination. The winds aloft would have scattered the remaining components in a rough straight line with the ballast masses first, then the balloon carcass, which had no parachute, only a streaming plastic tail. The relatively light flight computer hanging beneath its big parachute would land last, hopefully softly. We opted to fly to the balloon carcass first, gather the valuables from that site, and then hunt for the computer in a straight line past the carcass. We left the four lone hunters rustling through the trees. Back at the hotel, people were undoubtedly drinking beer.

Balloons are easy to find. The plastic lays a giant reflective disc over trees and shrubbery, in marked contrast to the dun landscape. We flew the wind line and as soon as the forest ended we saw it, not far from what must have been one of the most isolated farms in the state.

John and I yanked, cut, and swam through the ocean of sticky plastic, pulling out the giant valve at the top of the balloon. We took some pictures, gathered the cameras, and left the rest to be retrieved by a chase truck. It was getting toward dusk.

We loaded up, solemn and determined, focused on the flight computer. We'd use the remaining fuel to fly a figure eight over the wind line. It was perfect searching terrain, with nothing to distract: no hills, no trees, not even grass, just flat dirt. We flew to the limits of our fuel. Right turn, left turn, right turn, left turn. Occasionally someone would spot something that looked like color. It was always nothing. We didn't find our quarry.

I remained personally conflicted. The team had succeeded against poor odds and potentially disastrous turns of events, yet I felt apart from that success. I had logged two chase and recovery failures and regretted having joined the team of nay-sayers in the moments before the launch. I still would have said the launch preparations had been insufficient. It seemed like success was due to luck rather than planning, but we would never know, and I would cheer for a job well done with the rest. Go team, I guess.

As we flew home, we reviewed the numbers and wind speeds trying to figure out where the flight computer had gone. It was looking as though its parachute had not deployed, meaning the computer would have fallen upwind of the balloon carcass, where the ground team was still searching.

It made sense that the tracker would have flown off in the extreme wind speeds of the crash landing. It would explain why the second tracker wasn't working; it would have smashed into the ground at 120 miles per hour.

After parking the helicopter, we made our way back to the hotel and my funk lifted. After going more than 18 hours straight, we were done, our payload had flown. A ground recovery truck had made it to the main payload and got the cameras off during our hunt for the other equipment. Beers popped and excited engineers elbowed each other for a view of the nerd-porn playing over and over on a screen. We yipped and pointed as the videos from the payload cameras rolled through breath-taking views of the Earth from above and the wild high-altitude canopy deployment. The stratospheric blackness is unique. The orange canopy was lit up by the sun, but with no atmosphere to speak of, the sky behind it is black, not blue. But something seems wrong. There are no stars. In the stratosphere, and space for that matter, the light balance is just right so that the sky appears jet black. It is not quite lightless enough for even the brightest stars to poke through. The result is that the images look fake—ironically, doctored promotional images with stars look more real.

On a different day, debriefings would reckon with the crazy risks taken at launch, the communication snarls, and the difficult recovery. The parachute opening had been a bit faster and harder than ideal. Yet the experiment's success was undeniable. This victory pushed the World View team to a new level of confidence. For them, the big leagues were just around the corner.

Partway through the party, the final chase truck rolled in, the team we had left trekking through the forest. Refusing to return empty-handed, the group had retrieved all the equipment the helicopter couldn't carry from the balloon carcass site. In the bleary revelry only possible after 24 hours of chasing balloon equipment in the badlands of New Mexico, they had affixed a bull skull to the front of the truck. There was a hint of tribal rogue spirit among them and they, like me, would be questioned as to whether they had followed their orders. But not tonight. We took science cowboy pictures, holding high-tech pieces of metal in front of the bull skull and the mud-covered truck.

The next day, our theories about the fate of the flight computer were validated when Joe, Esteban, and their chase team found it upwind of the balloon carcass landing site, smashed to pieces after a 10-mile plummet from the edge of space. The videos would show that the gore line responsible for destroying the balloon had failed to separate after tangling on one of the many snaggy points of the frame of the flight computer and then snarled with the parachute, collapsing it in flight. The tracker ripped off by the high-speed winds was found miles away.

Superstition doesn't sit long in the minds of scientists, but it was hard to believe we hadn't used up some of our good luck that day. If unseen forces favored our progress, it was only just barely. We would proceed boldly—but carefully.

Late June 2014, Roswell, New Mexico: Wrapped up in a Very Big Balloon

While the previous launch had been touted as a flawless success, everyone on the team knew it had uncovered a host of problems, and was no triumph of robust engineering. The problems, some directly encountered in the flight and some uncovered by it, formed a terrifying matrix of issues that we would try to power through fast. Engineering designs we had spent years developing were being rethought in minutes and rebuilt in days.

It was no trick to realize why the press releases carried no mention or video footage of the launch itself, no images of the payload flipping out of its cart and cheese-grating its broadside face on an abandoned runway and out into the dirt. On top of the botched launch there was the issue with the balloon's flight computer smashing into the shrub forest short of the balloon landing site. To top matters off, I learned after the flight that a bad transponder caused air traffic control to lose sight of the balloon during the flight, making us beyond unpopular with air traffic control, who had to rely on phone calls and GPS coordinates to track the monster balloon during the mission. The list of problems was overwhelming, but management had tasted success and now had no sign of lifting their foot off the pedal.

Technological readiness aside, we had at most a couple weeks of marginally usable weather before launching season closed up for the summer. If we didn't do our remaining unmanned drop to prove out the new drogue system's ability to keep a pilot stable, our chances of launching Alan that year would shrivel. We were relentless in our determination to get a large balloon in the sky with our dummy payload beneath it before the heat of summer set in. We had to know if Ida would spin out.

We had to redesign the launch cart to make sure that what happened to the last payload at launch didn't happen to Alan. We needed a transponder that worked. Our balloon flight computer parachute system needed to be fixed if we were to stop spraying computer parts into the shrubbery. Most importantly, this issue with the scenario leading up to the flight computer's smash-up had raised a much larger concern that the long gore line paying out through a hole in the bottom of the balloon had a tendency to snag on things. That snagging had happened on the low side, at the computer, so even though the gore line failed to separate from the balloon-side flight computer, it had still successfully departed from the balloon, allowing the gore to rip. Had that line snagged on something upstream of the falling computer instead of on the computer itself, it could have arrested the computer's departure or broken the gore line off, either of which would have resulted in a rogue balloon, one that could travel around the sky for a long time.

Stratospheric ballooning is only a fair-weather game. Several pieces of the weather issue puzzled together to form the map of the launch windows. The launch window at the time was borderline on several counts. First and most simply, stratospheric launches need low wind. Standing balloons make an acres-wide sail, applying enormous forces to their attachment points. The big plastic sail bends in the wind, forming a curve called a catenary between the balloon head and the payload. Upon release, it swings like a pendulum, sending the payload diving into the ground or ripping the balloon apart, whichever comes first. Once the balloon has left the ground, high winds stop being a threat; the balloon simply moves with the wind, so wind speeds don't usually apply forces. The path where the wind will send the balloon through the tens of miles of ascent does, however, play a major role in whether any given day is a launch day. There are places the balloon can't land, like populated areas or military grounds. There are places a stratospheric balloon can't even fly over, like secretive missile ranges or big cities. If the flight path will send our balloon somewhere forbidden, we don't fly.

Drifting to the west out of Roswell was problematic because the terrain was rough for landing and because the missile range posed a huge north-south barrier. Combining all the restrictions, there were two windows during the year with sure-thing launch days. We were not in either of them. The better of the two was a couple of months away. With each passing day over the next few weeks, the weather got worse in multiple ways. The westerly stratospheric winds increased. Winds got stronger and more variable in general as the days got hotter, while nearly every day thunderstorms threatened to soak our ground cloths and make them unmanageable.

If the weather window closed, we would leave the waning spring season with too many tasks unaccomplished. The fall window, which we were hoping to use for manned flights, would get used up with dummy drops and training exercises, pushing the program another half-year into the future while we waited out the winter for another window in the spring. This summed to a drive to launch, even in marginal weather. Even though a balloon and its helium cost more than a modest house, this was an acceptable risk.

Summer days are hot and nights are cool, making the winds at the ground difficult to predict. Gusts are hard to gauge. "Light and variable" were the best winds we could hope for. Light and variable winds lead to tricky, shifting wind directions which disrupt layout and challenge our deepest theories about how our newfangled launches were supposed to work.

We had been in the desert for weeks. For the next launch, we were going to more than triple the balloon size and blast another beast into the sky out of season.

One of our first tasks after losing the flight computer to tangled line was to implement a solution for the tangled flight computer parachute. As engineering problems always seem to do, this one cascaded into a series of unforeseen problems with other systems. We now saw everything above Alan as a snag forest of metal corners and blocky little cameras on skinny stems.

We cycled through potential solutions at light speed. People threw out ideas about using ballast to gore the balloon. A mini extendable boom was considered for keeping the gore line out away from anything it could snag on, like Alan's SAEBER system. A shop that could test our transponder was identified. A permanent scared look remained on Zane's face and my own while we overturned the designs we had agonized over for years. We had checked innumerable intricate details, but neglected now-obvious design faults.

Solutions were implemented. A mock umbrella for the suit system was created to avoid the gore line snagging on the scraggly spreader bar that held the structural lines apart above Alan. The launch team added foam deflector rails to the flight computer and wrapped it in plastic so the structure would have some chance of sloughing off a limp line coming in contact with it. The transponder was tested at our new shop. The laundry list of major problems with systems was patched over in days, prodded forward by the fearless director Taber, who was now on site full-time acting, almost laughably, as our "safety officer." The man was a dynamic leader who deserves much of the credit for us getting through this wild push, but he was no safety officer. He was pushing us to our absolute limits, testing our endurance, mental stability and, most contrary to his title, our willingness to take risks and see how fast and scrappily we could throw together engineering solutions for extremely complex problems in high-altitude flight.

To add to the difficulties, the balloon we were using was gigantic. One of the available balloons in our inventory could achieve our target altitude with our weight beneath it. In fact, it could achieve an altitude quite a bit higher than our target with a heavier payload than ours making it acceptable, but stressful in new ways. It was substantially bigger than even our biggest balloons and would go higher. It would get Ida to 140,000 feet.

Our willing heroine Ida was built up again. This time she had two accelerometers, four cameras, two different types of GPS data loggers, an altimeter that turned on a light for the cameras at a certain altitude, GPS locators, and a flight computer with a secondary cut-down trigger and live location broadcasting. Amongst the madness of the other rebuilds, we scavenged her accessories from all over our builder's paradise, creating a host of new assemblies.

After this fast-forwarded frenzy, we were ready for flight and antsy for gaps in the variable weather to punch Ida through the livable atmosphere during a time of year almost no organizations consider acceptable for launching balloons. We started the routine: up in the middle of the night to prepare for a possible launch at dawn.

We began preparations at midnight. The suit team was executing a dry run of the full preparation sequence, but this time, instead of actually putting Alan into the suit, we were performing the rituals with Ida. When we had suited Alan up in the previous drop and marched him through the sequence while launching Ida, we couldn't properly execute the very final stages of the process when the sedan was rolled to the launch platen and our space traveler (be it Alan or Ida) was hooked to the balloon. So this time we would walk through the process only with Ida and be able to execute the dry run from inside the tent through to a real live launch. The only exception was the pre-breathe. We commandeered an unsuspecting helicopter pilot in order to get real data on the effectiveness of the process, data that we couldn't get from Ida. Alan came in with the late crew that morning.

In the absence of an actual suit-up, we walked through every motion, pretending to turn valves and pull pants and boots on piece by piece, checking each step off once it was done and calling the necessary steps into mission control.

We hoisted Ida with the BLV, hooked on the ground carts, and sent the backwards-facing BLV inching down Stratosphere Lane to the long-abandoned runway. The short, slow parade then turned onto the active runway (temporarily closed so airplanes didn't land on us). We staged, for the first time, in the area where the two runways intersected to create a flat space larger than a football field. We stopped at the edge of the huge clearing, unhooked the ground carts, and waited. We would stay at that location until that day was over. These turned out to be perfect seats for the rodeo.

Meanwhile, the balloon team had worked through the layout of the gigantic balloon. Its several hundred feet of plastic were laid out according to the wind direction predicted by Don, the weather sage. As the balloon team geared up to fill the balloon, which was several times larger than anything we'd attempted in the past, a new issue arose. The wind didn't appear to be shifting.

In the "light and variable" conditions, "variable" was of great concern. Well in advance of laying out the balloon, Don had to marshal a host of details affecting the complex, changing winds into an accurate approximation of the wind direction at the time of launch. Using that information, the balloon team had laid the balloon out in the exact opposite direction of the winds throughout the night. The prediction was that at sunrise the wind direction would flop 180 degrees and would then be going in the correct direction. We had seen this happen before. At launch, the wind is supposed to blow the rising balloon head toward the balloon base so that it leans away from the spool it rolls on and away from the spork vehicle.

The wind didn't shift. It was blowing in exactly the wrong direction. Changing the layout of the balloon would cost too much time and potentially compromise the acres of thin plastic. Since the balloon was already spent, we decided to attempt the launch anyway. We might as well try and see what happened.

This would affect the way the suit team hooked up Ida. The mounts on the launch sedan were designed to resist Ida's movement only in the direction we had expected the wind to pull on her during the stand-up and prior to launch. With the wind reversed, the dummy could slide easily out of the launch sedan and most certainly career Ida, and all her delicate accessories, into the concrete. We would have to reverse the direction of the cart so it would be facing the right direction prior to launch. This, however, put Ida facing the wrong way for her flight. In this orientation, the snag guards and antennas would all be residing in a different place than when they were tested. With emotions running high, we discussed whether this was acceptable. Answer: no. We would reverse the hook too. That way the launch sedan would be oriented so the mounts worked correctly, with Ida facing backwards. Then, as soon as she left the sedan, Ida would do a quick one-eighty, reorienting and leaving the correct equipment under the high-side flight computer when we released the equipment behind her as she rose.

The helium was discharged into the balloon head without incident. My team watched it twist gently from more than a football field away. The launch collar wrapped around the balloon just under the head to constrict the top of the balloon. The circumference of the balloon stalk was similar to that of a medium-sized tree trunk. The collar was tightened against the balloon. It kept the top of the balloon organized, tight, and pressurized such that it couldn't luff and spinnaker into the lightly gusting morning winds. It had a quick-release mechanism that would unhook it, leaving it to drop harmlessly to the ground just prior to launch. The balloon slowly rose as the spork vehicle inched forward.

Gusts arose. Not only were they too strong, they pushed the balloon in exactly the wrong direction, toward the spork vehicle and crew. Half the spherical balloon bubble inverted into the other half, turning the sphere into a thick bowl with the helium reorganizing in between the two sheets of plastic. The balloon luffed like a sail, looking amazingly similar to a spinnaker on a sailboat filling deep with air, ready to send the boat flying across the water or, if the wind was too strong, crashing into it.

The suit team stared like children witnessing a massacre and not yet understanding what was going on. Grinning stupidly, with little winces distorting our faces, we tilted our heads toward the impending balloon carnage at the other end of the runway. We eventually realized that this was no longer a launch but a serious situation that was growing terrifying for some.

The wind scooped into the acres of exposed plastic, creating thousands of pounds of force. The launch collar, intended to prevent exactly this, clearly wasn't doing its vital job. We would find later that the collar had been installed too low, leaving too much free volume to allow the plastic to invert and spinnaker. Then, in a big gust, the balloon collar popped free. The forces were too big. The canvas and webbing cone flopped into the air and down to the ground, leaving the huge beast free to flail.

The launch crew still wanted to launch. Most of the balloon was still on the ground. With moments left, the only option was for the spork vehicle to drive out of the mess. If the balloon got into the sky far above the spork vehicle, it might be able to stabilize again under the reefing sleeve and dampen the violent swings developing through the length of the stem. Getting the helium bubble into the air and away from the vehicle and driver was at that point likely the safest option as well. John ordered the spork vehicle to drive toward the launch platen.

The wild apartment-complex-sized balloon careened back and forth. The thick plastic stalk that was wrapped around the spool slid across it, while the driver darted the spool back and forth with the front-end loader, driving the spork vehicle like a go-cart, trying to keep it oriented under the flopping balloon. There was no saving it, though. The balloon dipped back toward the spork vehicle in a huge gust and pressed its plastic against the cab. That was it. Flight done. Right after the vehicle contact, another gust slammed the sailing balloon sideways, causing it to fly into the rail holding the spool drum and pinch itself between the spool and the arms that connected the spool to the front-end loader, the place it would stay until it was picked off by the cleanup crew.

The gusts kept coming, turning our wincing to real fear and prompting rapid discussions of what we should be doing. The balloon quickly caught all the corners of the vehicle and almost instantly shrouded it completely, making it look like a toy front-end loader that had been shrink-wrapped to the ground. It seemed like the strong winds gusting at the vehicle could drag the spork vehicle across the runway. It was holding, so far. From our vantage point, we thought the driver was still inside. The cab of the vehicle would not only be airtight, but its breathable air could have been replaced with suffocating helium. The balloon crashed in violent waves around the vehicle, complete with plastic spray.

We ran to the other end of the balloon to help. To our relief, we learned that the driver had escaped the cab before the vehicle had been engulfed, and so we were spared a dangerous rescue operation through the forceful, unpredictable rapids of flapping plastic, slashing through whipping load tapes and risking being shrink-wrapped ourselves. John ordered the crown valve to be opened. Meanwhile, the door to the vehicle had remained open after the driver escaped. The plastic grabbed it and sent shattering glass blasting across the runway. In a final moment of action, John sprinted into the maelstrom of slapping plastic and slammed the door shut before it was ripped off. Then we all stood a safe distance away, watching the draining balloon lay down its bashing form like a dying dragon that had failed to digest a front-end loader.

Toward the end of the deflation, the last of the helium was still trapped inside. Blikkies grabbed the gore line and ripped open the carcass from the center. We all dove in, slashing through mounds of plastic to release the trapped helium. Someone cut through the wires to the crown, crossing them and blowing up some circuitry. We hacked the last of the life from the bloodless beast, learning new lessons of balloon adventure at a stunning and very expensive rate.

It took the rest of the morning to clear the balloon carcass and scour the runway surface for every bit of glass and plastic spewed across the concrete. Alan crawled along the runway surface alongside the team, his nose a foot off the ground, searching for anything glinting. It was important to him to leave the runway the way we found it. Every single shard of glass and shred of plastic was bagged and removed.

Early July 2014: Highest Dummy Drop Ever; A Balloon Gone Rogue

The push was relentless. We had been working nonstop for weeks on end now, hoping for a window of decent weather among a sea of thunderstorms, wet runways, and howling gusts that could tear a stratospheric balloon right up the middle. Sebastian had us grit our teeth and keep at it. We chomped at the bit with nothing to do in a town we had intentionally chosen for its inactivity and relatively long distance from anything worthwhile. We ate our breakfast at an hour when most of us wouldn't have gone to sleep yet in normal times, debating over whether anything would really happen at daylight. Hopes rose, then fell. Our only attempted launch had been an epic failure. We were getting dazed from working nights. The weather was bad. We wanted to go home.

We kept busy. We designed and built a new launch sedan so that even in high winds our dummy wouldn't fly out of the sedan. We changed to floppy antennas so that they wouldn't break off if Ida did hit the ground. We improved and polished while we waited for the weather sages to let us know we could try again.

A favorable prediction finally came. We would try again. We awoke to a starless sky, but didn't feel confident as our black Suburbans rolled the empty streets at 11 p.m., with thunder booming and lightning streaking to the distant desert floor in every direction. This was a launch day? We arrived on site at midnight with no real hope we would launch. We started the launch day chores sloppily. It didn't take long for the call to come. No launch that day.

I spent that morning building a power station to use with the laptop in the helicopter. We needed a more reliable source of onboard power than the trickle of juice from the cigarette lighter. I wired two car batteries into a steel tool box with one of our long-distance modems and a power cord that went to a laptop. We fired it up. It didn't work. As the sun rose and the rain dropped torrents through the leaky roof of the tin shed, we concentrated on troubleshooting why the laptops wouldn't accept our exterior power source. We finally figured out that a combination of low-input voltage and the computer's internal power settings were causing the system to reject the 12-volt power after a certain threshold. We changed the computer settings and recharged the car batteries to top off their voltage—and everything turned on. Another system ready, another day gone. I got home by midday. Bedtime. Maybe tomorrow.

We arrived at midnight to begin a new day. This time we weren't inside a donut of thunderheads and the weather predictions looked promising. We went about our chores with a new sense of purpose. As the clocks ticked toward morning, it became apparent we would attempt a launch that day. Alan wouldn't be present.

We prepared the dummy as if it were Alan, attending to every step of our checklists. Although a couple of items actually required an action, most of the steps were fake; we mimed every action as if Alan and the suit were in our hands. We powered on the life-support pack, checked the sensors, meticulously checked the parachutes, and transferred Ida from her vertical orientation in her holding straps to the more comfortable 45-degree forward-lying position, all just like it was Alan. Zane, who was always painfully literal, would respond exactly as he would if Alan were in the suit. If I asked him to check the oxygen-monitoring equipment, he would answer without the least trace of humor in his voice, "Pilot is not breathing. Oxygen-monitoring equipment is not active." I would then have to copy back on the net: "Note this is a simulation. Disregard."

Zane took over leading the operation while I got the BLV, snatched Ida from the gantry, and wheeled her to the launch site. The weather still looked good, a perfect day for launching dummies. The never-disappointing desert sunrise started to show. At the launch site, we continued going through our checklists, occasionally doing something real to Ida. We switched to onboard power, turned on the cameras, and put our sensors into flight mode. The time was approaching.

Just like the last time, the winds were supposed to shift 180 degrees at sunrise. I had always found this nerve-wracking. Not only were we counting on a 180-degree wind shift, we also hadn't had very good luck dealing with the turbulence and uncertainty associated with waiting for the shift to take place. Shifting the balloon layout was out of the question. This time we planned to launch before the wind shifted. The balloon was laid out in the nighttime wind direction. We intended to have Ida flying before the winds wheeled around to the opposite direction.

The moment came. The balloon team scurried around hundreds of feet away, looking like ants beside the giant balloon bubble silhouetted against the pastel horizon. We heard the thunder of 3,000 psi of helium unloading to a 13 psi atmosphere through handheld aluminum cannons. The crown was released. The balloon flopped and jellyfished up into the air and into its stubby lollipop shape. The launch collar was installed to keep the head of the balloon tidy and out of the wind's way.

We stared and waited. The balloon ascended slowly and silently as the spork vehicle drove toward us, allowing the bubble to rise. When it reached its predetermined mark, we wheeled Ida to her first staging area. Then the bubble continued to rise and the spork vehicle got closer until its drum was raised above the nest of equipment at the balloon's base. The drum released, leaving the balloon standing straight as an arrow, pointing upward from a blank metal plate, aiming into the pale sky, home of the Unknown. We raised Ida onto the platform. We hooked her up. She was ready to fly.

The wind had not shifted in the other direction yet, but it was starting to push lightly sideways. This was a new one for us. We had thought through launching forwards and backwards, but there were no manuals on launching sideways. The long balloon arced slightly at Joe, who was poised to pull the final cord and let her go. There was no way to turn sideways because the tethers holding everything down were in the way. We'd just have to go for it.

John called, "Launch!" and Joe pulled the cord.

The initial jerk was straight sideways, and the cart made a strange attempt to bound 90 degrees to its right but couldn't. Ida dislodged from her mounts, but managed to stay in the cart while the oddly turning vehicle did a post-and-twist maneuver around the back wheels. She lifted up into the air, flying straight at Joe, who was standing with the pull cord he had just released still in hand. He ducked. Ida passed a few feet over his back and shot away with the same indifference she always showed about traveling to space, even though this was the beginning of the highest anthropomorphic dummy flight ever done by balloon.

The low-altitude winds were slow and varied so the balloon wasn't going to travel far from the airport until it was high in the sky. Higher in the atmosphere, the winds were aggressive, tracking a steady 70 miles per hour directly west, driving anything above 80,000 feet straight toward the strictly-controlled White Sands Missile Range and then on toward the Pacific Ocean.

Blikkies and I pulled down the aerostat flying weather station at the launch site and headed back to the tin shed. Ida was standing in for Alan, so we had to make a speedy arrival at the landing site to rescue her in the desert. While the balloon meandered above the airport, we gathered our disassembly tools and waited by the helicopters. Data came through from Ida's chestpack. We waited for mission control to tell us to take off. An hour went by. The balloon crossed into the tropopause, the coldest part of the lower atmosphere. This is where mission control would drop ballast if cooling helium contracted enough to slow the balloon's rise. We requested mission control to inform us if the ballast had been fired. Mission control responded they had not yet fired the ballast.

When the balloon crossed 80,000 feet, our helicopter got the order to fly. By now the balloon was moving hard to the west, and we would fly straight toward it until we were close. Once we got close, the plan was to circle underneath the balloon until Ida was released and then, during her four minutes of freefall and five minutes of parachute flight, we would try to spot Ida in the air.

The careful, familiar procedures make the situation seem boring. And then suddenly it wasn't. The helicopter raced at its maximum speed, 120 miles per hour, toward the balloon that was now flying Ida well above 100,000 feet. In the no-man's-land to the west of Roswell, we quickly lost our radio signal and contact with mission control. It was unclear whether the ballast had been released. The velocity of the balloon made it look like it had, but at last contact, mission control had said it hadn't.

The situation crumbled. Our cool helicopter pilot wasn't going to fly anywhere near the space beneath that balloon without knowing for certain a block of metal wasn't going to crash down from the sky. Without communication with mission control, we didn't know whether the ballast had been fired, when it was going to be fired, or if it was going to be fired at all. Ballast that wasn't fired at the tropopause was often fired toward the end of the mission just to get some extra altitude out of the balloon. That would be right now.

The pilot went from calm to spooked. In our obvious deficiency of situational awareness, lack of communication with mission control, and gentle in-fighting, things fell apart. We desperately needed to ask mission control a simple question. We had known the balloon would fly west and that radio cuts out to the west. Clearly, we weren't ready for that particular mission. It was no longer just about ballast, but about the fact that we seemed like amateurs playing a very real game. We questioned our five-mile circling radius and whether that was sufficient to prevent winds from carrying the ballast close enough to crash on us during its 120,000-foot descent. I was transferring the GPS location of the helicopter to the screen, tracking the balloon manually, but I couldn't do it fast enough to actually verify in real time we were staying five miles away from the balloon or accurately update headings to maintain the circle we were supposed to be flying. The balloon was a dot 20-some miles away. It was visible only out the top windows and looked like it was directly on top of us. What's more, we realized that without communication back to mission control, we had no way of knowing when the balloon would cut down and maybe send enough plastic to cover a small farm through the helicopter rotors.

In a helicopter, the pilot is in charge. The pilot made an executive decision that we were not going to close in on that balloon mark. Ida was not Alan; she wouldn't suffer alone in the desert. We didn't appear to have a clue what was going on. The helicopter turned and booked it away from the balloon just as the data stream from Ida's chestpack said she was approaching her max altitude. The bickering continued. I wanted to be closer. To me it's a big sky. The pilot was still on board with the mission but wasn't getting anywhere near that balloon mark until Ida was low in the sky. That day was not going to be the day we would show the world we could recover Alan promptly.

My data stream stayed strong. Quickly after float, at just over 120,000 feet, I saw the ascent rates for Ida turn negative and spike, meaning she was falling. At that point the squabbling stopped. Ida's speeds climbed for the next 30 seconds, going over the sound barrier in freefall. The pilot brought the helicopter into a large circle, turning back toward the action. The descent rates slowed as Ida hurtled into the lower atmosphere. I called the altitudes over the comm system. At a few thousand feet above the ground, I saw a sharp reduction in descent speed. The parachute had opened. The pilot was satisfied. We could chase the payload.

With the helicopter location on one screen and Ida's location on another, I furiously transferred the location data from one program to the other using pen and paper and taking tens of seconds for each updated heading. If I got one wrong, we'd fly in the wrong direction for a moment. I really wanted to see that parachute in the air, but it wasn't destined to happen that day. In the midst of my scribbling and re-punching numbers, the GPS cut out. Ida was on the ground and we weren't there.

Once Ida's movement stopped, my number transferring could stop too. We flew toward our last known mark. Within two minutes of scanning the ground around that area, we spotted her silver canopy lying in the desolate, radio-silent hill country west of Roswell. The chopper landed on a hill not too far away, and Blikkies and I poured out to see what had become of our Ida. The recovery time wasn't terrible, within 20 minutes for sure, but nowhere near the five minutes we wanted.

Blikkies assessed the scene while I used our backup iridium phone to contact mission control. It was too loud to use it in the helicopter. Blikkies' face above Ida looked somber. "There is no drogue," he said. Ida's stabilizing parachute was supposed to have stayed attached through the reserve parachute deployment, but it was nowhere to be seen. We had no idea why it wasn't there—it just wasn't. That drogue was attached with two-inch-thick webbing that could pick up a half-ton pickup truck. Somehow it had removed itself from our test article.

We collected the cameras, now fearing our test was shaping up to be a pretty monumental failure. I got through to mission control. They frantically asked me to look at the balloon. I looked up and saw it easily enough, a little white dot in the sky above. As I told them what I saw, the implications hit me.

"The balloon didn't destruct. We have no way to track it. We need you to get in the helicopter and maintain a visual."

Obviously, the balloon was not leaving the sky like it was supposed to. The balloon equipment module had been dropped, but the gore line attached to it hadn't done its job. With all the equipment dropped, there was no more communication with the balloon. There was a backup system, the crown valve, which was supposed to have opened before the balloon equipment module separated. It ought to be open, but at that altitude and with all the weight gone, there was little pressure to push the helium out the valve. The valve alone could take a long time to bring that balloon down.

We were guessing at these details at that moment. What we were told was to get in that helicopter and fly toward that balloon. That's what we did.

We were quickly gathering the entirety of the situation. The only tracking equipment left on the balloon was a small radar reflector on the beam underneath it. The balloon was now a hollow shell floating aimlessly through the high atmosphere. We got in the helicopter and told the now very wary pilot what we were instructed to do. We had already left this pilot's comfort zone long ago, and now we wanted him to charge over the Sierra Blanca Mountains toward the highly restricted airspace of a deeply secretive central New Mexico missile range where the balloon was heading.

We caught up to the balloon, a flying dot. If an average person were asked to find a high-altitude balloon at float, all they would be able to do is notice how many white dots seem to appear and disappear in the sky. I'd had lots of practice and Blikkies was an expert. We started burning our eyeballs against the sky, fixating on a dot.

Part of me was happy for the helicopter time. I'd already found them quite fun, and now we got to ridge-fly the thermals over a gorgeous New Mexico mountain range. I took turns with Blikkies keeping a heading on the balloon.

Soon it became unquestionably clear that our balloon was entering White Sands Missile Range protected airspace. Nothing was allowed in there, not even balloons flying 25 miles high.

Balloons aren't dangerous while they're high in the sky, though. There's nothing at that altitude except other balloons. Those don't ever hit each other because there aren't enough of them up there. It was quite likely that our balloon was the only object in the entire atmosphere cruising at 120,000 feet at that moment. Balloons only become a problem when they start to come down. We went to great lengths to make sure there was nothing we could damage within a dozen miles of where we thought a balloon would land—but when a balloon goes rogue, all bets are off.

The painful phone call to the secret desert missile range was made by mission control. It was understood and approved that the balloon would fly over the missile range. For the next 40 minutes we were on edge, hoping that whatever was happening up there didn't decide to let that balloon end its journey before leaving the secret base's airspace. If we dropped a balloon carcass into the missile range, we would seriously alarm the military personnel there, we would likely never get our balloon back, and we would wake a sleeping beast: the government.

As our helicopter approached the edge of the missile range, a radio call to the helicopter pilot came through informing us they knew the balloon was overhead, they could see it on radar, and that we were not to enter the missile range airspace under any circumstances. The missile range runs north-south to the west of Roswell, making hundreds of miles of east-west air travel in that area impossible. The prohibitions on air traffic, which make Roswell so ideal for launching balloons, were now working against us. We assumed our mission was over.

We broke back toward the mountains and landed at a beautiful mountain airstrip in the snowbird town of Sierra Blanca to refuel and touch base with mission control. With cell phones now working, I had my first crisp conversation with Sebastian and learned all the details. It was as bad as we thought. The balloon was over the missile range and it had no tracking equipment except the radar reflector, which was too small to be seen by the FAA office now taking over tracking our mission from faraway Albuquerque.

His panic was present in the communication. We needed to keep sight of that balloon which, while I paced around that airport talking to Sebastian, was barreling at 70 miles per hour across the missile range away from us. We needed an airplane. Airplanes fly high and fast. They can stay airborne for hours and cross the mountains that the balloon would easily sail over to the west. I barged into the control room of the little airport asking if there were pilots and planes for rent. I got a justified angry "No!" along with a look that implied I needed to leave that control room fast to avoid more of a predicament then I was already in. The airport was tiny; the options were few. The helicopter could only do 120 miles an hour, and there was a huge swath of land between us and the balloon. The helicopter was the only choice. We got our marching orders to fuel up the helicopter and do everything we could to keep sight of that balloon.

The pilot didn't like any of this. We were breaking the "don't be sketchy" rule of flying helicopters. He eventually bought into the plan, though. We fueled up, got in, and got on it.

The problem was simply keeping an eye on this tiny dot. If we lost sight of the balloon, the chase was over. Without knowing the balloon's altitude, no one could predict its flight path. All we had was this visual. I never knew the gooey part of my eyeball could hurt before.

We took turns staring at this little bit of nothing while the chopper shook and drifted and turned and swayed. The clouds came and went. We flew for hours in the wrong direction as the dot faded, until we didn't even know if the little speck we were looking at actually was the balloon. I would watch while Blikkies would blink ferociously and rub his eyes, gazing for a moment at the less bright and painful dashboard from the front seat of the chopper. Then I would describe with every geographic detail I could squeeze from the blank sky just where the little speck was until Blikkies could find it again and I could throw my jaw down and forward, closing my eyes hard like I was trying to crush rocks with my eyelids.

We turned the first corner of the rectangular missile range, not really knowing if we were then getting closer or further away from the balloon. It seemed to be southwest of us, heading toward Arizona, and we could now fly straight west and just maybe close in, with us doing 120 and the balloon doing 70, apparently headed dead-straight west toward the Pacific Ocean. Clouds started to creep in. A new battle now, losing and finding the little sky dot amongst the white wisps. Things were looking rather hopeless for us. I didn't want to be the one to tell Sebastian we had lost a plastic sphere the size of a football stadium and it was continuing toward the ocean—and Japan.

We turned the far corner of the range. Happiness is relative. In that musty helicopter cabin, we were elated at the prospect of flying straight at the balloon. The dot should get bigger. The pilot got a mysterious call from air traffic control that they had a fix on the balloon and that it was at 125,000 feet. Our only explanation is that the relay came from the missile range. Whatever the case, that confirmed for us it was going straight west, the exact direction of the stratospheric winds at that height. If we knew the altitude, we knew the direction, something to supplement our burning eyes.

The dot did indeed get bigger. We closed in. It almost seemed nice and close. As we hovered in for gas in the tiny town of Truth or Consequences, the balloon was only visible out the top windows of the chopper, indicating we were again nearly below the beast. We no longer had fears it would fall on us, the big-sky theory having prevailed. We wanted to stay underneath the balloon now that it was truly understood how far it was away from us.

We called mission control again. They were clearly all holed up in the mission control trailer doing everything they could to support us. They had wind estimates from different layers of the atmosphere and trajectory analyses for different gas-expulsion rates and were eager to add information to their arsenal. Despite all the information, the reality was that there was nothing much we could do except what we were doing. We looked at the balloon through binoculars, and it looked strange and stringy, like it wasn't a ball anymore. I told that to Sebastian, who seemed very excited, and I immediately regretted filling them with optimism. I had to clarify I had no idea what I was looking at. It was a tiny spit-wad in the sky as viewed through binoculars 50 miles away, shaking and catching sunlight. It might have still been intact, or maybe it wasn't. I had no real idea. All fueled up, we got back in and got on our way.

We chased. We followed that white dot for hundreds of miles. When we passed directly under the balloon again, it looked dismayingly round and fat, floating healthily in the heavens like it belonged there. As we approached the border of Arizona, storms brewed up over the White Mountains and we encountered peaks too big for the helicopter to go over. The pilot put his foot down. We rounded mountains, navigating in real time while the balloon meandered in and out of clouds. Finally, after an exhausting eye-beating run, we lost the balloon in building thunderheads. We had done our best, but we had lost it.

We had also reached the pilot's threshold for adventure, and without a poll for consensus he decided that for our own safety we would fly to the nearest airport to the west, in Safford, Arizona, to hole up and try to spot the balloon. If it was still up in the stratosphere going straight west with the stratospheric winds, that's where we would see it.

We texted Sebastian that the balloon was lost and that we were heading to Safford. I don't know what was discussed, but there must have been intense moments of contemplation in mission control while they worked out some very critical next moves.

While the balloon was still over some of the country's most sparsely populated land, mission control made one last attempt. A pilot friend of the crew in Tucson, which was now not that far away from the balloon, was scrambled. This individual just happened to be Mark Kelley, a prominent astronaut with a flair for this type of adventure. Mark went to the Tucson airport while we were making our way to Safford and hired an unsuspecting young pilot to take him on a ride. The ride just happened to be a scenic tour of Safford, Arizona, where a nasty storm was mounting, in order to find a balloon at an unknown altitude in an unknown location.

Our helicopter landed at Safford and we resumed our ritual of slowly and meticulously scanning the sky. We could see the storm circling us. In yet another turn for the worse for us, a fire raging to the west created another huge swath of restricted air space and hazy skies. We stood on the tarmac and stared as huge firefighting helicopters landed, filled with water, and took off. We were at the end of our line, running out of energy and eyesight. It was also getting dark. It was pretty well over for us.

As we scanned the sky, we talked dully about what would happen if we lost our balloon for good. We didn't even know for sure that the crown valve was open. If every destruct mechanism had failed, the balloon could circle the entire globe. It didn't seem crazy to think that our failure might put an end to the program, too. There were powers that be who might never forgive us for this one. We didn't realize it at the time, but when we lost the balloon it was heading straight for Phoenix, Arizona, where conversations about closing down Phoenix Sky Harbor airspace were starting.

While Mark flew around Safford in a Piper Cub with what must have been a terrified young flight instructor, in a wild stroke of luck and balloon-finding prowess Blikkies spotted the little speck of balloon from the dusky tarmac at Safford airport. It was northeast of us heading west-ish. Something was different, though, in a good way. By that time the balloon was supposed to have passed us, but it hadn't. It was also far north of its formerly straight westward path. This was the first good news we had gotten. It was no longer in the due-west stratospheric stream. It appeared to be coming down. Then, in another thrilling turn of events, a tracking GPS signal came through from a tracking unit that doesn't start working until its quarry gets below about 50,000 feet. Instead of making a call that our balloon had gone rogue, the mission control team was making a call to say we had several indicators that our balloon was heading down fast.

In no time we were back in the chopper, heading for the coordinates on the tracker. We got Mark on the radio and talked through what we knew. The storm, now curling in toward Safford, wasn't going to let us fly. As we turned around to head back to base, the crazy ex-astronaut took the poor unaware flight instructor straight into the storm to seek out the increasingly frequent tracking signals. We watched the balloon until it disappeared into the thunderheads. Before we landed, a text came through that the tracking signals were stacking in the same place. The balloon was on the ground in desolate unpopulated land.

Mark took the little airplane through the storm and verified that the balloon was down, reporting it wadded up, wet and broken, splayed across part of the forest north of Safford.

We picked up a courtesy car at the airport and went to a hotel in Safford. The driver seemed well accustomed to this type of routine. He took us to Walmart to buy socks and underwear. While we were driving, the storm that took out the balloon hit us with ferocious wind-driven splashes of water and sheets of sand that filled every inward-facing corner in the town, making everything smooth. The sand blocked the remaining light of the dusk, and I looked with tired eyes out the beat-upon car windows thinking about how weird my life was.

The day ended with Blikkies, the helicopter pilot, and me, brothers now, sharing a 12-pack of beer and two pizzas in a Safford hotel while watching the videos of our dummy Ida falling supersonic from the edge of space. She was amazingly stable. Our spin-control system had worked.

Somewhere into our second round of beers, the videos solved the mystery of the missing stabilizing parachute. Low in the atmosphere, the stabilizer picked up a resonance and vibrated so intensely that it rubbed through the heavy strap against the back plate of the parachute rig and flew away. It's probably in some farmer's UFO collection now.

Early in the morning, we flew to the landing site of the balloon. We crossed gorgeous mountain landscapes, forests glistening from the night's rain.

We found the balloon unexpectedly on our way to the GPS spot. It was as large as it was strange, lying across pine scrub and meadow grass. The balloon was wadded up with weird tentacles of plastic reaching out all around it. We trotted up to examine the dead monster. It was filled with water.

The screeching of the wet plastic was disturbing as we waded through it. We bundled up the 800-pound wet mass trying to find the crown valve. We also hunted through the plastic to see if the button that was supposed to rip out and initiate the destruct sequence was still there. We couldn't find it. We found the hole near the base of the balloon where the destruct line was supposed to pass out. It was ripped like something had pulled out of it, but there wasn't anything else to help us understand what had happened, no sign of the gore line. We collected the cameras. They would likely tell the secret of why that giant ball had refused to clump up and come home.

The chopper flew back to Safford for fuel, then started the long trip back. We stopped in El Paso where a young woman working the counter at the small aircraft center saucily asked what we were up to. I told her we had chased a rogue stratospheric balloon across two states in a helicopter, and now we were going home.

We chugged back around the missile range and arrived in Roswell six hours later. We packed our things to head for real home. Blikkies and I drove to Albuquerque, checked into our hotel, and met at the bar overlooking the landscape from the airport hill. We watched fireworks sprout up across the city. It was the Fourth of July.

After 30 hours of preparation, launch, and chase, the final team arrives back from the field to drink beer after our second large payload launch with recovered equipment. (Photo by Dave Jourdan.)

The team attempted to launch the iron dummy assembly to over 140,000 feet using a 14.5-million-cubic-foot balloon out of season. The winds changed direction and shrouded our spork vehicle in balloon plastic, causing a scary debacle on an active commercial runway. (Photo by Volker Kern.)

A payload hits the ground during a high-wind launch after the launch cart (a different cart than Alan's launch sedan) failed to stay under the payload through launch.

Looking up at a balloon at over 120,000 feet from the flight computer as it falls away from the balloon. The cord streaming behind the computer was supposed to rip the balloon in half, but it failed to do that, leaving the balloon to float several hundred miles across the Southwest, coming down in Safford, Arizona, leaving a track toward Phoenix.

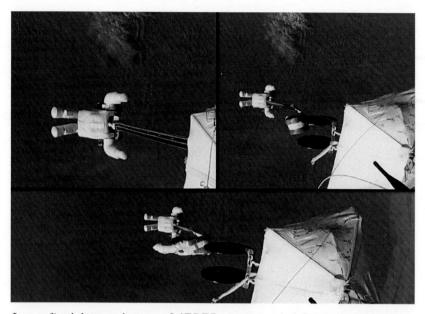

In our final dummy drop, our SAEBER system worked flawlessly, extending to create a rigid pole that kept the drogue parachute away from the dummy.

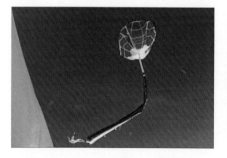

The moment our drogue parachute snapped away from Ida as she fell from 120,000 feet.

The spork vehicle completely wrapped in plastic.

A large balloon standing just prior to launch. (Photo by Dave Jourdan.)

CHAPTER 14

...

The Right Stuff

T he list of tasks that remained before Alan would start flying to the stratosphere was getting shorter. Alan needed to be better trained and then demonstrate his air-worthiness in skydives from airplanes. First we would run him through a rigorous testing regimen in the tin shed. We wanted to see him do everything he might ever need to do flawlessly. We wanted to find out what he couldn't do, and make sure his abilities went beyond the limits of the program. Then we would chuck him out of airplanes. Only then we would let him go to the stratosphere.

Late July 2014: Human Factors and Pilot Training II

To a certain degree, the point of the next series of tests was to inflict pain. We had been too easy on Alan in the past. We had a certain sick feeling about pushing him to his breaking point, but we had to know where that was. We had to test his fortitude for what would be one of the most intense trials a human being can experience: freefall from space. We had set aside four days for a session of testing human factors and pilot training. Three tests were scheduled, with the fourth day a buffer, which we always seemed to use. The training was to be combined with training in emergency extraction for our growing team of aerospace medicine doctors, most of whom worked day jobs in emergency rooms. We would string Alan up in our pilot-prep area in Roswell, give him tasks intended to exhaust him, and then see if he could still do everything he might have to do in flight, even though he was at the breaking point.

The suit team headed to the desert a week ahead of time to prepare hardware, run our phase zero preparation routines, and work through a test safety and readiness review. From here on out, all tin shed activities were performed in the midst of a sizeable mob of onlookers gawking and photographing as if we were exotic animals. The mob could smell the end. Once again we were in favor.

We settled into extended-stay hotel rooms. The preparations were seamless. We could prepare the suit in our sleep. We anticipated problems but knew how to solve them. By the end of the first day, the suit was hanging in the preparation area checked out top to bottom, ready for Alan to turn valves, pull handles, grab steering lines, and take his helmet off until it was second nature. Ryan wasn't with us. He had engagements back home, so his manager came out to take his place for this one series of tests.

Doctors would come into Roswell in waves. We needed several levels of backup because of their unpredictable schedules. At least eight doctors were to be fully trained so that there would be at least four doctors, two for each helicopter, fully ready to administer any medical attention necessary to keep Alan alive and safe.

Each doctor did four live training sessions with a real person in the real suit, either Alan or me. When Alan landed, a team from the helicopter would approach him. Either Mitch, Ryan, or I (depending on which team reached him first) would remove the bubble, inner helmet, and facemask of the suit and then let the doctors in. The doctors would call out one of the four levels of extraction—green, yellow, orange, or red—to alert everyone about the next steps.

Green extraction is the one to hope for. It is a normal extraction performed by the suit team. In a green extraction, all the doctors have to do is watch. A yellow extraction is not terrible, but not great. It's a doctor-driven extraction in the case of non-life-threatening injuries such as broken bones, in which the doctors guide the suit team to ensure a minor injury isn't exacerbated into a major one.

An orange extraction is bad. Orange means a spinal injury. Not only would we take Alan out of the suit in a way carefully dictated by the doctors, taking extreme care not to move his spine while maintaining clear access to his airway, but we would completely destroy the suit in the process, cutting things apart to accommodate the tricky removal.

The worst extraction is red. This would be a high-speed emergency extraction performed in response to an exposure to vacuum. If that occurred, Alan's thrashed lungs and nitrogen-bubbling blood would be causing all sorts of issues requiring immediate attention. Even simulating and practicing a red extraction was intense. We mimed chopping away all the rubber and plastic mechanisms attached to Alan's face and body, grabbing him and ripping him out of the suit by his knees to get him open and free in 25 seconds. We never actually cut the suit in the training sessions, but we did everything else we would do in a real emergency.

On the first day of pilot training, we tested normal configurations, doing the human work in the order the mission would progress so as to tire the right muscles in the right order. We threw in the extra extraction trainings to be sure Alan would be capable of more than we imagined could be required. We treated Alan like an engineering test article: worst-case loads in worst-case conditions.

We dressed Alan in record time with passive indifference. In the ascent portion of flight, Alan would have to repeatedly work the push-to-talk toggle, the heater toggle, and the purge valve. The flogging began. We could see the groan in his eyes as we pushed him to do things he clearly knew how to do so he could demonstrate that he could do them over and over again. We checked off our boxes.

"Move the temperature set point up 10 degrees."

"Now move it back down 10 degrees."

"Now open the purge valve and reclose it completely five times."

We worked through the ascent exercises in a hurry. It was good to rush him, tire him out. One of the doctors had to leave the following morning, so we moved into further extraction exercises that same day. We let him squeeze out of the suit, dripping with sweat, to take a short break, then suited him right back up for more. The extraction training was mostly for the doctors, but while Alan was there he would be the suit subject. We were trying to beat the shit out of him so we could ensure he could still function after getting wailed on for hours.

Alan lay on the ground in the suit and we pulled him out four times in four different ways. In the green extraction, we worked through removing the bubble, facemask, helmet, gloves, body seal, and boots before carefully and gently working Alan out of the claustrophobic bag. In yellow, the only difference was that the doctors, who were just learning how the suit worked, had to direct the extraction instead of us suit folks, who spent all the hours in all our days studying and playing with that suit. This took some training. "If you pull the latch your hand is on, that bubble is going to shoot across the room."

On to orange extraction. The bubble comes off and Alan tells them, "I can't feel my legs." They then walk us through the pretend chopping up of the suit without moving Alan's spinal column. This time Alan is instructed not to help or move. He gets pulled out over a bumpy back-massager of regulators, pressure sensors, and aluminum structural rings.

Then finally, the dreaded red extraction. For these, Alan wasn't to help at all. He had to mimic unconsciousness with perhaps minutes left to live. In this scenario, we adopt a "life over limb" philosophy and focus on nothing other than timeliness. Alan gets ripped out of that suit in a ferocious hurry. A special respirator developed by an aerospace doctor named Forrest Morten Bird, capable of delivering oxygen to severely damaged lungs, is applied to his mouth. For the exercise, we call out the things we would cut. "Cut the mask off. Cut the chin strap. Cut the helmet." We mimic removing these items fast, with only a slight regard for the real human head in our simulator. "Gloves off!" (Those are easier to remove than to cut.) "Waist ring open. Cut the water lines. Cut the electrical cord." In this case we leave the boots and pants on and just yank him out. "Ready to pull." We lift up his arms so they don't grab on his armpits, Mitch grabs behind the knees, "Pull!" Alan gets pulled out of the suit like a wad of weeds getting ripped out of a stuck drain. First the suit tightens up. Then it pops and loosens. Daylight.

That was day one. Alan succeeded at all the human factors tests for the ascent. We succeeded at wearing him out.

Day two began early in the morning with another extraction training and a new set of doctors. I could have taken a turn in the suit, but Alan was a good sport. I think he was catching on to our secret agenda. Into the suit three times and then back out again, straining his neck each time so his face would miss hardware on the way through. After he came out the third time, we moved into the descent portion of the test for a series of exercises we expected to take three days.

We put him back into the suit for the training we should have completed before we ever let Alan jump from an airplane a year ago in Coolidge, when he couldn't depressurize the suit or reach the steering toggles. We got him into the suit in 35 minutes. The whole process goes faster when we stop trying to be gentle.

We started with the drogue fall portion of the flight. Blikkies rigged the drogue parachute so we could hang him up from the drogue bridle going to a hook on the gantry instead of the little parachute. We didn't want an accidental handle pull to drop him on the floor. This wasn't a perfect representation, because in a real freefall he wouldn't just be held by the little parachute. Much of the force stopping him from accelerating would have been coming from the wind hitting him, but it was the best we could do. In this drogue fall configuration, Alan would need to do a few things, the most important of which was to pull his parachute, a task he had yet to excel at.

We started with the main parachute pulls. He not only had to grab the handle and get it free, but also yank it forward, maximizing the pull stroke. The pull handles were plastic loops, about half an inch thick, placed on the chestpack where he could easily reach them. The handles connected to cables. The cables ran through a steel tunnel called a housing to the parachute pack. At the parachute pack there are two parachutes, a main and a reserve, each of which have their own compartment, called a container. The containers are held closed by four flaps that each have a hole and a grommet. The flaps are closed around the packed parachute and a loop is pulled through all the holes. A pull cord is then passed through the loop, and that pull cord keeps the container closed. When the handle is pulled, the flaps are free to fall open and the parachute free to fly out of the pack.

There were two identical main parachute pull handles on either side of the chestpack. They both went to the same loop. Those were the lower handles on the suit. The two higher handles were used only in emergencies. The upper right handle, the "cutaway," would separate the main parachute from the system, which would be necessary if the main parachute fouled during deployment. The other handle deployed the reserve.

Alan had to be capable of performing a second pull in the bone-seizing panic that comes after pulling a main parachute handle and having nothing happen, a panic Alan had felt once. For the test, we had installed special pins to keep the parachutes from barfing out of the bag and needing to be repacked every try, but otherwise everything was rigged exactly as it was for flight. We made Alan pull the left and right parachute handles 10 times each, a total of 20 pulls. This time he had it. He ripped the plastic handle out of the springs in the handle guard over and over, then wagged his arm back and forth until the rip cord pulled through the closure loop.

While in his drogue parachute freefall configuration, Alan also had to work the purge valve. If the helmet bubble was going to fog, this was going to be the time. In the mission, negative-100-degree-Fahrenheit air would be barreled at the front of the helmet bubble, and moist hot air from the panting, sweaty human inside would be less than an inch away from that freezing airflow. The purge valve would blast dry oxygen into the fogged helmet bubble. All Alan had to do was reach over and open the purge valve and close it again. Five times. Not such a problem, but he was starting to get tired. Every time I said, "Do another," the manager standing in for Ryan looked back at me like I was telling him to torture a puppy. Ryan would be the only one talking to Alan on flight day, so his stand-in had to give the orders, for better or worse. An hour went by. It was time to switch to parachute mode.

At this point in the flight, Alan would have pulled his parachute and would be hanging from the parachute risers, so that was what we would simulate. In our first attempt, we found that our mock parachute riser system didn't work with the ground oxygen lines attached. We had to use the flight oxygen tanks instead. There were only a few hours of flight oxygen available so we had to be fast. We momentarily set Alan down on his feet, holding up a couple hundred pounds of suit and suit equipment while we switched the hoist hook connection. Blikkies pulled the parachute risers out of the parachute container and hooked them up to a metal spreading assembly we had made to simulate the spread that the parachute would apply. The top of that hooked up to the hoist. Then Alan was lifted back up and put through parachute moves.

This was another critical sequence for Alan. In the central Arizona desert, our system had so blatantly failed that Alan hadn't even been able to touch the handles on the parachute risers. Blikkies had redesigned the risers so the handles were much larger and hung lower. Alan had to be able to reach them while pressurized, even though we were confident the new depress valve handle by the suit helmet would be much easier to operate than the turn knob on his hip. We tested as though those modifications hadn't worked. We wanted to subject him to the same conditions he'd experienced when the depress failed at Coolidge. This time he managed the handles beautifully, even with the suit fully pressurized. Stiff as a robot, he grabbed the larger handles and worked them to steer the canopy. Blikkies had added Velcro fasteners onto the risers so that if Alan needed to let go of the handle in flight, he wouldn't have to worry about them blowing behind him and out of his reach. Blikkies had also built a neat little contraption to apply counterforce to the steering toggles during the test to further wear Alan out before he got to the part where he would take the helmet off. Alan did five cycles removing the steering lines from their stows and executing a simulated controllability check, left turn, right turn, stall. He did this five times in a row while Blikkies pulled against the steering lines, forcing Alan to muscle the suit against the counterforce.

Alan's exhaustion started to show at this point. He had been in the suit for hours and was covered in sweat. There was an edge of annoyance to his voice when he asked if all this was necessary, since he'd shown he could depressurize the suit. Ryan's stand-in was told to report the bad news. Alan had to do it all, no shortcuts.

Depressurizing the suit is a whole new assault on the senses. It's like ascending thousands of feet in an airplane almost instantly. The ear-popping and gut-expansion are extreme. We didn't make Alan fully depressurize five times because the re-pressurization process takes too long. We let him simply open the valve, let the suit start to depressurize, and then close it again. He did it five times with no trouble. The failure that had threatened his life in Coolidge had been hanging over us for a year. Now it was behind us. On the fifth of those depressurizations, we had him leave the handle open and vent the suit to ambient pressure.

For the next round, the suit would remain depressurized. At this point in the process, we were starting the activities we had previously assumed would happen the following day. Alan would feel like he was wearing a thick pair of coveralls and had a 260-pound baby gorilla clinging to his skinny body. The parachute work was repeated, Blikkies pulling on the back end of the steering lines to resist while Alan pulled the handles over and over. It was the same set of tests he had just done. Depressurized, it was easier. He grabbed the toggles out of the stows, turn left, turn right, stall. Then we would reset and make him do it again, five times.

Next, the emergency procedures. If the main parachute failed, Alan would have to first pull the cutaway handle and release the failed main parachute above him. Then he had to pull the handle that would deploy the reserve parachute. Five times in a row he found the handles, grabbed, and pulled, wagging the handle back to break it free of the springs. Then he pulled the rip cord out by yanking up and down.

By the time the last of the handle testing was done, every one of the springs previously holding the four handles into their pockets was mangled and stretched out from being exercised so hard. Clearly tired, aggravated, and ready for this long, hard testing to be over, Alan had gone into beast mode, destroying eight stainless steel springs by brute force. We kept pushing his patience and made him operate the push-to-talk toggle, something he had done hundreds of times. Now he had to do it under the parachute to report he was okay during his parachute ride.

The last step before dropping Alan to the ground was to do the steering toggle checks under the reserve parachute. When the reserve parachute deployed and the parachute bag emptied its contents, Alan would hang differently under the risers, so we needed to be sure he could still operate the toggles. The flogging continued.

We removed the reserve parachute from the pack and had him go through the same actions of removing the reserve steering toggles from the stows and pulling them against a now-tiring Blikkies over and over again. He opened and closed the purge valve five times under the reserve parachute, another action he had done many times and knew he could do. Initially, he seemed inclined to refuse the test, asking the suit tech if the test was necessary. The suit tech looked at me. The test wasn't done until all the boxes were checked. Ryan's stand-in passed the word: "We have to finish all the steps." Alan opened the purge valve and then closed it again five times.

The afternoon wore on. We were not the same team we had been a year ago. No more shortcuts.

Alan was now exhausted, aggravated, and extremely uncomfortable. Which was exactly where we wanted him. If he could do the final critical steps in this condition, he was ready for his mission.

Alan was so successful completing tasks that we realized that we were about to finish the grueling human factors session that we thought would take three days in a little more than one day. The doctors stepped in. They grilled Alan to make sure he wasn't in danger of anything more serious than exhaustion if he continued on. The answer was no. We conferred with the doctors and convinced them that the more tired Alan was, the better. We wanted to evaluate whether he was physically capable of operating the suit when his life depended on it. In the real flight, he would be this tired by the time he got back to the ground. The doctors gave us the all clear to put Alan on the ground and continue with the final critical and strenuous phase.

First we wanted to make sure that no matter how he landed, Alan could always roll himself onto either his chest or his back. We laid him on his side with his arm pinched beneath him and left him to squirm. He figured out how to get his feet down and support a backward arch, lifting the heavy chestpack into the air while rotating and plopping back down on top of the parachute pack. Success. We did some quick checks to make sure he could access and operate the depressurization lever on the ground so that if he didn't depressurize in the air he could do so on the ground. He accessed the lever easily in any position. The final test was lifting off the helmet, the test that would lift our fears of lonely desert suffocation.

We started the tests with Alan lying facedown. Because the ground-support lines go through the front of the suit, we had to power it down, so he had no cooling. During this last grueling trial, he'd be heating up and have no displays. We also removed the voice radio antennas to keep them from getting broken off during the rolling around, so he was without communication as well. With Alan hot, tired, and more alone than ever, we started him through the paces. I flashed a thumbs-up at the helmet bubble. The first attempt cheered us. He reached up, found the lever, and yanked it, dropping the bubble into Mitch's hands. Oxygen squirted. The rest of us pumped our fists and smiled. Two more on the chest, then three on the back.

On the second attempt, he was clearly starting to struggle. We were finding his physical limit. The latch was physically located by his left ear. He had to press the two safety buttons simultaneously to release the latch. Once released, the latch needed to be pulled to unlock the helmet. He tried once, fumbling with the safety buttons. It was a stretch to get his arm high enough. Then he had to push little buttons through the 13 layers of fabric and insulation between his fingers and the latch. I knew from my own time in the suit how the heat and claustrophobia get to you, how everything feels the same and everything fights you. Alan finally managed to drop the helmet for the second time. The third attempt was even more of a battle. Alan would try for a while, then let his arm fall down by his side while he took a break before trying again. He finally dropped the helmet on his chest for the final time. Now to repeat that sequence on his back. We were worried. He looked done for.

We let Alan breathe some normal air with the helmet open, turned him over, and hooked the cooling back up. We granted him a rest before the final assault. If he could open the helmet three times on his back, he'd be done. He was sopping wet. Sweat-saturated air emanated from the open portions of the suit. We might have pushed too hard. He did not appear capable of the last test. He panted on the ground. We were all exhausted. But we were so close. And the doctors were right there.

Alan went back in. With the helmet closed, we gave him the thumbs-up. The first pull was encouraging. His hand went up, found the safety buttons, pushed them, and yanked the helmet latch. Now we saw a glitch this time. With Alan on his back, gravity would not assist. Alan was back-bent over the parachute pack staring at the ceiling. The helmet didn't fall off. Alan brought his other arm up to bat at the back of the helmet, trying to swat the now-unlatched dead weight off the suit while muscling against the spring-loaded latch with the other hand. If the latch were released, the spring would close and lock the helmet again. It came off and fell to the ground. His face showed only exhaustion. Two more to go. We snapped the helmet in place and flashed the thumbs-up. It was painful to watch. He moved like an arthritic old man lifting a forkful of peas: painful, trembling, and strained. A few tries and the safety buttons were pushed. He managed to pull the latch. His slow batting at the helmet pushed the helmet out of its metal lip. Second success. Down the helmet clanked. One more to go.

The end of the testing was so close we could feel it. Alan raised his shaking arm. He couldn't find the buttons. He tried again and again. Resting, he attempted to shake out his hand. We saw two simple buttons, but for him they were impossibly far away through the clenching suit and its bulky fingers. Alan rested and tried, tried and rested. The little buttons wouldn't push. We had been at the helmet test for the better part of an hour now. He swiped his arm, the signal that said, "I'm done." The suit tech yanked the helmet. We had found his limit. We discussed it like soldiers negotiating for a middle ground after a battle. Nobody wanted to quit. Nobody wanted to fight anymore. We cracked a deal.

Alan had got the helmet off five of the required six times. It was an astonishing effort, but we couldn't check the box. Dozens of exercises and a secret mission to push Alan to the edge had worked too well. We universally agreed that several hours of brutal nonstop physical suit checkouts were unrealistically stressing. There was no way Alan would be that tired on the ground after his mission. We decided to let Alan finish the checkout during our upcoming airplane jumps. For now we would check off everything except the helmet removals, and as long as Alan went three for three removing his own helmet the next three times he got in the suit, we'd check him out to fly.

I felt a bit awkward, like I should be ashamed of our unrelenting beating. We'd made a pilot so tired he couldn't pull a little latch. That was the goal, though. It wasn't a secret anymore. Alan knew we'd been out to find his limits.

The truth of the matter was that the man was a tank. We, the five-man team that executed these tests, were ourselves on the brink of collapse. Alan had completed in six and a half hours what was supposed to take three days. Every person close to the program had doubted at some point or another whether Alan was capable of executing his mission, one that had gotten the better of young, muscular daredevils that base-jumped for a living. From that day on, not one of us would question his ability again. Alan was the right man for his jump. He was the only man for his jump. He was strong enough, fit enough, resolute enough, and light years smarter than necessary. He was the right stuff.

August 2014: Airplane Jumping Session II

Maybe it was to justify this strange existence, but I adopted more readily, and at times more aggressively, an almost religious view of what we were doing. Alan was ascending not just into an unexplored place but into a deeper Unknown. I don't think I'm unique in my fascination with what isn't yet understood, and so I find it unsurprising that many religions place a god above us, since the bulk of the unknown, by a vast margin, resides above, rather than below, or within our achievable horizons. I had long considered it a meaningless cliché to think that God was in the sky, but I had changed my mind. God was the Unknown. He was in the sky, and we were going to find him, and in finding him, make him further away.

In Coolidge, the last time we tossed Alan out of an airplane in the spacesuit we had designed for the purpose, a cascade of failures sent him reeling somewhere into a veiny spread of desert while our response team was incommunicado, trapped by fences and thorn-covered washes holding us away from our goal. Just two weeks after the pilot-training session, we organized a trip to Roswell for the purpose of throwing Alan into the deep blue for the second time.

We started our trip like we started every trip, checking into the hotel in downtown Roswell and heading to the airport for a full day of prepping, cleaning, and inspecting every one of the thousands of components that make up our suit. With the shell off of the front, the life-support pack looked like a space machine that belonged behind a rope fence at a museum.

Wires and tubes spaghettied everywhere. You could only wonder if the thick aluminum cage that just barely extended over the garble would really protect it in case of impact.

We all had the same worry. What would happen if Alan couldn't land the suit gently? Alan was well trained to fly in his angled position and accomplish a post-and-twist landing that would allow him to turn around and lie down on his back when he met the ground, instead of chest-slamming the Earth like he had in his first jump. Tandem parachuting instructors used this landing when the human strapped to the front of them is unconscious. The instructor is supposed to flare the parachute near the ground, pulling down the tail of the airfoil-shaped parachute to increase the lift and drag of the wing, slowing both its forward and downward speed. In the first stage of that flare, as they are gliding forward next to the ground, they stick a leg out to catch the Earth and flip 180 degrees so that they face up. They drag backwards, protecting the floppy student affixed firmly to their chest. Our chestpack had lived through one face plant, but it wasn't a test we wanted to repeat.

The airplane test was more stressful than the final flights might be. The flight would have had years of planning behind it. The equipment was all designed and built for the exact purpose it was going to fulfill. The support team had thought through every possible scenario. These test jumps were ad-libbed. We planned them well, but we planned them in weeks rather than years. When something didn't work, we improvised on the spot instead of taking weeks off to design and test a solution. Our equipment appeared to be in perfect shape, though. The only direction was forward.

After we had pressurized the suit for our final phase zero checkout, Mitch and I grabbed a weed-whacker and spray paint to mark out a landing circle for Alan and the support divers. We cruised around in a golf cart, hacking down the thick weeds around the disguised hazards, such as half-buried rusty pipes and poles. We marked the main landing circle with orange paint. It sat in the center of a rectangle the size of a football field at the end of one of the runways.

For this jumping session, we would be joined by two new safety divers. One was Trevor Cedar. Trevor ran the student skydiving program at the drop zone in Deland, Florida, where the parachute factory was and worked with United Parachute Technologies regularly. Trevor was British, lanky, and a symbol of competency in skydiving. He filled his days jumping from airplanes and his nights in wind tunnels teaching people the art of falling. The other new safety diver, Luke Evens, led a similar life; he ran photography and video at Skydive Deland and often jumped with Trevor with new skydivers leaving an airplane in the air for the very first time.

Because these jumps were being performed at a different airport than the last ones, and because it would be the first time anyone involved in the program would jump at this airport, the first jump would be an orientation run. Luke, Trevor, Blikkies, Alan, and myself would all take a skydive to test out the new landing area. (I was slated as an emergency responder from the airplane if the recovery didn't go as planned, so this orientation was part of my training.) The plane would fly a typical course, show us the landing zone from the sky, and let us go at 18,000 feet above sea level, the ceiling for most normal skydives. While we tried to maintain a clear focus on preparations, spectators started arriving, making the upcoming days some of the most stressful of my life. Those days would be another kind of test, preparing us for what was to come as the tasks and stressors of the manned balloon flights crept up on us in front of a live, inquisitive audience.

We started at the normal time with the annoying cat-herding required to get the now-sizeable crew of people out of the hotel and headed toward the airport. We had gotten used to the balloon exercises having a big crew and lots of bystanders. The suited airplane jumps had now graduated to sufficient thrill levels to warrant their own extended mob. We had to learn to endure tripping over people at every turn, and be polite at extended meetings filled with crisply-spoken, half-informed, and unnecessary questions intended to dangle someone's inquisitive intelligence in front of the documentary people.

At the airport we went through the morning brief, typical except for one detail. Taber was turning 50. His wife, Jane, had wrangled behind the scenes to send him for a tandem skydive for his big over-the-hill birthday. Tandem skydiving doesn't require any substantial training. We had fitted out a tandem rig in secret and organized the necessary equipment to take him on his first jump while we did our orientation dive. I had slipped the waiver that Taber needed to sign into the slides for our morning brief; I would break the news in front of the whole team like a marriage proposal at a football stadium. I walked mundanely through slides showing aerial images of the airfield where we would land, where the hazards were, and the plan for each day: we leave the hotel at 4 a.m., airplane fires up at sunrise, and we step into the rushing air stream with the sun well above the far recessed horizon at 18,000 feet. Then I pulled up the waiver and informed a whooping room that Taber would be joining us on the jump.

The morning burned into existence with an insane bustle. Two helicopter pilots wanted to know where to go and what to do, while the airplane pilot shuttled back and forth preparing his plane. Last-minute suit-preparation details cropped up. Fortunately, our permission to use the airport as a drop site only extended until noon, so we were able to brush a lot of bystanders away by saying, "We gotta jump now." In the holding area we fit checked a brand-new pilot-loading ramp Joe had built. This involved a certain amount

of scurrying after hardware amongst the towers of boxes filled with parts
and equipment amassing in the tin shed.

Now into the plane. We talked through the skydive in a wild hurry. Taber
and Blikkies would reach the weight limit of the equipment at 500 pounds
between the two of them. Taber was shorter than Blikkies and would be on
the front, making the two of them a bit more aerodynamic. They would fall
very fast. Luke and Trevor would film the birthday boy tandem, and Alan
would jet along next to them while I tried to fly as fast as I could to keep
close to the cannonball crew. I was slow. Lanky people have a big surface
area to create drag, and not much weight to push in the other direction. Alan
should have been slow, too, but he was a much better skydiver than me and
could get himself pointed head down like a missile. This left me likely to be
up above the pack struggling to keep up and breaking off to steer away early
to avoid crashing through an opening canopy below me. The plane spun up
its props and took off into the desert sky.

This would be the highest skydive I'd ever done. We'd be more than
14,000 feet over the ground, just under 18,000 feet above sea level, a tiny
fraction of the distance to where Alan was going. On the way up, I taught
Taber the special handshake that skydivers do so he could learn the full ritual
of joining souls with a group of people before experiencing first terror,
then the indescribable freedom of falling and flying through the open sky,
unlocked from the rules that bind humans to the Earth. Alan joined the
brotherhood along with the safety divers.

Luke opened the giant tailgate, and the Roswell desert zoomed wide
below us. Here the ground isn't lined by washes but scattered with farm
circles, separated by expanses of bare dirt and scrub grasses. We gave our
final look while Luke stepped out to film the exit. Taber was strapped to
Blikkies' chest, facing the same direction and just a bit lower than Blikkies
in the harness so Blikkies could see over his head. The green light came on,
and Taber and Blikkies stepped off, flipping through a football-field-length
back-flip across the sky. When the duo completed the rotation, Blikkies
threw out a stabilizing drogue parachute typical of tandem skydiving
systems. Alan and I ran out of the plane behind them, soaring into the wind
that tore across the airplane belly and pointing our heads toward the Earth
to try to keep up with the pack.

This was my peace for the week. For a full minute I was calm, loose,
and free. As expected, I couldn't keep up. I went head down for a second
and started gaining on them, but made what was probably a wise decision
to pull out before catching them to avoid launching into the group without
full control of myself, especially with a drogue parachute trailing Blikkies
and Taber.

At around 8,000 feet, a couple hundred feet above the four other divers,
I peeled off and tracked across the sky toward the landing area. The track

position, with arms back and body rigid, is the closest a human body can get to achieving flight. With no other jumpers around, I was free to tear across the sky without worry of collision, likely reaching speeds near 150 miles per hour. I flew to the landing zone and put my arms back in front of me, assuming the traditional skydiving arch to slow down. About 4,000 feet off the ground, I pulled my main and the new parachute blossomed smoothly above my head.

In the distance, I saw the other parachutes opening up near each other. We all released the steering lines on the canopies and pointed them toward our freshly prepared landing circle. I formed a square pattern to the landing area just in time to see Alan attempt his post-and-twist landing. He flipped hard onto his chest into the ground, wrapping once into the ends of the parachute lines, and got up laughing, just in time to watch Blikkies and Taber similarly face-dive into the ground. I ran over and hugged Taber, who was dirty but radiant. Luke and Trevor were all smiles and high energy too. It was a perfect kickoff for the next, more terrifying, phase of our testing.

We headed home exhausted, elated, and tense. Tomorrow we would push a pressurized spacesuit from an airplane with a man in it. We couldn't purge the Coolidge jump from our minds. We had to be better this time.

Leaving the hotel in darkness was a routine of our job. The small tin shed city buzzed with floodlights and glowing buildings. We moved through our morning brief and into suit preparations. These preparations would use the balloon flight procedures, but would skip unnecessary steps and add-ons that weren't required for balloon flights. The dance had new steps; the checklists had new boxes. We had to make calls to mission control to ready the airplane, and to cue a helicopter. Alan suited up in his undergarments. We primed the ground equipment and readied the outer layers of the suit. The doctors went through Alan's pre-flight checkout and applied the on-skin equipment for monitoring his vitals. He didn't pre-breathe for these tests. He wasn't going high enough to need it, and for this particular test we decided the extra practice wasn't worth the complication.

People were everywhere. Despite a stern lecture about staying out of the way, a stream of onlookers popped in and out of our clean preparation tent, bumping into us, undeterred by our sharp looks. The weather looked good and from what we could tell the jump was going to happen.

Alan emerged from his prep tent into the larger tent ready to don the suit. We informed the airplane pilot that we would be meeting him on the abandoned runway within the hour to load our pilot. Alan ducked into the suit pants and then the upper half. We hooked him to the ground oxygen supply and buttoned down all the seals. He was alone. We blurred around him, sliding on the parachute pack, connecting the pull handles, this time for real. Our first hitch: part of the parachute pull handle had fallen loose. Mitch, a true master, stepped in calmly with special pliers, normally used to clamp arteries, provided by the medical team. He reattached the loose part by slipping a nut deep behind the chestpack shell and refastening a nut on the other side. Alan had to hold perfectly still while Mitch executed the maneuver. It was like watching someone perform surgery on a conscious patient. Success. We moved on to the final steps, readying to move Alan out of the tin shed.

We had to change Alan over to the rigging harness that held him at a 45-degree angle. My stomach fell through to the floor as I stared at the blank space next to the suit where the assembly was supposed to be.

In all the chaos we had managed to leave the metal holding assembly for the suit on the other side of the country, in Florida. The unit was being worked on and had traversed the US several times in the previous month. Somehow we had been working for three days in and around the area where the unit usually hangs and didn't notice it wasn't there. The word "abort" hit my mind instantly. We couldn't continue without that unit.

As fast as I had that thought, I saw Blikkies, looking clever, holding the new stabilizer parachute attachment web. Since the redesign for holding Alan more vertically, there was a very convenient attachment point that would hold Alan at a suitable angle to have him hauled out to the tarmac and set down while connected to ground support. Blikkies rigged it up.

We unzipped and pulled open the giant doors to the tent, then the enormous door to the shed, and I climbed into the BLV to carry Alan toward the tarmac. We emerged from the shed in a train. The pilot hung from the BLV over a long tow bar that trailed the two carts holding the mass of tubes and wires that provided cooling fluid, oxygen, and power to Alan for the familiar trip down Stratosphere Lane. About halfway down the road, we recognized the Skyvan airplane heading toward us.

It is pretty unnerving to have a huge twin-engine open-prop airplane power straight for you. Just as it did before the dummy drops, the plane swung a one-eighty at the last minute to present its gaping back end to us, rear door wide open.

Everything gets wild when the sound of a running aircraft 30 feet away is thrown into the mix. People only communicate what is vitally necessary. The fair-weather bystanders start to edge back toward the buildings. We got permission from mission control to remove the cooling lines, leaving Alan to bake while Mitch swapped the existing launch sedan mounts with a new rollerblade wheel system for rolling him out the airplane tailgate. I donned my parachute rig on the off chance that worse turned to worse and I would have to jump to help Alan in the desert.

We got permission to transfer Alan to suit oxygen. It was time to load him.

"Big turn to the left. Line up with plane. Up the ramp, feet first. You hold feet, I'll push. Got it?"

"Got it."

We made a big sweeping turn, trying not to stress Alan's wheels. Alan remained still. Any movement would throw us off. His only view was of rough, old concrete sliding under his face a couple inches from his bubble. Then his head tipped down as wheels pitched his feet up the ramp. The grip stripes on the loading ramp ran under his face, then came the tie-down cleats and smooth tan flooring.

We anchored him with crisscrossed straps, just like the dummy. I knew exactly what to do, no thinking necessary. He was secure. Taber poked around, behaving like a safety officer. Sebastian called for the final go/no-go poll before passing control to Blikkies. We yelled over the roaring engines.

"Safety, this is a go/no-go poll to pass off the pilot."

"Safety is go."

"Surgeon."

"Surgeon is go."

"Chase."

"Chase is go."

"PSA, this is flight."

"Flight, this is PSA. Go ahead."

"You are go for pilot pass-off."

"Copy that."

I yelled to Blikkies, "You're in charge!"

Blikkies did a comm check with Alan. Trevor closed the door to the airplane. A moment of panic: I couldn't find my closeout checklist. I wouldn't fly without it. The stakes were too high to trust my brain alone in the heat of the moment. My special pressure suit assembly pants had too many pockets. After digging through every one of them, I finally found it. We gave the pilot the thumbs-up.

The pilot taxied toward the active runway. Alan moved his hands through the air as if he were skydiving, practicing. The sound of the engines rumbled into my chest. I felt nauseous, as though the spinning engines pulling the manned pressurized suit backwards into the sky were pulling up the contents of my gut.

Skydiving planes pitch back hard off the runway. Everything wants to fall toward the door. I thought about the straps and the cleats they were tied to. I wasn't sorry the door was closed. We lifted off the runway and reared hard toward 18,000 feet. The crop circles and pecan groves lay in the dirt and grass in every direction around the tiny city.

At 6,000 feet above the ground, I started through my checklist. Luke and Trevor sat still, while I ran laps around the suit. I checked valves, tube connections, displays, oxygen levels, thermal flaps, access doors, everything. At one moment I thought there was a problem with the suit pressure but was reminded by Blikkies that the pressure goes down as we go up: physics. Blikkies finished off the closeout with a radio check. I sat down. All I had left to do was remove the straps and push. We completed the critically important step of sliding our hands against each other's palms and fist bumping. Blikkies included Alan in the ritual after getting his attention by waving in front of the bubble. At 18,000 feet, the yellow light came on.

Luke opened the giant door, exposing the spread of open desert and a glimpse of our airport landing zone. Blikkies and I removed the straps while Trevor held Alan's legs. The plane remained slightly pitched back, urging Alan to leave at all times. After the straps were off, we drew him back across the fat red line on the airplane floor. Luke stepped off the back of the plane and onto a metal platform behind the door to signal when the spot was good. We were over the landing zone. I waited for Blikkies to nod his head and signal "Ready." At that we would pull back, signifying "Set," and then push, the "Go."

At this point my mind was clear, as if I was already skydiving. I had crossed over from the state of fear to the point of no return where the body clears distraction and trades the energy it was spending on holding back for focus, strength, and survival. What was Alan feeling? I counted down from 20 over and over again, skipping number 17. Everyone but Alan was working hard to breathe at 18,000 feet.

The yellow light turned off and the green came on. We were over the landing zone. As soon as Luke fine-tuned the spot, Alan would depart.

My mind contained nothing but a schematic for the extremely simple tasks ahead.

Luke stepped out. I stared at Blikkies. His head went up and then down. We pulled Alan back. We pushed. The wheels sent him accelerating fast toward the gaping door, and with a slight tilt he plunged into the blasting air stream. Two black shadows swept to either side of me. Blikkies and Trevor were away.

I lay on the bed of the aircraft with the air stream skimming my face and my eyes drying in the rushing air, refusing to blink. I counted. 10 seconds for the first 1,000 feet, five for each 1,000 feet after. 10, 15, 20, 25, 30, 35, 40. The bodies shrank to spots. One spot bloomed to an orange rectangle with a white stripe. Alan's main parachute had deployed. Another canopy bloomed open. Blikkies was out to help Alan to the ground. I popped up and sprinted to the pilot to euphorically report, "The main is out!" so he could relay it to the ground.

I hovered around the cockpit of the airplane as the aircraft turned toward the jumpers so we could watch through the front windows of the plane. The orange canopy made its first turns; Alan had control. The parallax tricked my perception. My heart dove through my chest as it seemed like Alan was heading for a crash with the airport terminal. It was a trick of the eye from the altitude. He was far from the ground and far from the terminal. We saw a helicopter hovering above the city to the north as Alan circled in. Blikkies made a clean approach, and we watched his parachute fold against the ground, where he would stand and guide Alan in on the radio. I became ecstatic, watching the perfect landing pattern. Alan's shadow showed up on the ground opposite the rising sun as he pulled in for a landing a stone's throw from the waiting ground crews. The landing looked nothing but peaceful. Alan's body met his shadow at the perfect location. The stiff orange and white wing folded itself softly to the ground in the morning sun.

The helicopter landed close enough to ruffle the canopies. I buckled up for a quick ride down. The plane lunged at the ground in a banking turn and cleared the remaining 4,000 feet in a couple minutes, landing in front of our freshly grounded pilot. I ran from the plane toward the landing site a few dozen feet away. Alan was still lying facedown in the depressurized suit, helmet off. The suit was dirty, but people were smiling. We pulled Alan out of the suit in the normal fashion. No issues. We put our gear in clean white bags. I saw some damage on the suit shell: one of the valves was bashed and on the verge of falling off. There was dirt in everything.

There was an element of shellshock behind people's smiles, a tension. Riding back to the landing site with Blikkies and Alan, I felt like there was something nobody was talking about. But Alan was alive and unharmed. We got back and drank coffee. Luke, Trevor, and the ground crews loaded up the video. The story of the jump and landing unfolded.

Alan had left the plane rocking back and forth like a potato chip falling through the air. Something in the dynamic of the suit's shape, or the drogue parachute sliding in and out of his wake, was causing him to pitch back and forth in what must have been nauseating repetition, making his head smack against the bubble on the first heavy swings. Luke, Trevor, and Blikkies swooped beside him in seconds, freefalling alongside him. Alan started to turn. In failed attempts to arrest the turn, Trevor bopped him. Then it was pull time. In an unwelcome reenactment of scary memories past, Alan found the pull handle, pulled, and no parachute appeared above his head. Somehow, the line had locked up. Alan yanked the handle just like he was trained to do, back and forth. It didn't let loose. The fall continued. Luke intervened and snagged the other handle. It released, and sent the life-giving parachute blooming above Alan's head while Luke and Trevor rocketed away hundreds of miles an hour toward the Earth.

The suit was depressurized without an issue. The canopy ride was as elegant on video as it looked from the plane. Alan had it. The parachute turned and maneuvered and he flew his spacesuit to the landing site. Blikkies guided him in through a perfect landing pattern over a huge empty airport. He turned in for a base leg and approached a landing site just dozens of feet from the waiting ground crews. The last left turn rotated to a slow, peaceful cruise toward the final moments of flight. As Alan approached the ground, he executed a flare to stall the parachute and arrest the forward and vertical speed threatening him and his suit.

About a third of the way through the flare, his foot collided with the ground. He rotated just under 90 degrees before body-slamming the life-support pack into the powdery dirt. He flipped onto the suit helmet bubble with his feet rotating past his head. The momentum of those centrifugal feet arched his back onto the grinding bubble, cartwheeling the suit half sideways to land in a dirty ball of dust. We had just seen our second face-plant-style landing in a spacesuit that lived the rest of its life in clean rooms, touched only gently by white-gloved hands. That was the end of our day. Everyone was fine. Alan was smiling and giggly about the crash landing. Per usual, he was the least shaken person there. We'd clean up the suit and go again tomorrow.

We were outside the paradigms of the spacesuit world. NASA has spent millions of dollars on special equipment designed to prevent the catastrophe of a training astronaut falling down. We were slamming pressurized, manned spacesuits into the ground at glide speeds upwards of 30 miles an hour and resetting to go again. We felt like we were finally treating a spacesuit the way it needed to be treated. The science community wants to build suits for Mars in which people would move through daily life. How can they do that if they are too cautious to risk that an astronaut surrounded by technicians could take a tumble in a lab? We were helping to connect a disconnect in the bureaucracy. Spacesuits will someday need to be durable. Intentionally or not, we were helping to pave that road.

We analyzed the damage to the suit. In Alan's twists and turns, the life-support pack had angled into the worst possible orientation. The belly of the pack was clean and smooth, designed for laminar airflow and built with the face-plant-style landing in mind. The back was a parachute rig that can drag through the dirt all day. The sides, however, were a snag forest whose delicate scraggly attachments had no hope of surviving an encounter with the ground. All together, we had learned that if Alan landed on his side like that again, we could expect most or all of the suit's skinny protrusions to be damaged when they dug into the desert floor. Miraculously, our plastic aeroshell had survived, despite the guards for the parachute pull handles scooping into the Earth and bulldozing up a little mound of dirt, the same action that had cracked our aeroshell and ripped off the handle guard in the previous jump.

Despite the fact that we were faced with hours of delicate repair, a huge load was lifted from my shoulders that morning. This jump had roughness around the edges, but it was certainly not a repeat of our prior near-deadly jump in the central Arizona desert. We had gotten to where we should have been before attempting that wild flight.

The mood was light. We laid into the suit with wrenches and vacuum cleaners. We disassembled all the major components to clean the dirt out of the guts of the life-support pack and suit components. In a matter of a few hours, we had replaced the thin bent fingers of metal from the side of the tank that had met the ground. All the structural elements of the pack had done their job; there were no warping or bends in any part of the structure itself.

While we were working on the suit, Blikkies was digging into why the pull handle hadn't let the pull cord out when Alan yanked it. The handle itself had released from the springs that held it down without any worries, but something bound up the cable on its way out. It wasn't actually clear from the videos, or Alan, whether Luke had pulled the handle or if Alan had reached for it and Luke had snatched it from his hand right as he finally got it. It was clear, however, that it had taken more force than desired to clear the handle. When Blikkies got through his investigation, it appeared that some combination of the housing accumulating some filth in shipping and the cable binding on the edge of the housing had made for a hard pull. He thoroughly cleaned the cable housing and pulled some housing through the clamp that held it to the chestpack, creating a smooth tunnel for the cable. When Alan yanked on the handle the cable would not scrape or bind across an edge.

After a celebratory lunch, we started to reassemble the hardware and perform our outstanding checks. In one day, five people refurbished a crashed spacesuit. It was a task that seemed, at the time, to have become simple. We could have been mechanics in an auto shop replacing components on a busted car.

With some hesitation in our voices, we agreed to reset and attempt another jump the following morning. Alan and the safety divers went through the dive flow. We headed home for an eight-hour break before returning in the dark to try again.

The next morning was tense. We had implemented what amounted to major changes across a span of hours in the heated aftermath of a jump that was spectacular in all things, including its incredible smash-and-tumble finish. We were on edge, tired, and in all reality probably didn't want this jump to happen that day. But we had our deadlines. Alan had to leave at the end of the week. If we didn't jump, Alan might not get through all the skills in the available time. We pushed through a brutal wake-up to begin the suiting process.

Across the span of a couple hours, Alan was in the suit and looking ready to go. Before this suit-up process, we switched to some newly arrived painted parachute pull handles that were intended to be our final flight versions. They were candy apple red and stood out against the suit with a shine.

We had been peeking outside, watching the sun clear the horizon and worrying about a cloud layer lurking above us. Before exiting the shed, we checked with the tower, who told us that the cloud ceiling was at 12,000 feet, too low. With hopes it would break or that we would find a hole, we hooked the BLV up to the suit and I began to drive it out, pulling Alan and the support carts to the flight line.

The crane beeped as I backed it down Stratosphere Lane, punctuating the airplane roar that filled my tired head. Suddenly the tarmac came alive with yells and waving arms.

I took my eyes from the spotter behind me and slammed on the brakes. I watched the suit lurch. Aside from the sloshing he was getting, Alan seemed fine. Why were they yelling? Everyone who was supposed to be watching the suit was gaping at the chase truck. I grabbed the control stick for the boom on the crane, ready to drop the suit on the ground, an action that wouldn't harm the pilot but would mangle our ground-support hoses. Now I saw the reason for all the yelling. One of the camera crew from the documentary was wedged underneath one of the chase trucks, and the team of doctors training for Alan's mission was extracting the downed cameraman from the truck that had apparently just run over him.

Luckily for that cameraman, he was sent home on some crutches. Our most severe injury so far.

With the team shaken by an accident some 20 feet from the BLV and the weather failing to improve, Sebastian initiated a "weather hold" that the suit team interpreted as an abort. We started into some tests that would render the suit unusable that day. We wanted to see those new red handles pull the cord to release the main parachute. We locked out the pack so that pulling the handles wouldn't actually deploy the parachute and told Alan to pull. He reached with his favored right arm for the main deployment handle and with a sharp tug was able to remove it. With a couple swings, the pull cord released, verifying a good fix. After that he switched to his left hand and we learned for the one millionth time why we test. He grabbed the red handle and gave it a jiggle. It didn't leave the guard. He reached in again and yanked back and forth, but the springs holding it in were refusing to let it go. The apparently slightly weaker left arm, combined with a bit of fatigue, appeared to be preventing him from getting the handle to release. After a few more tugs he gave up.

We moved to have him pull the other two handles, the ones that cut away the main parachute and released the reserve. We again found ourselves shaking our heads in raw engineering shame. The handle to cut away the main parachute was connected through the housing that Blikkies had just moved to solve the problem of the hard-to-pull pull handle. Moving the anchor back made it so the housing could wag back and forth. Now it was clear that the original pull cord was too long; there wasn't enough stroke to pull the handle. That was a screw-up that could have spelled disaster in the event of a bad main parachute deployment. We were lucky that the cameraman had wedged beneath the chase truck and let us escape what happens when a pilot can't pull his parachute or actuate one of the critical emergency systems. We were lucky that day had ended how it had.

The next morning turned into a full day of work we had previously thought was done. We removed one of the two springs that held the pull handles and made them easier to pull. There were theories that the new red handles had been harder to pull because they were made of a stiffer material, or perhaps that the paint was sticking to the shell slightly. Regardless, we only had the red handles to use, so we tested the configuration repeatedly, updating the hardware on the suit to have a single spring instead of two. Blikkies also revamped the anchor system and tested the pull cord stroke until he was confident the system could repeatedly do its job and release the required cords. We filled the day and went home late—but confident that we had working hardware.

These airplane tests were done with all the risks of freefalling and deploying a parachute from a much-modified rig, but with a tiny fraction of the precautions that went into the process of developing the hardware because the intended use was a balloon ride to the stratosphere, not rollout from an airplane. We knew that two of the closest brushes with disaster in the Red Bull Stratos program had been in their airplane jump program. I'm certain their close calls were at least partially due to the lack of preparation that comes with preliminary testing as opposed to the real deal. We noted our own close call.

Had we gone ahead and launched Alan that morning, he likely would have failed to pull his own parachute and once again, one of the safety divers would have swooped in to save the day. Scarier still but far less likely was a scenario where if the main parachute had failed, the cutaway probably would not have worked, leaving Alan only the chance that he could have successfully dumped a reserve into whatever tangled mess may have been above him. I do truly believe that day was headed for an abort. It wasn't right. We weren't ready. We were strangely thankful that someone had been run over by a truck.

The next day the weather was excellent. This time faster and with fewer spectators, we started working in the darkness to prepare our glowing white suit. Alan put on his protective cup, adult diapers, and liquid thermal garment.

The bubble went on and he was sealed away. We installed the parachute rig and dangled Alan at 45 degrees. I got the BLV, trying to focus on Mitch and his thumbs-up leading me out, not the image of the cameraman pinned under a pickup truck. The airplane roared in. We knew our tasks so well, we completed them in silence all the way until the plane took off.

Throughout the final round of checks during the climb to 18,000 feet, Alan kept moving his arms, pretending to skydive. With no view of the lights and no outside sounds penetrating the bubble, Alan had no indication he was about to get launched out of the back of the plane until he saw the floor moving under him. Luke was already out. Blikkes followed Alan. The last diver had to jostle past me as I gaped at the plummeting bodies below.

I lay on the tailgate of the plane staring at the shrinking white dot surrounded by the three black specks. I counted the seconds. Somewhere around 40, a canopy came open, but it wasn't orange and white. An instant later the colors I was waiting for bloomed. I jumped up and trotted to the cockpit to relay word that the main was out.

The plane spiraled down to 4,000 feet, where I could still jump if needed. Blikkes landed. Alan's canopy raced toward his shadow, deformed in a healthy flare, and folded itself neatly to the ground. The helicopters were on the scene in seconds.

By the time I got to the group, I found smiles and a very dirty suit. Clearly there had been another face-first smash down. In the hour that followed, we heard the tale of the third skydive in the StratEx pressure suit.

Alan rocked into a solid drogue parachute inflation and once again, the potato chip rocking bucked on. Alan started turning again and wasn't able to stop it. The freefall transitioned to parachute flight at just the right time, so the safety divers didn't need to intervene. Alan flared into the center of the landing patch and made an attempt to turn the suit around. His foot clipped the dirt, but instead of turning over onto his back, he once again skidded on his side of the suit, mangling solid steel and ripping valves out of their brackets. Alan was again unscathed. He took the helmet off by himself, as was mandated by the previous tests. He came out of the dirty banged-up suit with a smile and a joke in the classic Alan style.

The real beauty, however, was a small but significant motion 6,000 feet in the air. In the third jump of the program, in as real a scenario as we could create without taking Alan to space, he finally performed a function critical to the completion of the program. Alan had pulled his own parachute.

Early September 2014: Airplane Jumping Session III

Grasshoppers are some of the strangest creatures I've ever seen. During autumn in the desert Southwest they are everywhere. They spring into the air, reaching wild heights in comparison with their own size. They would

crash onto the half-century old tarmac of the Roswell airport making
no attempt to land with any type of control. They landed like crash test
dummies, letting themselves flop and deform against the ground. Then
they put themselves back together, reorganizing their limbs to their correct
positions for another jump. All day long. One imagines that any jump could
be the final jump for one of these bugs, but the more we watched them the
more it became obvious that would never happen. Somehow they always
got back up and went for another hop.

We broke from jumping for a week. Blikkies and I went to Florida to
hack away at the never-ending hardware list. We holed up in the engineering
loft at the parachute factory, reassembling rigs and building a prototype
umbrella device to go over Alan in flight. This device was intended to
deflect stray line from grabbing the spreader bar which oriented the straps
holding the suit to the balloon base. After Alan had departed the balloon,
we didn't want any chance of entanglement that would prevent the gore line
from failing to rip the balloon apart because it looped around something
while it fell. We worked from before the sun came up to hours after it went
down. Between cutting, sewing, and assembling, we would sneak in some
fun by bolting together $CO2$ canister launchers and firing rockets into the
sunset over the factory.

Alan's inability to pull the new red parachute handles after doing it so
easily in the human factors training was a conundrum. We decided to go
back to the original ones. After I had begged the shop to build us a pile of
3D-printed parachute handles made of exotic carbon-filled nylon and paint
them candy apple red, I had to beg some more, this time to fill the order
in the plain white nylon we had originally used. When the week was up, we
returned to Roswell with new gear, ready for more jumps.

We refurbished the spacesuit. Our unprecedented method of smashing
the suit into the ground at full speed and rebuilding it in a matter of hours
had a strange payoff: the more we abused and fixed the suit, the tighter it
got.

Alan arrived early for more training. We got him into the suit and
hung him from the gantry. Luke, Trevor, and Blikkies bashed him around,
spinning him in circles and pushing his legs up and down to simulate the
potato-chipping motion that was beating him up in the air.

During this testing session, Luke and Trevor shared an epiphany they
had had while watching the videos from the previous flights. Alan would
regard this discovery as one of the most significant of the program and for
him as the pilot. He credited it entirely to the two safety divers. Luke and
Trevor had blown minds in every drop with their command of their own
bodies while in freefall and their understanding of the aerodynamics of
awkwardly shaped objects that changed geometry during flight. Now they
focused on an instant during the previous drop when Alan had reached one

hand down to the parachute handle on his chest while the other hand was above his head. When he did that, they perceived a slight slowing in his spin. From these few seconds of footage, they built a new theory of body positions that could reliably induce and stop a turn. This theory was put to practice in commands to point an elbow or an arm to various extremes in the direction of the turn. We had Alan practice the motion during this testing session with the intention of trying the method in flight.

These responses were exactly the opposite of the ones ingrained from his skydiving training. The revelations were in alignment with what we had learned long before in the wind tunnel testing. We had certainly failed to properly assimilate that knowledge. The motions did, however, have new subtleties: it was an exact motion with a precise curvature of arm that was able to successfully steer the suit in a predictable way. Blikkies and the divers simulated every chaotic motion they could imagine while hammering his brain with new commands until they were confident they had reversed his instincts and ingrained the motion that would allow him to turn. Now he had to prove his knowledge in freefall.

We still had to tackle the issue of Alan opening his own helmet. He was the one who came up with a practical and easy solution: simply remove the thumb from the over-mitt that had been added to the suit during thermal testing. When we ran the tests with the thumb just tucked back, the buttons and the latch were easy to operate. So we cut the thumb off the over-mitt, leaving only the electrically heated glove to warm his left thumb. Getting the helmet off trumped a cold thumb. Alan never had a problem removing his helmet again.

We ended the training with more handle pulls, this time with the plain white plastic ones, which did seem more bendy and easier to free from their springs. We had also refined all the pull cord lengths. Alan was fresh, and not in freefall. He was once again able to pull the handles. We loaded the handles up, let Alan rip them out, then loaded them back up and made him do it again. When we were all sufficiently worn out, we stopped. Alan had new instincts for flying. He could pull the parachute handles and remove his helmet. It was time to test in the real stress of freefall.

We made some changes to the flight plan. We gave up our dreams of a "post-and-twist" landing in which Alan flipped around and slid in on his back. Perhaps it was always a happy delusion, an idea that soothed the executives who wouldn't have accepted a plan in which Alan bulldozed sagebrush with the chestpack at the end of every flight. From now on, however, Alan would stay pointed forward and skid in on the chestpack shield like a penguin sliding down an ice chute, but with significantly more friction. Alan would then be able to focus solely on flaring the canopy to slow himself down in the final instants. We hadn't analyzed or designed the system to handle a full-blown face plant. We were saved by our conservative "best effort" to make the chestpack strong, as well as our arsenal of spare parts and growing ability to make fast repairs.

We planned to send Alan out of the plane feet first this time in hopes of minimizing the potato chipping that was proving a difficult flight feature to shake. Alan was much more rested than for earlier flights and much better trained. We expected to see a difference.

The teams poured into their positions in the dark. Doctors arrived to run ground support and continue their training. Mission control lit up with computers. The meteorology team scrutinized their weather charts. The suit came together. Alan slowly entered it. The suit vitals came live as systems were turned on and connected.

We pulled him down to the tarmac in the usual Stratosphere Lane parade while the airplane pilot rolled in and drenched us in exhaust. Mitch bolted the wheels onto the suit's chest. We accomplished it all with hand signals amidst the impossibly loud prop wash. Joe hooked up the ramp, and this time we pushed Alan headfirst into the wide rectangle of the airplane rear. One strap over the butt and another over the shoulders. Boxes were checked. Control was passed to Blikkies. Time to go. I stared at Alan. Alan stared at the floor.

When we left the runway, I could guess our altitude by watching the ground. At 1,000 feet, it became difficult to distinguish individual people. At 5,000 feet, cars started looking like ants. By 10,000 feet, cars were difficult to see at all.

Per usual, we unclipped our seat belts at 7,000 feet. I started through the in-flight checklist, closing valves and checking sensors. Alan rehearsed his skydive, move by move.

The plane leveled out at 18,000 feet above sea level. Cars had disappeared and roads were only visible as the dividers between patches of farm. Blikkies and I circled each other, removing the straps draped over the suit and tossing the ends to each other like we were docking a sailboat. Blikkies set the drogue parachute on the static line, clipping the little bag to the long cable that ran the length of the plane's cabin. When Luke opened the door, I blocked Alan with my leg to stop him from rolling out. The yellow light came on: three minutes. Then came the green.

The series of head nods cascaded from Luke, out behind the door, to Blikkies to me.

"Ready!" We pushed forward.

"Set!" We pulled back.

"Go!"

The rollerblade wheels carried Alan at the perfect speed to glide, not fall, out of the airplane. The drogue snapped to life from the static line pouch.

Blikkies let the momentum of his push carry him, running, right out the door. Trevor sprinted the length of the cabin and dove behind him.

I took my position on the tailgate and counted the seconds past the moment when I should have seen Alan's parachute. Only one parachute had bloomed and it wasn't his. What was happening? Why were the safety divers opening without Alan open? Before the full panic set in, an orange rectangle popped into view 12,000 feet below me. I could just barely make out the white stripe: the main. Our fourth freefall was over.

When I finally arrived at the scene, parachute still on my back, the landing scene was familiar: one happy pilot, one broken, dirty spacesuit, and half a dozen doctors and suit technicians back-patting and laughing about the latest face-planting, helmet-sliding landing.

Alan sunk under the drogue and immediately knew the face-first exit hadn't fixed the potato chipping. After this dive, we would decide that the rocking motion, like the facedown landing, was something we could tolerate. Alan did, however, exhibit a newfound ability to control the suit. Rocking up and down and falling away with Luke and Trevor surrounding him, he pushed an elbow into the air stream and turned around, then flawlessly stopped the turn and spun in the other direction. He repeated the routine with full arm turns, executing the maneuvers with purpose, pushing the air above him into invisible corkscrews.

Luke and Trevor's theory on how to fly the suit in and out of turns ended up being correct. We hoped the theory would translate to stratospheric heights and that a dipped elbow would indeed arrest a turn. Through this long flight, Alan learned he could implement a turn and seconds later tuck in his arms and bring it to a stop. That was important. It removed our concern that the length of a stratospheric dive could make spinning inevitable.

The maneuvers took up precious freefall time. Unbeknownst to me, Blikkies had passed all his remaining duties to Luke and Trevor and pulled his chute early. He watched from above with plenty of sky to meet Alan under chute and guide him in. This was the action that freaked me out from above, seeing Blikkies' parachute open before Alan's.

Alan's freefall did continue below the mark, however. Occupied with so many maneuvers, he passed through his pull altitude in a fluster. Reverting to instinct in the face of panic, he plunged his hand for his hip like he was wearing a normal skydiving rig, even though his pull handles were fixed to his chest. After a couple of belated swings and smacks on the chestpack, he had crossed the altitude where the safety divers were instructed to intervene. In a display of mind-exploding ability to command precision flight with only the human body for control, both Luke and Trevor turned and thrust at the side of the suit like fighter jets and snatched the parachute pull handles from either side of the suit simultaneously at virtually the exact threshold altitude.

The precision involved in that action was otherworldly. The suit is built with totally redundant main deployment handles, one on each side. Alan was falling at about 130 miles per hour when the altitude threshold was crossed. The two safety divers instantly matched their fall rates to that of the suit, accounted for the time to cover the distance between them, flew in, and snatched the handles in perfect unison at an exact altitude measured in feet, while 190 feet ticked by every second. Luke and Trevor could swim literal circles around what they had to do out there. Alan was in good hands.

We got our morning comedic experience watching the suit headcam video of the landing on repeat while eating breakfast. It was Alan's softest landing so far. Without trying to twist around on the ground, he was able to focus his attention on flaring the parachute. He slowed his air speed much more and managed to keep himself straight through the belly flop. This time he hit the ground with his legs, then his knees, rolling toward a summersault until plowing six feet of dirt with the smooth plastic helmet, legs pointing straight toward the sky. He plopped back on to his belly and snapped off his helmet himself.

The two metal switches on the top of our oxygen tanks, an inch of solid steel a quarter inch thick, were wrapped around the front of the tank covers like question marks. A problematic valve once again broke loose. Easy to fix. There were no holes busted through the shell and the side of the pack was intact. Alan didn't have a scratch.

Alan had commanded the suit through the air with remarkable proficiency. We wanted to be done. The fact of the matter, however, was that we had one more box to check before Alan could be called a ready spacesuit skydiver. He was one for four on pulling his own parachute. We would send him back to the sky.

We filled our afternoon with suit removal training with a new batch of doctors, three extractions per doctor: yellow, then orange, then red. Alan and I shared suit duties.

Before heading back to the hotel, the team executed the fastest spacesuit refurbishment in our history, reducing what is ordinarily an outlandishly laborious process to a few hours. We inspected every element, replaced all damaged or worn components, and did a full functional test, including pressurizing the suit and executing a pressure decay leak test. Once again, the leak rate was reduced. Our one and only suit had endured more than twice the normal usage duration as its space station counterpart and was improving in durability. Some humans will one day find themselves in a place where going outside means wearing spacesuits. This testing served as a testament to how hardy they can be, and how fast they can be fixed when broken.

There was one jump to go. Alan tried to convince us that he could have pulled the parachute handle if he hadn't been so busy practicing sky maneuvers. We granted that he had done an amazing job controlling the suit, but he hadn't demonstrated proficiency with the handle pull. We agreed that if Alan repeated his commanding heading control on the next jump and got his own handle pulled, we'd all go thumbs-up to move on. Sometimes two for five is good enough.

This jump would be the 44th suit run of the program. Our operations were fluent and clean. The shadows of Coolidge had faded.

We suited Alan up the next morning with repetitive ease. We repeatedly launched latex weather balloons to get extremely detailed wind profiles above the airport, a luxury most skydivers wish for and none receive. Because of weather concerns, we would launch the plane before the sunrise on the ground, such that the jumpers would leave the plane as the sun rose at altitude, about 20 minutes earlier than the sun cleared the horizon on the ground.

Luke had spent his free time the previous day creating a tongue-activated switch he could put in his mouth to take high-definition pictures while blasting through the sky at 130 miles per hour.

Teams ran like clockwork. Light was just beginning to play at the fringes of the desert as the crane met the plane at the end of Stratosphere Lane. We clicked through the routines with ant-like collaboration.

When the door opened at 18,000 feet and the green light flashed, Blikkies, Alan, and I ended an era. It was the last time we would skate that suit out of a plane.

Alan executed a flawless dive. Luke and Trevor casually twitched their arms and legs, maintaining a healthy paternal distance from their graduating pupil, who executed a 360-degree turn in either direction before reaching calmly to his side, pulling the handle, and squirting the parachute to bloom orange and white overhead.

Luke clicked his tongue, snapping the shutter of a full-size SLR camera fixed to his head. Later we would see stunning pictures of skydivers silhouetted against a sunrise high in the sky while nighttime still lingered on the ground.

Alan executed a perfect landing pattern in a normal, now less spectacular, cloud of dust. I didn't sprint to the doctors and suit techs congregated around the suit when we got back to the ground. I knew Alan was fine. The part of my life when I worried over a man in a spacesuit pushed from the back of a plane was over.

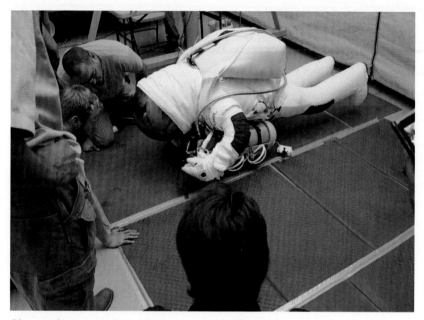

Human factors training. Alan is trying to depressurize the suit.

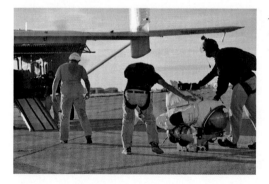

Alan being rolled onto an aircraft in preparation for airplane jump testing.

Mitch installing wheels onto Alan's suit before he is loaded into an aircraft for his second set of suited airplane jump tests. (Photo by Volker Kern.)

Mid-jump test in the sky above Roswell International Air Center. The spacesuit is fully pressurized and configured as it would be in a high-altitude flight for training. (Photo by Luke Evens.)

*Mid-jump test in the sky above Roswell International Air Center. (Photo by
Luke Evens.)*

*Mid-jump test in the sky above Roswell International Air Center. (Photo by
Luke Evens.)*

Alan heading out the door on one of his airplane jumps from 18,000 feet above sea level at the Roswell International Air Center.

Alan under parachute after an airplane jump test. (Photo by Dave Jourdan.)

Another crash landing in which Alan flipped all the way over onto his back.

Alan's parachute opening as viewed from the ground during an airplane jump test. The two safety divers, Luke Evens and Trevor Cedar, are falling away as the chute opens. (Photo by Dave Jourdan.)

Alan crashing into the ground on one of his airplane jumps. This landing was typical. Every jump in the StratEx suit resulted in a tumble over the life-support pack.

Alan approaches the landing site with acute control of his parachute. He landed remarkably close to the intended landing site on every drop. (Photo by Dave Jourdan.)

More epic face plants. It was after this landing that we abandoned attempts to have Alan turn around while flaring the canopy. From this point on Alan would intentionally lie down on his chest during landing.

CHAPTER 15

...

Preparations

I was not a normal human anymore. I was living in an extended state of meditation in which I could sustain prolonged focus without the social nourishment that my peers outside the project enjoyed. The biggest link to real life I was able to maintain was with my girlfriend back home. She had taken me back. I was able to explain in my weird way why the project was so important to me—what I was doing wasn't just work. She understood the difference. She is an engineer too. My love for her compounded as she learned to sail with me in the strange waters of my altered reality.

The balloon team was working on the balloon-destruct problem from a different angle. The team had learned that our rogue balloon, the one had that traversed a substantial portion of the United States, had failed for a troubling reason. When mission control commanded the destruction of the balloon everything properly fell and the gore line was pulled, but the gore line failed to rip the balloon in half. A small hole was created near the top and a long slice at the bottom, but the catastrophic failure needed to put the balloon into freefall was not created. Amazingly, the bottom half of the balloon was totally ripped open and there were two manhole-sized holes at the top (the open crown valve and the hole created by the gore line), but the thing still roamed the sky for almost seven hours. 10 million cubic feet of helium takes a long time to vent. They attributed the failed destruct to a combination of the lower weight of the flight computer (as compared to the payload that normally pulled the line) and the fact that the balloon was rising when the computer was dropped. The worst part about the discovered failure was that there was not an easy way to ensure it wouldn't happen again.

The team decided they would add yet another destruction system for the balloon. If the gore line failed, they would burn the top off the balloon with cannon fuse, a type of mild explosive-laden cord. John Straus was responsible not only for the act of launching the balloons, but also for the engineering of the balloon system itself. Because the destruct systems weren't working, he led the charge to fix them. The launch team tested the fuse idea by taking pieces of the many balloon carcasses boxed up scattered around the site, attaching various types of fuses to them, and sending them to the stratosphere where they would light them off and watch how well they destroyed balloon plastic. Pieces of polyethylene balloon were now the payload beneath latex balloons. They couldn't test the destruct methods on latex balloons because they pop when they get to their target altitude and so don't float away too far or require their own destruct system. Each flight was also a training run for helicopters that helped the chase team hone in on their ability to track a payload coming down from the stratosphere and land next to it.

The balloon team investigated everything from detonation cord, eliminated because actual explosives are a bureaucratic mess, to a type of cheese-cutter idea, all in search of a third method to destroy a balloon in case the first two didn't work. They ended up choosing a Chinese-made cannon fuse, similar to one that might light off a large firework.

September 2014: Meeting Moses

One of these test payloads did a zigzag pattern up to altitude and happened to land back in downtown Roswell. It was plucked from the middle of a road by a squat, fiery Hispanic man with a pocket chain dangling past his knees. His name, we would learn, was Moses. The camera was still running.

Later we would see him on video, grabbing the payload and bringing it to a huddle with his friends to discuss what it was and what they should do.

A notice on the side of the payload promised a reward for its return, and Moses wanted it. He called the number provided and reached Rolfe, who informed him that a truck that had been tracking the payload via satellite was turning down his street. Moses yelled, "Can you see me through this camera?" and took off running. Rolfe assured him that no one was watching him, that the camera was just recording. Moses didn't believe that, and kept asking for confirmation that we could see him. Rolfe asked whether he wanted to return the payload and whether they could make some arrangements.

"Arrangements!" hollered Moses into the phone. "What the fuck you talkin' 'bout, arrangements?" He started making dubious claims about how the payload had hit his dog and wanted to know who was going to pay for its care. He said his grandmother had been hit by a UFO. All the while he was managing to dodge the chase truck. He circled back behind his house and went inside to discuss with friends how much money our modified Walmart Go-Pro camera was worth (200 dollars was the answer to that) and whether that number was more than the 1,000-dollar reward. They bickered; the camera audio recorded. Should they steal the camera or return the payload and hope for the 1,000 bucks? They chose both.

Moses called Rolfe back, informed him that he would like to return the payload for the reward, and gave him directions to his house. He then proceeded, with the camera still recording and perfectly framing his face, to cut the camera off the payload. Only then did he find the "off" button.

The recovery team met Moses to make the deal and immediately spotted the saw hole where the camera used to be. They told Moses that the only thing they really cared about was the camera footage—without it there would be no deal. The reward offer stated the payload needed to be "intact." Moses suggested that the camera must have broken off on landing. The recovery lead ran his fingers across the clearly sawed edge of the hole where the camera had been. Moses rushed them off the property, noting, "I've been to prison twice, and the second time I liked it."

While the recovery team was on their way home, another call came in. Moses had found the camera. He would return it, but not in exchange for the promise of a check. He wanted cash. I was dispatched from the airport to withdraw 1,000 dollars from the bank, wondering how this was going to look on my expense report.

Armed with the cash, the recovery team set up a rendezvous with an increasingly paranoid Moses. He showed them an intricate scene, complete with a ladder placed against a tree with several broken branches where he claimed to have at last found the camera, which had apparently broken off. They swapped the camera for the cash. We never saw Moses again, except on the video of his low-altitude payload rescue, captioned and digitally enhanced as a record of the weird adventures inherent in high-altitude ballooning.

September 2014: Finishing a World-Class Avionics Suite

Dan McFatter, who had rebuilt our entire flight computer in a pinch after the pull-out of our original communications contractor, worked out of a nest in a corner of the dusty tin shed. Tangles of wire braided around and through waveform generators, power sources, and space-rated electrical circuits, all undergoing mad overhaul while he held the organization of it all in his amazing brain. He was refining the machine that performed flawlessly in the communications test and turning it into a bulletproof, highly redundant work of art capable of releasing our pilot in three different ways, bringing down our balloon in three different ways, and maintaining a mind-boggling set of communications signals across dozens of instruments all operating on the public band without the need for special frequencies licensed by an unpredictable outside contractor. Esteban helped him, and together they solved communications problems few people had considered—because few people had ever wanted to communicate with devices high in the stratosphere.

GPS devices read signals from a constellation of orbiting satellites to triangulate their position. We needed to know the real-time location in three-dimensional space of the balloon and every device that would separate from it. In addition, because GPS clocks are among the most accurate on the planet, all of the systems' timestamps came from GPS readings.

Since the beginning of the program, we had been warned that making GPS work reliably above 50,000 feet was a challenge, especially for fast-moving objects such as Alan, who was expected to shatter the sound barrier at Mach 1.3. Dan had slowly encountered each of the issues reported to us from the members of the Red Bull Stratos team, industry partners, and the Fédération Aéronautique Internationale, which certified records like the ones we were trying to break. GPS signals don't stop working as the things they are tracking get really high, it's just that the software in devices that interpret GPS signals stops knowing what to do and the units start failing to process the data properly.

In a design-and-test process across dozens of flights to the stratosphere while the launch team was experimenting with ways to destroy balloons, Dan went down to the chip level, designing a GPS unit the size of a deck of cards that would perform in environments no other known system could. He had designed and built the highest, fastest GPS system we knew to exist in the public domain. It worked every time. The official record observers from the Fédération Aéronautique Internationale were stunned when, after months and years of hair pulling trying to get the Red Bull Stratos system to work, Dan's little deck of cards could capture GPS tracks in beautiful smooth curves at high speeds in the very top of the stratosphere.

The second major improvement to the avionics suite was the addition of a new aviation transponder. Transponders tell air traffic controllers where airplanes are. It is a box that transmits a set of coordinates that can be read by the controllers so they can guide airplanes around. Balloons can't be guided around, but air traffic controllers still really like to know where they are.

Our last balloon went rogue for a very stressful portion of a day. Aside from one spotting that seemed to come from deep within a secretive missile range, its little spherical radar reflector proved ineffective as a tool to inform air traffic control of the location of our balloon. Realizing how close we had come to a disaster, we assured air traffic control that a transponder would ever after reside on the balloon, even after the avionics package fell away. If we ever again set a football-stadium-sized trash bag free in the stratosphere, human eyes scanning the sky for a dot wouldn't be the only hope of knowing where it was. There was only one problem: transponders stop working before the stratosphere starts. This doesn't have anything to do with distance, temperature, or pressure. Someone writing code for the FAA at some point in the past recognized that airplanes don't fly above 50,000 feet and didn't code in the functionality needed for such altitudes to be recognized by their system.

Dan used his newly developed GPS technology alongside a very modern type of transponder, working in concert with a new piece of software implemented at the FAA to make a transponder that would work deep into the stratosphere and even into space. Dan's system was tested on little balloons throughout the summer and fall of 2014 and became the first transponder to be functional throughout the stratosphere.

That system worked in its early tests when it was relatively alone on a balloon, but for our flight, it would be one more signal in a shooting gallery of potentially conflicting signals that needed to be tested for interference before we could move on to manned flights. We decided we would need to do yet another long-distance communications test. I would hang from the BLV in Alan's spacesuit once again, while a little trailer parked above a gorgeous vista read and sent a rainbow of radio signals weakened appropriately by distance.

This test was an afterthought. It never made it onto the schedules. It didn't need to. It was so fast and easy for us to set up that we were confident we could do the prep in hours and knock it out in days. We threw together a makeshift test-readiness review so our distant supervisors would be informed we were going to be donning the suit. I would hang from the BLV and try to communicate with a trailer on a mountain 70 miles away.

Sebastian set up the trailer in the mountains while the rest of us slept. In a drab morning mood, I put on the suit and was sucking bottled air before the sun came up. John drove the BLV. My belief in the value of simple experience was reinforced as I took in the desert sunrise through the helmet. John set me onto the launch sedan, picked up the balloon equipment module, and lowered it over me. I was hooked to it, then together the equipment module and I were hoisted into the beam of radio waves emanating from the hillside 70 miles away.

I walked through the steps. "Flight, this is pilot with a 10 count: 10, 9, 8, 7, 6, 5, 4, 3, 2, 1."

Then Sebastian in the mission control trailer on the hillside responded, "Pilot, this is flight with a 10 count: 10, 9, 8, 7, 6, 5, 4, 3, 2, 1."

In between counts, tens of minutes rolled by while mission control ran through their checklists verifying the signals flying in and out of the chestpack and the flight computer above my head.

Soon the last comm test was over. I crawled out of the suit onto mats laid on the dusty tarmac. It was so fast and free of stress or hitches that it was hard to decide whether it merited our normal celebration routine. We didn't spend adrenaline, but it was still a victory.

September 2014: Human Spin Testing

With one test remaining before our manned campaign, we entered a period of reflection. We were all forced to think and talk about the odds of whether our pilot and friend might die because something we made didn't work. I felt like I should start smoking cigarettes or drinking whiskey at work to demonstrate I was someone with more to worry about than emphysema or the rules of the workplace.

Another topic we had kept shoved to the sidelines arose. Would the program continue if we didn't succeed during this window? The weather would turn bad again at the end of October, pushing the next launch opportunity five months out. We learned in a briefing that Alan's wife wouldn't tolerate much more, so if it didn't happen in the fall, maybe it wouldn't happen at all. Someone asked whether the program could continue with a different pilot. John put his face awkwardly close to mine in an obvious mocking stare. Taber said that wasn't something to discuss before it needed to be discussed, and then added, "Alan's wife does always ask why it has to be him jumping." John kept staring at me. I pretended I hadn't heard.

We were well into September, with roughly four weeks of usable weather remaining. We had four potential balloon drops ahead, a test drop with Ida and then three successively higher drops with Alan, the last one at 135,000 feet.

The days were a blur. Helicopters spun up around us like it was a wartime outpost, training for chase or picking up one of the near-daily payloads we were floating to the stratosphere to test remaining components. Some days we sent up two balloons and tore across the farm-covered countryside after them. I kept reminding myself that these days were profoundly unique.

On one of our missions we tested a comm system we had installed on a local radio tower to improve the communication between ground crews and mission control during chase. Joe and I flew hundreds of miles in all directions in a powerful helicopter that bristled with antennas, probing the limits of the new communications system. We counted to 10 over and over again. The tower-based antenna competed with a flying antenna that was sent to altitude. The area had record amounts of rain and the landscape was pocked with shimmering pools splaying reflections of the industrial wellheads submerged within them.

The flying system came down at sunset in a cornfield. We landed the helicopter nearby and set off to find the owner of the field just as he came skidding around the corner in a rattling pickup truck, furious that we had landed there. It was his land, after all, and his corn. We tried to explain who we were and that our payload had landed in his field. He angrily yelled, "Well, go get it!" We treaded nervously through an eight-foot-tall corn forest, ankle deep in muck. We found our lanky payload spread out across the corn tassels. We picked at it until it all came down, slithered our way out of the corn, and got back in our helicopter to go home.

We prepped Ida for her final launch before her retirement. We glued on limbs and packed her yellow chestpack with sensors to monitor every portion of her upcoming voyage. Alongside that effort, the launch team finished outfitting the biggest balloons with their cannon fuse destruct systems that would burn the tops out in case our primary destruct method failed. It was decided that I would do another fairly terrifying exercise in the suit to assess the human impacts of spinning.

We didn't want Alan throwing up into the facemask if he were to get into a spin. The doctors suggested building a tolerance to spin by actually having Alan practice spinning in the suit. I already had experience with how much more comfortable something can be after trying it just once. My first time hanging from the BLV I bobbed and hung, swinging back and forth, trying not to puke. All it took was that one exposure and it wasn't so bad anymore. My last ride was delightful.

I generally agreed it was a good idea, but as always it was far more complicated than the higher-ups who proposed the idea understood. If we did this connected to the big tanks we normally used for ground operations, the hoses would twist up while the suit spun. We didn't want to spend our flight oxygen on spin training.

We developed a secondary oxygen system in a matter of days, using pony bottles about one foot tall. We rigged an attachment system and a pneumatic assembly to both fill the bottles and tap them into the suit's oxygen system. This was a complete sea change from the NASA-style engineering most of the team members had spent their careers doing. Building a secondary oxygen system for a government spacesuit test would have occupied dozens of people for months. Zane and I bought the parts on the Internet and built this one in two days.

The fast-rigged hardware still required a pre-test before Alan could rely on that oxygen while he tried to get used to spinning. People joked about how new systems got tested on Alan's cheaper, more expendable body double before they were used on him. We knew it was only joking, though. It would waste precious time to bring Alan for spin practice only to find out the oxygen system didn't work. Besides that, we knew Alan was the one taking the real risks.

We made a test plan: spin left a few times, spin right, buck the suit in the potato-chipping motion, and bring it all together with some spinning while bucking. Then cap it all off with a mild swinging to try to capture the resonant frequency of the suit hanging from its tether for a last-minute analysis to make sure there was no time during Alan's fall when the potato-chipping frequency matched the resonant frequency, something that could cause utterly out-of-control bucking.

It would be my 21st time in the suit. The team was rougher with me than Alan. The process was more casual and faster. I never warranted a peanut gallery, so we didn't have onlookers pretending to troubleshoot. No one asked, "Hey! Is that thingamajig on straight?" We didn't have to throw anyone out of the tent.

After the suit was on, the team set me down on the ground before transferring me to the drogue bridle strap where I would hang during the spinning. We'd gotten used to this shortcut. The system weighed 430 pounds, but the suit itself had some structure when inflated, and behaved like an exoskeleton. I just had to stay balanced.

I was lifted up by the drogue attachment. Blikkies strapped the pony bottles onto the parachute pack while Zane routed the flexible tubes up over my shoulders into the tanks. Schematics and images of pipe fittings and one-way valves rushed through my brain like a bad horror movie montage as I reviewed Zane's and my very quick design, trying to decide if we had done everything right. Was my oxygen going to shut off when they hooked on those bottles? Think, think, think. I snapped my head back and forth, trying to see if they were doing it right. Click. The new tank was connected and I was still breathing. Thumbs-up.

Mitch whapped my leg to get me turning around the swivel at the top of the bridle. I was supposed to give a thumbs-down rather than barf. The world spun. Mitch gave another whap to get me going faster. The room flew past in sequence: door, Zane, Mitch, Ryan, ground cart, Blikkies, door, Zane, Mitch . . . Vision was my only reliable sense and not sensible enough to convince the brain that what I saw was real. It was like bad virtual reality. The scene blurred.

I went thumbs-down quickly. Mitch blocked me to a sudden stop. The world kept spinning, which was worse than the spinning itself. It was as if I had so much inertia that stopping me made the Earth spin. Then it was over and time for round two. Taber had stopped by to watch and suggested I look at my altimeter instead of out at the moving world. The whaps began and I was spinning in the other direction. To my surprise and great relief, it appeared that staring at something that wasn't moving was hugely effective at fending off the nausea I was terrified of. The doctors were also right; just a tiny bit of experience goes a long way. On that second run they calculated my rotation rate at over 60 revolutions per minute before Mitch jumped in to stop the spin. Once again, stopping was worse than the spinning itself. The world spun and wobbled while a wave of nausea came and went.

That was just the intro. Now it was time for the real thing. They wanted to know the limits, so instructed me to go thumbs-down only when I truly couldn't take it anymore, not just when I felt uncomfortable. For two sessions, first spinning right and then spinning left I sustained somewhere between 15 and 30 seconds of spinning at over 100 revolutions per minute, peaking at 120. It was a fast enough spin that the suit started to flatten out in the classic flat spin position weighing heavy in the mind of every stratospheric jumper. Our new understandings of principal inertial axes were confirmed as the suit went from an angled position in which the bridle was vertical to a horizontal position in which it was angled. The system element with the most mass was dominating the motion. As the rotating system gained energy from Mitch's slapping hand, the suit moved onto its stable spin axis.

On the final round, the strange feeling that everything was still spinning after I stopped was particularly bad. The urge to swipe the air and be free to vomit on the floor instead of into the facemask that contained my breathing air filled my mind as everything seemed to be rotating around my body and spinning around my head, but I made it, no puking.

The rest was easy. The potato chip motion that Alan experienced in the air felt ordinary; I could do it all day. When they added the rocking motion, it wasn't so bad. It was soon clear that the suit could not both spin and rock hard at the same time, because the angular momentum of the spinning damped the rocking. It looked like a true rocking spin was impossible, at least when the only thing to induce it was a person whapping the suit.

The session ended with a gentle swing-set ride in which accelerometers attached to my body established the resonant frequency of the suit. All I had to do was lie there and let the complex instruments do their thing.

I felt some nostalgia on being removed from the suit. We were on the cusp of the final adventure; if all went well, I had just taken my last ride, in which, despite the most fiendish efforts of the suit crew, only my sweat had made its way into the inside of the suit.

Late September 2014: Ida's Retirement

Our next dummy run would be similar to the last. As the Suburbans slipped through the night toward the early morning balloon launch, we all knew that if this went well there would be no question that we would begin the manned drops. The suit team's biggest concern was the new drogue bridle attachment. The drogue had broken off in the last test, allowing the dummy to freefall at high speeds before the parachute came out. We used the reserve parachute with Ida because it was outfitted with an automatic opener. If Ida had been relying on her main parachute, it would not have deployed. The break occurred low in the atmosphere where spinning was less of a threat, but it did break. We thought we'd fixed it. We had to test it.

The bridle was now thicker and sandwiched in heavy nylon so that nothing could rub through it as it had on the last drop. The most important aspect of this drop for the collective team, though, was the chase. We had yet to demonstrate a successful chase operation with a real payload dropped from very high in the sky. We had done well recovering the little flight computers after small balloon flights, but our track record with full-size balloons was not good. On our last drop, the operation was muddled. We wasted time bickering in the cabin of the helicopter, screwed up the final moments, and took three times longer than our target for getting to Ida. We were there in 15 minutes. It was supposed to be five.

The dressing of the dummy was routine. Alan wasn't there, so we had a doctor pre-breathe. Right off the bat we ran into a problem. Not everyone's face has the same shape. We had always known that the masks came in a variety of sizes, presumably for this exact reason. But Alan and I had always pre-breathed with the same mask, never encountering a problem because our faces were similar enough that the facemask fit us both. When the doctor put on the mask, normal air came through the side of the rubber facemask. We were reading the nitrogen from the air instead of the nitrogen that was trapped in the blood of the person using the system. We went through two doctors and one helicopter pilot before we found a good enough match with Glenn Patterson, the lead helicopter pilot, who then served as the pre-breathing double for Alan.

When Glenn's blood nitrogen content was down to an acceptable level, we prepared the dummy and the nonexistent suit. It was a morning full of gaps while we struggled to remain vigilant and focused even though we had little to do. Finally, it was time for me to get the crane and move Ida out of the tin shed and onto the tarmac.

I had become much more in tune with the weather since the project started. I could tell the strength of the wind just by feeling it against my face. Even in my daily life outside of work, I couldn't shake the habit of assessing whether the wind, the clouds, or water on the ground would threaten a launch. Today was a good day.

The launch crew had the balloon laid out as I pulled the crane to the side of the launch platform. We talked and checked and waited. Before Ida moved, the balloon had to be stood up. Once that had been accomplished, we wanted to improve our fluency in setting Ida on the launch sedan and pushing the sedan under the standing balloon.

The stand-up was smooth. The bubble filled and rose into the sky, catching the pink light skimming up from the horizon. The spork vehicle driver waited for the launch collar to be installed before he could pull forward and release the remainder of the balloon into the air. After the collar broke in a cascade of failures in our last attempt, the new one had been outfitted with stronger straps. A temporary launch collar was first affixed to the balloon by a crew standing on the rails of the frame that held the spork vehicle drum. It kept the plastic tight and bundled while the spork vehicle driver drove forward and exposed a new neck of plastic so the real collar could be put on. That collar was set in place with a yellow trigger line routing through several release mechanisms.

The vehicle continued forward, pushing the bubble further into the morning sky. As soon as it crossed the halfway mark between its starting point and where we waited with the launch sedan, we began pushing our dummy into the launch area to hook her up. The timing was perfect. We pushed the cart onto the launch platen and settled Ida underneath the big standing balloon. The slightest wind will make a balloon shake and twist, but this balloon stayed tall without even a shimmer or ripple. It stood in a pristine column of stagnant air hundreds of feet tall.

Blikkies and I were active now, running through checks, pulling off safeties, and connecting cords. Instead of the approval from the launch director to do the final hookup, we received an unexpected hold. Something was wrong. Why wouldn't mission control let us hook Ida to the balloon? After several confusing minutes, we were told that all of the GPS signals had failed. No location data was reaching mission control, just a few hundred feet away from where Ida sat.

Mission control asked us to move out from under the balloon so they could do more checks. We pulled Ida back while they looked for interference in the signals between Ida and the balloon equipment module. This continued for over 20 minutes. On a day with normal wind, the balloon would have been beating itself to death, but the air remained eerily still. We moved Ida in and out from under the balloon while the team in mission control tried to isolate the problem. Our luck subsided as a light wind rose. The bubble moved gently sideways and the whole stock leaned. The wind was in the wrong direction.

Two debates began, one about whether we could launch the balloon without a GPS fix and one about whether we could launch Ida backwards. Neither of these were new discussions. GPS cut out all the time, and it was common for winds to turn around 180 degrees right after the sun came up. New or old, these were not discussions you want to have under a sailing balloon the size of a small skyscraper tugging to escape.

The GPS discussion circled around how we could execute the balloon destruct and be sure it didn't drop somewhere dangerous if we weren't sure where it was. The backwards launch discussion centered on what factors drove the direction Ida was facing when hooked to the balloon. Taber, the safety officer, pushed in his typical fashion to get the launch off, even though the situation appeared to be crumbling. I very hesitantly went along.

We had seen over and over again that when one thing doesn't work, a whole series of things don't. I found this to be the result of two things. First is the fact that one failure tends to breed a cascade of other failures, the way the GPS problem had allowed time for the wind to pick up. The second factor was a product of the fact that all the teams were on similar schedules with similar resources, so one team not being ready reflected how none of the teams were really ready.

We rethought hundreds of hours of engineering in a matter of minutes and turned Ida around. Inexplicably, mission control stopped receiving a signal from the transponder. The debates rolled on. The wind shifted. We turned Ida back around again as the balloon waved in the air above us.

We repeated this dance multiple times. Unexpectedly, the communications problems fixed themselves. To this day we don't know why the GPS failed, nor what fixed it. Suddenly it was time to hook everything up and send Ida on her way. We rolled onto the launch platform for the fourth time, but now we got our clearance to hook her up. We connected the electrical connections, hooked the main hook onto the balloon equipment module fitting, and did our checks. We backed away to allow for launch.

John made the call to release the launch collar, which would be followed immediately by the launch. The release cable was pulled, sending the yellow cable that strings up to the release mechanisms inside the collar falling to the ground. The launch collar didn't go anywhere. For some reason the new launch collar had failed to let go of the balloon and continued to choke all the plastic into a nice tidy bubble.

If the launch collar stayed on the balloon, the balloon wouldn't rise more than a few thousand feet before the bubble overpressurized and the balloon popped in a pretty catastrophic way, bursting like a wad of air-filled bubble gum and crashing the payload. Ida had an automatic parachute opener, which would only make things worse. If the balloon popped a few thousand feet off the ground, the automatic opener would spit out a parachute while Ida was still hooked to the balloon.

The trajectory of the balloon in the early parts of the flight was to the north, back toward the city of Roswell, no place to crash half a ton of metal and balloon plastic.

The balloon team got under the balloon and shook the plastic, hoping the collar would fall free. Blikkies, who had made the collar, was consulted. Would it come off on its own once a substantial amount of pressure was placed on it by the expanding bubble? The short answer was, "I don't know."

It really seemed we couldn't let this balloon go, no matter how urgently we wanted this drop. More people got up onto step stools and shook the balloon as hard as they could, but the collar was hundreds of feet high, separated by hundreds of pounds of plastic from the people doing the ineffectual shaking. A decision was finally made for the spork vehicle to try to back the balloon down so the collar could be released manually. The irony of the situation was that the reason to put a collar on is to prevent the bubble from acting like a spinnaker in the wind. The day was so remarkably still that a launch collar hadn't been necessary.

The spork vehicle driver would get his extra amount of practice that day. It wasn't even known whether a balloon could be backed down out of the sky, but we were going to try. Small gusts started to kick up at two or three miles per hour, not sufficient to cancel the launch but enough to scare us while we tried to back the balloon down. Ida was pulled a safe distance away from the operation. The spork looped around the balloon and the drum was fastened on the other side so that the big vehicle could drive backwards and roll the plastic around the drum, bringing the balloon down against the upward force of the bubble.

It looked like this operation was going to work. The spork backed up and the bubble started down. A slight shift in the wind caused the vehicle to have to turn. The vehicle started in a direction where there were no ground cloths to protect the balloon from the rough concrete of the abandoned runway. We scrambled to lay new ground mats down behind the vehicle and stuck new pieces of tarp around the balloon. Things turned from normal to chaotic very quickly.

Nobody knew what was going on. The driver didn't know how to drive the vehicle backwards, and the drum jerked back and forth. The tarp wasn't fully under the balloon, and the rough concrete rubbed the plastic like a cheese grater. The balloon slipped from one side of the drum to the other with thousands of pounds of force. It looked like a mess, and it was probably a dangerous situation to be close to. The balloon stalk was the diameter of a large tree trunk, hundreds of feet long, and jerking across the runway. The balloon slipped all the way off the side of the drum, catching itself around the bearing between the drum and the tractor arm. The vehicle kept backing up while we all screamed for the driver to stop. Hundreds of pounds of plastic were tensioning up like a rubber band pulling against the launch plate, which weighed as much as a heavy truck and was anchored with concrete barriers. The vehicle stopped before anything lifted up or the balloon snapped. The operation was over.

The huge bubble of the ruined balloon floated high above the drum. The crown valve was opened, and the sky behind the flowing helium rippled: tens of thousands of dollars' worth of helium visible to the naked eye. It still wasn't draining fast enough. The shrinking balloon head was muscled to the ground and the crown valve cut out, leaving a hot-tub-sized hole at the top. The plastic was released and the balloon shot back up to fully vertical for a split second before the last of the helium poured out and it collapsed in a wad. There were hard conversations in store for us.

We had failed in a pretty messy display on the eve of our great manned flights. Of the remaining balloons, only one was the right size for this flight. We hadn't tested our drogue bridle. The chase team was still where they had been all morning: at the airport.

Early October 2014: Preparing for Manned Flights

The risks to Alan's life weighed heavy. If all the untested systems worked, we would carve a place for everyone involved in the project in the history of aviation. If they did not, we would bury our dear friend.

We had to decide if we would attempt the dummy drop again. There were more whispers about this being our last season. We argued about the rebuilt drogue bridle and whether a system as critical as a main attachment tether could go untested. We argued about high-altitude flight dynamics and whether Ida actually needed to go as high as Alan to prove that the system wouldn't spin like the painfully absent and relatively uninformed review boards had suggested.

Just before our meeting, Alan gave a small speech about how cool it would be just to accomplish the first flight to the very bottom of the stratosphere, around 60,000 feet, in a spacesuit. He promised it would achieve our very original goal of suspending a person, alone and exposed, into the stratosphere to explore. The speech sounded half-hearted to me, like he was trying to make a disappointing reality settle easier. We knew his family wouldn't get behind another launch season. Maybe I was projecting my own feelings into his speech. I was internally conflicted. I knew a long, multi-step flight campaign that baby-stepped through ever-higher altitudes was the right choice to keep Alan safe. But it rendered our chances of breaking the world record for the highest balloon flight and freefall slim.

In churning discussions, we made momentous decisions in mind-searingly short periods of time. Taber led the talks. The ultimate decision was made in one meeting with all the leads: Sebastian, John, Taber, Norman, and myself. Alan wasn't there; he had already agreed to abide by our decision. There was aggression and hurt feelings. Of course everyone didn't agree. We were talking about omitting a test that we had previously deemed necessary, because we thought it was the only way we would finish the program. Our biggest lesson from our earlier brush with disaster in Coolidge was never to compromise the predetermined test plan—which was exactly what we decided to do. Ultimately, we all took responsibility for the final decision, though Taber was the main voice in the discussions and delivered the news to Alan. I agreed with the final judgement. Doing great things requires risk. The drogue bridle would be further reinforced to the point that nothing in the whole angry atmosphere could destroy it. Then we would go into manned flights.

Because Ida had failed to leave the launch pad, we had blown our opportunity to execute one full-on chase exercise. We wanted a best approximation to go down once before the real deal. We would send up a foam-padded communication payload under a latex balloon and chase it with all the real gear: two helicopters, a helicopter-fueling station, two trucks, and a skydiving plane. The fixed-wing aircraft would fly above the helicopters during the chase to simulate the part of the mission when Blikkies jumps after Alan.

Given Alan's brutal, rambunctious landings, we needed assurance that Blikkies could get to him in the sky so he could guide him to a good landing location, face him into the wind, and tell him when to flare. We needed to find a helmet-mounted communication system that would make Blikkies' atrocious South African slang understandable in flight. We bought every system we could find that would ship to us within days and started rewiring them and testing them out in skydiving helmets, then swapping components and testing again. We found a set that seemed like it would work and took it to the sky for real-life testing.

We started the preparations by skydiving from a helicopter to let Blikkies practice meeting up with a person under canopy, and to test the communication system he would use to communicate jumper to jumper. With Glenn in command, we suited up with the new comm system in our helmets. Glenn had removed the doors from the mid-size helicopter so that we could ride to altitude and easily step into the void. We tested the comm system while walking around in our jumpsuits.

We walked to the helicopter and strapped in. We got the run-down again. We would go to altitude, then Mitch, who was riding side-seat, would signal

Blikkies and me to step out onto the skids. With the helicopter moving slowly forward, we would get a 3-2-1 from Mitch, then simply let go of the airframe and let our bodies rotate off the skid into the mile of open space below us. We needed to go simultaneously, being careful not to push off or bounce on the skid because the helicopter could dip and destabilize.

The chopper powered up and took off. My faith in the comm system wavered as we rode up when Blikkies said something to me and I couldn't pick out a word of it. Maybe it was because I was staring deep into a long sky, contemplating stepping off the skid of a flying helicopter.

We reached our altitude. We got the three-minute call. I carefully removed my seatbelt and then buckled it back into itself so it wouldn't flap and beat the door frame to death when the helicopter descended. I stepped onto a skid. Blikkies stood on the other skid, radiating fierce intensity. I would time this right. The one-minute sign came from Mitch. I held the square edge of the door frame. Then the all clear signal came. Mitch shot a hand back with three fingers showing, then two, then one, then I let go of the helicopter frame.

There was a peacefulness to that moment I'd never experienced in other skydives. As soon as I let go, the noise was gone. The wind was gone. It felt like I was perfectly still while the machine above me shrank at an incredible rate. I turned all the way over in a long, arching backflip. Nothing to do but wait. Until the wind picked up I couldn't control myself anyway. I floated and fell in peace.

After a 125-mile-per-hour air stream developed around me, I wriggled myself into a facedown position, reached for my parachute pull handle, and pulled it. Parachute deployed, we could execute our test.

I was pretending to be Alan so I wasn't supposed to talk much, just follow Blikkies' commands. He told me to go right, then left, then right again. As I approached the ground, he sent me flying straight at the airport terminal. I almost bailed on the exercise to turn away from the buildings before he finally gave me a call to flip away from the terminal and back to the nice big landing patch. Touchdown. Test success.

We made plans to do the test again, this time with the fixed-wing airplane involved. I would go up in the helicopter while Blikkies went up in the plane, which would fly away from the airport. I would jump out of the helicopter and get my parachute out. Then the plane would turn and fly back to the airport to find me in the sky. Blikkies would jump over me, get his canopy out, and meet me in the air. It was the best simulation we could think of for the real thing. Also, before the test, we established a smaller list of commands for Blikkies to give me for turning directions so I would have to do less work deciphering his accent.

We ascended again. I dropped away through the still calm, this time flipping backwards several times before smacking the air stream I needed to lever against to right myself. Once I got my parachute out, it wasn't long before that familiar South African accent came across my radio: "I see your canopy." Blikkies had hopped out of an airplane a few thousand feet above my head and skydived and parachuted right to me. I saw him swoop in front of me on his way to the site he would choose for both of us to land. He talked through the commands. "Left 90, right 90, 180, left 90." He worked me slowly to the ground, and I landed about 50 feet away from him and our recovery truck. It was flawless.

For the next test, the balloon crew readied a latex balloon with our communications package beneath it and sent it to the sky. A full chase crew stood by to sprint across the raw desert after it. We took off as the balloon cleared 15,000 feet and followed it east. Right off the bat, the tracking software crashed. I cycled the equipment, changed plugs, and brought it back online. We flew through the clear skies to the east until we got ahead of the little balloon and landed to wait and save some fuel.

While we were on the ground, the fixed-wing had trouble seeing the helicopters. We bounced communications back and forth, helping the pilots and Blikkies find us 6,000 feet below.

We took off, flew further east, and then landed again. Mitch updated the pilots every couple minutes with new coordinates, heading, and distance to the balloon. It was going faster than the models had predicted, zooming at over 60 miles per hour straight east, toward Texas.

We had a secondary mission objective with our chase run, which was to fire one more fuse and test the tertiary balloon destruct. As the balloon cleared the 100,000-foot mark, we got word that the fuse was fired. The payload would be released immediately after. We were notified as soon as it started making its way toward the ground.

We left the holding point early, concerned that the payload under canopy would keep flying hard to the east. We were right. Mitch recited his coordinates more frequently as the balloon meandered down from the heavens through a quick 45 minutes of descent. We arrived below the balloon as it passed the 10,000-foot mark. We spotted the payload under parachute and circled in as it hit the ground. The other helicopter was right behind us. We had uneventfully and successfully chased a payload through a trip deep into the stratosphere and back to the ground, reaching it before it landed.

The helicopter was too low on gas to make it back to the airport. We landed next to the road. The Chase 1 team loaded into trucks to go back while Glenn waited for fuel. It was the first time he'd landed short in 17 years of flying. Now more than ever, we needed to get comfortable pushing the limits.

The last check-off in our final preparatory period was spin training for Alan. We would repeat the same training I had done in the suit earlier.

Basically, we would buck him around and spin him until he told us to stop, giving him a chance to practice methods of reducing a spin's effect on him.

We suited him up in relatively good time, put on the parachute pack, hung him from the center of the gantry, and switched over to pony oxygen bottles. We started with bucking, the easiest exercises. We pushed his legs down, rocked his head up high, and let him swing back down, getting higher and higher like a kid on a swing set. When he was at his highest, we started turning him around and had him alter our turn inputs by pushing his hands against a pretend air stream. He did well. We followed that with some high-amplitude "chipping" to give him a taste of what it might be like if that motion got really bad up at altitude. His head bashed repeatedly against the top of his helmet. Not a word from the man. He powered through.

Last was the spin, so he could get accustomed to the motion. We didn't expect him to spin in the suit, but if it did happen, we wanted him prepared.

He was instructed to look at his altimeter while he was spinning because that had helped stop my motion sickness. Mitch initiated the spin. We spun him fairly slowly for about 15 seconds, and he seemed okay. That was the warm-up round. We spun him in the other direction for about the same amount of time, and things didn't go so well. In a rather troubling outcome, Alan signaled he did not want to continue. He was feeling queasy. We stopped. It was a pretty mild session and its outcome did not increase our comfort level. It appeared that Alan was not good at handling spins. He had fared well enough, though. We wouldn't make him do it again.

The days before we started the manned campaign would blend together. It was a somber period for most of us, especially Alan, who was mentally readying himself for a trip to a place where no person had gone. The closeout seemed muted and unemotional.

The flight-readiness review was the biggest and most important review of the program. This was the culminating proof, demonstrating to the powers that be that the system was ready. Even though this review was supposed to be the most critical of all, it seemed like a mere formality. It was remarkably smooth and had no events worth noting. No objections, no actions. The longest meeting of the program had been a test-readiness review in the first year that lasted 17 hours. With a very real understanding of the uselessness of never-ending meetings packed with half-informed onlookers, Sebastian brilliantly structured this end-all of meetings so that it was over in under three hours. No questions.

We ran pre-flight checks on the suit. Mitch went on one more small chase exercise to verify the updated tracking equipment while the rest of us did a leak check. The suit had the smallest leak rate yet seen. I felt sober and straight-faced. I reviewed checklists at a hotel desk with unblinking determination. It was time for Alan to ascend.

Helicopters taking off for chase training exercises. (Photo by Dave Jourdan.)

Blikkies looking down at my parachute, during an air-to-air parachute communications test, after jumping from a helicopter over Roswell International Air Center.

The lead helicopter pilot Glenn Patterson riding his helicopter like a bull.
(Photo by Volker Kern.)

Launching a latex weather balloon before a chase exercise.

A balloon deflating after our final dummy launch failed. The balloon was wedged between the arm of our spork vehicle and the drum meant to guide it out.

Jeff Davis fills a helicopter with fuel from the mobile fuel station. (Photo by Dave Jourdan.)

Blikkies and I after a successful mid-air meet-up. I jumped from a helicopter and Blikkies jumped from an airplane 4,000 feet above me. Blikkies was able to dive to my altitude and open his parachute to meet me in the air and guide me into a landing. (Photo by Dave Jourdan.)

Blikkies the parachute master hooking into a landing at Roswell airport. (Photo by Dave Jourdan.)

CHAPTER 16

...

The Wild Black Yonder

All engineers know that if something they design doesn't work correctly, it could kill someone. I'm sure a few people have died using blenders, but not many. People die in cars and airplanes all the time, but lots of people use them and live. In our situation, only a handful of people had used equipment resembling ours—and nearly half of them had died. If Alan was injured or killed, we couldn't hide behind committees or bureaucracies. We had built the thing. We were responsible for what it did.

Exactly three drops were left in the program. Alan would ride to successively higher altitudes in a spacesuit attached to a balloon and skydive from the stratosphere.

October 5, 2014: Exposed in the Stratosphere at 57,000 Feet

We woke up at midnight. The night sky waited, cool and calm, for the aeronaut to go further than most. Alan would be the fifth-highest skydiver. He would go higher than anyone ever had without support from a capsule or gondola. For over two years we had imagined the sight of our fragile suit hanging below a plastic inverted teardrop, but now all I could imagine was a feeble white cartoon character against the black-infused blue fringe bouncing over the top of the troposphere.

Before the jump we still had communications work to do. I'd had trouble understanding Blikkies in our previous jump tests, but I thought that was more about accent than equipment. We set up another test jump for Alan and Blikkies so Alan could assess for himself whether he could understand Blikkies' punk South African slang while flying under parachute. After the jump was all set up, Blikkies came down with a really bad head cold. With all the paperwork filed and the plane ready to go, Blikkies pushed to have me jump in his place. This made very little sense, but I wasn't going to turn down an early-morning skydive with Alan on the eve of his first record flight. So I would go in Blikkies' place and command Alan to make turns and flare to land under parachute. Alan wasn't actually going to follow my commands, because I'd probably steer him into a building. We'd just make sure he could understand and get some practice with our shortened repertoire of commands. Blikkies was only allowed to say "right," "left," and "flare" along with some number of degrees tied to all the lefts and rights, so that deciphering his accent though the scratchy air-to-air comms was possible.

Alan and I suited up in jumpsuits, our parachute rigs, and the helmets with the communications gear wired into them. A button plastered to my hand with Velcro fasteners would activate the microphone. The wires that snaked from my hand to the helmet were scary. I checked them compulsively, worrying they could somehow wrap around something that screwed up my parachute deployment. I was experiencing a mixture of angst about jumping while wrapped in wires and thinly veiled excitement about my role in vetting stratospheric parachute systems. I tried not to think about how this was unambiguously a pinnacle of my life. I had to focus. It was a job. It just happened to require jumping out of an airplane.

A Kodiak skydiving airplane and its Canadian pilot team were waiting at the intersection of the abandoned and active runways. We walked up the wide ladder to board the airplane, just as I was used to doing at skydiving centers, except that only two people got into the plane. It ascended at an impressive rate. With only two passengers there was nothing holding it back.

I tried to test our comm system while on the plane, only to be reminded why nonessential talking is a bad idea. I opened the line. "Pilot, this is chase for a comm check," and got back a blank stare. The plane was too loud. Then the confusion started. Alan didn't know why I was trying to talk to him—was something wrong? I tried yelling into the microphone, with no success. We finally pulled the helmets off and leaned our faces close to each other. I shouted, "I was just trying to do a comm check." Alan responded, "Oh. Okay," as if to say, "Why the hell are you confusing the situation with a comm check? We did that on the ground." Point taken. No more talking.

Near the drop altitude, the pilots yelled, "Three minutes!" from the cockpit. In a commercial skydive, the plane would be unloading a whole line of people and would start to drop jumpers as far from the airport as possible. Not this time. We would jump directly over the airport. No worries of making it back, no worries of crashing into other jumpers. Alan and I performed the skydiver handshake. The yellow light turned on to let us know we were near the airport. We opened the door and looked down 7,000 feet at the big X of the airport. The green light came on and the pilots looked back to affirm their go-ahead.

We stepped into the door. We looked down at the ground. Alan shook my shoulder straps to signal he was ready. I nodded. He pushed me into the doorway, pulled me back, and then lunged out, still holding my shoulder straps and shoving us both into the air stream gushing past the side of the plane. We leveled out and locked eyes, freefalling as a perfect pair. We were laid out with our bodies parallel to the ground. Alan was holding my shoulder straps and I was holding the side of his jumpsuit. Alan nodded to indicate I should pull my parachute. Alan kept ahold of my shoulder straps while I let go with one hand to reach back for my parachute. I experienced my first "pull in place"—when a linked skydiver pulls a parachute while still holding their buddy. I felt the backpack open and the release of the deployment bag, which floated up until the lines were fully extended and the parachute bloomed out of the bag. Alan was ripped away. He faded to a dot. I slowed under my parachute while he continued at over 100 miles per hour toward the sandy airport.

Once the thin nylon sheet developed over Alan a few hundred feet below me, it was time to carry out the test and talk. I started by telling Alan my parachute was out and I saw his parachute down below me. Alan's helmet didn't have a microphone, so in flight he couldn't talk, only listen. In flight he would have to let go of a steering toggle and reach for a button near his shoulder to talk, something he'd only do if necessary. I started to run through the commands: right 90, left 90, right 45, left 45, 180, flare. Below me, his parachute wobbled and turned. I was running through commands way too fast for any action to be completed.

We were also testing out the use of a new type of smoke bomb on landing, which the chase crews would set off near the trucks. A thick plume of smoke rose into the sky at a prominent angle, showing us the direction of the wind. The wind was stronger than we had expected. and we both adjusted our landings downwind of the originally planned spot to compensate. Alan landed gracefully below me, despite having lost all his good flying altitude carrying out my maneuvers. I flew straight in. We rustled up our dusty canopies.

Alan left in a waiting helicopter for a pre-flight tour of possible landing sites. The helicopter chase team flew the prospective balloon path, with him stopping to assess how good various spots were for landing.

When Alan returned, the flight director Sebastian, lead pilot Glenn, Alan, and the chase director Dave hovered over maps discussing where to drop Alan. At this point in the year, all flights would ultimately go east toward Texas. If all went as expected in this first flight, the landing zone wouldn't be far from the airport. A close landing site simplified everything; it made for a shorter chase and easier communications. We went to our hotel rooms to sleep through the afternoon before getting up at just before midnight to start the run.

Before every early-morning test, the suit team met at the local IHOP to find our groove before stepping into the furnace. We always sat in the same places and got the same meals. We didn't talk much. Other teams in the midst of similar rituals might be arriving, eating, or leaving, but we never sat together or talked with each other. This was part of a meditation that closed our minds to outside influence, blinding us to the white distractions that lead to mistakes that lead to disaster.

We went back to the hotel and picked up Alan. There was a small pack of outside observers for this flight. The leaders of our parent company were on site to observe, charged with staying out of the way. I strove for focus. I went into the office to grab cereal bars, coffee, and clipboards, then out to the tent to set up for pre-breathing. Alan mingled with the observers. He was calm. I was not calm. I flashed annoyed looks at the minglers and pushed in an obtrusive, "Need you in the tent in 20," intended to puncture the lightheartedness of the crowd. I only wanted to see focus for the next six hours.

Alan made it to the tent on time, but the doctors and surrounding crew remained painfully chatty with him as the suit team scurried around, hooking tubes to machines and cycling equipment through its checks. The scheduled time to start the pre-breathe passed. We kicked a gaggle of doctors out of the tent and parked Alan on the cheap recliner. Dr. Clark and Alex, Alan's designated pre-flight doctors, went through his checklist, suiting him in the undergarments and privately discussing the details of his immediate state of health. Medical clearance was granted. Alan put on an oxygen mask and began what would be four hours of breathing pure oxygen to push the nitrogen from his blood. It wasn't actually necessary to pre-breathe that long on this particular flight because the pressure in the suit wouldn't get that low and it wouldn't be that long, but this flight was all about practice, so we did everything in the same way we would do it on the final flight.

A few minutes late but well within our built-in time buffers, Alan listened to Simon and Garfunkel on an iPod, stretching every 30 minutes to help break the nitrogen free from muscles so it could travel through his blood to his lungs and out his mouth. We readied sensor assemblies and checked oxygen sensors. We removed covers and tested emergency shut-off valves. For the first time we sealed fancy high-speed, high-altitude GPS loggers. These were the units developed by Dan and sealed by the official observer from the Fédération Aéronautique Internationale. The observer verified that the unit had not been tampered with.

Alan sat peacefully and maybe even slept a bit wearing the oxygen mask in the recliner in his special tent. The nitrogen levels in his blood meandered down toward nothing on the graphs from the mass spectrometer hooked to his facemask. There would be brief spikes in nitrogen when he moved around a lot. Especially when he turned over to pee into a bottle. This always caused a nitrogen spike, which we attributed to a shifting facemask. Soon enough it was time for Alan to duck into the suit and assume the 45-degree position.

Alan walked out, draped in hoses like an alien catfish. He removed the mask and battled the yellow tunnel to enter the private universe. All was going remarkably smoothly. Then, at step 547 of a 1,922-step procedure came the inevitable hitch, the thing we hadn't thought of.

Sometimes when you put on a ski glove, a finger can get twisted around and resist every effort to straighten it out. That's what happened. We couldn't get Alan's pinky into the right-hand glove. I took the glove and tried to put my hand in it to flip the pinky finger around. I pushed my little finger into the pinky hole of that glove until I thought I had pulled a muscle and still couldn't flip that bladder out. We decided to close Alan into the suit and pressurize it so the pressure would pop the finger out. With the suit at full pressure, it still wouldn't flip. In another blow from Murphy, our spare glove happened to be in Houston undergoing a repair on its heater.

The minutes of our well-schemed timeline fell away. I tried again to use my hand to free the pinky; Mitch and Ryan pulled out plastic integration rods to try to push through the sticky rubber. We speculated about whether the glove had gotten hot and stuck to itself. We reviewed everywhere the glove had been for the last few days to rule that out. We tried for a second time to pressurize the suit to pop the finger straight. The glove didn't pop, but Alan's ears did. It was no fun to be cycled up and down like that.

We had used up our time holds. The launch team was now officially waiting on us while we fussed around with a pinky. We were on the verge of an abort over a stuck finger.

At this point Mitch, a man seasoned in spacesuit construction and testing, suggested we take apart the glove. We wouldn't break any seals but we'd unstitch the cover layers and peel back the insulation and heater assemblies to expose the bladder and flip that finger over. We requested permission to perform emergency surgery on the hand of our spacesuit about to take its maiden voyage to the stratosphere. Permission granted.

Mitch carefully unstitched the glove's cover layers. Government safety officers would have hemorrhaged. The black cover layers, advanced insulation, and heater assembly were laid over the top of the glove, exposing the rubbery bladder. Alan watched through the bubble while we cut apart a glove that his life very directly depended on. Mitch fiddled. The morning ground thin. Mitch put a flashlight inside the glove and saw the pinky twisted into itself at the tip. After over an hour of wrestling, Mitch got the pinky flipped with some flashlight tricks and a plastic integration rod. Alan put the glove on, and after some battle with the still-not-quite-straight pinky bladder, all the fingers were back in. At the current moment, with what was likely one shot at patching this mess up in time to attempt a flight, Mitch proposed we pressurize the suit and hand-sew the cover layers back onto the suit with the suit under pressure. It would be tight with the bladders filled out, but faster.

The suit pressurization was good, Alan was in what we hoped would be his final pressurized state, but the plan was a bust—the pressurized suit was too tight to be sewed. The suit was depressurized once again. Mitch calmly hand-tacked the cover layers back together, missing the pressurized bladder with the sewing needle every time he plunged it through for another stitch while Alan held his hand steady as a marksman and watched.

For the fourth gut-condensing time, Alan was pressurized in the suit. We would still attempt the stratosphere.

We paced through the rest of the process barely inside the weather window. We had missed the pristine weather that comes at sunrise. It was already getting light as we put on Alan's parachute pack, hooked up his parachute handles, and cycled through the last of the functionality checks before connecting the spreader bar to his back. We mounted up the hopefully indestructible SAEBER system. In half the time it had taken us to coax Alan's hand into that glove, we walked through several dense pages of checklist. In the gathering light, we gave our final call to mission control for clearance to move to mobile operations. Clearance granted. The crane was pre-staged in front of the tin shed waiting for us. The launch team had been sitting in their trucks for the last hour listening to us talk about how Alan couldn't put his glove on.

At Zane's direction, I lowered the boom of the BLV, drove into the shed, extended the boom into the clean tent, and snatched Alan up off the gantry. The team hooked up the ground carts. I backed slowly out.

The excitement was back. The sun frosted the desert grasses in the distance as the train made its quarter-mile stroll to the launch site. The balloon team had set up with the bubble right where Stratosphere Lane met the runway, making our drive shorter than normal. I parked with our wheels just barely on the concrete. Normally at this point we sat and waited, but not today. Others had waited instead, and now it was time to move.

The balloon looked tiny. Although it would be the size of an apartment building when it flew, this was the smallest zero pressure balloon we had ever filled. It seemed dauntingly little, as if its stature would make it all the feistier.

We took Alan off his cooling hoses, disconnected his flight power, and dropped him on his launch sedan while the balloon bazookas thundered to life. The two people holding the crown valve let go, and the balloon bubble whumped into the air above the spool.

The preparations continued. We were shocked several times when Alan moved, forgetting that there was actually a human in the suit. Between our history with inanimate aeronauts and how stoic a person can become sitting bound in a spacesuit, Alan's movements had the effect of a stone statue reaching at you in the night.

The redesigned balloon collar was installed, cinching the plastic and defending the system against the dreaded spinnaker. The spork vehicle approached.

The suit team settled Alan into the launch sedan and transferred him to suit oxygen. The sedan, with Alan on board, was pushed toward the rising balloon.

In a stingingly predictable turn of events, the GPS in the balloon equipment cut out. We were rocking on our heels, ready to push Alan to the stratosphere, and now there was another hold. No GPS, no launch. In his normal dry fashion, Sebastian acknowledged that we were sucking on flight oxygen and issued the direction to go back to ground oxygen while communications got worked out.

The balloon snapped around and whapped itself, lashing and whipping in little tantrums. It was hard to tell if it was a healthy balloon or not. It was scary to watch and even scarier to consider hooking a human to. John and I discussed whether the balloon was safe to launch. John had calculated the safe winds for launch with each balloon size, and the winds were staying below the limits. Taber and Sebastian in mission control had the final discussion as to whether this was acceptable. Even though the angry plastic sheets were flapping against the balloon belly, the stats said she was harmless. We put our faith in the math. We would launch.

The GPS came back. I ran back to my team. We pushed on the little sedan to move it beneath the balloon, necks straining upward because we couldn't take our eyes off it. Blikkies and I attached the flight hook and plugged in the main power cable to the pyrocutter. John administered the final checklists, which Blikkies and I carried out. We stepped back to watch Alan's first launch under a zero pressure polyethylene balloon. Mission control turned on their cameras. And called a hold.

This was truly unexpected. The reason for the hold was mission control was not able to see Alan's arms through the live flight camera. This might seem like a trivial detail, but arm signals are an integral part of the mission's operations, the backup if there are any voice communication problems and the means for a "yes/no" system. The balloon continued to twist, while a launch technician ran in circles around it to prevent the trigger line for the collar from wrapping up around the stalk.

Rolfe scurried in with the plan to cut the camera free of its housing and adjust its angle in real time, but it was quickly clear that the camera wasn't moving without minutes or hours of work. Mission control called an audible. Alan was told that whatever the procedures said he should do with arms, he should to do with his legs instead. And that was it. Flight ops changed: pretend your legs are your arms for all comm signals and continue on to the stratosphere.

For the second time we stepped back. The angry swirling orb continued to aggress the space around it, whapping at our nerves. The calmest person there was Alan, leaning his head against the suit helmet bubble waiting for whatever it was we were doing to end so he could get his flight under way.

The mess had subsided. Calm settled in. We all quieted down. John yelled, "Collar!" At the pull of the initiation line, the canvas collar popped off the bubble and swayed to the ground. With the balloon now free to spinnaker and truly rip itself and its surroundings apart, there was no more time. John lunged back a step and called, "Go!" Joe pulled the cord. The ground tethers released. Alan was in the sky.

After all that angry thrashing, the balloon went nearly straight up without so much as a quiver. Cheers erupted, but not from me. I didn't like people cheering while Alan was in the dangerous black zone. I would cheer to myself silently in four minutes when Alan was high enough to use his parachute.

The balloon slowly untwisted. Alan waved at us each time he turned a circle. A scrap of plastic from the wrapping around the balloon stalk freed and floated to the ground. In a burst of leftover adrenaline, Jacob sprinted after the piece of litter.

Mitch and I waited in a chase truck for the balloon to clear the airport grounds. We had been instructed by mission control to wait for the balloon to get to 10,000 feet, then drive to the chase helicopter and move the chase to the air. We stared at the plastic glowing in the morning sun. The chase helicopters spun up their rotors.

The radio calls rolled through as mission control ticked Alan through the milestones of the early flight.

"Pilot, this is flight. You have crossed 4,000 feet. You are out of the black zone."

"Pilot, this is flight. You have crossed 7,000 feet. You will now abort to your main parachute."

"Pilot, this is flight. You are crossing 10,000 feet above ground level. I will now switch to reporting altitudes above sea level."

That was our cue. We drove to the helicopter, hopped in, and flipped open the computers. Sweet, sweet data was flowing. All systems normal. All data live. Without chitchat, we pulled the doors closed. Glenn stepped into the cockpit. We were joined by the two flight doctors. It was the real chase. Mitch took up his tablet. He would navigate until we found Alan somewhere to the east. The airport dropped down below as the balloon ascended above us.

We had trained chasing little latex balloons. Those balloons were the size of a grand piano when they took off and the size of a small house at float. This balloon was a league above that. The latex balloons were visible in the sky to a very well-trained eye and only on the clearest of days with a proper orientation to the sun. This balloon was visible to all who looked, probably including some UFO conspiracy theorists. It's so much easier to chase a balloon when you can look out the window and see if it's where the computer says it should be.

About five minutes into the chase, my data feed cut out. No need to panic. The data feed was still live at mission control and the other chase vehicle. We fell to the number two position as Chase 3 leap-frogged to cover a potential abort while I attempted to debug the software. All the data in the helicopter was linked through my machine; when my connection failed, everything cut out. I rebooted with no luck. I cycled through the communications ports trying to find what was confusing the computer while Glenn kept north of the balloon by the visual. I swapped the antennas to different plugs. Bam. Data back.

Everything else went amazingly smoothly. The suit was operating flawlessly, hand-stitched glove and all. Alan didn't have a single complaint and was using his feet to communicate, an apparent improvement. Lifting the voice toggle was arduous, while lifting a leg was easy. We would hear Sebastian say something like, "You are now crossing 30,000 feet." Then, without a word from Alan, we'd hear Sebastian say, "Copy." The routine calls rolled on as we helicoptered over eastern New Mexico farm country. They reported the altitude from the ground and adjusted the system heater settings. Alan reported in interviews later that the only thing he spent substantial time on during the flight was thinking through his emergency procedures and trying to relax. He did take a moment to comment on the beauty of the upper troposphere.

The chopper pulled in front of the balloon, and Glenn set it down in a green field while we waited for the call for the cut-down to parachute flight, when we'd go airborne again. The balloon shined to our right.

The balloon was going faster than we had expected. The landing surveys had indicated that we needed to cut down well before the nasty terrain surrounding a geographic feature called Mescalero Ridge. Alan was streaming toward that ridge as the stratospheric winds picked up.

A discussion opened up between Alan and Sebastian about whether to cut away early, before the balloon topped out and started floating, or to stay in through float and wait it out until the balloon was over the grasslands beyond the ridge. The conversation was casual. Alan seemed matter of fact and distracted. After all, he was surrounded by a blue-black sky that had been viewed only by his few predecessors in ballooning, a few pilots of extreme high-altitude aircraft, and in rumbling glimpses by astronauts going in and out of orbit. They made the decision to cut down before the ridge, as had been planned. Alan was coming home. We would learn later that at the moment Sebastian started Alan's countdown to end his first epic journey, the balloon just barely pierced the bottom of the stratosphere. Alan was the first human to experience the stratosphere at rest and outside of a vehicle.

As the countdown approached, the radio traffic got frustratingly busy. Alan and Sebastian prepared for release in one of my ears, while in the other Glenn wrangled the two other choppers into position and directed the fixed-wing aircraft that would dump Blikkies out over Alan. I had my CIA-style earpiece from the flight radio connecting to Alan, Blikkies, and mission control inside the larger headphones that went to the helicopter comm system. All the while Glenn and all the other pilots relayed positions to mission control to verify they were close enough for the med teams to reach Alan and far enough away to be sure not to hit him. In the final moments, Alan sheepishly requested a countdown before release to prepare his body position, something that I don't believe was explicitly in the plan before that. The verifications overlapped the mobile air traffic control, which overlapped the pre-flight countdown. All while Mitch and I sent our own inter-helicopter commands to Glenn so we could maintain our holding pattern upwind of the balloon.

"Mission control, we're at negative 110.96—"

"Affirmative, three. Move to posi—"

"Pilot, this is flight approaching landi—"

"Three, this is one relocated to altitu—"

"Balloon is heading 35 degrees east of north at 5.3 mi—"

"Pilot, this is flight. Prepare. I'm going to be counting down."

"Five, this is one. Maintain that head—"

"Pilot release in five, four—"

"Five, this is one. Prepare for drop on that head—"

". . . three, two—"

The cacophony swirled in my head. I wanted silence ahead of the drop.

"One. Pilot away."

I got my silence. The numbers on my computer screen went wild. The pilot ascent rate exploded into the negative thousands as Alan accelerated toward the Earth. My heart pounded. I stared at the computer and called altitudes into the radio.

"50,000 feet."

"40,000 feet."

The radio from mission control opened up. Something was wrong.

"All chase vehicles, please advise. The balloon has destructed. The balloon is falling."

Fear swept through me. My bones locked. For a brief second, I imagined Alan was attached to a falling balloon, plummeting with a death streamer in tow. A second call came through to clarify.

"Pilot is safely away. The balloon destructed after release."

The balloon had ruptured itself from the shock of release. We had proved remarkably bad at bringing balloons down when we wanted them down, and now it appeared that we were remarkably good at making them fall when we wanted them to stay there. The helicopters were circling in a pattern about three miles from the point of drop waiting for a parachute. We turned our heads to the sky, surveying the blue between the rotors for a growing wad dancing toward us. All the while Sebastian called altitudes out to Alan as he descended.

"30,000 feet. 20,000 feet."

On my computer, the descent speeds flattened out.

"Parachute is out."

Mitch went back in go mode as the radio universe erupted again. The helicopters turned 90 degrees and raced toward the center of their perimeter where Alan was now under parachute. Mission control informed us that the balloon carcass was on the ground a safe distance away. Blikkies and his fixed-wing airplane closed in overhead for the dive toward Alan. We closed the three-mile gap. The fixed-wing airplane came over the radio.

"Flight, this is five. Jumper away."

Blikkies was in freefall. We shouted headings at Glenn, closing in.

"20 degrees south of east at 1.1 miles."

Seconds later Alex, the doctor in the front, shouted, "Canopy 1 o'clock!"

Straight in front of us was a bright orange canopy with a white stripe down the left side, Alan's main. Good news, no emergencies. The altitude at which he pulled the chute was perfect. The hard part was over. Alan was safely under canopy in safe thick air with multiple chase assets locked on.

Blikkies came on the radio to start telling Alan where to go. I heard the commands flow through my headset and watched Alan execute them out the front window of the helicopter in beautiful synchrony.

"Left 90."

Alan turned his canopy 90 degrees to the left.

"Right 45."

Alan turned the canopy 45 degrees to the right.

A plume of white skydiver smoke crept upward from the field where it looked like Blikkies was taking Alan. The chase trucks were in position at a good landing site and had deployed the smoke so Blikkies could better judge the wind.

The helicopter circled the canopies as they very slowly made their way back to Earth from 13,000 feet above ground. The two parachutes danced around each other, circling a wide-open grazing land with an occasional fence or farmhouse, but no truly problematic obstacles. A perfect flat landing site.

Blikkies sent a couple final commands, then spiraled to the ground to look up and guide Alan in. The first canopy set down. We heard the call to Alan to start into his landing pattern. Blikkies was sending Alan in a different direction from where he landed to stay away from some power lines.

Alan made his final turn at Blikkies' call and glided in to make what appeared to be a beautiful soft landing under a nice flare in the middle of a pleasant grassy field.

Our helicopter landed about 100 feet away. We sprinted in toward the orange parachute and a raised thumbs-up sign. Mitch popped the bubble. I turned off the tanks. We flipped the facemask off a happy, dirty stratospheric skydiver. We yipped and hooted, our eyes shining, making odd little hops of electric excitement. We had sent our man to the stratosphere and he was back safe on the ground.

The doctors called their official "green extraction," indicating all was well in the suit. Mission control could start their celebrations. Alan came out of the suit sweaty and glowing. We bundled the unscathed suit back to the tin shed for refurbishment.

Alan flew home and enjoyed the night with his family. Before leaving, he noted to us that the drop had "made the program." And added that he had "tremendous confidence" in the team.

The teams enjoyed themselves thoroughly that night. We roasted a pig, drank beer, told and retold our stories. We repeated Alan's descriptions of the depth of blue in the space between the troposphere and the stratosphere, and the serenity of extreme high-altitude balloon flight. We talked through Alan's description of a truly stable flight, how the SAEBER held the drogue parachute away from the suit and how it stabilized him for a spin-free, 250-miles-per-hour descent. We talked about Blikkies' flawless midair meet-up, and Alan's most gentle landing to date. The suit team relived the tremors of dissecting a glove on the flight line. There were many versions of the moment of seizure when we thought the balloon was in freefall with Alan. We reveled late into the night, and toward morning shaved in Mohawks to commemorate all the weirdness of our circumstances.

October 15, 2014: Manned Flight to 107,000 Feet

I think that people like records and big events because we remember our lives as a series of big events, not as a continuum of rolling existence. Furthermore, we trump old exciting happenings with newer ones that make the previous ones recede. This happens personally for individuals, and publicly in collective memory. Either way, we walk into some kind of darkness, shine a light, and set records.

In hot, tired discussions following our first manned balloon drop, we entertained the idea of blasting straight into the next flight while within the current weather window. Our experience of good weather taught us to expect windows that were about three days long. We had launched on the first day with predictions that indicated two more ahead. We seriously debated whether we should go straight to our hotel rooms for one solid day of sleep and then crank into another launch, squeezing two stratospheric missions into the equivalent of a long weekend. Ultimately, good sense prevailed. We needed rest and emotional respite. The team packed up and took a breather for a week, then reconvened in our dusty palace, most of us still sporting Mohawks.

With this launch we had checked a giant checkbox. I had come to favor the idea of incrementalism in the art of doing things that could easily kill you. Baby steps. Skipping the middle and leaping to our final launch to the very top of the stratosphere seemed like a step too far. Not everyone agreed. Some argued that because every launch includes some degree of risk, multiple launches create an environment that is riskier overall.

The incrementalists argued harder. If Alan were to spin on a somewhat higher flight in a way that was extremely uncomfortable but undamaging, it would indicate to him and the team that going to full altitude with the existing system could result in an injurious or deadly spin. It's better to learn about damage without encountering it. We also argued that every increment includes learning and reduces future risk. If Alan was exposed to incrementally more difficult stratospheric conditions, the experience of having managed the lesser versions would give him the skills and calmness to respond properly and have a safe flight. For me, the strongest argument was historical: of the few people who had attempted such flights in the past, the ones who took an incremental approach tended to live.

Ultimately, it was decided to insert an intermediate flight between our scary-but-smooth first flight and the hopefully glorious final flight. It was the right thing to do, but in all ways it felt like a stepping-stone. Few spectators came or tried to come. It was back to the old core team. In some ways this would be the finale of our long lonely stay in a crumbling city intentionally chosen for its isolation.

The only engineering change between the first and second flights would be to accommodate Alan's complaint that he had had a very hard time keeping an eye on his wrist altimeter. We would put a new altimeter onto the dashboard display panel of the suit. We took a shotgun approach to the design. While most of the others were taking a break between flights, Mitch and I created potential altimeter mounts which I would test in the suit. My nostalgia about ending my suit time had been premature.

Mitch returned to his shop in Houston and built a fully configurable version of the prototype mounting system while I modeled up a 3D-printed plastic version. We both still wore our Mohawks. Two days into our fervent build, Alan called me to discuss it and said he wanted the final pull altitude, about 10,000 feet above ground, to be at the top of the display. It took some begging to get the mounts remade with the lower numbers up at the top of the display. In a total of three days Mitch and I had designed and built half a dozen prototype altimeter mounts which could be configured in multiple ways to hold an altimeter in front of Alan's face. They weren't truly prototypes, because we were going to pick one and use it. We were back in the desert with them in less than a week after the successful balloon flight.

We scheduled an early-morning suit session to test all the altimeter mounts and choose one to go onto the suit. We would also run another rocking session to solidify the resonance numbers for our aerodynamics models of that pesky potato-chipping motion Alan kept experiencing. That rocking test would validate our altimeter placement because I would make sure I could still see the altimeter while rocking.

Once I was in the suit, all the inner layers on, neck dam sealed, facemask secured, and helmet bubble locked, I hung there from the drogue bridle while the team zipped around me mounting and unmounting various altimeter configurations and having me analyze and score them. Early in the process of mundanely and slowly going through each of the mounts and commenting on their visibility, I started feeling light-headed, and then spiraled into a paranoid fear. I thought through every element of the oxygen system, dizzying myself with terror. I suspected at one point that the mask wasn't on right and I was getting CO_2 poisoning from rebreathing my own exhaled air.

This was a catch-22. Noting my light-headedness and voicing a concern that perhaps something wasn't right in the suit could delay the program for weeks. So as I'm certain hundreds of pilots and test subjects have done in the past when feeling the pressures of environments very strange to their body, I kept my mouth shut for the sake of the program and for my own sake as a good test subject. I couldn't think of anything that could be going wrong. I powered through until an altimeter was chosen.

The last part of the test was the part where I got seesawed back and forth for one full minute to gather data on the suit's resonant frequency. Now that we had long-duration data from the first flight, I wanted to know if the resonance of the potato chipping seen in flight matched the overall resonant frequency of the system. We had attempted to get this number during the spin testing, but the data wasn't complete. For this test they strapped an accelerometer to my chest and captured the time when my motion reversed at each end of the swinging cycle. A match between that frequency and the swinging motion in flight would suggest that the swinging was produced by the drogue and was unlikely to change at higher altitudes. The information would tell us whether changes in Alan's body position would have a major impact on that seesaw motion he normally encountered.

I harbored serious fears I would pass out during this test, then told myself it was only one minute; I could do it. I took long awkward breaths trying to grab as much oxygen as I could from the loud helmet regulators before Mitch pushed my feet toward the floor. I stared at the new altimeter as my head pulled up, dropped down, pulled up, dropped down. Surprisingly, I calmed down.

That simple suit run was one of the most uncomfortable of all, and to this day I don't know why. I had left the previous test with mistaken nostalgia, thinking it was my last one. On that day, I couldn't get out fast enough.

Right when we thought we were ready to launch, in what was perhaps the pinnacle of our teams' impromptu testing exploits, Taber pulled an audible.

We had gone in circles since the outset over whether our launch sedan concept was going to work. When the payload skipped out of the launch sedan sideways and took a 30-yard skid on a previous launch, many became permanently discouraged about the sedan idea. It had been updated with the turning wheels moved to the front and the addition of new, more stable mounts. We didn't get much of an idea about the performance of the new version on the last flight because the balloon had lifted straight up and didn't stress any of its traveling features. For the next flight, we'd be under a balloon tall enough to sag like a hanging chain and potentially drag Alan a long way if the cart didn't work.

On the morning after our altimeter test, when we were set to begin preparations for the next flight, Taber pushed calmly to settle the debates once and for all. He wanted us to put a fully rigged Ida, who was enjoying her well-deserved retirement, into the launch sedan and yank her out with a helicopter to see if the sedan really would track the ground with the balloon's motion like it was supposed to. Two years earlier, this test would have taken two months to set up. Now, we skipped the rounds of test reviews and interminable insights from rooms of reviewers and did the test 24 hours after thinking it up. We consulted with the helicopter pilots who ate their meals with us and worked out of the same mobile office. We asked them if they would drag our dummy around in the launch sedan with their machines. They said yes.

We gathered a baker's dozen of our most battered GoPro cameras to stick all over Ida and her cart. The test plan called for half a dozen runs picking Ida up with the crane, setting her in the launch sedan, signaling a helicopter to hover above us, and attaching a 100-foot line to Ida. The helicopter would then yank her around in every way we could image a balloon pulling on a payload.

I drove Ida out to the flight line with the BLV and set her down while the helicopter started firing up. Of course everyone wanted to watch us pull an iron dummy out of a wheeled cart. We leaned into the helicopter and the pilot pulled out an earmuff while we went over the plan again. I shooed a videographer off the concrete.

The first two would be normal. The pilot would hover over Ida until she was hooked up, then creep about 15 feet, then accelerate forward to simulate the motion of a balloon lifting a payload in a 10-knot wind. This test would represent a situation we had struggled for two years to model with mathematics. The helicopter pilot wanted to try setting Ida right back down in her cart after the test to avoid the extra step of having the BLV do it. We told him it was worth a try.

The first test was wild and raw and beautiful. With me in the BLV and Jacob on the ground, we dropped Ida into the cart. With her secure, we pushed the cart onto the X in the center of the tarmac while the van-sized helicopter rose up into a hover over our heads, pulling the 100-foot line up off the concrete in the process so it hung straight, gently swaying. The pilot flew the hook to Jacob and me. We attached it to Ida using the old beat-up spreader bar left over from Alan's first flight. We all backed away.

The pilot leaned eerily out of the helicopter door staring down at Ida in her cart, making sure not to yank up and bunny-hop her out of the cart prematurely. The helicopter moved into position a dozen or so feet in front of Ida and lowered the hover, dipping the line into the signature mathematical curve, a catenary, that balloons make when experiencing a wind. He glanced down at us, then punched it forward and up, tensioning the line at an angle, then moving the cart forward. Ida, locked in by her mounts, rolled forward until the cart caught up with the helicopter and she lifted into the sky, swinging through nothing but cool gentle air. The system worked perfectly.

We validated unimaginable amounts of work in that first improvised session. John and Jacob had spent two years on this. John had developed elaborate models of mathematical arcs representing long, thin balloon stalks leaning into the wind on test rigs that Jacob had built and pulled around parking lots behind trucks. They had built a Rube Goldberg gantry-like contraption that yanked Ida into the air with pulleys. They had pulled Ida around with the BLV. Once they let the sedan gain a little too much speed and poked a hole in the side of a truck. Even so, they'd never managed to pull fast enough or high enough to simulate a balloon. Not until this test.

We cycled through the operation again several times. The idea of resetting Ida into the sedan with the helicopter was our only failure. To avoid the risk of destroying the sedan with a misplaced Ida, we accepted the slower process with the BLV. By the third test, we were yanking Ida out sideways, the way Alan might move if the wind unexpectedly shifted. The sedan turned and followed the helicopter. We had the pilot fly fast, just to see if the sedan could handle a 20-knot ride, something that was impossible since a 20-knot wind would shred a standing balloon. Ida never once touched the ground. No matter how the balloon tugged on the sedan in the wind, we were sure it would take Alan for a smooth ride through the turbulent transition from Earth to calm sky.

Over the next day, we prepared for the second of our three planned flights. Everything was routine. Alan arrived the day before the flight to conduct his landing site survey. A higher flight would send Alan substantially further to the east than the last one. He needed to decide whether he would float over Mescalero Ridge or drop early to safely.

Oxygen was also an issue. On the last flight, Alan breathed hard. If he breathed too hard on this flight as well, the models might run to negative margins for the final flight. If that happened, the program would need to halt while the team did something to reduce the oxygen consumption rates or increase the oxygen supply. Either of those options would certainly push us out of that year's weather window. It would be better for Alan to spend this flight practicing breathing more calmly than trying to push his limits.

We started the morning of our second stratospheric flight with our usual convention at the IHOP. Contrary to tradition, we chatted. My neck muscles were a bit less tense than they usually were at pre-flight breakfast gatherings.

The planned altitude for this flight would make it the highest drogue-stabilized freefall ever done, officially breaking Joseph Kittinger's record. The record for highest balloon flight and highest overall jump would still be held by the very recent jump of Felix Baumgartner, who had not used a drogue parachute.

In the tin shed, the balloon consultant from India sat in a folding chair looking over a double crown valve plate the size of a hot tub lid. He was looking at the carcass of a balloon that had recently been inflated with over 1 million cubic feet of spirited helium. With a heavy Indian accent, he spoke.

"He is not in a capsule, like a womb, protected." Then he flexed his arms downward, saying, "Testosterone. He is like Rambo from the sky."

This flight was our most elegant performance. We went through our checks with steady hands. Alan got dressed and started to pre-breathe on time. This was the first really critical pre-breathe of the program because Alan was going high enough for decompression sickness to become a concern. Above 100,000 feet, the pressure in the suit would drop low enough to cause serious damage.

During the pre-breathe, Zane panicked whenever Alan moved around and the gas analyzer showed his nitrogen levels shooting up. Nitrogen was either sneaking in through the side of the mask or being purged from his muscles. There is no physical privacy in a suit operation. Alan's weight was minutely tracked and announced over the net so the balloon fill could compensate for changes in mass. Whole roomfuls of people discussed his eating habits and speculated about fecal consistency and trapped intestinal gasses. His pre-flight meals were interpreted in terms of vomit consistency. He ate a pill that read out his exact temperature. Now someone outside the room was telling him not to move around so much while he peed.

During the pre-breathe we had our first meaningful run-through of sealing the record-keeping GPS units. The official observer came in to watch the sealing process and take some pictures. The call to seal the record-keeping units drew the first swarm of onlookers into the tent. The units were sealed by covering the data cards with a specially numbered sticker that would leave an unseen residue of a different number when removed. If the sticker was removed in secret and replaced with a different one identical on the outside, the wrong hidden number would appear under the sticker and reveal the ploy. The observer from the Fédération Aéronautique

Internationale had flown all the way from Virginia to watch us put that sticker on and take a picture of it. I threw everyone out of the tent when he was done. We went back to checking our boxes.

As the pre-breathe finished, Mitch and I drove to the flight line to see where we would be bringing Alan with the BLV in a couple of hours. The launch team was in the midst of an immaculate calm progression themselves. The heavy launch platen was in place and the concrete barriers down.

The suit-up was fast and straightforward. Backup gloves were at the ready, but the primaries went on just fine. Blikkies led the process of putting on the parachute pack while Alan hung back with his legs lightly crossed, looking like a cowboy leaning on a fencepost in a spacesuit. Mitch hooked the once torturously difficult chest strap clips under the life-support pack in one try. The SAEBER was connected. Alan transferred to the flight spreader bar, and that was it. We were ready to go to the flight line over an hour before our mission call.

With the balloon process ahead of schedule, John and I agreed to move Alan out early. For the first time, Alan rode to the launch site in the full dark of night in the center of a floodlit parade. Taber came out for final checks and then, with a full hour of schedule buffer, we stood around chatting over coffee and donuts. Alan went to sleep.

Temperatures were dropping. Alan woke up and for the first time ever asked us to turn on his heat on the ground. We never ran the heaters on ground power except to test them in our pre-flight check sequence. We didn't want to drain the flight batteries. This was a first in the astronaut world. Spacesuits on the ground are too hot, never too cold. We gave him the thumbs-up and raised the heater set point to warm him up. We disconnected the cooling lines.

A launch technician from the equally idle balloon team came over, and just for something to do, we practiced moving the launch sedan on to the platen. We waited for sunrise.

At the very first signs of light, we saw movement at the spork vehicle. A trickle of chatter came across the radio. The sleepy team came to life as Joe and Jacob made their way out on the long carpet pathways to the ends of their balloon fill lines to start the fill process. We perked up and hollered at straggling teammates to make their way back and get ready to start.

We turned Alan so he could see the balloon being filled, tying his leg to the crane so he would stay in that position. The sedan was positioned roughly under Alan to make the transition quicker. We waited and watched.

The balloon fill nozzles roared. Butterflies rose in my stomach as the bubble took shape. The bulging blob rounded out in the early-morning sun rays, creating the beyond-gorgeous glistening pink inverted teardrop that

I was starting to miss already. After the last spurts of helium, the fill lines were tied off.

The suit team stood ready. We would informally request clearance from mission control to remove the ground oxygen so we wouldn't waste one drip of oxygen in the transition period if something invisible to us was amiss. The balloon collar was installed to contain the head. The spork vehicle crept toward us.

This was not the biggest balloon we had launched, not even close. But it was a big balloon and looked grandiose standing up into the air. I had become so aware of the movement of the air I knew which types of grass moved at two or three knots of wind and which moved at five or six. Branches of trees start moving when winds get above 10, pine trees sway above 15 and make a full leaning arc above 20. Today nothing moved; even the flat-bladed tall grasses that normally rustled at just one or two knots were still. The balloon rose while we stood fast. There was little chatter because there were no hitches.

We made the call to remove the ground oxygen lines and off they came, followed by turning on the cameras and the other instruments with limited life. We pushed the launch sedan under the balloon seconds after the spork flung away as intended. Alan was hooked to the balloon equipment module. The rounds of okays were made in seconds. Joe got the launch command and pulled the cord. The tethers released and Alan rose straight up out of the sedan like a puppet being pulled into a perfect jump. He floated straight up over the airfield under a perfectly shaped balloon in the completely windless lower atmosphere.

Alan ascended for the first time beyond dark blue skies into complete blackness. I got in my assigned helicopter and monitored the flight on a well-integrated helicopter-mounted mobile mission control station that operated without even a minor issue. We pumped through the clear skies over still grass fields under a pilot who was ascending at the exact right rate. There was nothing to report.

"Pilot, this is flight. You are crossing out of the black zone."

"Copy."

"Pilot, this is flight. You are crossing through 20,000 feet."

"Copy."

"Pilot, this is flight. You are now in the stratosphere."

"Copy."

"Pilot, this is flight. You are crossing through 75,000 feet."

"Copy."

"Pilot, this is flight. You are crossing through 100,000 feet."

"Copy."

"Pilot, this is flight. You are passing through the altitude Joe Kittinger did his jump from."

"Copy."

"Pilot, this is flight, we are preparing for release, I need a verbal confirmation you are ready for release."

"Pilot is ready for release."

The helicopters were in position. The two chase helicopters made a three-mile circle around Alan's point in the sky while the fixed-wing, holding Blikkies, circled further out 10,000 feet above us. We were looking up and right at the little plastic wad hanging in the sky almost 20 miles above us through the perfect cloudless atmosphere. The medevac helicopter waited down range for a call.

"Pilot, this is flight. You are releasing in five, four, three, two, one."

"Pilot is away."

The near-zero ascent rates on my screen plunged to negative tens of thousands of feet per minute. Alan was hurtling to the Earth, getting up to just under the speed of sound in less than a minute. In this long flight Alan turned around a few times, experimenting with tiny motions of his elbows to counter the subtle, harmless rotations as he swung back and forth in his normal oscillations through the increasing sound of rushing air.

Sebastian called Alan's altitudes again as he came down. The altitude calls were a sort of audible altimeter to back up Alan's display-mounted barometric altimeter, which backed up his wrist altimeter, which backed up his GPS altimeter, which backed up his bright-light altimeter, which backed up the ultimate last-resort pressure-driven automatic parachute opener.

None of that was needed, though. At the exact right time, the numbers fell to about 1,000 feet per minute. Alan was under canopy. He had just completed the second-longest, second-highest, and second-fastest skydive of all time. Because he was wearing a drogue parachute, he had set a new world record for the highest drogue-stabilized freefall of all time.

Blikkies sprang from the fixed-wing airplane circling above us around the time our flight doctor spotted the orange canopy and shouted, "Canopy 2 o'clock!" And then, "Canopy 5 o'clock!" Blikkies was located also.

The wind had picked up slightly since launch, which was actually a good thing; a canopy pointing into the wind moves slower in relation to the ground.

The ground trucks released their smoke. Blikkies landed. He circled Alan into a nice clear field. Alan faced into the steady 10-knot winds and executed, for the only time in our program, a smooth lay-down landing that could have been interpreted as intentional.

We landed our helicopter and ran in. Mitch and I pulled the helmet and turned off the oxygen to find a happy, sweaty, now world-record-holding skydiver ready to fly again. Pilot and suit were completely undamaged.

The elated team swarmed. We packed up the suit. The trucks and helicopters went back to the airport 40 miles away, windows open, the air of victory blasting our faces. It was a truly flawless effort that very few people outside our team or the skydiving community will likely pay any attention to.

After the team's perfect preparations, Alan had executed a picture-perfect piloting of the suit from launch pad to grassland. Alan also set to rest our worries about oxygen consumption. He slowed his own breathing to the extent that instead of losing margin, as we had feared, we gained some back. If Alan breathed at the same rate in his final flight, there would be oxygen in reserve on top of the built-in contingency reserves.

We had made ourselves a chromed machine through meticulous practice and repetition over years—and in that instance everything operated perfectly. We built backup after backup and used none of them, not even the minor ones. The flight was reportedly without a hitch for Alan as well. In interviews after the flight he said, "If I had known it was going to be that easy, I would have skipped it."

Maybe conditions were just ripe that day. From that day until our final flight, which without any question we now would attempt soon, we would just need to keep Murphy on our side.

October 20, 2014: A Surprise on the Launch Pad

We were set to pull off the unthinkable: three manned flights in the span of a single month. We found ourselves speaking like the final jump was already done.

This time we would change nothing about the suit before readying it to return to the stratosphere. It worked through all the testing. Nothing was amiss or out of place.

The balloon team prepared two balloons. One had two crown valves in the top set into a plate the size of a small trampoline, even though the balloon team really wasn't relying on those valves. A balloon that big with little weight under it and open valves would float for dozens of hours, maybe days, before coming down. The balloon team was putting more stock in the fuse system, which would burn a triple cord of Chinese cannon fuse around the top of the balloon and lop off the entire crown, leaving a hole 15 feet in diameter. The fuse was sandwiched between the paper-thin balloon plastic and an insulating sheet to direct the heat from the burn into the plastic.

Some questions remained with these fuses. They hadn't been tested above 110,000 feet because all of the testing had been done with latex balloons. With less oxygen in the atmosphere at higher altitudes, the fuse burns slower the higher it goes. The compound that is burning has a built-in oxidizer, but the team learned during their testing that despite some magnificent sparkling, other factors, such as ambient oxygen and convective heat transfer, are at work on the ground. Every time a test was performed at higher altitudes, the fuse burned more slowly and less ambitiously. The next balloon would go some 20,000 feet higher than any previous test, so the team worried that the fuse might fizzle out. The worry was not new; it had crept in and out. With the day upon us, the team was implementing a fallback plan.

On both the full-size balloons they were preparing, they installed two fuse systems, one outside the other. The previous balloons hadn't had an additional fuse because they didn't go as high and the oxygen was thicker where they needed to be used. In the event that mission control initiated the first fuse and it failed, or it only partially lowered the balloon, they could wait until the balloon descended under the valve system or because of holes created by the partial fuse fire. When the balloon dropped to an altitude where things were better tested, they could initiate the second system. The solution was executed with little discussion. It was a decent plan, but it did feel last minute. Software was quickly updated to allow for two separate fuse fire events.

As far as the suit team went, life was calm and easy. We felt ready. We started well ahead of the effort with normal routines, from the adjustment of sleep schedules to breakfast at IHOP.

More people had flown in to watch. Alan's family and best friend from college were there. Several of the engineers originally involved with the project came. The weather report was patchy. The launch window might be as small as a few minutes. There was an unspoken sense that it wasn't going to happen on the scheduled day.

The suit-up process went incredibly well. Alan started his pre-breathe, then we pulled him into his suit. It was likely the cleanest, most issue-free suit-up we'd ever done, thanks to hundreds to thousands of hours of training.

We were in the midst of functional checks, walking through each critical system when the first weird thing happened. I got tapped by Alex, the doctor. He told me he'd received a text saying the fuse on the balloon had failed. It made no sense. The testing was done. The fuse wouldn't have a chance to fail until Alan was released. The only way it could "fail" now was by going off early, and that obviously hadn't happened or else the whole balloon would have lit on fire. I was annoyed. This was an example of helpful people inserting wrong information through wrong channels in communication. I told the doctor to put away his phone and stick to procedures. The last thing we needed was some big rumor-fueled confusion.

We continued with the functional checks. I made the call requesting permission to go mobile. Permission denied. Issues with the balloon. Wait, was this real? Had they lit a football-stadium-sized balloon worth a hundred grand on fire on the flight line? Yes.

Sebastian came out to the tent to give us the full story. When the system was plugged in, the balloon fuse had fired on the ground and ignited the balloon on the flight line. Apparently some bug in the hastily implemented software issued the "fire" signal to the balloon prematurely. Everyone on the flight line yelled, "Fire!" as the fuse tried to burn a huge hole in an uninflated balloon with far more oxygen present than would have been the case at altitude. The first fire extinguisher they grabbed didn't work. Thanks to quick thinking on the part of a ballooning sage on loan from NASA, they used the balloon canvases that the balloon was lying on to bat out the burning plastic. The balloon was completely destroyed.

Mission control called a hold while they decided if they would take out the second balloon. As crazy as it sounded, they had prepared two balloons so that if something unforeseen happened (like a balloon suddenly bursting into flames on the flight line?), they could turn around quickly and keep on going.

The same thing was on everyone's minds, though. Did they understand why the fuse fired? Dan was frantically batting at a laptop outside our tent where the other balloon was sitting. It was clear that some sort of problem in the hastily written software associated with adding the second fuse had caused the combustion, so a hastily written fix wasn't very reassuring. Obviously it mustn't happen again, especially not near the ground, where it would spell disaster for Alan.

On top of that, we only had two balloons sized for the final altitude left, and the weather wasn't good. We were getting updated moment to moment, and the predicted launch window was still only minutes long.

We sat around on folding chairs in the tent with Alan as the sun came up. Mostly we stared at walls. The official decision came over the radio: we would prepare the second balloon for a launch. It was not clear there would be a launch, only that we would ready the balloon.

Dan whacked away at his computer, his face grimly twisted, determined not to have his malfunctioning code blow the day. He found the problem and got through the updates. He reloaded the code. By now, watching Dan hack his way through lines of codes with his pale stare, we all knew with near certainty that it wasn't a good idea to keep on with the launch. Dan kept crunching, sitting awkwardly on a low wooden box, hunched over like a distraught kid sitting on a curb.

In the midst of the confusing lull, Alan's sisters wanted to come in and see him in the suit. Mitch asked Alan if that was okay. He said that was all good. The sisters were given permission to see Alan hanging from the gantry in his white cocoon, and they were followed by a mob 15 strong with cameras and smiles and "give me a thumbs-up" enthusiasm—an enthusiasm not shared by the folks in the tent. They were quickly kicked out.

Dan finished coding. I paced around outside the tent, pretending I wasn't staring at him. He ran some tests with spare hardware to make sure the "go" signal wasn't active when the system was initiated. It wasn't. In minutes he tested the new code a few times, and all appeared to be checking out. Near the same time, behind Dan, the team was finishing up the balloon preparation. There was light spilling into the tin shed as the morning became full. The daylight made everything feel even more real. Mitch was amped up, and I tried to let his energy fuel me into an optimistic state. The new balloon was moved onto the trailer and made ready to be pulled out to the flight line. The suit team was told to be ready to move the pilot out to the flight line as soon as the BLV had moved the balloon box onto the trailer.

When the crane was ready, we removed the forks and parked the vehicle outside the tent, all set to move the pilot. Then another hold was called while mission control looked at the weather. Our skin felt tight around our chests as the long morning kept creeping across the foggy and overcast pastel grasslands.

The medevac helicopter, which was usually on standby, was held up because of visibility problems. Normally we wouldn't launch without the helicopter on site and on standby to quickly respond to an emergency. The helicopter was grounded for weather somewhere en route to the airport. More tension, more things that weren't right. The weather at our site was poor as well: overcast had socked everything in, and wisps of low fog were drifting over our heads. We got the call that in 10 minutes they would tell us whether we were going to launch that day. I think by that point most of us hoped the answer was no.

There were only two balloons left. 10 minutes passed: abort. We took Alan out of the suit, keeping the equipment clean and carefully handled.

The day ended with a long debrief in which tired heads rested on hands as we walked uncomfortably through lighting our balloon on fire, then scrambling for another launch attempt. There was clear discomfort with how the software glitch got missed. We were a team, though, through and through, and as a team we shared the responsibility.

Alan was happy that we aborted. There were too many issues in one morning for a good launch. It had gone unspoken how dangerous it would have been if a fuse fired mid-flight. Alan of all people understood software bugs, they're a bitch.

October 24, 2014: Scratching at the Wild Black Yonder; Final Flight

Putting Alan in a spacesuit that would take him higher than any before him, followed by a 26-mile descent to a rocky, thick meadow halfway to the next state, just days after burning up a balloon on the launch pad made me feel like a leather band was squeezed around my heart.

There was a madness to what we were doing. Bolt by bolt, we had made a human-shaped spaceship. Alan would wear it to escape into the atmosphere and nudge us all to escape imaginary bonds that tell us where humans can and cannot go. Chunk by chunk, layer by layer, we were uncovering the wrappings surrounding the things we don't yet know about our universe.

We weren't sending Alan to band camp, but to a place where it is black as night all day long, both boiling hot and freezing cold, filled with a nothingness that would literally pull everything out of you. Someday, thanks to people like Alan, the stratosphere will become a place as familiar as the sky that is traversed by airplanes. But the stratosphere wasn't that place on October 24, 2014. Alan was going to the place just beyond the place we could reach.

We met up at the IHOP in the middle of the night. I ordered three eggs with wheat toast, no butter. Ryan got an omelet and sausage. Zane ordered crepes and Mitch had an omelet. As always, Blikkies was finished when we got there.

Alan drove his own car. This represented optimism, superstition, or both. When he left his car at the hotel, he was assuming he'd be spending more days with the team because we would fail. He drove when he anticipated leaving town after a success. The suit team met him outside the airport and drove in to the tin shed together. We didn't talk. The fleeting comfort of conversation wasn't worth the risk of conversation's consequences.

The aerostat and pie ball balloons were mind-bogglingly high in the sky. Those balloons, raised to the final height of Alan's stratospheric balloon, helped the launch team gauge the wind at the balloons' crown, several hundred feet above the ground. It was remarkably calm. Particularly because our "guests" would stay out of our way until 4 a.m.

Alan came into our clean tent while we were powering on the equipment. He had been to mission control. The day would have some unique elements. First, ground fog would cover some of the terrain under the flight path, posing a threat to both the helicopters trying to land in an emergency and Alan, who would have to land blind in the event of an early abort. The whole of mission control wanted a nod from Alan about the risk. Informed consent, I called it. He'd said yes, so the suit-up continued.

That day would also have extremely fast stratospheric winds. The beginning part of the flight would be a slow loitering near the airfield. Above 70,000 feet of altitude, the balloon would pick up speed flying directly east, toward Texas, gaining more speed until it reached its final altitude. Then it would be flying at over 150 miles per hour, faster than the helicopters could go. The predictions said Alan would leave the balloon somewhere near the border between New Mexico and Texas, some 80 miles east of the airport. This would be our furthest flight yet. This troubled me and the other mobile mission control console operators because long distances meant that communication with mission control could drop, in which case we could be charged with executing life-critical commands to bring the pilot down.

We had made special provisions for the particularly far-flying flight: in the event of a loss of communication with mission control, a command would go out over the net and on text message to our phones with the words "Chase is flight," meaning Dave Jourdan, the chase director, would assume the role of flight director because the mobile mission control consoles on chase would be physically closer to Alan than mission control and still able to monitor the system and execute commands. At that point any calls to "flight" would be referred to Dave, and the chase crews would take over mission control. If the trucks lost range, the responsibility would go to me, in the fastest helicopter, and a communications chain would string across the desert to our team to issue the final commands. This was all unlikely. We were not violating our tested system range, but there was something very eerie about the idea that the balloon would be going so fast that if we were 30 minutes late leaving to chase it, it would be too far for mission control to reach it and moving too fast for the helicopters to catch it. The balloon would be floating away with our pilot.

Alan came into the tent with the same calm demeanor he had shown through all the other flights. He was at our disposal. He did what we said and he didn't ask questions. At this point his life was in our hands, and any intervention in the well-proved process, even by him, could have consequences. He sat in his pre-breathe tent waiting for us to tell him what to do.

We started working through our start-up procedures. We turned on GPS location tracking units just before we turned on the GPS units that would capture the world record. Because of the importance of the record, the units were independently verified by the representative of the French record organization, who had taken them to his hotel room, run them overnight, then downloaded the data, making sure they indeed showed that they had been in his hotel room the whole night. He sealed the units with the intent of us putting them directly into the suit. We weren't about to fly the sacred units with week-old batteries in them, though. In our clean tent, as the night came to life, we opened the units with a crowd of onlookers taking pictures as we removed the batteries and put new ones in, leaving the meticulously validated data card untouched.

The ground carts came alive, beeping and winking. We did all our checks. We pre-chilled the equipment in hopes it would keep Alan just that tiny bit colder so he didn't sweat and potentially fog the mask. Alan hit the bathroom for his last chance at a toilet for the next seven hours of pressurized stress. The life-monitor chest strap went on and started logging his vitals. He put on his athletic cup, his diaper, then finally the liquid thermal garment that would flow thermal fluid around his body. The little pill that monitored Alan's core body temperature refused to work. We got clearance from mission control to continue the suit-up regardless. We will never know how warm or cold Alan really was that day.

By 2:30 in the morning, we were ready to start the pre-breathe. Alan lay back in his recliner listening to Simon and Garfunkel while we bustled around him manipulating machines. The pre-breathing mask was routed from the gas analyzer and oxygen regulators into Alan's tent and strapped to his face at 2:45 in the morning, 15 minutes early. We could launch ahead of schedule if winds threatened the mission. That meant we would be ready leave the ground as early as 6:30 a.m., a time which coincided with our FAA rules not to launch before civil twilight, 30 minutes before actual sunrise.

There wasn't much for the suit team to do for the next couple hours. Simon and Garfunkel played on while pure oxygen poured through a tangle of steel hoses. There was no talk. Anything not on a checklist was a distraction.

Every 30 minutes Alan did a round of stretches to help break nitrogen loose from his muscles. We stared at the laptop screen to make sure his nitrogen levels didn't go so high we had to report it to mission control. He drank fluids and peed, trying to stay hydrated. I liked the silence.

I went to the main trailer in search of food for the crew. A member of our chase crew was making a long line of sandwiches. He gave me the relevant updates: fog was still an issue but looked passable.

After munching sandwiches in our folding chairs, Mitch and I went to the flight line to see where we would be driving our ground carts in a couple hours. The launch team was positioning the concrete barriers that would hold the launch plate. They showed us the glowing wand marking the spot where Alan would ultimately hook to the balloon. We convened with the balloon equipment module team, Rolfe and Esteban, and negotiated that they would move to the other side of the launch platform so that we could pass next to the concrete barriers without leaving the runway.

We went back to the tent. Alan slowly traded the nitrogen in his blood for oxygen. Soon he would enter his spacesuit for the last time.

At about 4 a.m., Taber and a couple of photographers came into the tent for the suit-up. Alan walked out into the larger room to sit on a folding chair while mission control polled the site for approval to suit up. The radio squawked a go-ahead from each of the team leads. Everyone was on track.

The radio chatter told us that the launch team was plugging in the balloon fuse system. This was the moment when the last balloon had caught fire. In a second it was over, fuse plugged in, all systems normal.

Alan stood up, ready to go in the suit. I walked through the process, reminding each person what their job was. Then we swung into action. Oxygen mask off, duck down, into the rubber tunnel, head through the neck dam, adjust neck dam, inner helmet on, facemask on, adjust helmet, adjust mask, thumbs-up, outer bubble down, oxygen tanks on. Alan was sealed away. The process was smooth—there were no jitters, no pauses, only two minutes off oxygen. Ryan and Mitch sealed the pants to the suit torso. The gloves slid on like butter.

While we were adjusting the straps to the parachute pack, the poll came over the radio asking for approval to lay out the balloon. We were ahead of schedule; we were a go. We asked permission to pressurize. Permission granted.

We held the parachute pack straps up high against the suit shoulders and closed the suit pressure controller. Ryan told Alan to bring the suit to pressure at his own pace using the depressurization valve. His giant mitted hand cupped the yellow valve handle and slowly turned it closed as his persistent slow breathing motivated oxygen into the suit, which climbed to 5.4 psi above the pressure the rest of the team was experiencing in Roswell, New Mexico.

With Alan at pressure, we could take him off his feet and move him to the position he would stay in for the next five hours. We hooked up the spreader bar linking in our SAEBER system and lifted Alan up into the air with the hoist. We hooked him to the static webbing strap and dropped him to hang at 45 degrees. The bland landscape in front of the helmet would soon be replaced with far more interesting spectacles.

Blikkies tacked the stabilizing parachute bridle to the parachute pack with break cord to keep things tidy, standard procedure. He poured through his visual and tactile checks while we did thermal checks. We raised the temperature set point in the suit and waited for the computer to kick on the heater, then lowered it back down. Alan turned his glove heaters on and back off again to make sure they were working. On it went, all systems go. Alan the space man was fully ready to go to the stratosphere.

I made the call for a status on the BLV. It wasn't ready. We were early. We opened the giant zip-up doors of the tent, exposing Alan to a predawn horizon while the launch team rushed the BLV back.

In an unexpected call, mission control came on the net to ask Alan if his pilot, Richard, could fly his jet with another on-site pilot (the ex-astronaut Mark Kelly) to survey the flight path for ground fog. Apparently the fog issue wasn't going away. Alan agreed. Mission control said they weren't sure if they were actually going to do this, but that they wanted the option. Alan's plane was fast and would make the 80-mile survey in a hurry if they decided they needed it. The BLV arrived.

We were 30 minutes ahead of schedule. Factoring in our 30-minute buffer hold at the launch site, we were set to arrive about an hour before launch, keeping everything in a place of calm, with no schedule pressure clouding our minds. We ran the poll to mobilize. Permission granted.

I hopped in the BLV and drove through the two doors to Zane's stop signal and lowered the boom into the tent to grab our man. I snatched Alan and the other attachments were let go. The ground carts were hooked to the tow hardware. We knew our marks down to the inch.

Our lighted procession backed into the darkness toward the runway. It glowed like a distant city, its lights reaching into the sky above the airfield. I drove down Stratosphere Lane at a slow peaceful pace. Alan hung a few feet off the ground, his first new view for several hours. Taber came over the radio to warn me there was a team of photographers posted next to the runway partway through our drive. No issue.

Because this balloon was so big, its layout spanned both the active and inactive runways, meaning we would have to drive almost twice as far as normal. Throughout the slow half-hour drive, we squinted against the frenzy of camera flashes from the mob of photographers capturing pictures of Alan in his boring pose.

At the staging area, we relocated the launch sedan so we wouldn't have as far to push Alan before the launch. It was time to wait.

The sky looked amazingly calm. We were 50 minutes from the official launch time, but the launch team could elect to push it up as much as 30 minutes, making our potential launch window a tight 20 minutes away. So much for early.

A launch tech and I did a dry run with the launch sedan, walking it from where Alan was hanging to the huge metal plate we would bounce the cart up onto. We watched the launch folks, a few hundred feet away, scurry around with solemn purpose.

Alan hadn't asked for any cooling since we had left the shed, so we removed his cooling lines to get him that much more ready for his transition. We decided that this time, driven by experience from our previous launches, we would remove the ground-power line and drop Alan onto the launch sedan as soon as the launch team installed the launch collar.

About 10 minutes before civil twilight, still with no sign of sunrise on the horizon, John came over the radio discussing the balloon fill with mission control. 400 hundred feet away, we saw the launch team break their final huddle and scatter in a star, readying lines and machines to start the raising of a monster balloon.

The colors of sunrise limned the horizon as Joe and Jacob walked to their respective fill tubes, grabbed their helium diffusers, and started unloading a semi-truck worth of compressed helium into a plastic bag the size of a large football stadium. The tubes swelled and roared. The orb of the balloon began to form. We shifted Alan so he could watch the fill with the rest of us. Two people held down the giant valve until it looked like the bubble was going to lift them off the ground. They let go. The bubble surged and pulsed like a jellyfish into the brightening morning sky.

The fill continued. We were all game face now. No action without direction, no word without purpose. One fill tube was tied off in a simple overhand knot that would hold it all the way to space. The other tube stayed alive, erect and pointing to the massive bubble, while John squeaked the last bits of helium from the truck into the balloon, perfecting the volume so the ride would be neither too fast nor too slow.

From behind the spork vehicle, Jacob and our veteran balloon expert tied two temporary ribbons around the balloon stalk to hold the balloon tight and tidy until the launch collar was affixed between them. The spork vehicle crept forward, rolling the ribbons around the spool and exposing the tight midsection where the collar could be tied. Jacob laced on the launch collar. We stared in silence a football field away.

When Jacob took the top ribbon off the huge balloon, the plastic shot open. The expansion hit him square in the face, knocking him off the metal platform he was standing on. He got up. The mission continued. The vehicle moved again and the second ribbon was removed. The balloon was ready to rise into the twilight.

The light of morning was otherworldly. The acres of plastic reflected the sunrise colors, distorting the space behind it like a prism. The headlamps and floodlights dimmed against the encroaching dawn. It felt like we had been watching too long. The launch team had decided to pause for weather with the balloon partially standing. It was maddening.

At a launch site it is bad etiquette to ask questions for which the answer won't change the outcome of an operation. I wanted desperately to know what they were waiting for at the other end of the balloon, but it wasn't my department; I had nothing to offer. I stewed in agony for 20 minutes while the balloon bubble sat straight and perfect in the rising sun. Not a blade of grass wiggled. It turned out the winds at 500 feet were substantial, and John made the call to wait until the winds came down before hooking Alan to the monster stalk. That time came soon enough.

The aerostat set high in the sky at the final elevation of the balloon was slightly offset from its base, providing mission control with the information that winds in the sky were about 10 knots and dropping. When the winds dropped to eight knots, the stand-up proceeded.

It was time for us suit folks to remove Alan's ground support. We pulled the ground power and prepared to lower Alan onto the launch sedan, leaving his oxygen hooked up and flowing. I jumped into the BLV while Mitch disconnected the ground-power cable. The strap was disconnected from the BLV; now Alan was connected to the earthly world only by two oxygen hoses.

We completed our closeout checklist, with only one unchecked box remaining for the oxygen hoses. The cameras started recording. The data-logging sensors turned on. The suit was alive in every way. The spork vehicle moved toward us, and the balloon moved high into the air.

We would wait until the spork vehicle crossed the runway line about 50 feet from us to disconnect the oxygen and push the suit forward. The balloon rose gently and calmly into the orange sunrise. It pushed farther into the sky than we'd ever seen a balloon go, bending the balloon stalk as the wind stream hundreds of feet above our heads pushed into it. The wind leaned the balloon away from the laid-out plastic, just as it was supposed to do. It would pull on Alan's suit mounts and roll the sedan perfectly under the balloon until it lifted him away.

Mitch and I switched Alan from ground oxygen to suit oxygen, removing his last connection to Earth's natural atmosphere. The final box was checked.

The large drum swung open. Mitch and I settled Alan beside one of the cables holding the concrete barriers to the launch platen. One push onto the platen and we would send him away. The spork backed away to give us room. There was nothing but mission on the faces of the crowd.

It was the steepest balloon angle we had seen since the launch in which we dragged our payload across the ground. We all strained our necks continually staring to gauge our comfort with the wind. John had Esteban stand below the balloon head so we could visualize the potential swing of the payload. It was a shocking distance, over 80 feet. John called a hold.

John pulled me aside to feel out my comfort level, while the balloon sat remarkably still but dipping heavily toward the ground. The situation really looked eerie, but passable. The balloon was shifted exactly in the right direction. The helicopter tests two days prior had assured us the sedan would do its job correctly and roll along the ground until the force vector was substantially vertical and Alan went into the sky. We said go for it.

John initiated the poll to hook up. Our go/no-go process was so streamlined by this point that it was no longer a call-and-response. Answers flew back from the leads.

"Launch, go."

"Suit, go."

"Safety, go."

"Surgeon, go."

"Fight, go."

"Meteorology, go."

We began the final motions. The hook got clipped, pyrocutter plugged in, and white tape wrapped around the connection. Mission control crackled through the radio that the pyrocutter was showing live.

An issue arose, a problem we hadn't seen since the high-wind launch that crashed its payload. The balloon was leaning at such a heavy angle that the attachment rigging was loose. We tried to pull Alan back onto the plate to tension the lines into the direction of pull, but the wheels were caught between being on and off the platen. Through the commotion, John and Blikkies finished their final checkouts of the rigging.

John ordered the huge cucumber-sized turnbuckles to be extended so that the system could better tension. In my anxious state I repeatedly, and quite inappropriately, told John to let them out all the way. Blikkies correctly told me to let John figure it out. I shut up. Over the next minute, John did extend the buckles all the way out. The straps were almost taut but not quite. The sedan was still balanced half on and half off the platen. In an instant, and mostly silently, we decided to let the sedan go to the concrete, off the platen, allowing the lines to slacken. This reassured us that the sedan would not roll off the platen and turn the casters in a wonky direction. This did mean, however, that we would have to suffer the brief jerk of the lines taking up tension. It was time for Alan to take to the sky.

John scanned our faces with determination written all over his forehead and yelled to Norman, "Pull it!" The collar fluttered to the ground like paper from a balcony.

The balloon was still, but canted into a wind we could not feel. Then John said, "Go!" Joe pulled the cord.

Alan hugged the push button knob for the glove heaters like he was supposed to, guarding the knob from a snag while the balloon tensioned with its new freedom. Blikkies shuffled sideways in a blur, keeping the spreader bar positioned correctly so the straps tensioned evenly in a beautiful swoop. The sedan lurched slightly forward, then rolled just like it was meant to for 20-some feet until Alan's legs lifted up, leaning him forward, jamming the suit mounts into the mount receptacles before his whole body freed itself from the sedan. The departure might have been an instant too early, but it played out in fluid precision. Alan hovered over the ground, accelerating forward for an uncomfortably long surge, going straight, not up, for most of the 80-foot distance to the spot underneath the balloon bubble. Then all turned vertical. Alan ascended.

I never let myself get captured. Through the full flight campaign, I intentionally enjoyed nothing. I smiled little and hooted only at the end of missions. A launch was just the beginning. The flight was still to go.

My mind was still filled with the sound of flapping plastic rushing by me as Alan planed out across the ground, flying forward in what seemed a purely horizontal motion toward the dead airplanes that occupied the rest of our runway. I drifted backwards in short awkward steps while it drifted upwards. It was never easy to tell if the balloon was rising at a healthy rate or not. It always looked the same at any given moment, so it was necessary to create a sort of composite of mental imagery to gather that it was getting smaller and indeed going up. That was all I allowed in my brain until the call came that Alan had cleared 4,000 feet, the black zone. I shuffled backwards like a crippled penguin away from the launch platen. The balloon was going up.

It was time to go to the helicopters and wait. I forced a smile and shared the high-fives. The morning still held plenty of adventure.

The trajectories promised that the balloon would loiter within the airfield for a long time. Not until the second half of the flight would it pick up horizontal speed, but by the end of the flight it would be moving so fast that our highest-powered helicopter (of which we now had four) would not be able to keep pace with it. The Chase 3 helicopter carrying Ryan and company had taken to the sky prior to launch to cover an abort within the airfield. Shortly after we climbed into our chopper, the pumping blades pulsed the sky as they came in to land and wait behind us. We would be covering the abort from the safety of our home field until the balloon cleared the tropopause above 70,000 feet and took off straight east for Texas.

I wanted everyone to shut up and focus. I wanted those lighthearted people to quit pointing at the balloon and stare at the screen. I watched the screen and listened.

10,000 feet went by. Now Alan would use the main parachute in an abort instead of the faster opening reserve. Every time Sebastian told Alan something, there would be a pause and Sebastian would say, "Copy." Alan was literally alive and kicking. The balloon ascent rate was slightly above average, which was good.

The computer was running smoothly for a change, no drop-outs. The oxygen levels remained maxed out. We had filled the tanks about 25% higher than the maximum possible reading on the gauges, which meant that for the beginning of the mission all we knew was that the tanks were above the maximum pressure. Several of us started having the same little concern that somehow maybe the pressures would never start dropping—what would happen then? What if Alan got halfway through the mission and the tanks were still reading max? It was an unfounded concern but it was there in front of us; gauges that always moved weren't moving.

Sebastian made the call that Alan was crossing 20,000 feet, about 15 minutes in. The only significance of that moment was that the altitude calls would switch to being reported in height above sea level instead of height above ground level. They turned on the heating system.

The balloon crossed 30,000 feet half an hour after launch. I sat in the cab of the helicopter staring at my screen. Oxygen pressures finally started to fall. There would be plenty of oxygen. This was happening.

The balloon neared 40,000 feet, and we were given the go-ahead to get moving. The balloon was south of the airfield, still loitering in sight from the ground. At 70,000 feet, just over an hour into the mission, the balloon would start booking it to the east.

The pilots gathered us up for one quick planning session. Glenn explained with a hint of apparent annoyance that if a helicopter fails over ground fog, all of its occupants would eat it when the chopper augered into the ground. The pilots didn't want to launch with fog present for fear they would have to fly over it. I don't know what was discussed that morning, but at some point it was decided that the mission would proceed, despite the presence of ground fog. We all went back to the helicopter and sat down. I wanted to do whatever we had to do next, even before we actually had to do it, as if I could somehow finish the entire mission by performing my own tasks quicker.

We did our headset checks around the horn. I was sitting in the exact same position I'd been in since launch, staring at a laptop screen covered in circles with little fake digital needle gauges showing all the life-support vitals. I pulled my door shut, minding the wires that snaked out the window to antennas held on the roof of the chopper with tape and magnets.

The engines came to life with the familiar mid-pitch turbine yell of the system coming up, accompanied by the slow shadow-striping turn of the main rotor over our heads. The camera bird, call sign TV, started into the air and skimmed down the road first. Glenn, from the captain's seat of call sign One, was not only the captain of our bird but the coordinator of the entire flying brigade.

Glenn told each of the other pilots when they should be taking off in the sequence and how. The choppers would get in formation and break east. The fixed-wing and Blikkies would wait at the airfield for another half an hour until the balloon picked up horizontal speed.

We followed TV and would be tailed by the second chase helicopter, call sign Three, which was trailed by the medevac helicopter, call sign Med. Glenn was a flying air traffic control coordinating the formations and directing the birds in and out of the fuel station, which had left the airfield several hours prior to stage in the east.

We took off down the road, and the excitement built. The helicopters pulled to the north of the city, rising way up above the ground for a beeline across the ominous patch of ground fog beneath. The balloon was still in plain sight over 10 miles above us and a few miles south. The helicopter pilots flew in a slow formation toward the long patch of fog. We would clear the fog and wait on the other side for the balloon to come over toward us in the rising winds it would soon encounter. The communications between Sebastian and Alan kept coming across clear and docile.

"Crossing 57,000 feet. You are now above the altitude of the first flight."

After a pause: "Copy that."

The life-support vitals looked incredibly docile as well; nothing so much as hinted at an issue. The suit was rock-solid stable. My focus briefly shifted to the fog crossing.

I never would have imagined that helicopter pilots fear ground fog the way they do. Glenn was stern and focused like I'd never seen him as he coordinated the flying fleet to haul across the fog to the other side. It came into view like a glistening silver lake across the desolate grasslands. Its fingers filled the gentle contours of the land just like water. My fears rose with the pilot's. If the pilot was scared, I knew I should be too. Glenn briefed us quickly on the fact that he didn't know what was beneath him, not offering any recourse, just informing us we were done for if there was a mechanical issue in that next 10 minutes. He then pushed the stick forward. The chopper leaned forward while the fingers of fog curled into a continuous shine. Soon there was only fog below. Sometimes the sight of a rooftop would let us know that the fog was indeed right next to the ground. Soon enough, in minutes, we saw the other side of the shine and were out of it, slowing to more modest speeds. We were out from over the fog, but the balloon was still behind us. If Alan aborted into the fog, it would be bad news. We set down very briefly on a little farm road while the balloon made its way toward us, picking up speed.

Glenn talked nonstop, coordinating the air team. Right as we crossed over to the meadows on the far side of the fog, the fixed-wing, call sign Five, came into the radio chatter attempting to keep an eye on the helicopter formation from two miles above. I stared at my eerily normal system values while the balloon crossed out of the fog behind us. One worry gone.

That particular day in the place where the balloon was rising, the stratosphere started around 60,000 feet. Alan was well into it. The sky was likely starting to deepen to black while his balloon swelled. The altitude calls kept coming, followed by the response that indicated Alan had answered with a leg motion. They were more a forced contact to verify that Alan was conscious and alert than they were an actual communication of altitude. Alan had three altimeters within view.

"You are now crossing 80,000 feet."

"Copy that."

"You are now crossing 90,000 feet."

"Copy that."

"You are now crossing 107,000 feet, higher than your previous drop."

"Copy that."

Alan remained remarkably calm through the entire mission. The oxygen-pressure sensors showed his slow breathing rate, and in interviews after the mission he reported, "In some ways [the final flight] was the most relaxing. I was savoring every one of the pieces. It was the first time I spent lots of time looking at the layers of the atmosphere. I spent less time thinking about emergency procedures. It was very peaceful and relaxed."

The choppers had begun alternating making fuel stops while the balloon picked up speed to the east. We knew that over the next half hour the balloon would transition into the very top parts of the stratosphere and the winds would convey it toward Texas at ever-increasing rates until each helicopter, from the under-powered, over-filled Three to our most powerful One, lost the ability to keep pace. The next terrifying prospect was of the balloon drifting out of sight and out of signal range before the release was actuated. There were multiple backup release mechanisms, but nobody wanted to try them.

We took our turn to swoop in for a drink of fuel. Everyone had caught on to my seriousness by this point. No words without purpose were exchanged. After fueling, we burned fast to the east to get ahead of the balloon while it made its haul to the finish.

The balloon was still an easily visible splotch in the sky while we raced to get ahead of it before it rose into the fast winds. Mitch and I alternated validating each other's values for heading and distance, correcting Glenn's heading to guide us to a point about 20 miles ahead of the intended release, a location where we could still command the balloon to let go of Alan if mission control ran into problems. If the release was normal, we would retrace our steps to cover the landing.

Alan crossed 129,000 feet to become the highest balloon occupant of all time. There was only one way down. He would soon experience the longest descent of all time. I saw it on my computer, and the final call came. He had reached float. At 136,000 feet, his ascent had ended.

Alan would later describe seeing distinct layers of the atmosphere as thin slices of blue. He was surprised by his inability to see extremely far. Per line of sight, he should have been able to see both the Gulf of Mexico and the Pacific Ocean, but he could not see either. We later concluded that because Alan was just above the atmosphere, he still had to look through lots of air at an angle to see long distances. This is in contrast to the space station, where the astronauts see the surface of the Earth at nearly a right angle.

View Through the Atmosphere

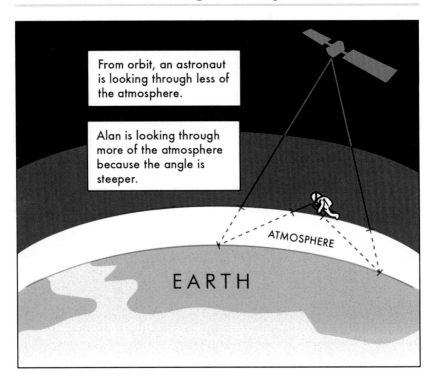

From orbit, an astronaut is looking through less of the atmosphere.

Alan is looking through more of the atmosphere because the angle is steeper.

ATMOSPHERE

EARTH

The radio calls continued. Alan said something about cranking the heater up to warm the suit before the fall. I assumed they had complied, but later learned they actually turned the heat off so that if Alan lost consciousness during the fall he would not overheat lying on the ground. Mission control then made a call we didn't hear requesting positive verbal affirmation that the pilot was ready for the drop. Mission control had lost the video feed and could no longer use the leg-lift method to receive affirmation from Alan. They would soon lose the radio feed as well if the flight wasn't ended.

At this point we were so far from mission control that we could hear Alan over the radio, but not mission control. From way up high, Alan still had communication but it was patchy; 26 miles above us, he pressed a push-to-talk knob to tell mission control he was ready for release but was blocked out by a radio that couldn't connect. The balloon was so far away that communications were beginning to fail. Alan was flying away at 150 miles an hour.

A second serious issue was forming during the release. The balloon was aimed directly at Lubbock, Texas. Mission control needed to get Alan released and destroy the balloon. The envelope was certain to enter the space above the sizeable city if the balloon wasn't destroyed. At the limit of the communications system, leaving the balloon to float over Lubbock and destroy it on the other side wasn't an option.

After several tries the transmission took. We heard Alan tell mission control he was ready for release. We heard nothing after that. We were too far away.

The release was coming. We turned around and booked it back west to retrace the 20 miles we had just covered, bringing us close enough again to hear mission control just in time for the countdown to release scratching through the radio like it was a Saturn Five shuttle launch that had been re-recorded several times and was now playing in some old movie.

"Five."

"Four."

"Three."

"Two."

"One."

If the release command were to fail, it would be now. The comm link was teetering. I stared in singular focus at my screen, waiting for the now flat-lining ascent rates to rocket. They blasted into the thousands of feet per minute downwards. The pilot was away.

Alan hugged his chestpack while he slipped away from the giant balloon. The carbon fiber SAEBER tube pulled off its spool and erected into a 10-foot-long pole holding his limp parachute away from him while he accelerated into the darkness. He was floating weightless. It was a full 26 seconds before the camera microphone recorded any sound. He was falling in total silence.

The pull of the SAEBER off the spool nudged him into a gentle back roll. He saw a vast expanse of planet Earth with the atmosphere frosting the curving horizon. He slowly rotated backwards, seeing the round balloon hovering above him. Then the parachute SAEBER rod caught his shoulder, giving him one quick glimpse of the stabilizing parachute at the end of the carbon fiber pole resting peacefully against a bright round balloon. The parachute was floating like a plastic bag in the ocean despite the fact that it was traveling at hundreds of miles per hour.

After a second slow roll, he crossed the sound barrier. All was still completely silent. As the first whooshes of sound were picked up by the camera microphones, the stabilizing parachute inflated, righting Alan and pointing his knees at the Earth in the orientation we had intended. At that point he started into the slow, pulsing, rocking motion that would accompany the rest of his journey.

The buildup of sound was fascinating. Alan later corroborated the camera microphone data, stating that at the beginning of the journey, the experience was entirely silent. Even as he rocketed into supersonic speeds, the experience was barely audible to him. Air lightly whistled around the chestpack as he became the second person in history to break the sound barrier outside of a vehicle. The sound transitioned slowly to the loud roar of freefall as he crashed back through the sound barrier, this time from high speed to low, and in much thicker air. With two sonic crossings behind him, he remained stable, no spinning. Our system had worked. The most frightening minute of the four-and-a-half-minute freefall was over.

This flight, and that of Felix Baumgartner two years prior, proved in practice the bizarre physics of stratospheric skydiving. The air densities are so low during the crossings of the sound barrier that they had no perceivable effect on the pilots and were not audible. Crossing the sound barrier and flying at supersonic speeds was imperceptible. The forces of freefall, and the sound heard by the pilots, changed based on equivalent air speed, not true air speed. This would explain the relative silence and peacefulness of the first crossing of the sound barrier: there was simply no air.

Alan continued to plummet toward Earth, quickly descending from a maximum speed of 822 miles per hour toward low-altitude terminal velocity at 130 miles per hour. He gently dipped his elbows into the air stream to maintain a heading. It was a remarkably stable flight.

Highest Flights

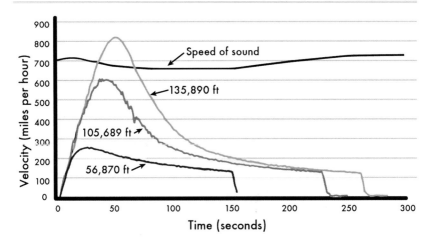

Glenn charged the helicopter, commanding the fleet to do the same, toward the last GPS point we had received before losing contact in the radio shadow beneath Alan's falling body. The trucks arrived at the prospective landing site and entered the radio clutter. One of the trucks came on the net to report they had heard a sonic boom. It shot adrenalin into the mood. Soon Alan would approach the ground and our adventure would be over.

The signal came back. With Alan dropping lower, the cone of the null radio space below him shrank. I fixed my eyes on the computer screen, watching one number exclusively, burning the screen image into my retina. If the numbers slowed too fast, it could mean the reserve had come out early, which could spell disaster. If descent rates failed to diminish, we'd be relying on an automatic opener that had just taken a trip to a vacuum in temperatures that don't happen on Earth.

As Alan approached the pull altitude at 10,000 feet, Sebastian called for Alan to prepare to pull his parachute. We heard the calls.

"10,000 feet. Pull your parachute."

"You are past your pull altitude. Pull your parachute at any time." Our hearts stopped.

Then the descent rate slowed. My computer showed a descent rate that buffered right down to a comfy 1,200 feet per minute: Alan was under parachute. He had unintentionally missed his pull altitude by just enough to break Baumgartner's freefall distance record, but not enough to create any real problems.

Alan depressurized the suit handily with the depress valve and threw the safety pin that locked the valve shut somewhere between Roswell, New Mexico, and Texas. Our headings were updating, and we could bring the helicopters in to cover the landing.

We flew in a three-mile pattern around the GPS spot where Alan was supposed to be. Alex, the doctor in the front of the bird, spotted the orange canopy and yelled, "Canopy, 2 o'clock!" The parachute looked good.

Blikkies' voice came on the net around the time the doctor spotted the second parachute. Blikkies had executed a perfect freefall over our heads through the eye of the circling helicopters and opened a parachute over Alan. The trucks released canisters of smoke. Blikkies used his abbreviated comm protocol, issuing short, understandable commands: "90 degrees right." He dropped a smoke canister of his own from under canopy, creating another skinny cone of smoke leaning cleanly into the wind.

Blikkies directed Alan into his final approach. Glenn circled the landing site and lowered toward the ground. We all readied our headcams and prepared to spill out and sprint toward our man.

During the landing commotion, 26 miles above us, the stadium-sized balloon was still floating. Mission control sent the signal to release the flight computer from the balloon, the action that was supposed to split the balloon and initiate a rapid descent. Nothing happened. Focus had squarely shifted to a huge balloon nearing the edge of mission control's broadcast range and heading directly at a large Texas city.

Mission control immediately fired the first of the two fuses installed on the balloon to burn the top off. What they didn't know was that with the suit away, the enormous balloon, now above 140,000 feet, had started to rotate. This balloon was so big it needed multiple reinforcing layers at its top called "caps." Those caps were so heavy that without Alan's balancing weight, the monster had turned on its side. In an almost comical miss, we had all failed to realize that the top of the balloon was heavier than the bottom, and that once Alan fell away, a sphere that could fit a city block would begin to invert. When the flight computer was released, the balloon was nearly upside down in a mounting bracket it was supposed to fall away from. Gravity was holding it in. The ground crews tending to the landing of their hero and anticipating great celebration had no idea that mission control was watching, for the third time, as a monster balloon became a potential menace to the lower world. Sebastian later said that this moment was "the most nail-biting part of the final two flights."

In a quirky turn of events, the parachute intended to carry down the little flight computer shot out from a spring-loaded canister 13 seconds after the release command. The little parachute bounced along the thin plastic of the balloon's light bottom skin until it broke through and cut a slice in the celestial sphere. The balloon began to descend, but very slowly.

The mission control team waited in painful suspense as the balloon approached closer to the dense populations of western Texas. The plan was to use the second fuse only at 110,000 feet or lower, where there was more oxygen. That is the altitude that the fuse had been tested to work at. Sebastian and John made a crucial game-day decision to light off the second fuse early, slightly above the specified altitude, in a last-ditch effort to increase the descent rates before the balloon drifted into populated areas.

To this day, it isn't clear exactly what happened. Somewhere between the small parachute slicing the balloon, the two fuses burning their way around the balloon crown, and the flight computer eventually falling from its mounts as the balloon swayed back and forth, the carcass fell into a rapid descent and landed on unpopulated ground in western Texas. John and Sebastian theorized, after watching the available video footage, that the slice from the small parachute had initiated the slow descent, and the first fuse very slowly burned through the top, causing the rapid descent right around the time the second fuse was initiated. Perhaps the final yank that destroyed the envelope was the heavy crown valve falling out of the balloon as the fuse burned around it. Both fuses were fully burned when the balloon was found on the ground.

When the balloon began to descend, mission control erupted into cheers. The documentaries and photos later pictured that scene of elation as a celebration of Alan safely reaching the ground—but in reality he had long since landed.

25 minutes prior to the balloon destruct, and 26 miles under the place in the sky he had just departed from, Alan flew under a perfectly formed canopy toward two trucks 50 feet from his guide and friend Blikkies, who yelled "Flare! Flare! Flare!" as Alan approached the ground in the perfect clearing 70 miles east of Roswell International Air Center. Alan clipped his feet and bashed against the ground, mashing every forward-facing part of the suit, chestpack, and helmet into the Earth before rotating right on past vertical and falling onto his back. A big clump of grass and dirt grabbed the top of one of the oxygen tanks as he rolled through the landing, decorating his shoulder like a badge of accomplishment.

Headcams rolling, we sprinted toward our man with the sun on our faces and the wind at our backs. No ankle-busting rocks could slow my stride as I ran through the tall grass, knowing nothing that could hurt us now.

The bright white suit lay on its side in the golden field. Alan grabbed the clump of dirt and grass from his oxygen tank and chucked it sideways. Blikkies ran up and they shared a high-five that had been earned over years, sometimes in bargains with death itself.

The rest of the team sprinted on, knees high. Mitch, Ryan, Blikkies, and I shared glances, and then Mitch popped the helmet off. Alan reentered our universe. The flight surgeon asked Alan if he was okay, and Alan answered, "I'm tired but healthy." The doctor called a green extraction. People swarmed the suit with trucks and boxes and hugs. The limp space-age fabric lay on the ground, used up, in ultimate release. All the trucks had made it. Every helicopter had landed. We gathered around Alan like the family we were.

All of us, including you, reader, must continue our mission. As a species, we will fight on to find the end of the darkness. Forego our daily rest and tiny battles with the darkness on Earth and find the darkness up high. Continue to snip the bands that hold us to this beautiful, fragile planet. With wide, bright eyes, we will stay awake, laugh, and claw at the boundary that divides us from the Unknown.

Layers of the Atmosphere and Historical Jumps as of 2016

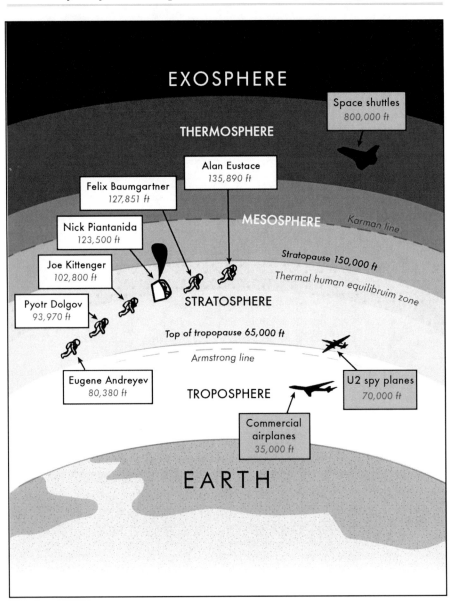

On the tarmac hooking Alan up for his first stratospheric balloon flight to 57,000 feet. This balloon will hold 106,000 cubic feet of helium when fully inflated. (Photo by Dave Jourdan.)

The team preparing for the 107,000-foot flight. (Photo by Dave Jourdan.)

Alan waving goodbye to us on his second journey. (Photo by Dave Jourdan.)

The 107,000-foot balloon on the launchpad. (Photo by Volker Kern.)

Esteban Garcia and Patrick Pasadilla hold down the crown of a balloon before releasing the bubble.

Alan rising into the air on his second flight to 107,000 feet. This flight set the official world record for the longest and highest freefall performed with a stabilizing parachute. (Photo by Bill Gibson.)

The team standing up the balloon that will carry Alan to 107,000 feet, well into the stratosphere. This balloon will hold 1,700,000 cubic feet of helium when fully inflated. (Photo by Dave Jourdan.)

The 1.7-million-cubic-foot balloon tearing in half after Alan has departed on the second flight.

The launch crew performs final checkouts on the dummy assembly prior to a trip to the stratosphere.

The view from 107,000 feet.

Sunrise from the stratosphere.

*Mission control was linked to Alan and chase crews through the
communications trailer, which is shown in the top corner of the image.*

*Part of the suit team stands with Alan waiting for our launch window on
the final record flight day. (Photo by Volker Kern.)*

The chase helicopters for the final flight waiting for departure to the east to chase Alan. (Photo by Volker Kern.)

The final balloon being prepared for launch to 136,000 feet.

Alan ascends into the air on his way to the top of the stratosphere for the highest balloon flight of all time.

Josh Hect cheers as Alan flies across the ground in his final launch. (Photo by Dave Jourdan.)

The final balloon being stood up on October 24, 2014. This balloon will hold over 11 million cubic feet of helium when fully inflated.

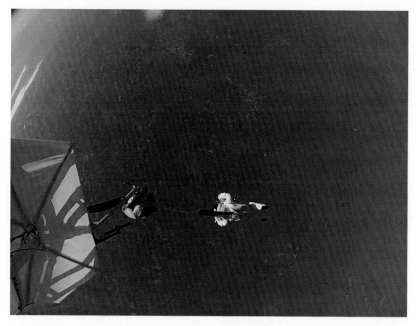

Alan falling away from the balloon at 135,900 feet.

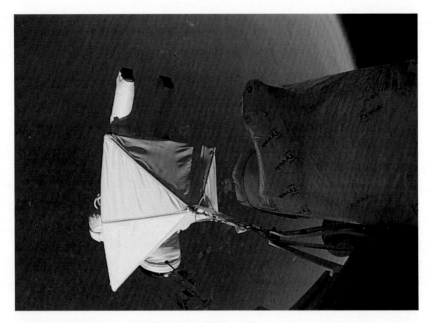

Alan releasing from the balloon at 135,900 feet at the start of the highest and longest freefall ever performed.

Looking through Alan's helmet bubble from a GoPro camera at the black of space at 135,000 feet. Alan is the only person ever to experience this part of the atmosphere outside a spacecraft.

Looking from a GoPro camera mounted at the bottom of Alan's chestpack, down his legs, at the balloon that carried him to altitude as he falls away. The balloon in this frame is large enough to fit a pro football stadium inside of it.

Coming in for a landing in the field east of Roswell near Texas. Alan is starting his flare to slow the canopy before he crashes for the final time. (Photo by Dave Jourdan.)

The team cheers when the "green extraction" call is made, meaning Alan is on the ground and undamaged. (Photo by Jim Harris.)

The team that pulled it off. (Photo by Jim Harris.)

The final balloon wadded up on the ground after the final flight. (Photo by Dave Jourdan.)

A balloon carcass being carried back to the Roswell tin shed under one of the helicopters. (Photo by Dave Jourdan.)

The End (for now).

EPILOGUE

...

In October 2014, the StratEx team executed three manned flights to the stratosphere in rapid succession, within a span of three weeks. The last of those three flights was the highest balloon flight and skydive of all time. There was well-grounded skepticism as to whether the project could be completed in the one-month window, or whether it would be completed at all. Through 35 major tests spanning years, we didn't have a single success with first attempts until the final jumps: two were completed successfully on their first try. After more than 25 people had worked for over two and a half years designing, testing, rejecting, and re-designing equipment, only 21 days were spent on the final stratospheric flights.

Alan set three official parachuting world records and one unofficial ballooning record. He achieved the highest "Exit Altitude" of any parachutist at 135,890 feet, the "Distance of Freefall" record at 123,414 feet, and the "Vertical Speed Attained with a Drogue/Stabilization Device" record at 822 miles per hour. (Alan did not fall faster than Felix Baumgartner, whose freefall speed record, achieved without a stabilizing parachute, still stands at 844 miles per hour.) Because Alan did not land with his balloon, he was not awarded an official record for the highest balloon flight of all time, though he is unquestionably the highest-flying balloonist ever to survive his feat.

Alan's final landing was followed by an uneventful suit-doffing and a trip back to our Roswell tin shed, where 20-some spectators met the 25-person operations team for celebrations. Our afternoon was filled with hugs and high-fives and developed into a final night of partying in Roswell. For the first and only time in the program, the suit was not refurbished after crashing into the ground.

The program ended remarkably abruptly after the final jump. The team dispersed within two days, leaving piles of equipment in the tin shed. We came back a week later to tear down the site and remove all the equipment. Most of it was packaged into storage containers and shipped back to Tucson, where it would await sorting and dispersion. The site was returned to the management of Roswell International Air Center. There our new clean room remains, next to the medical room installed by the Red Bull Stratos team. Hopefully the next team attempting a world parachute record in Roswell will refurbish another room in the World War II–era metal shed and, with a few more records under its belt, the facility will become a modern stratospheric skydiving facility.

The StratEx suit was the first commercially developed spacesuit to be used in practice. It is the first spacesuit designed for a private citizen and the first new spacesuit design to be tested in a vacuum since the 1970s. The suit was accepted into the Smithsonian Air and Space Museum and was delivered in 2015 for permanent display. The display is intended to debut by the end of 2016.

Stratospheric exploration and skydiving substantially changed during this short era from 2012 to 2014. The number of people to successfully skydive from the stratosphere doubled after over 50 years of inactivity. When this program started, half of the people who had gone to the stratosphere with the intention of skydiving back had died in their endeavor. Stratospheric skydiving became profoundly safer during the period of this project. Prior to 2012, four people had attempted 15 jumps from the stratosphere, and two of those jumps resulted in a fatality. After the StratEx and Red Bull Stratos programs, six people attempted 21 jumps from the stratosphere, with the fatality rate staying steady at two.

Both the Red Bull Stratos program and our StratEx program were nominated for the Collier Trophy "for the greatest achievement in aeronautics or astronautics in America" the year following the jump. Neither team won the award. But in 2015, the StratEx project won the Laureus Action Sports Award, the Crystal Eagle Award, and the FAI/Breitling Milestone Award, and Alan was made an Honorary Golden Knight.

Alan intentionally avoided the media throughout the project. The final jump was attended by one reporter, John Markoff of the New York Times, who covered the story in depth. On the day of the jump, the project made the front page of the New York Times' Science and Technology website and was reported worldwide in hundreds of publications and news outlets. It was an ESPN "Play of the Day" and made the cover of Parachutist Magazine. But after the flurry of media attention subsided, few people seemed to remember it. To this day, it is still regularly confused with the Red Bull Stratos project. A common response when I tell people I worked on the StratEx project for the highest balloon flight and skydive of all time is, "Oh, the Red Bull thing—that was awesome."

Alan was remarkably undamaged throughout the entire program, enduring not so much as a scratch through years of intense suit training and jumping. A few months after the jump, Alan retired from Google. He remains fascinated with space, aviation, parachutes, and the stratosphere. He continues to fly his airplane and went on to get a helicopter pilot license.

He is currently working on everything from machine learning and weather modeling to new space parachute systems and, with his daughter, safety devices for bicycles.

A few months after the jump, Blikkies was promoted to production floor manager at United Parachute Technologies, where he now oversees the manufacture of a substantial portion of the world's parachute systems.

Taber and his wife Jane continued the development of the space gondola idea we helped them test partway through the program as the founders of the company World View. The goal is to bring paying customers to the stratosphere in a pressurized capsule under a balloon. After Alan's jump, the space gondola could rightfully be thought of as a continuation of the StratEx project and the use of balloons to give people access to the stratosphere. Taber and Jane left Paragon Space Development Corporation to devote all their time to the new system. The capsule is envisioned to carry six passengers, one crewmember, and one pilot to over 100,000 feet to view the Earth from above. Soon after the end of the project, most of the core StratEx team, including me, joined that company to pursue this next adventure.

BOOK ACKNOWLEDGEMENTS

...

This book was made possible by a group of hugely supportive individuals. When I first presented this work as a rough draft to Alan Eustace, I had no idea if it would be—or even could be—published. The support that came after was overwhelming. Alan allowed me to share the technical details of his suit and air the insides of a sometimes gruesome story. He not only let me make this experience public but wholeheartedly aided me through the entire process.

The main structural editor of this book was Andy Wolaver. Andy took on this project years before it was finished—for free, and with little hope of the book ever being published or widely recognized. Andy had an incredible ability to pick up the technical details of the project and help me meld them into a fluent story. Andy did an amazing job, taking an overwritten and overstated manuscript filled with engineer's jargon to a real book. Thank you, Andy, for your long effort to make this a reality.

My girlfriend Kayla Maranjian was a cornerstone of this book. For years, she was the only person aside from Andy who knew it existed, and she provided advice and help throughout the whole process, including helping me make the decision to publish the book. Aside from continual advice and read-throughs, Kayla edited several sections of the book behind Andy.

Line editing and further structural editing support was provided by Nancy Casey of Moscow, Idaho. Nancy put in another giant effort behind Andy and Kayla to untangle the book's themes, characters, and redundancies while smoothing the flow at the sentence level. Final copyediting was performed by Robin DuBlanc, who put the final touches on the project.

All graphics and layout were provided by Jenna Westbrook of JMK Design Studio. Jenna did an incredible job explaining in pictures concepts that took me years to understand. Jenna was a unique find: a talented graphic designer with an engineering background and strong technical ability. Thank you, Jenna, for lending me your wonderful talent as a graphic designer and for helping me understand the book-making process.

I started this project knowing close to nothing about the process of writing and publishing books. I was extremely privileged to be surrounded by great authors who could help me along. Dave Jourdan was my guiding arrow. An integral part of Project StratEx, Dave also happens to be a great writer of books recounting his own adventures. Dave showed me how the book-publishing process works, providing detailed information on everything from editing to budgeting. Dave collected all the photos from the project and was the main force behind the photo selections presented within. James Hayhurst from the Fédération Aéronautique Internationale also helped with editorial advice and editing—Jim not only certified the StratEx official records but is also a seasoned author. Other authors close to me who provided editorial advice include the CEO of my current company Jane Poynter and astronaut Ron Garan.

Many project members reviewed early versions of the book and provided edits and advice. Thank you to Alan Eustace, Josh Hecht, Ryan Lee, Christie Iacomini, Dr. Jon Clark, Julian Nott, Sebastian Padilla, and Taber MacCallum.

PROJECT ACKNOWLEDGEMENTS

...

I truly consider this book's actual writing only a tiny piece of the sum of its value. This work exists and is worthwhile because an unbelievably talented, motivated, and brilliant group of people made a spacesuit that changed my life.

Several companies took a big risk on this project. Paragon Space Development Corporation was the prime contractor and leader of the incredible effort. They fought through years of uncertainty and difficult decisions to make this project a reality. ILC Dover put their spacesuit technology to the test and allowed one of their most senior engineers to work on the project nearly full-time. United Parachute Technologies also had to make do without a very important member of their team, and they offered the use of their Sigma Tandem technology. ADE Aerospace Medicine provided doctors, for free, to support the jumps. Aerowestern helicopters flew our helicopters and supported us wholeheartedly, even living in Roswell with the team for the final push. Finally, World View Enterprises supported our launch efforts partway through the program and provided on-site assistance at the end of our journey.

Thanks to Alan Eustace, the man with the plan. Alan had a dream and he made it come true. He used his own money and time to create an incredible piece of engineering, and dozens of people were allowed the honor to work on that suit along with him. Alan is the man I hope someday to be.

The leaders of the project were the backbone of the effort. Taber MacCallum's unending enthusiasm, drive, and endurance pushed us to be the team we were and was the brain behind many of the program's major decisions and architectural elements. The leaders who guided us on this mad adventure, fighting the ongoing battles, taking the first hits, and clearing the path, were the fearless Sebastian Padilla as program manager and flight director, Gary Lantz as the initial program manager, and Norman Hahn as the chief engineer. Jane Poynter and Grant Anderson led our company back at headquarters. Barry Finger drove the early proposal and initial architectures. Christie Iacomini guided the initial design of the suit, and Paul Damphouse was the original operations director.

Our suit team worked tirelessly for years, making huge sacrifices to make the suit come true. That suit team included Zane Maccagnano, Ryan Lee, Daniel (Blikkies) Blignaut, Mitch Sweeney, and myself, as well as flight doctor Alex Garbino (during final suit ops) and, early in the program, Dave Graziosi.

The launch team, the people who made the floaty things float, was led by John Straus. The deputy launch director Joseph Levy was on the fill team with Jacob Dang. The "Diesel" team included Patrick Pasadilla, Esteban Garcia, and Brian Richardson. Early in the program Ernie Arispe and Brit Lee stood up the big balloons.

Testing was led by Rolfe Bode, often assisted by Ernie and Esteban. Rolfe and Esteban also made up the BEM team during launches.

Mission control was led by the big guy Sebastian as flight director and occupied by Dr. Jon Clark on the flight surgeon console, the miracle worker Don Day and Robert Redinger on the meteorology station, Zane on the life-support console, Ryan Osborn on the communications console, the avionics sage Dan McFatter as the flight engineer, and Taber in the flight safety seat for the final flights.

The chase crew was led by the chase director Dave Jourdan, with Josh Hecht, Travis Palmer, and Norman helping the effort after the departure of Jeremy Sotzen, the original chase director. The chase team directed the helicopters flown by the helicopter lead pilot Glenn Patterson along with Johnny Stevensen and Todd Rosignol. Alan's flight support was provided by Richard Myer, and the fuel truck crew was led by Jeff Davis.

Skydiving support was truly lifesaving at times. The main support jumpers were Luke Evens and Trevor Cedar, with support during the first jump by Louis Palomares and Derek Vanshboten. Blikkies jumped in all dives. Parachute support came from Ty Bowen during the high-altitude parachute launches, and tons of parachute system management support came from Mark Procos and Bill Booth. The parachutes themselves were provided by Performance Designs, with technical support from John LeBlanc. Wind tunnel support in Colorado came from Derek Vanschboten and Peter Baney.

Medical support came from ADS aerospace medicine, including an incredible team of doctors assisting the program on leave from their hugely busy day jobs. The doctors who supported flights and the team included Sean Norton, Anil Menon, Erik Antonsen, and Cameron Decker.

A huge team of engineers supported the team from back in Tucson at headquarters, with Jason Brockbank, Rebecca Tate, and Walter Harrington helping the build and test of countless parts that were always on rush. Lab support came from Laura Kelsey. Analysis support came from Chad Bower and Jim Harrell. Javier Lopez supported analysis and also helped with the early design alongside Aaron Powers. Parts were checked by the inspection lab, which was run by Danny Wise and Carlos Rios.

James Hayhurst from the Fédération Aéronautique Internationale certified our records. The on-site support in Roswell was consistent and invaluable, with help from the Roswell Fire Department, Roswell FBI, and Bureau of Land Management. Air ambulance support was provided by PHI Air Medical.

Finally, I thank my incredible parents, Mike and Cheryl Leidich, whose unending love and support pushed me to be the person I am, with, my love of engineering, knack for tinkering, and insatiable desire to experience the world. Thanks to my wonderful sisters Kari Reigner, Celeste Cizik, and Aimee Leidich for their lifelong support, my brothers-in-law Matt Reigner and Nico Cizik for instilling in me a sense of adventure, and my girlfriend Kayla Maranjian, who is always there for me, through the good and the bad.

BIBLIOGRAPHY AND NOTES ON ACCURACY

...

This book was written as a first-person account from my own perspective. A rough copy of the book was provided to all the major team members for review several months before publication and all questions of factual accuracy were reconciled prior to publication.

This work was generated in two major sections. First, around the time of the events described in what became chapter 4, I began taking notes and making outlines with the intent of eventually creating a book. After that point, nearly everything was written as it actually happened, and so the information is more detailed than in the beginning of the text.

I wrote this book almost entirely in secret; it was known only to my girlfriend and one of the editors, a close personal friend, until roughly one year after the project ended. During the writing process, this work was not influenced by a corporate agenda and was not written with the promotion of any organization in mind. I hope and believe that this created an honest account of the project.

Historical information included in the book came from the sources listed below.

"Adventurer Crosses English Channel Using Helium Balloons." The Telegraph, May 28, 2010. http://www.telegraph.co.uk/news/newstopics/howaboutthat/7776724/Adventurer-crosses-English-Channel-using-helium-balloons.html. Retrieved July 7, 2016.

"Audouin Charles Dollfus, 1924–2010." http://astrogeo.oxfordjournals.org/content/52/1/1.44.full. Retrieved July 13, 2016.

Azriel, Merryl. "Jim LeBlanc Survives Early Spacesuit Vacuum Test Gone Wrong." Space Safety Magazine, November 28, 2012.

Federation of American Scientists. "X-38." http://fas.org/spp/guide/usa/launch/x-38.htm. Retrieved September 20, 2006.

Jenkins, Dennis R. Dressing for Altitude: U.S. Aviation Pressure Suits—Wiley Post to Space Shuttle. National Aeronautics and Space Administration, 2012.

Kittinger, Joseph. Ryan, Craig. Come Up and Get Me: An Autobiography of Colonel Joe Kittinger. University New Mexico Press, April 16, 2011.

Knacke, T.W. Parachute Recovery Systems. Defense Technical Information Center, 1987.

Leidich, Jared, Daniel Blignaut, and Robert Alan Eustace. "Human Stratospheric Descent System: Architecture and Design for Safe, Stable Flight." American Institute of Aeronautics and Astronautics, Aerodynamic Decelerator Systems Technology Conference, Daytona Beach, FL, April 2, 2015.

Leidich, Jared, et al. "StratEx Pressure Suit Assembly Design and Performance." American Institute of Aeronautics and Astronautics 45th International Conference on Environmental Systems, Bellevue, WA, June 15, 2015.

NASA. "Preliminary Report Regarding NASA's Space Launch System and Multi-Purpose Crew Vehicle." January 2011. http://www.nasa.gov/pdf/510449main_SLS_MPCV_90-day_Report.pdf. Retrieved May 25, 2011.

NASA. "President Bush Announces New Vision for Space Exploration Program." http://history.nasa.gov/Bush%20SEP.htm. January 14, 2004, Retrieved August, 23 2016

Padilla, Sebastian, et al., "StratEx Mission Overview." 45th International Conference on Environmental Systems, Bellevue, WA, June 15, 2015.

Parachuting World & Continental Records.
Retrieved October 18, 2012. http://www.fai.org/record-parachuting

Part 101: Moored Balloons, Kites, Amateur Rockets and Unmanned Free Balloons. Chapter 1, Subchapter F, Title 14: Aeronautics and Space, Code of Federal Regulations

Rhian, Jason. "NASA's EFT-1 Mission Slips to December."
SpaceFlight Insider, March 14, 2014. Retrieved December 7, 2014.

Ryan, Craig. Magnificent Failure: Freefall from the Edge of Space.
Smithsonian Books, October 2003.

Ryan, Craig. The Pre-Astronauts: Manned Ballooning on the Threshold of Space. Naval Institute Press, March 31, 2003.

Ufarkinym, Nikolai V. "Hero of the Soviet Union Pyotr Dolgov: Heroes of the Country." Патриотический интернет проект "Герои Страны. http://www.warheroes.ru/hero/hero.asp?Hero_id=1875 Retrieved September 6, 2011.

U.S. Senate Committee on Appropriations. "VA-HUD and Independent Agencies Subcommittee Hearing of FY05 Budget Request for NASA: Testimony of Sean O'Keefe, Administrator, NASA." Hearings & Testimony, March 11, 2004. Retrieved January 29, 2007.

U.S. Standard Atmosphere, 1976. U.S. Government Printing Office, 1976.

APPENDIX

...

Major tests and events in Project StratEx:

Event Name	Date
Alan Meets Luigi Cani	August 4, 2010
Alan Develops the Lone Suit Idea	August 2010 – October 2011
First contact between Taber and Alan	October 2011
Paragon (and the author) begin work	February 2012
Wind Tunnel testing with Loaner LEAI Suit	April 30, May 1, 2012
Design and Build of StratEx Suit	May – October, 2012
Cluster Balloon Tests	July 2012
Dart Testing	October 30, 2012
Pre Delivery Acceptance Testing	November 30, 2012
Unmanned Vacuum Testing	April 10, 2013
Manned Systems Checkout	April 25, 2013
Manned Thermal Test 1	May 2, 2013
Coolidge Airplane 1	May 9, 2013
70K Balloon Stand-Up	June 19, 2013
Manned Thermal Test 2	August 2013
Long Distance Comm Test 1	September 22, 2013
93,000 Foot Dummy Drop	October 10, 2013
Human Factors / Pilot Training 1	November 1, 2013
Life Support System Rebuild	November 2013
Vacuum Chamber Testing	December 2013
Manned Thermal Test 3	January 2014
Airplane Dummy Drops 1	February 2014
Attempted Comm test 2	February 14 2014
Airplane Dummy Drops 2	March 2014
Communication System Rebuild	March – May 2014
Manned Long Distance Comm Test 3	June 6, 2014
Tycho 120,000 Foot Test	June 18, 2014
Failed 412K Test	June 29, 2014
120,000 Foot Dummy Drop (Rogue Balloon)	July 6, 2014
Manned Airplane Jump Testing II	August 19,21 2014
Manned Airplane Jump Testing III	September 2,3 2014
Preparing for manned drops	September 2014
Manned Stratospheric Flight 1	October 4, 2014
Manned Stratospheric Flight 2	October 15, 2014
Manned Flight 3 Attempt Fail	October 20, 2014
World Record Stratospheric Flight (Flight 3)	October 24, 2014

Contributors to Project StratEx:

Role or Function	Name
Pilot, Founder, Funder	ALAN EUSTACE

PARAGON SPACE DEVELOPMENT CORPORATION

Role or Function	Name
Program Manager and Flight Director	SEBASTIAN PADILLA
President and Chairwoman, Co-Founder	JANE POYNTER
CEO and CTO, StratEx Safety Officer, Co-Founder	TABER MACCALLUM
COO, VP of Engineering, Co-Founder	GRANT ANDERSON
Project Engineer, Navigation Engineer	NORMAN HAHN
Equipment Module IPT Lead, Flight Recovery System IPT Lead, PSA Operations Lead	JARED LEIDICH
Flight Vehicle IPT Lead, Launch System IPT Lead, Launch Manager	JOHN STRAUS, PH.D.
Chase Lead, Logistics	DAVE JOURDAN
Environmental Control and Life Support Systems (ECLSS) / BEM & Ground Cart Designer, Ground Cart Operations, ECLSS Engineer	ZANE MACCAGNANO
Power, Avionics & Electrical Interfaces Lead, Flight Engineer	DAN MCFATTER
Test Readiness, Communications System Design, BEM Team Operations	ROLFE BODE
Design Engineer, Fill Team Operations	JACOB DANG
Operations & Procedures, Deputy Launch Manager, Fill Team	JOE LEVY
Manufacturing Technician, BEM Team Operations	ESTEBAN GARCIA
Logistics Support, Launch Diesel Operations	PATRICK PASADILLA
Deputy Program Manager, BEM Team Operations	TRAVIS PALMER
Launch Diesel Operations	BRIAN RICHARDSON
Chase Team Support and Logistics	JOSH HECHT
Design & Build Phase Space Suit Lead	CHRISTINE IACOMINI, PH.D.
Director of Programs	VOLKER KERN, PH.D.
VP SQ&MA	HENRY KONOPKA
Quality Assurance	DANNY WISE

Role or Function	Name
Contracts	KATHLEEN MCCLARD
Subcontract / Vendor Manager	MICHELLE CAMARENA
Marketing and Communications Manager	CAROLE LEON
Initial Program Manager	GARY LANTZ
Manufacturing Technician, Former Launch Diesel Operations	BRITT KAYNER
Test Technician, Former Launch Diesel Operations	ERNIE ARISPE
Former Deputy Program Manager and Chase / Recovery Operations	JEREMY SOTZEN
Integrated Analyses / Pressure Suit	TOM DURRANT
Thermal Engineer	TOM LEIMKUEHLER, PH.D.
Manufacturing & M&P	VANESSA THOMPSON
Initial Safety Officer	ROBERT DUBOSE
Initial Operations Lead	PAUL E. DAMPHOUSSE
Engineering, Manufacturing, and Logistics Support	TYLER BALL
People department	KRISTIN BEHRENS
Lab support	PHILL BENJAMIN
Analysis support	CHAD BOWER
Engineering and manufacturing support	JASON BROCKBANK
Shipping and receiving, logistics	MIKE CAMARENA
Engineering management support	STEPHANIE CHIESI
Engineering, Manufacturing, and Logistics Support	THOMAS COGNATA
Engineering, Manufacturing, and Logistics Support	AARON CORCORRAN
Information technologies	ARNOLD CUELLAR
Shipping and receiving	JIMMY DEZUBELDIA
Manufacturing support	MICHAEL DENARO
Administrative support	GIOVANNA DIETZ
People department	JENNA ELMER
Engineering, Manufacturing, and Logistics Support	NEYRA ENRIQUEZ
Life support expert and advisor	BARRY FINGER
Structures expert and advisor	JAMES HARRELL
Lab support	WALTER HARRINGTON
Engineering, Manufacturing, and Logistics Support	BRAD HARRIS
Quality control	MO HERNANDEZ
Engineering, Manufacturing, and Logistics Support	HARDY HOUSTON

Role or Function	Name
Finance support	JOEL JOHNSON
Engineering management	TIM KAST
Engineering, support	CHUCK KEIERLEBER
Engineering support, lab management	LAURA KELSEY
Engineering, Manufacturing, and Logistics Support	JOSH LIEN
Engineering design	JAVIER LOPEZ
Engineering, Manufacturing, and Logistics Support	TERRY LYTLE
Administrative support	DEBRA MAGRUM
Engineering, Manufacturing, and Logistics Support	JUSTIN MARTIN
Administrative support	RHONDA MUMFORD
Engineering, Manufacturing, and Logistics Support	TOM PALAMIDES
Information technologies	MELISSA PALMER
Engineering, Manufacturing, and Logistics Support	DENVER POWELL
Engineering design	AARON POWERS
Engineering drawing support	KATHY RICHARDSON
Quality control	CARLOS RIOS
Shipping, receiving and logistics	JENNIFER ROBERTS
Finance support	MARISA RODRIGUEZ
Engineering, Manufacturing, and Logistics Support	ROLLIN ROOS
Engineering, Manufacturing, and Logistics Support	WILLIAM SARNACK-ALLEY
Engineering, Manufacturing, and Logistics Support	MARC SPENCER
Lab support and manufacturing	REBECCA TATE
Engineering support	TAD THENO
Manufacturing support	ART TRUJILLO
Engineering, Manufacturing, and Logistics Support	GLENN WAGUESPACK
Engineering support	ALEXANDER WALKER
Engineering	SCOTT WEILER
Manufacturing support	ROGER YOUNG

CONTRACTORS AND SUPPORT

Role or Function	Name
Communications System Technician, Communications Engineer	RYAN OSBORN
Launch Advisor	FRANK CANDELARIA
Chief Medical Officer, Language Advisor & Flight Surgeon	JONATHAN CLARK, M.D.
Chief Meteorologist and Ballooning Flight Advisor	DON DAY, DAYWEATHER INC.
Balloon Chase Pilot	CAPT. MARK KELLY
Medical Advisor	RICHARD JENNINGS, M.D.
Decompression Advisor	DR. ANDREW PILMANIS
Independent Safety Review Board	EDWARD LU
Independent Safety Review Board	DONALD WHITE
Meteorologist, Former Navigation Engineer Operations	ROBERT REDINGER
Advisor, FAA Relations	KEN SASINE
Security and Logistics Support	ERNEST SANCHEZ
Land Access Liason	BILL MARLEY
Embedded Software Developer for StratEx Flight Computer	JOHN DAVIDSON (JD)
Technical Advisor	CHRISTOPHER STOKELY
Safety and Operations Consultant	DANNY BALL
For Roswell International Space Center, Air Center Manager	JENNIFER BRADY
Airport Superintendent	KEVIN SYKES
USPA Director of Competition, FAI Observer	JAMES L. HAYHURST
Executive Director, USPA	ED SCOTT
Logistics Support	ALAN TREVOR
Generator Technician	QUENTIN DAY
Wireless Communications and Embedded Systems	ROD KRONSCHNABEL
Vigil USA, LLC	CANDICE PROCOS
World View Public Relations	ANDREW ANTONIO
Scientific Balloon Technology	JULIAN NOTT
Safety Sky Diver	TREVOR CEDAR
Safety Sky Diver, In-flight photographer	LUKE EVENS
Safety Sky Diver, Wind tunnel operator	DEREK VANBOESCHOTEN
Safety Sky Diver, parachute engineer	LOUIE PALOMARES

ADE AEROSPACE MEDICINE

Role or Function	Name
Medical Team Member	ALEX GARBINO, MD, PH.D
Medical Team Member	ANIL MENON, MD, M.P.H
Medical Team Member	DEREK MATTHEW NUSBAUM
Medical Team Member	ERIK ANTONSEN, M.D., PH.D
Medical Team Member	MATTHEW TURNEY, M.D., FAAEM
Medical Team Member	SEAN NORTON
Medical Team Member	SHAWN GOUGHNOUR
Medical Team Member	DAN BUCKLAND
Medical Team Member	GIUGI CARMINATI
Medical Team Member	CAMERON DECKER
Medical Team Member	ANDY PILMANIS M.D.
Medical Team Member	JAMES PATTARINI, M.D.
Medical Team Member	REBECCA BLUE, M.D., M.P.H
Medical Team Member	SHARMI WATKINS M.D.

ILC DOVER

Role or Function	Name
Pressure Suit Design Leads and Field Operations	RYAN LEE
Pressure Suit Design Lead and Field Operations	MITCH SWEENEY
Pressure Suit Design Lead and Field Operations	DAVID GRAZIOSI
Pressure Suit Manufacturing	GUADA MORRIS
Pressure Suit Manufacturing	OLGA BUSTOS
Pressure Suit Manufacturing	NICOLE BRAZIL
Pressure Suit Manufacturing	WHITNEY LOWERY
Pressure Suit Manufacturing	MACEE CHRISTENSEN
Pressure Suit Manufacturing	GARY CHILSON
Pressure Suit Manufacturing	DONNA ANSBACH
Pressure Suit Manufacturing	BROOKS GRIFFIN
Pressure Suit Manufacturing	JOHN TOBLER
Pressure Suit Manufacturing	MIKE LOREA ROBERT BAKLEY

Role or Function	Name
Engineering and Management Support, ILC Dover	PHIL SPAMPINATO
Engineering and Management Support, ILC Dover	DAVE CADOGAN
Engineering and Management Support, ILC Dover	JAMIE GIL
Engineering and Management Support, ILC Dover	BOBBY JONES
Engineering and Management Support, ILC Dover	JOEY SUNG
Engineering and Management Support, ILC Dover	GREG MULLER

ROSWELL FIRE DEPARTMENT

Role or Function	Name
Fireman	SHANE ADAMS
Fireman	BRIAN POWELL
Fireman	CHAD HAMILL

TATA INSTITUTE OF FUNDAMENTAL RESEARCH

Role or Function	Name
Retired, Scientist-in-Charge	SREENIVASAN SHANKARNARAYAN
Scientist-in-Charge	SUNEEL KUMAR

UNITED PARACHUTE TECHNOLOGIES

Role or Function	Name
Lead Designer, Engineering, Manufacturing, Safety Sky Diver	DANIEL "BLIKKIES" BLIGNAUT
General Manager	MARK PROCOS
Owner	BILL BOOTH
Designer, Engineering, Manufacturing, Test Support	TY BOWEN
Designer, Engineering, Camera/Safety Sky Diver, Manufacturing	LOUIE PALOMARES
Manufacturing	BRAD SAYLOR
Manufacturing	APAPORN KAWCZK
Manufacturing	CONNIE VANDENBERG

AEROWESTERN HELICOPTERS

Role or Function	Name
Lead Pilot, Chase One	GLENN PATTERSON
Helicopter Pilot	ERNIE SMITH
Helicopter Pilot	JOHNNY STEVENSON
Helicopter Pilot	TODD ROSIGNOLL
Helicopter Pilot	NATE MAPLESDEN
Helicopter Pilot	ADAM MOORE
Re-Fueler	JEFF DAVIS
Cineflex Camera Operator	DOUG HOLGATE

RIEDEL COMMUNICATIONS

Role or Function	Name
Chase / Recovery Communications	MATTHIAS LEISTER
Chase / Recovery Communications	CHRISTOPHER STREET

DEL E. WEBB HIGH ALTITUDE CHAMBER FACILITY

Role or Function	Name
Chamber operator	BRENT CROW
Chamber operator	EDDY MILLAN
Chamber operator	GAYLA MARSH
Chamber operator	RON DIEDRICHS

WIN AVIATION

Role or Function	Name
For Win Aviation	ANDRI WIESE
Airplane Pilot	NICK BEALE
Airplane Pilot	NICOLE JANKUTA
Airplane Pilot	DYLAN TODD

ATOMIC ENTERTAINMENT

Role or Function	Name
Documentary Crew	JERRY KOLBER
Documentary Crew	ADAM DAVIS
Documentary Crew	TREY NELSON

FAI World Record Claim

CLASSIFICATION: Class G – Parachuting
SUB-CLASS: Performance Record – as described in SC-5 - 3.1.1 (2)
PERFORMANCE RECORDS CLAIMED: Exit altitude, Distance of fall and Vertical speed
- 3.3.3 (1) Exit altitude (absolute)
- 3.3.3 (2) (b) Vertical distance of fall with a drogue/stabilization device
- 3.3.7 (1) (b) Vertical speed attained with a drogue/stabilization device

CATEGORY OF RECORDS: General

EXIT ALTITUDE: **41,422** METERS

DISTANCE OF FALL: **37,623** METERS

VERTICAL SPEED: **1,320** KM/HOUR

PLACE OF JUMP: Roswell, New Mexico, USA
DATE OF JUMP: 24 OCT 2014
TIME OF EXIT: 15:09:29 UTC; TIME OF LANDING: 15:23:48 UTC
NAME OF JUMPER: **Alan Eustace**
GENDER AND CITIZENSHIP: **Male, USA**
FAI SPORTING LICENSE: **P198870**   EXPIRES: **30 SEPTEMBER 2015**
AIRCRAFT: **Aerostat, free balloon**   IDENTIFICATION: **N508LJ**
CONTROLLING NAC: **National Aeronautic Association of the United States (NAA)**
AEROCLUB DELEGATED SPORTING POWERS: **United States Parachute Association**
DATE FAI NOTIFIED: 24 OCT 2014

CERTIFICATION:

In accordance with GS 4.2.1, I certify that the claimed record performances were made in compliance
with the FAI Sporting Code. The record file meets all requirements of GS 6.8 and the precision of
measurement standards set forth in GS 7.3, as specified in SC-5, 3.3.3 (6) (9) and 3.3.7 (2) (3), with a
description of the recording devices, proof of chain of custody, evidence of the accuracy of data and
overall margin of error.

James L. Hayhurst
FAI Official Observer
USPA
5401 Southpoint Centre
Blvd. Fredericksburg, VA
22407 jhayhurst@uspa.org

Smithsonian
National Air & Space Museum

February 27, 2015

Julian Nott
Santa Barbara California

Dear Julian:

This is to confirm that the Collections Committee of the Smithsonian National Air and Space Museum has voted unanimously [and with virtually no debate] to accept Alan Eustace StratEx equipment, pressure suit, parachute ancillaries into the national collection. The highest praise our Museum can give is to include a person's work in its permanent collection. At the Smithsonian we are lucky enough to be able to select from the very best from all over the world. The Museum is extremely selective and turns away all but a very small percentage of the important craft that are offered. Mr. Eustace honors us with the donation of the suit that kept him alive during his record breaking achievement. We look forward to sharing the equipment, and the story, with the millions of visitors who will pass through our doors in the decades to come. Let me extend my best wishes to the StratEx team in the consideration for the Collier Trophy.

Sincerely,

Tom D. Crouch, PhD
Senior Curator, Aeronautics

SMITHSONIAN INSTITUTION
Paul E. Garber Facility
Bldg 21 MRC 531
3904 Old Silver Hill Rd.
Suitland, MD 20746-3190
301.231.1600 Telephone